Artists Working

From Life

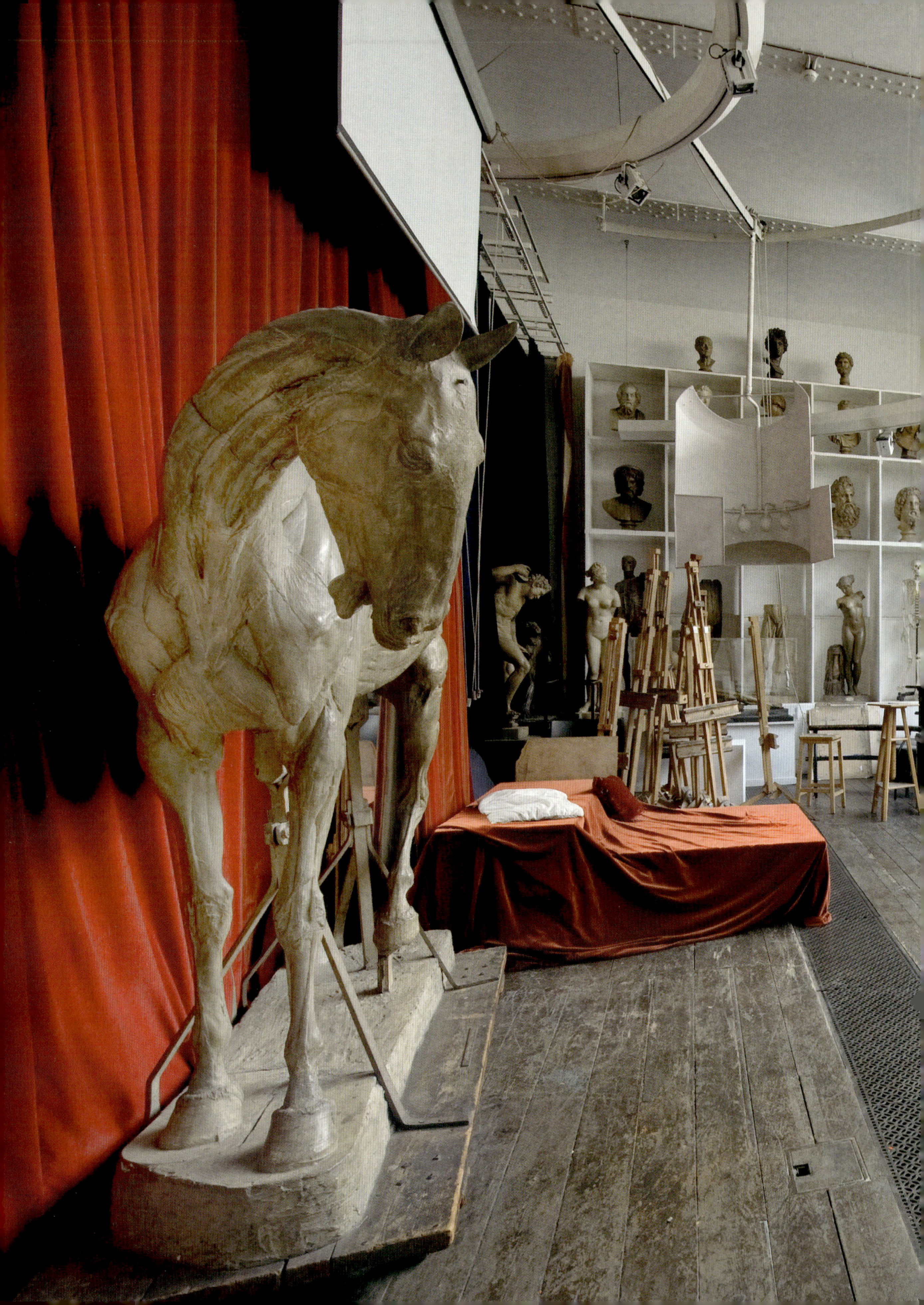

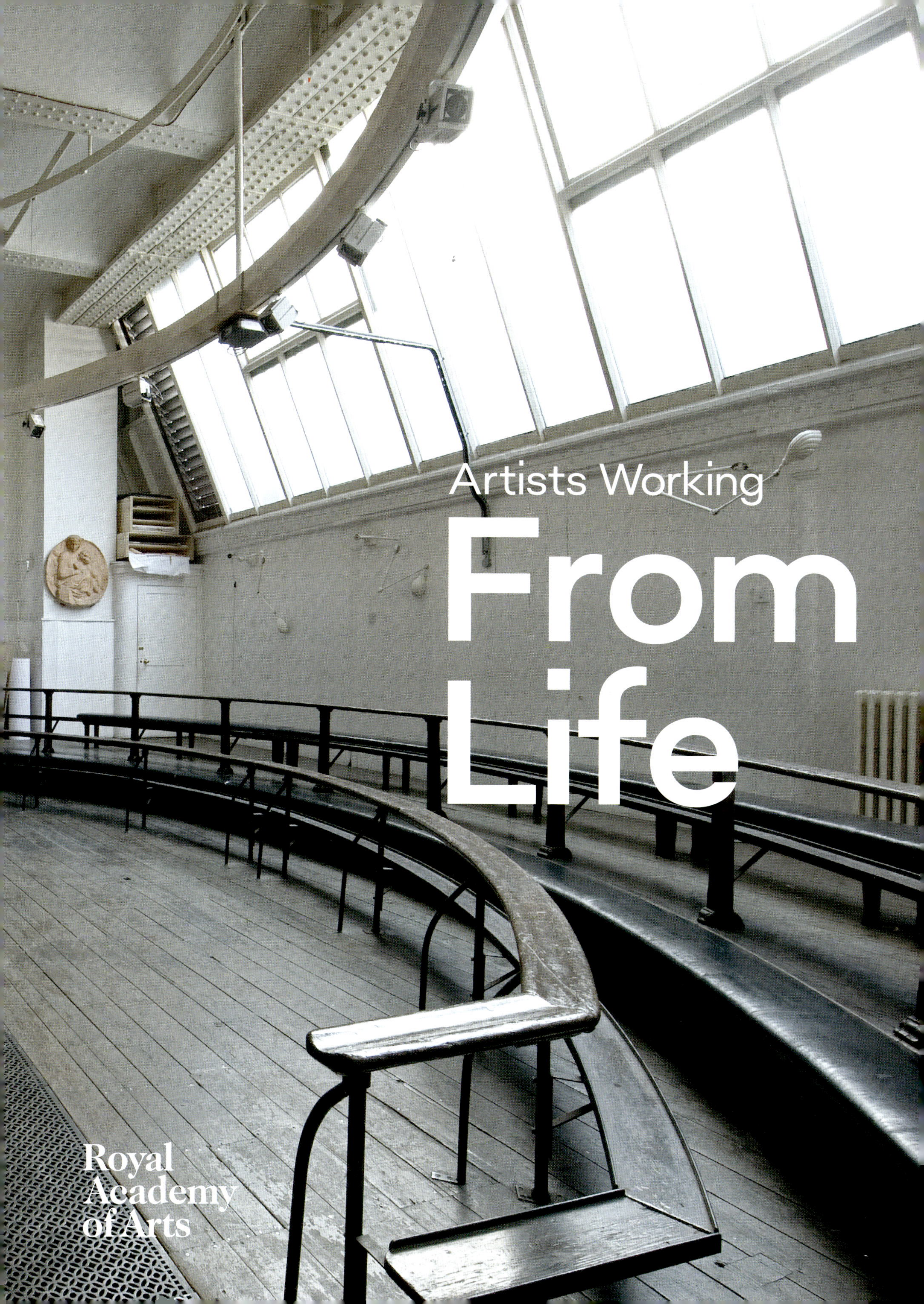

Artists Working From Life

Royal Academy of Arts

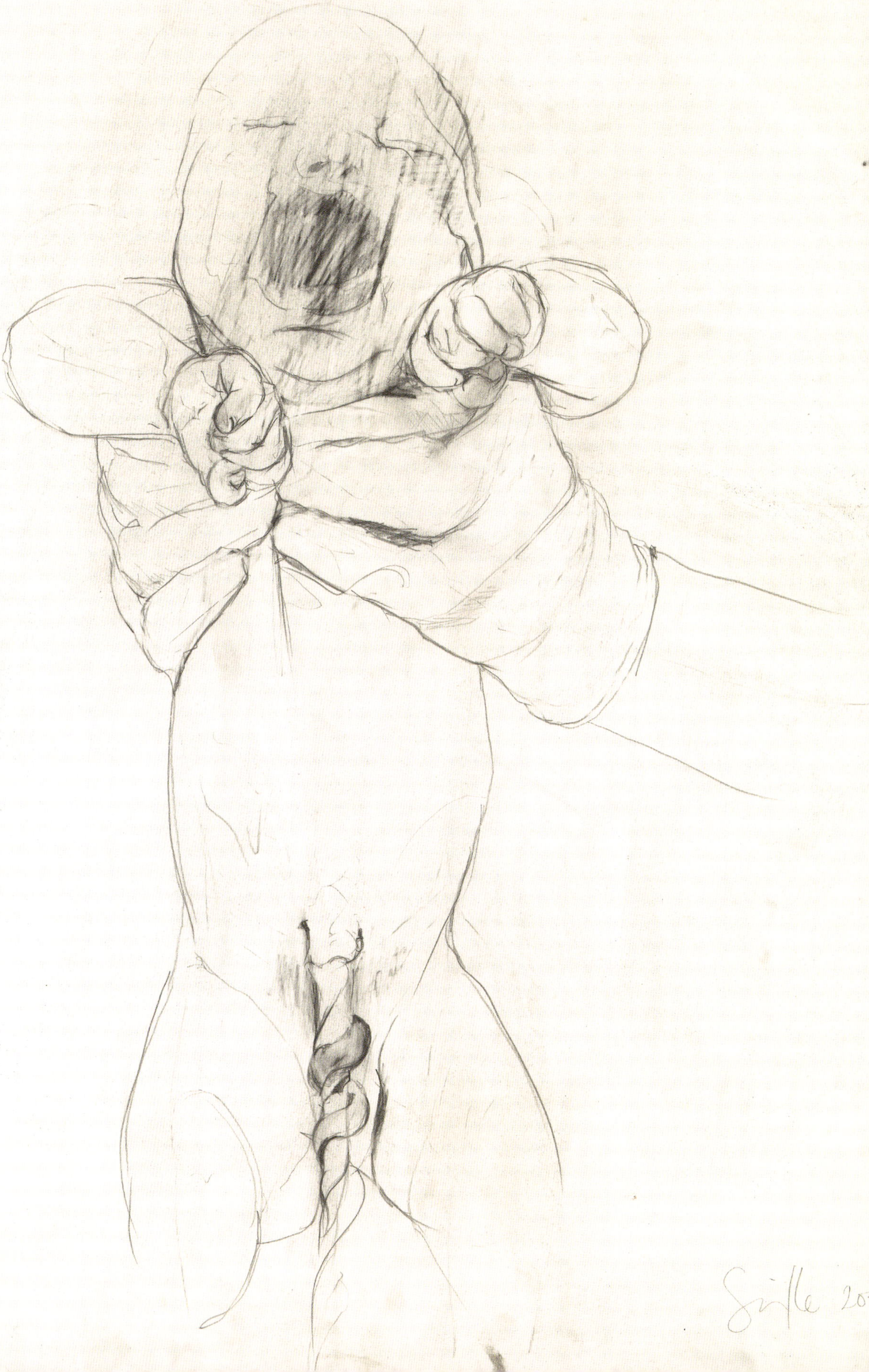

Contents

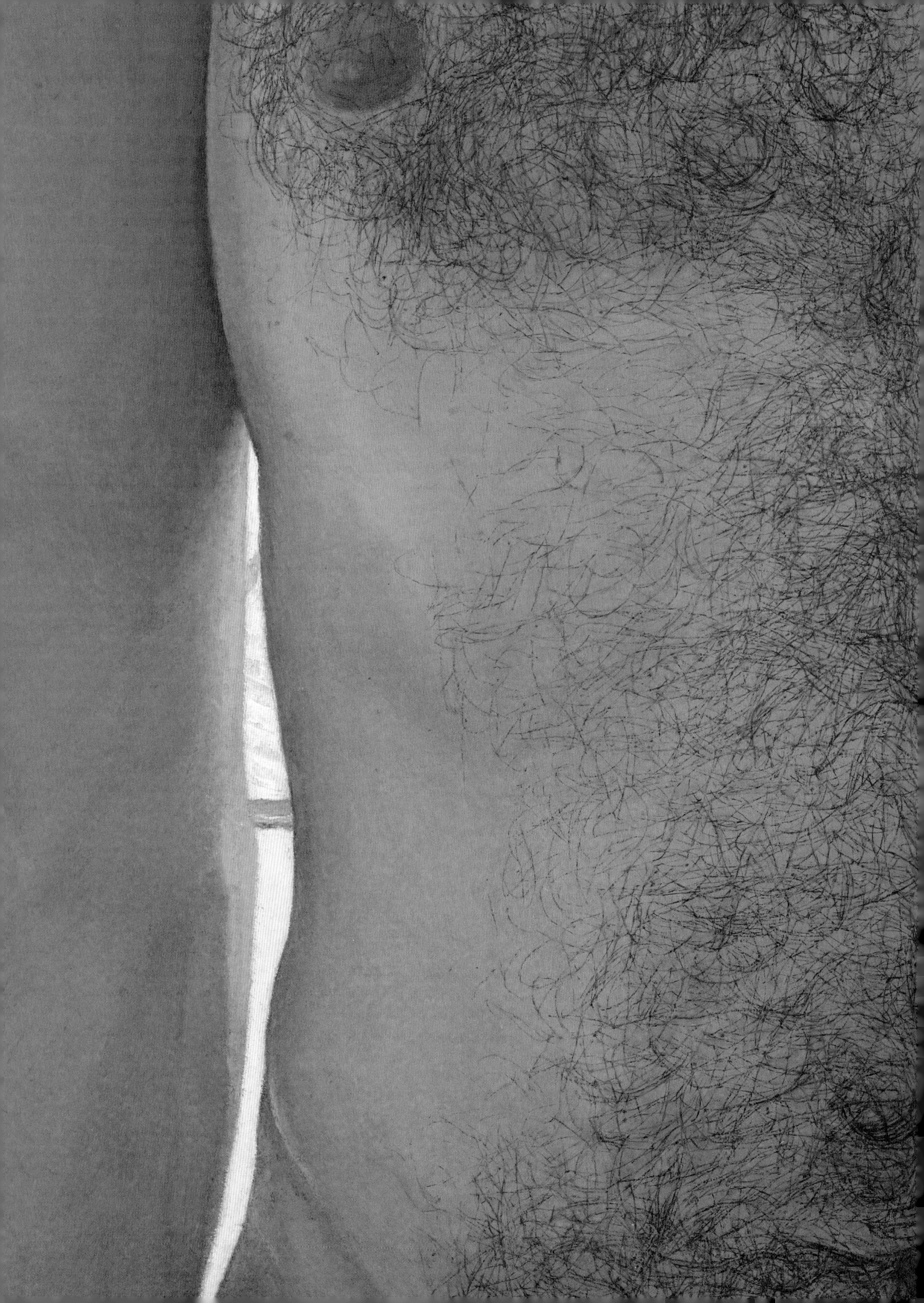

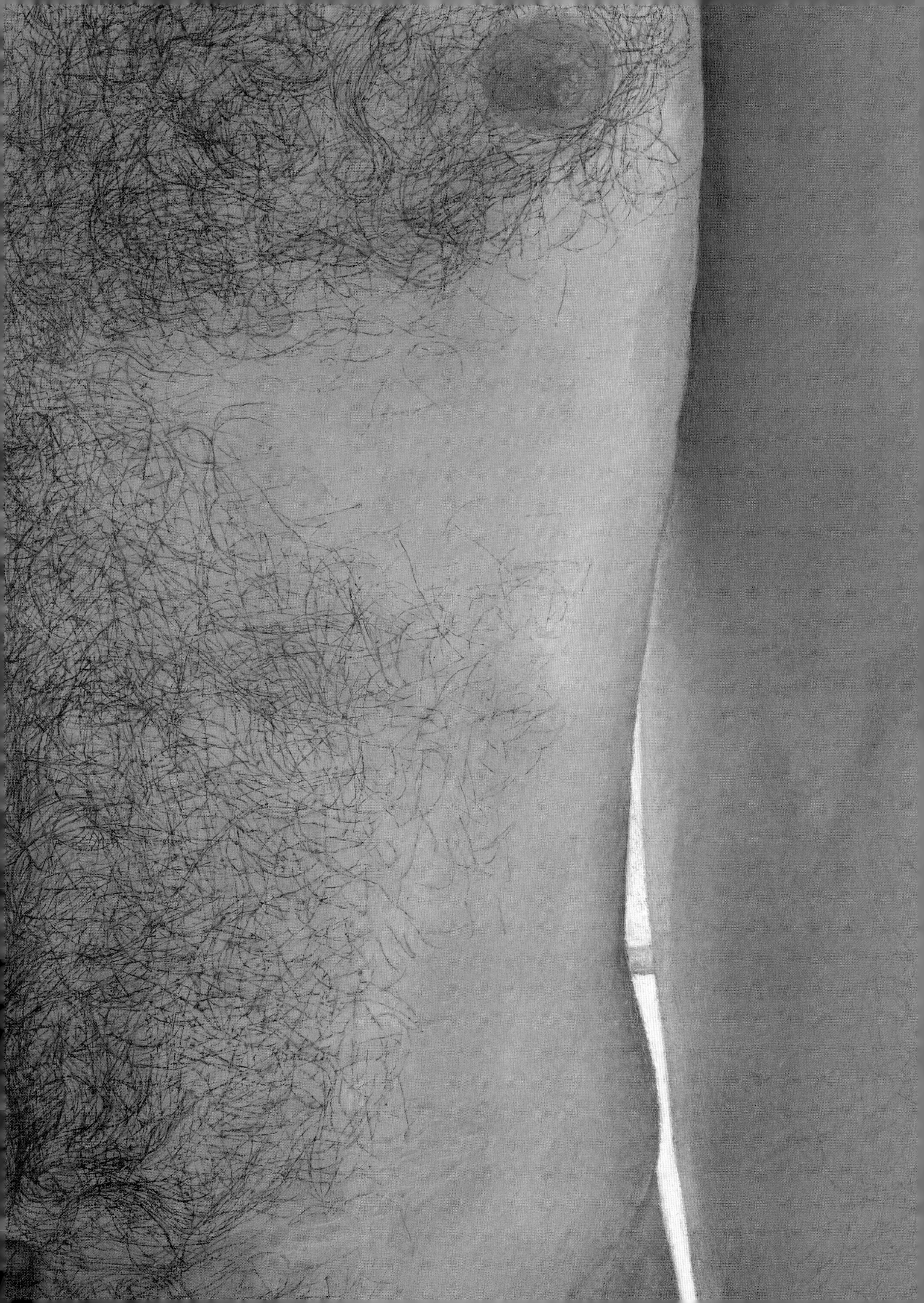

Introduction

Rebecca Salter,
Keeper of the Royal Academy

The representation of the human body through direct observation, otherwise known as 'working from life', is the emblematic practice of traditional artistic training. An art school has been at the heart of the Royal Academy of Arts since its foundation in the eighteenth century, and that school has always had a Life Room, where nude models are drawn or sculpted. Today's RA Schools Life Room is pictured on the cover of this book: tall velvet curtains act as a backdrop to the model's stage, which is faced by two rows of curved wooden benches where students sit and work if they are not standing at an easel, flanked by casts of classical sculptures, as well as écorchés and skeletons to assist with anatomical study.

The Royal Academy is an association of artists, and since its inception, one artist has assumed the position of Keeper, becoming responsible for the Schools. Since I took up the role in summer 2017, I have been learning about the Keepers who came before. George Michael Moser was the first, and he brought a passion for life drawing with him from the St Martin's Lane Academy, an informal precursor of the RA. The drawing reproduced here, now in the Royal Academy's own art collection, is testament to his talent. Annette Wickham describes in her following essay how the Academy developed Renaissance traditions in its instruction of artists, and how life drawing had a central place in its studies as a result.

Yet while working from life is entwined with the RA's history, it has not been compulsory at the Schools for decades, nor at most major art schools in Britain. A small number of students attend life-drawing classes regularly today; the RA Schools Life Room now has a varied role, and is as much a space for lectures and socialising as an arena for scrutinising models. During my foundation course in fine art in the 1970s, my teacher picked up on my struggles with traditional life drawing and suggested I might not be accepted on a degree course; tutors no longer expect to see any depictions of the human form in a young artist's portfolio. What constitutes fine art has, of course, radically broadened.

As this book of interviews shows, working from life has broadened too. It persists in new forms. Practitioners across disciplines – in painting, sculpture, photography, installation and performance, and even architecture – are inspired by its traditions, as they rethink what the body means and what constitutes 'life' in a world of rapidly evolving technology, such as virtual reality, where the boundaries between the physical and digital worlds become blurred. This publication brings together artists with consummate drawing skills with those who rarely draw; figurative painters with conceptual artists; a sculptor who works in steel with an artist who is happiest with a pastel in hand. It has developed from a special exhibition project at the Royal Academy, 'From Life', which features many of the artists in these pages. The show is curated by Adrian Locke and organised in partnership with HTC Vive, Sky Arts and Google. As well as a three-month exhibition, the project includes a varied series of artist-led classes in the RA Schools Life Room.

So what does working from life mean today? For me, it is all about looking – an essential skill that we often neglect – as well prioritising the external world above our interior states. But as this book demonstrates, there are as many answers to this question as there are artists.

George Michael Moser RA
Life Drawing of a Male Nude
c. 1745–50
Red chalk on buff laid paper
57.6 x 38.7 cm
Royal Academy of Arts, London

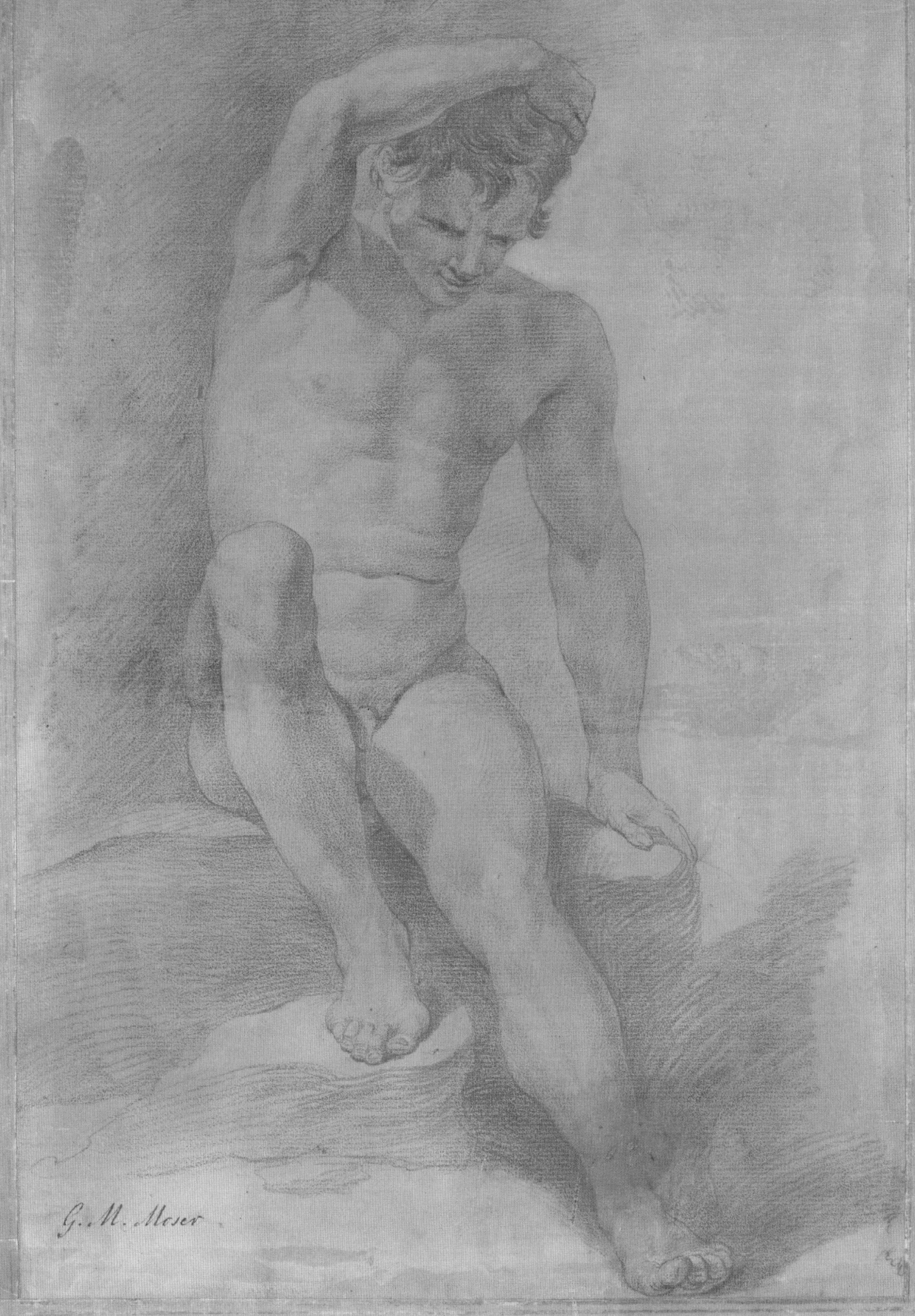
G. M. Moser

Looking at Life Drawing
From the Renaissance to the Royal Academy

Annette Wickham,
Curator of Works on Paper

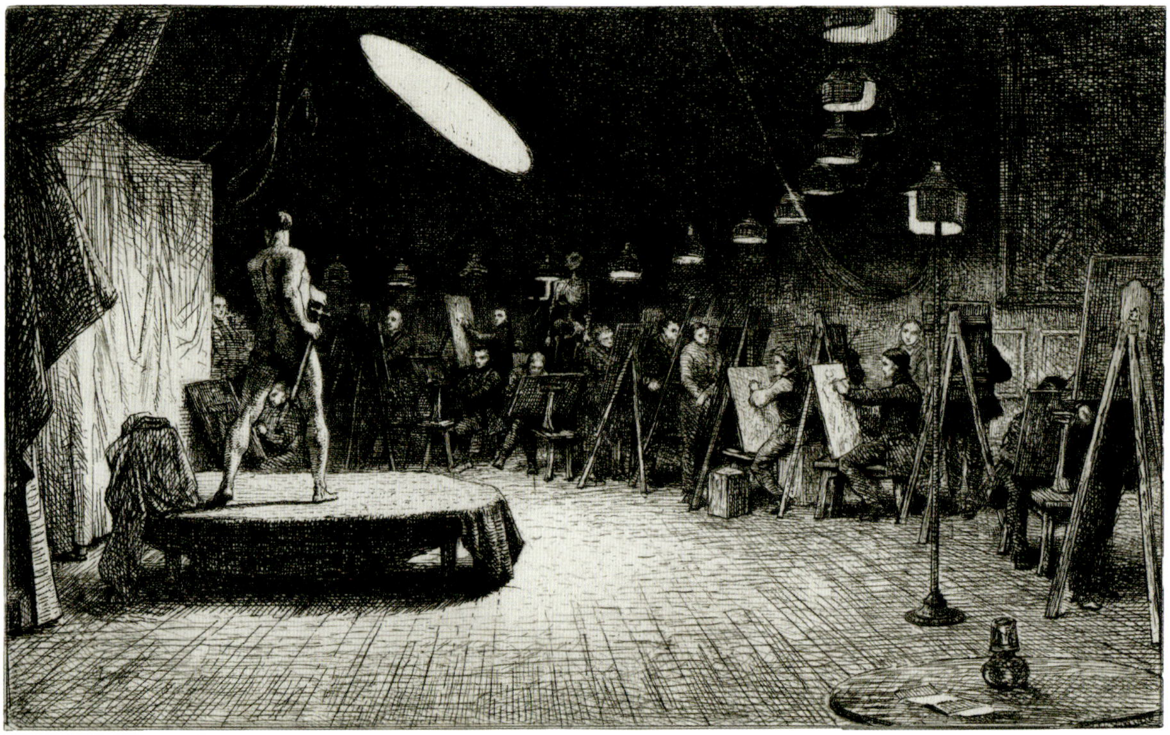

Charles West Cope RA
Life School,
Royal Academy
1865
Etching
15.2 x 24.7 cm
Royal Academy of Arts, London

Charles West Cope RA's depiction of a life class taking place at the Royal Academy in 1865 is an evocative image that seems to sum up the conventions of traditional academic training. The young, exclusively male, art students sit at their easels in a semicircular formation, facing a nude male model who strikes a heroic pose on a dramatically lit platform. The atmosphere among the students appears to be one of intense concentration on their task, which is to render the figure before them in black and white on a standard-size sheet of paper. Although traditional, these conventions give rise to various questions, especially if one looks at the scene with no prior knowledge of art history. Why, for instance, is life drawing usually a collective activity? Why do the models invariably have to be nude? And why was the life class – for centuries – the mainstay of art education, even for artists who did not intend to spend their career depicting figures?

The answers lie in the Renaissance origins of life drawing. Like so many other innovations of the Renaissance, the evolution of the life class was inspired by the art of the classical world. As more and more ancient Greek and Roman statues emerged from excavations in Italy and beyond, it was immediately clear that their naturalistic yet highly idealised forms were the work of artists with a thorough understanding of the human body. Direct observation and

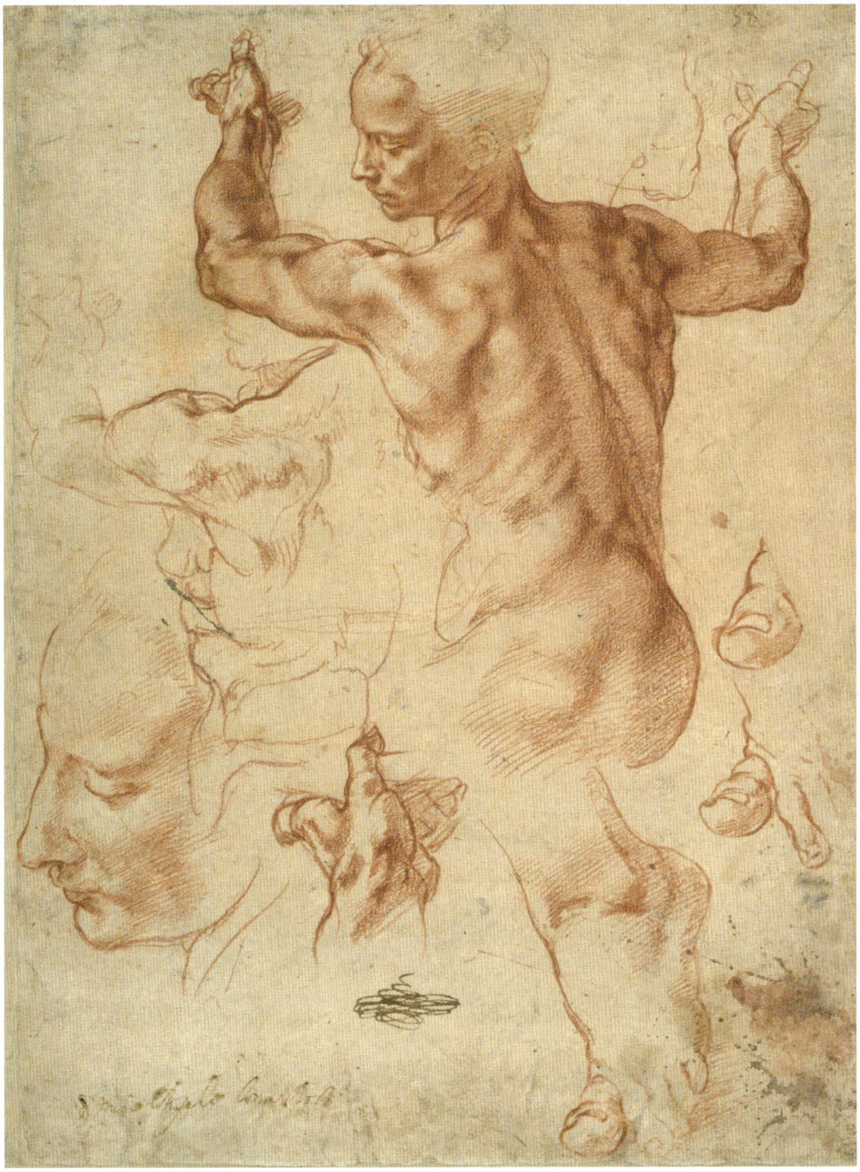

Michelangelo Buonarroti
Studies for the Libyan Sibyl (recto)
c. 1510–11
Red chalk on paper
28.9 x 21.4 cm
The Metropolitan Museum of Art, New York

study of the figure, Renaissance artists concluded, were the key to achieving similar results or even surpassing them. Michelangelo, in particular, was a prolific draughtsman whose surviving works include many striking figure studies and preparatory drawings for his major works.

It was a logical step for artists to study anatomy and to draw from nude models, despite moral qualms over both. Theoretical justification was provided by the Italian architect Leon Battista Alberti in his treatise *On Painting* (1435). He recommended the following process in preparing a figurative painting: 'Before dressing a man we first draw him nude, then we enfold him in draperies. So in painting the nude we place first his bones and muscles which we then cover with flesh so that it is not difficult to understand where each muscle is beneath.'

As Alberti suggests, life drawing was not seen as an end in itself, at least not for students. It was the ultimate stage in learning to draw, and was only to be approached after a prescribed course of preliminary studies, among them copying prints and drawings, drawing from ancient statues (or plaster casts of the same) and studying anatomy and the theory of perspective. This established progression is synthesised in an illustration in Diderot and d'Alembert's eighteenth-century *Encyclopédie* (see overleaf). Students' familiarity with the approved body types, poses and expressions of antique

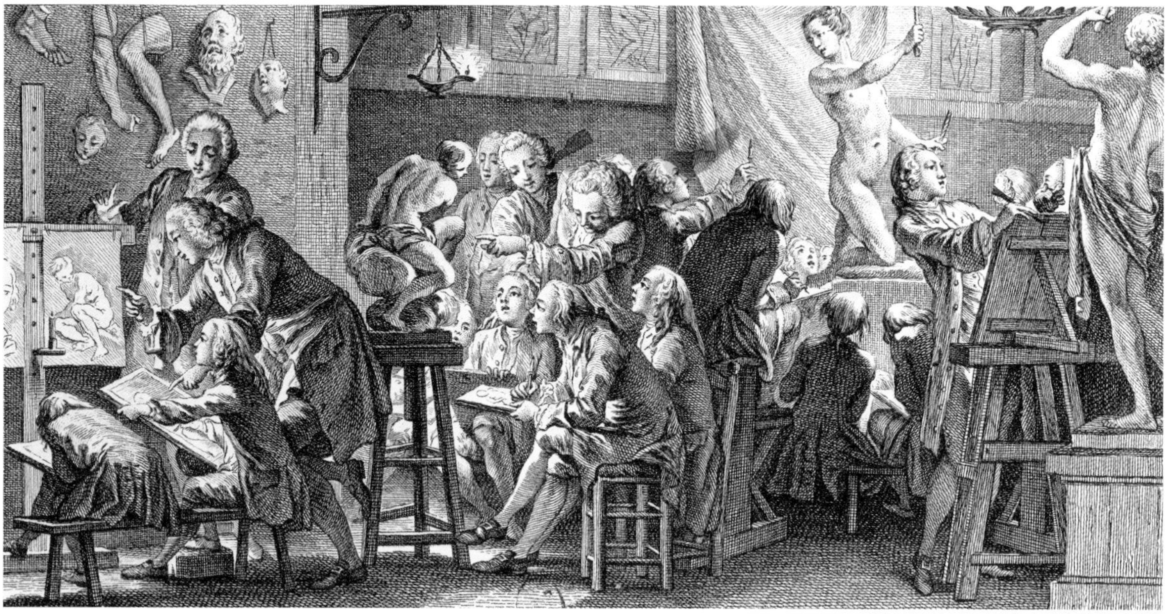

sculpture, so the theory went, would help them learn to 'correct' the quirks and flaws of real human bodies – like a pair of rose-tinted, classicising spectacles. A famous classical model for the relationship between the real and ideal appears in a text by Cicero; the Roman orator and writer described the Greek painter Zeuxis making studies from five of the most beautiful women in his city in order to create one ideal woman to represent Helen of Troy. As Cicero relates: 'he [Zeuxis] knew he could find no single form possessing all the characteristics of perfect beauty, which impartial Nature distributes among her children, accompanying each charm with a defect.'[1]

The life class developed in the studios of artists and craftsmen who took on pupils, but it assumed a more formal status in the first art 'academy', which was set up by the painter and art historian Giorgio Vasari in Florence in 1563. Not primarily a teaching institution, the Accademia e Compagnia delle Arti del Disegno (Academy and Company of the Arts of Drawing) also served as an artists' association and, patronised by the influential Medici family, as a prestigious place of intellectual debate. Nevertheless, it proved highly influential in its codification of the hierarchical system of teaching drawing that was subsequently adopted in other academies that sprang up in Italy and, eventually, across Europe and the Americas.

The most significant national academy to open after the Renaissance period was the Académie royale de peinture et sculpture in Paris (later the Ecole des Beaux-Arts), founded in 1648 by King Louis XIV. Initially, the only practical instruction offered at the Académie royale was in drawing, making the life class the apex of the whole course. This emphasis on drawing stemmed from the humanist belief that the discipline was the foundation of all the visual arts. As Michelangelo put it: 'Design, which by another name is called drawing ... is the fount and body of painting and sculpture and architecture and of every other kind

Benoît Louis Prévost
Ecole de Dessin
c. 1751–77
Etching
An illustration for Diderot and d'Alembert's *Encyclopédie*, after a drawing by Charles Nicolas-Cochin
Bibliothèque Nationale, Paris

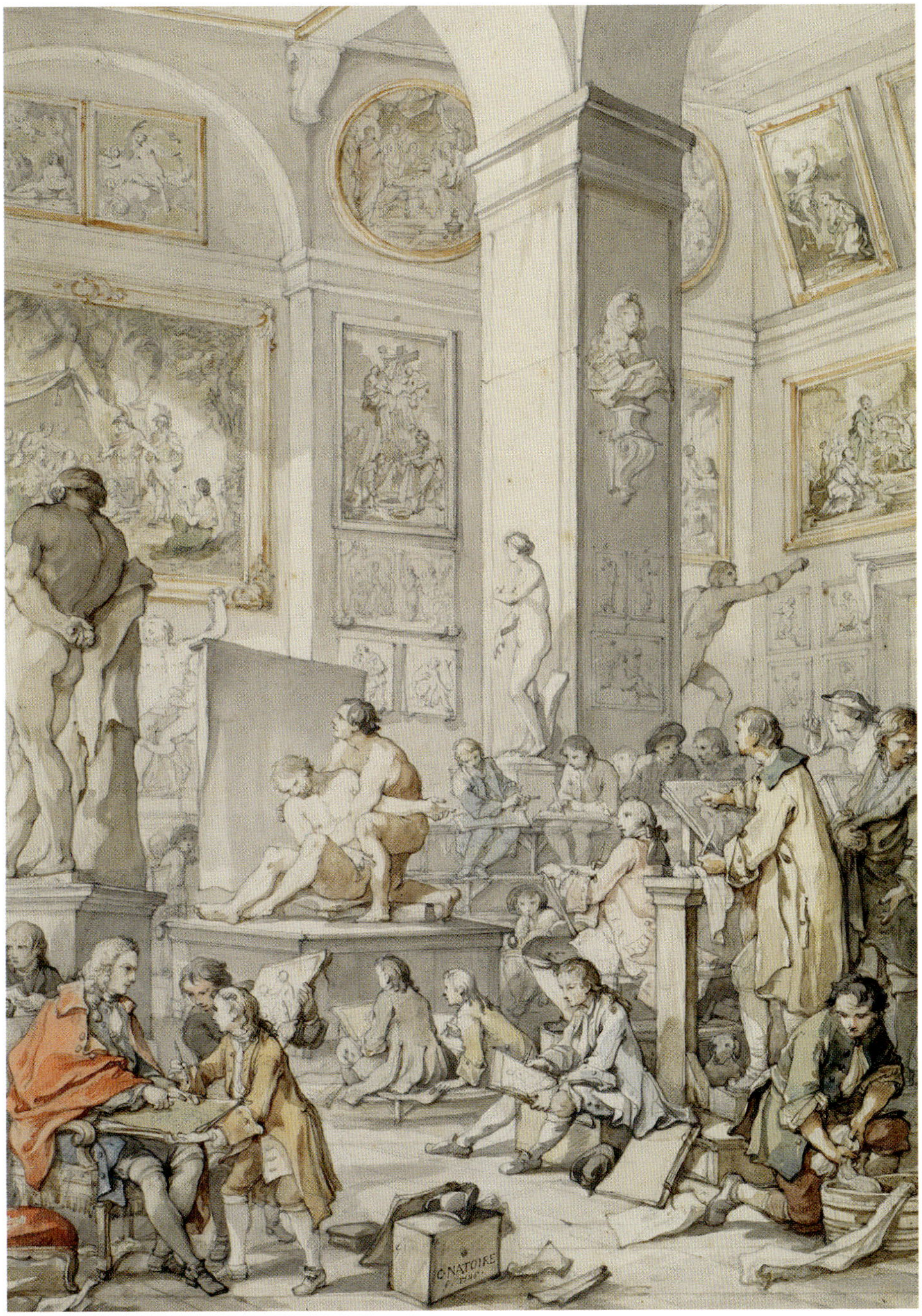

Charles-Joseph Natoire
Life Class at the Académie royale, Paris, with Natoire as an Instructor
1746
Watercolour and chalk on paper
45.3 x 32.3 cm
The Courtauld Gallery, London

of painting and the root of all sciences.'[2] Drawing – or 'disegno' – also carried intellectual weight as the medium in which an artist's creative power is first expressed and through which his or her thought processes are developed.

The Académie royale was granted a monopoly on the practice of life drawing, which greatly increased the method's prestige and sense of exclusivity. A drawing by Charles-Joseph Natoire offers a behind-the-scenes glimpse of its famous life class in action, although it is thought to be more of an 'idea' of a class than an attempt to record accurately the appearance of the room. Natoire, who later became Director of the Académie de France in Rome, included himself on the left (in the red cloak) as the tutor correcting students' work. He would also have been responsible for setting the pose of the two male models apparently wrestling, perhaps in loose imitation of the famous antique statue *The Wrestlers* (Galleria degli Uffizi, Florence). The continuing importance of classical sculpture is also emphasised by the presence of casts after the Farnese Hercules, the Venus de' Medici and other canonical works.

An anonymous 'young painter at Paris' in May 1764 described the Académie royale life class: 'there were at least 200 students, in a large hall ... all busy copying from a living man, who was placed naked in a reclining posture ... There are two rows of benches round the room; the highest for the statuaries [sculptors], the other for painters; every one has his own light placed at his right hand ... There are students here from all parts of the world.'[3] This British student had seen nothing quite like it at home. That is because a century of debate over the advantages and disadvantages of academic art education in Britain preceded the foundation of the Royal Academy of Arts in London in 1768. Several less formal art schools and associations, some providing life drawing, existed in various parts of Britain before this date, but the Royal Academy was the first state-sanctioned art school in the country to be set up along the lines of continental academies. As such, it aimed to raise the status of British artists and equip a new generation of art students with the necessary skills to produce paintings, sculpture and architecture that would be on a par with the achievements of the Old Masters and their classical precursors.

Life drawing was crucial to this mission. When Johan Zoffany celebrated the foundation of the institution with his group portrait of the Academicians (1771–72), it is revealing that he chose to depict his fellow members gathered together in their Life Room. George Michael Moser, the first 'Keeper' (or head of the RA Schools), is busy setting the pose of the model. Intriguingly though, closer inspection reveals that none of the artists looks as if he intends to do any drawing. It has been suggested that Zoffany was playfully echoing Raphael's Vatican *School of Athens* and tapping into the idea of an academy as a place of debate. Even though they are not actually drawing, there is a sense of the artists' shared pride at having finally secured a national academy in Britain to promote the practice.

The two curious oval portraits of women on the right of Zoffany's painting are also significant. They depict the Royal Academy's two female Foundation Members, Angelica Kauffman and Mary Moser. Unlike their male colleagues, they could not be shown attending the life class on the grounds of moral propriety, but Zoffany managed to shoehorn them in at one remove. The Academy's attitude to women artists was only to become more problematic as time went on. Despite numerous women exhibitors at the annual exhibitions, no more female Academicians were admitted until the twentieth century. Likewise, no female students were enrolled in the Schools until 1860, when Laura Herford applied, giving only her first initial and surname. It was assumed that L. Herford was male and 'he' was offered a place. To their surprise, the Academicians found no written rule excluding women and Miss Herford was admitted. Others followed, but the women were initially confined to drawing casts and it was not until 1893 that they were allowed to draw from the male model – and then only if he was wearing a voluminous length of fabric thoroughly wrapped around his bathing trunks.

There was one role in which a woman was welcome in the early days of the Royal Academy: as a model. This was a significant departure from continental academic tradition, which focused exclusively on the male figure, following the Renaissance theory that upheld the male body as the 'perfect' measure of all things (epitomised by Leonardo da Vinci's *Vitruvian Man*). The Royal Academy preferred to follow the tradition of its less formal predecessors in London, including the private drawing school run by William Hogarth, which had always featured models of both genders.

Once it was taking place in a group setting at an official teaching institution supported by the King, the practice of drawing from the female nude became more socially acceptable. However, the

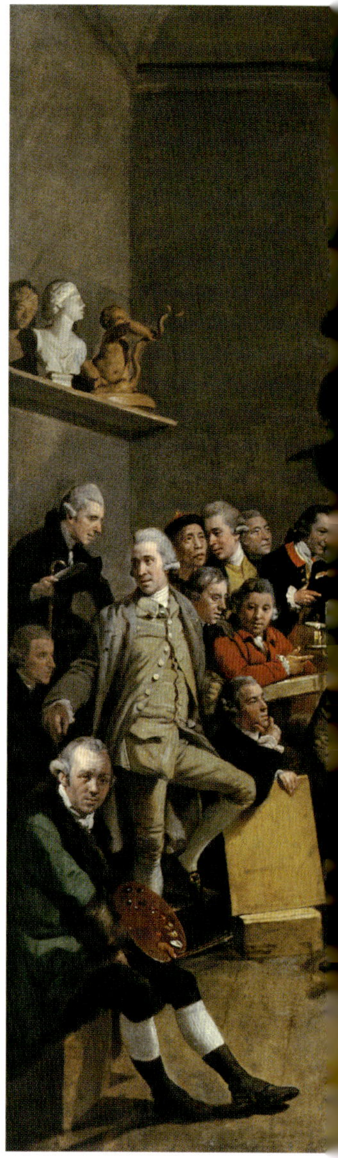

Johan Zoffany RA
The Academicians of the Royal Academy
1771–72
Oil on canvas
101.1 x 147.5 cm
Royal Collection Trust, London

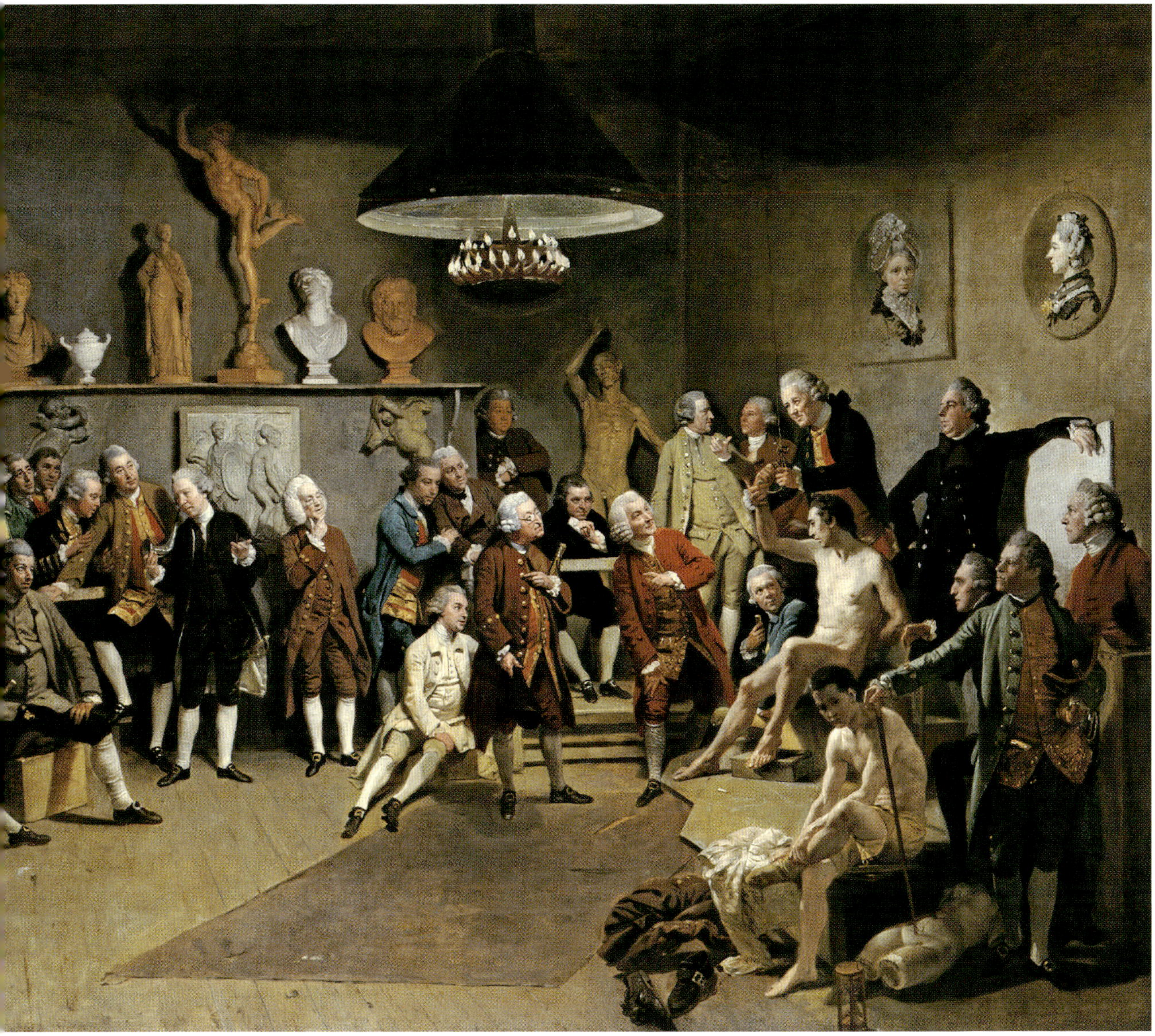

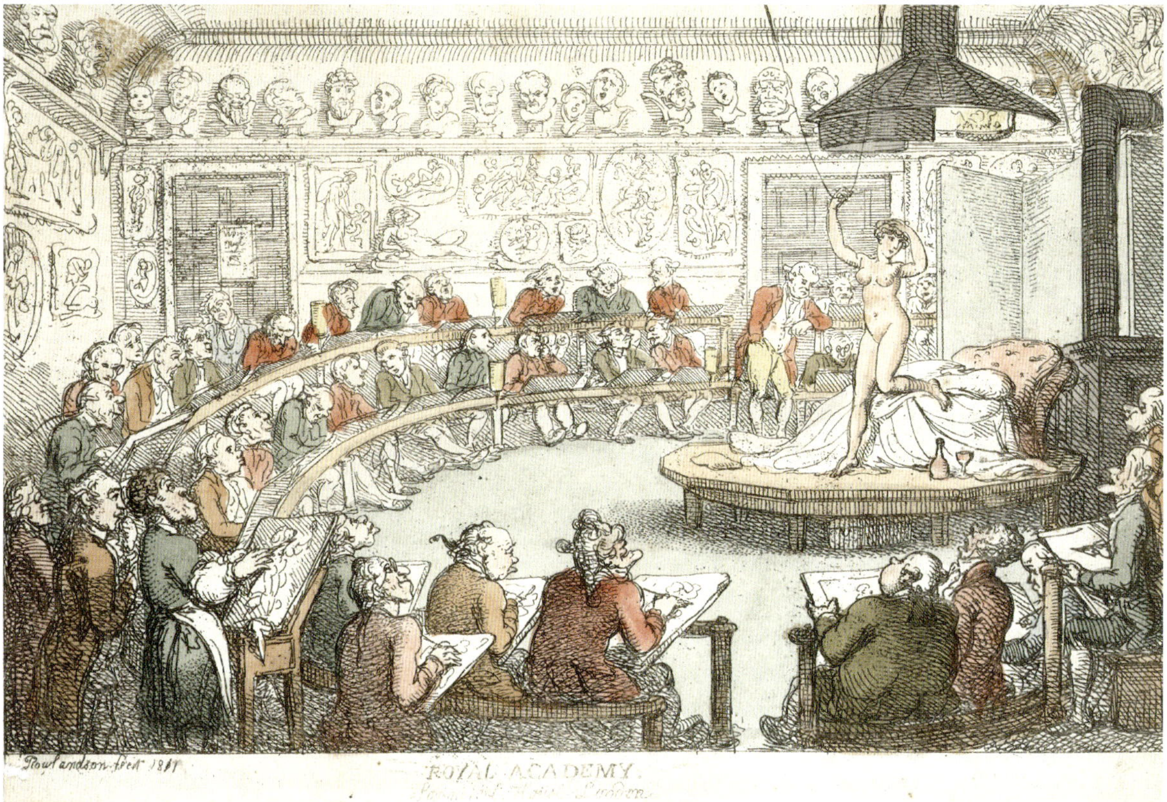

Thomas Rowlandson
A Life Class at the Royal Academy, Somerset House
1811
Hand-coloured etching
13.7 x 21.8 cm
Royal Academy of Arts, London

Academy stipulated that students must be over 20 years of age or married to attend when a woman model was sitting. Despite this, behaviour was sometimes problematic. Although women were paid more to sit – as 'shame' money – they were often assumed to be prostitutes and treated with less respect than the men. A depiction of the life class by the caricaturist Thomas Rowlandson hints at this attitude. (Indeed Rowlandson *would* know, having been almost expelled from the Royal Academy Schools for firing a pea shooter at a female model.) Similarly, the painter James Northcote RA recalled that although students were absorbed in their work during the class, some would 'watch the women out' at the end. He added that certain young men had even been 'lured into a course of dissipation and ruined by such connections'.

In Rowlandson's depiction, one of the artists – on the left, wearing an apron – appears to be painting instead of drawing. This again deviated from strict academic tradition but it was sometimes allowed in the RA life class, depending on the teacher. Records suggest, though, that painting was generally considered a practice that 'seduced' students away from draughtsmanship and, as such, was only recommended at an advanced stage. Painted life studies also tended to raise moral hackles. Even a series of impressive flesh-toned chalk studies by William Mulready RA were denounced as 'vulgar' and 'bestial' by the critic John Ruskin. Queen Victoria disagreed, however, and bought one.

The variable approach to life drawing at the Royal Academy was a direct result of the teaching system that had been put

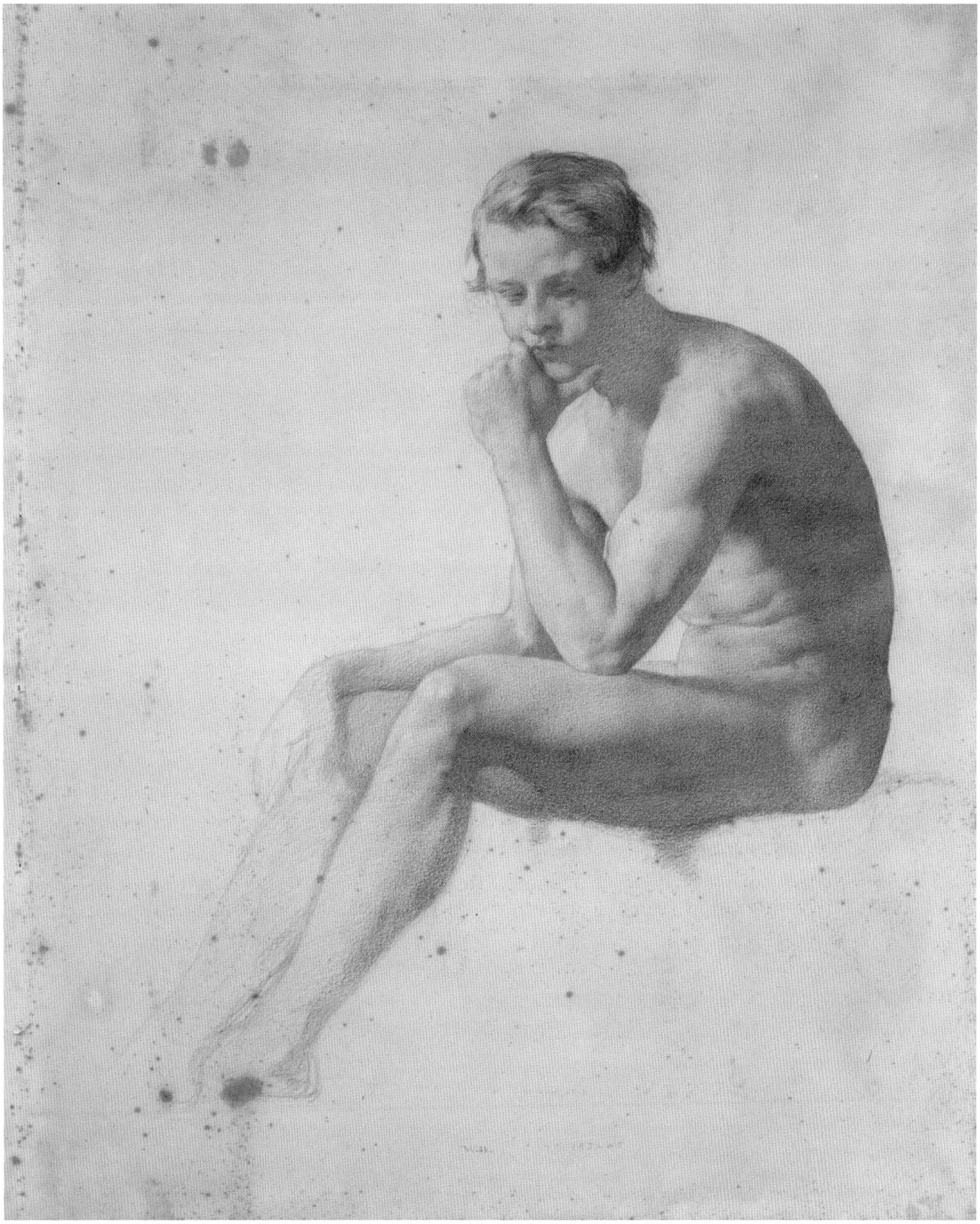

William Mulready RA
Seated Male Nude
Mid-1850s
Red and black chalk
on wove paper
53 x 43.6 cm
Royal Academy of Arts,
London

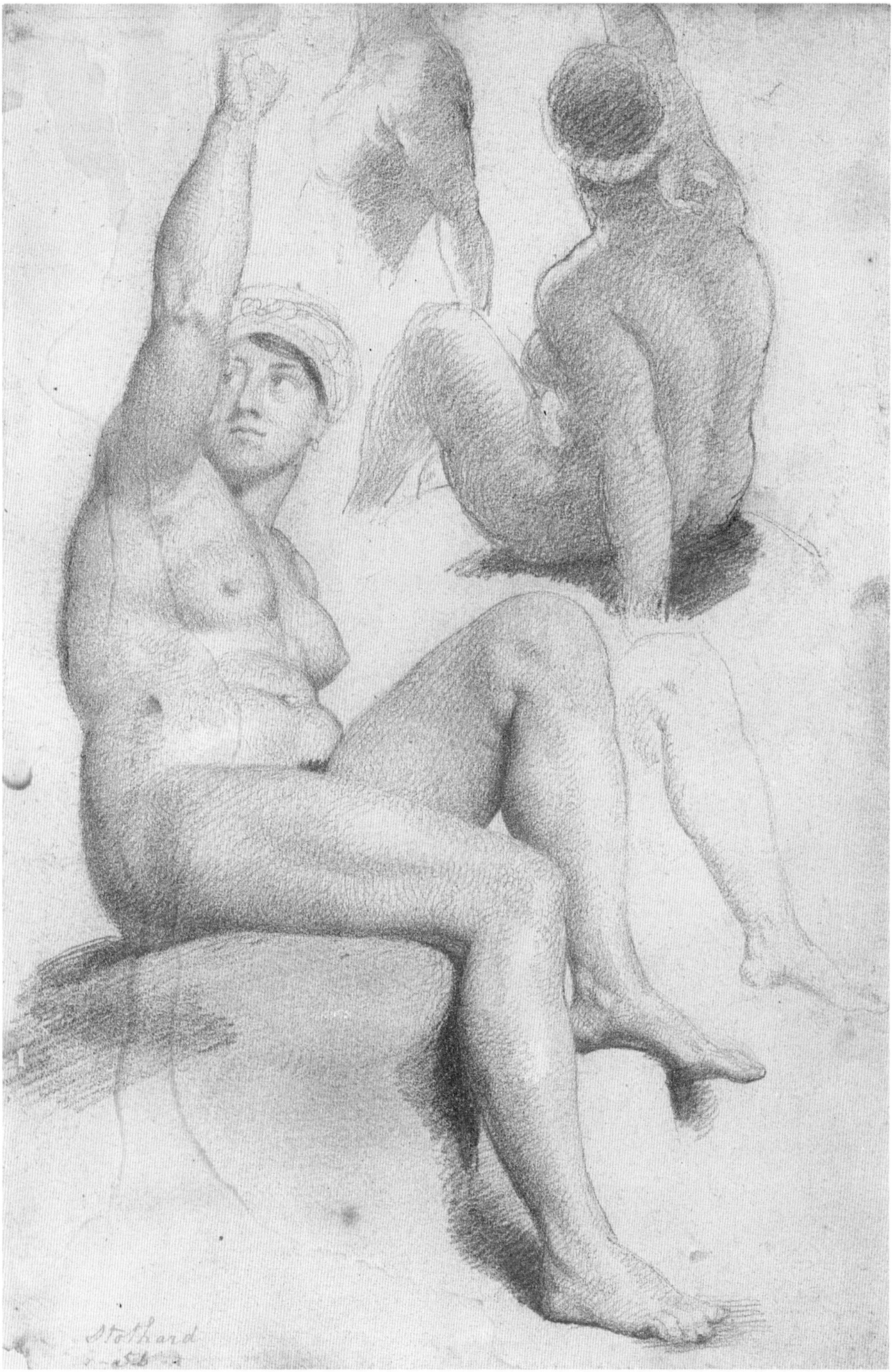
Stothard

in place at the outset. There was no specialist teacher for the class, which was overseen instead by a series of 'Visitors'. These were nine Academicians elected annually, each to take a turn at teaching the class for a month. The intention was to avoid the students being overly influenced by one particular artist or style. The RA's founding President, Sir Joshua Reynolds, felt that this had been a problem at some earlier academies, remarking that one of the great advantages of the new Academy was that it had 'nothing to unlearn'.

Classes were two hours long and models often held the same pose for several nights in a row. Luckily an hourglass was always on hand to ensure they had regular breaks. The Visitors set the pose of the model and some would watch over the class closely and correct drawings. Others, notably Mulready and William Etty, also taught by example, sitting down and drawing among the students. Mulready wrote: 'I think it is beneficial to the students for the Visitor not only to say, "Go in such a direction", but to go in that direction himself.'[14] Some Visitors, however, more or less opted out. The Victorian painter Sir Edwin Landseer, for example, was told off by his father, the engraver John Landseer, for reading *Oliver Twist* while his students drew. This situation was eventually to draw heavy criticism from commentators, the press and even the government, yet many students appreciated the relaxed approach, which they felt was a form of 'wise neglect', and the Academy continued to run the class this way until the 1930s.

Certain Academicians attempted to enliven the experience of academic life drawing. John Constable set up a bower of greenery in the Life Room to aid the representation of the model as Eve in the Garden of Eden. William Etty devised a 'living picture' with several models posing as 'Venus Sacrificing to the Graces'; the *Morning Herald* described the scene, noting that it raised the 'enthusiastic feelings' of the students 'almost to ecstasy'. Others pursued less dramatic methods. Thomas Stothard, for instance, developed an approach similar to the exercises that often feature in life classes today. While the model held a pose, Stothard – as Visitor – moved around the room taking different viewpoints and making small rapid sketches in a variety of media. Advanced students may have been encouraged to do the same. J. M. W. Turner, for one, produced drawings that were very similar to the sketches of Stothard, one of his teachers at the RA Schools. Turner appears to have followed his RA teachers closely; one of his Academy life drawings (see page 20), now in the Tate collection, is also a close match for one by James Barry (Visitor from 1794 to 1795) in the RA collection (see page 21).

During the nineteenth century other art schools emerged in Britain with very different approaches to life drawing.

Thomas Stothard RA
Studies of a Seated Female Nude
c. 1800
Pencil on wove paper
18.9 x 12.4 cm
Royal Academy of Arts, London

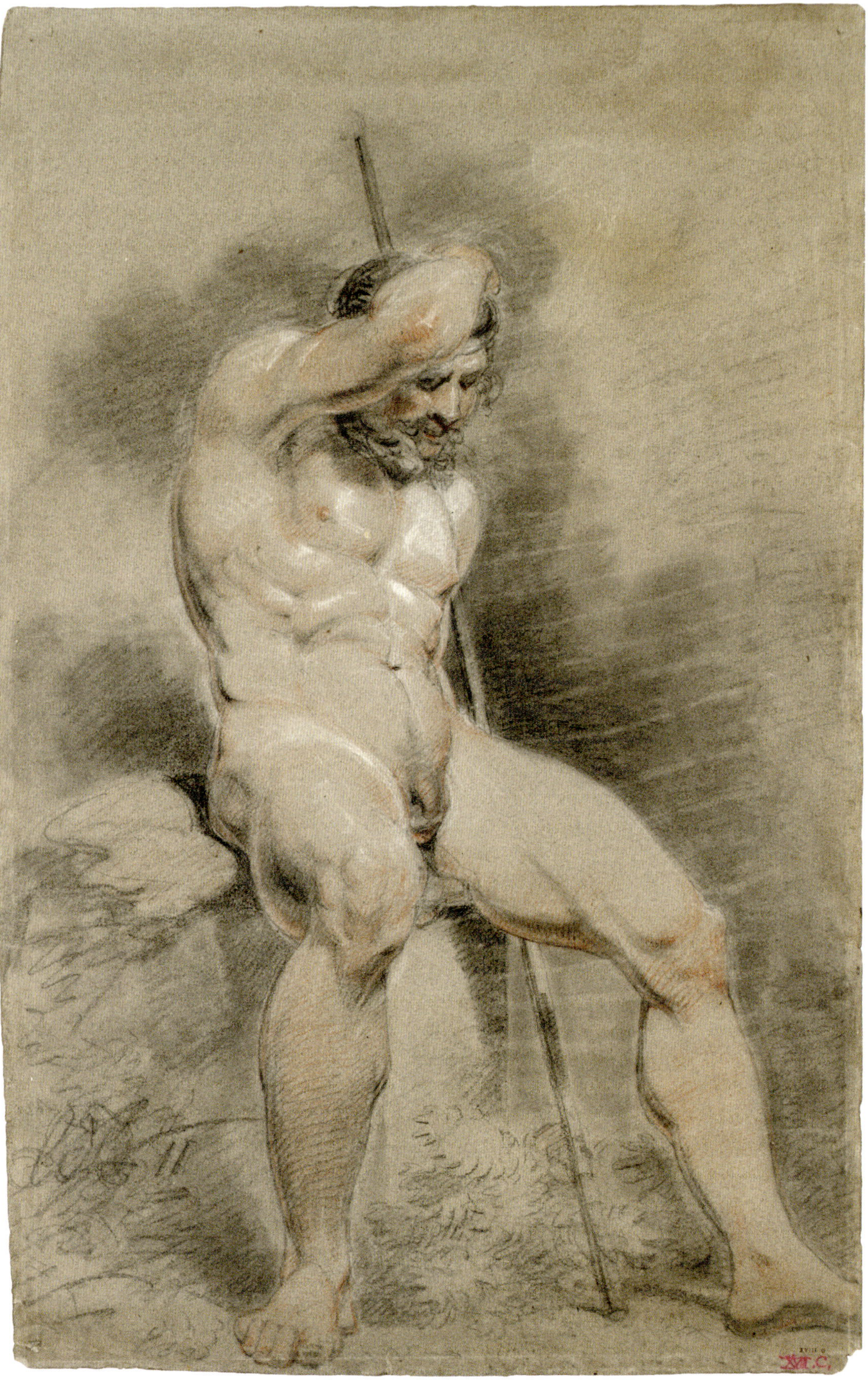

J. M. W. Turner RA
A Seated Male Nude with a Staff and with Right Arm on Head, in a Landscape Setting
c. 1794–95
Chalk on paper
46.3 x 29.6 cm
Tate, London

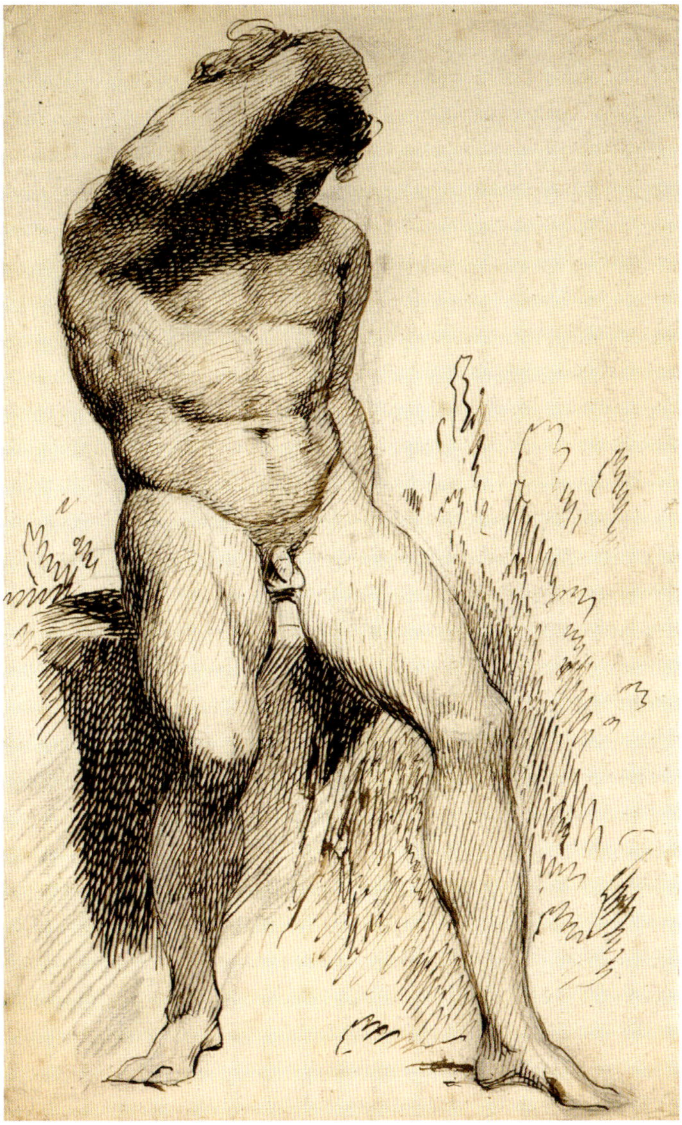

James Barry RA
Male Nude Sitting on a Rock
c. 1794–95
Pen and ink over black chalk on cream laid paper
51.6 x 31.9 cm
Royal Academy of Arts, London

Founded in 1837, the Government School of Design (later the Royal College of Art) originally aimed to offer designers and craftsmen a thorough grounding in drawing and, as a result, promoted study from plaster casts of natural forms, ornamental designs and fragments of architecture and sculpture above life drawing. Conversely, the Slade School of Art, founded in 1871, was intended to train fine artists, and recommended 'constant study from the life model', in the words of its first professor, Sir Edward Poynter Bt PRA. Slade students did begin their studies with a short stint of drawing plaster casts, but drawing and painting from the live model were the main focus of the course. Close observation was encouraged but studies did not need to be laboured to be considered 'finished'. The Royal Academy Schools belatedly followed suit, reducing the amount of time students had to spend drawing the (by then dreaded) casts, and introducing a broader curriculum with practical tuition in painting and sculpture.

In the twentieth century, however, life drawing also began to suffer from its elevated status within the academic canon. It had always had its critics; William Blake, for instance, had reportedly dismissed the static productions of the RA life class 'as looking more like death, of smelling of mortality'.[5] By the 1960s, when state art education in the UK was being overhauled, this sense of its staleness had spread. Jon Thompson, who studied at the RA in the 1950s, was not alone in objecting to the practice of life drawing as 'an ideologically loaded tool for making students conform to a certain philosophy of art'.[6] The traditional art-school curriculum of practical tuition, including life drawing, was entirely dismantled to be replaced by the more theoretical focus of the new Diploma in Art and Design. Ron Bowen, Reader Emeritus at the Slade, has stated: 'Observation simply ceased to be of interest to most students and tutors. Even here, where the

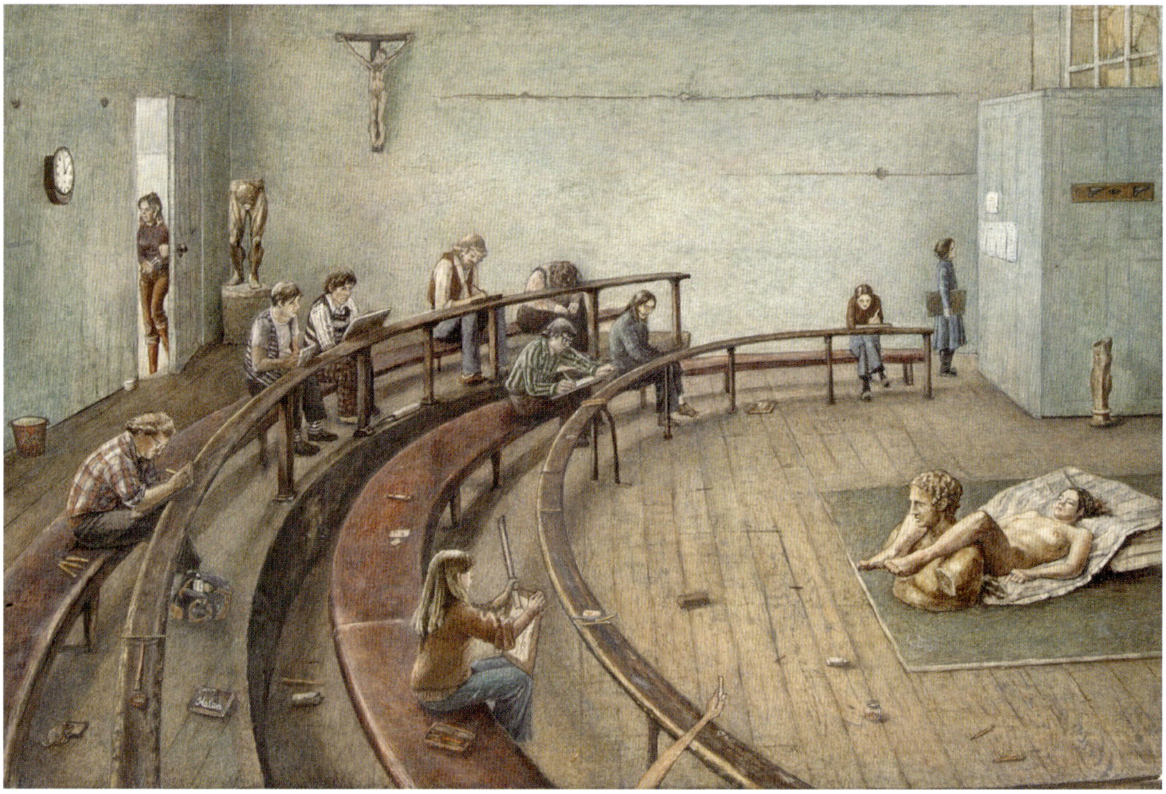

Helen Clapcott
Life School at the Royal Academy
c. 1979
Tempera on board
20 x 29 cm
Royal Academy of Arts, London

life class has remained central in the education of students, its role was challenged.[7] Being outside the state system, the Royal Academy continued with its life class nevertheless and all students – despite being postgraduates – were expected to attend for at least a term. The redundancy of this pursuit, at least for some, is conveyed in a *c.* 1979 portrayal of the Life Room by Helen Clapcott.

The Royal Academy eventually dropped compulsory life drawing, though it remains an option for Schools students, and practical courses are now offered to the public, including sessions where participants draw from life using iPads. Significantly, the Academy's historic Life Room has been retained, set up with its rows of semicircular, paint-dashed benches and staffed with the apparatus of a traditional art school: anatomical figures, busts of Roman emperors, heavy velvet drapes and a formidable set of spotlights. It is also used by students as a place for meetings and lectures, parties and performances, installations and exhibitions.

And as life drawing has become disentangled from its historical academic context, it has been gradually reinvigorated, as is demonstrated by projects like Jeremy Deller's *Iggy Pop Life Class* (2016; see page 38). It has even been reintroduced in some art colleges. Bryan Kneale RA, as the first Professor of Drawing at the Royal College of Art, described how he encouraged students to try life drawing, advising them to approach the practice of drawing the model 'from as many different viewpoints, physical and philosophical, as possible'.[8] Life drawing is now less about achieving a heroic, classical ideal and more about the quirky, the individual and the vulnerable, an exploration not only of the human form but also of the human condition. As Henry Moore put it: 'You can't understand life drawing without being emotionally involved ... It really is a deep, long struggle to understand oneself.'[9]

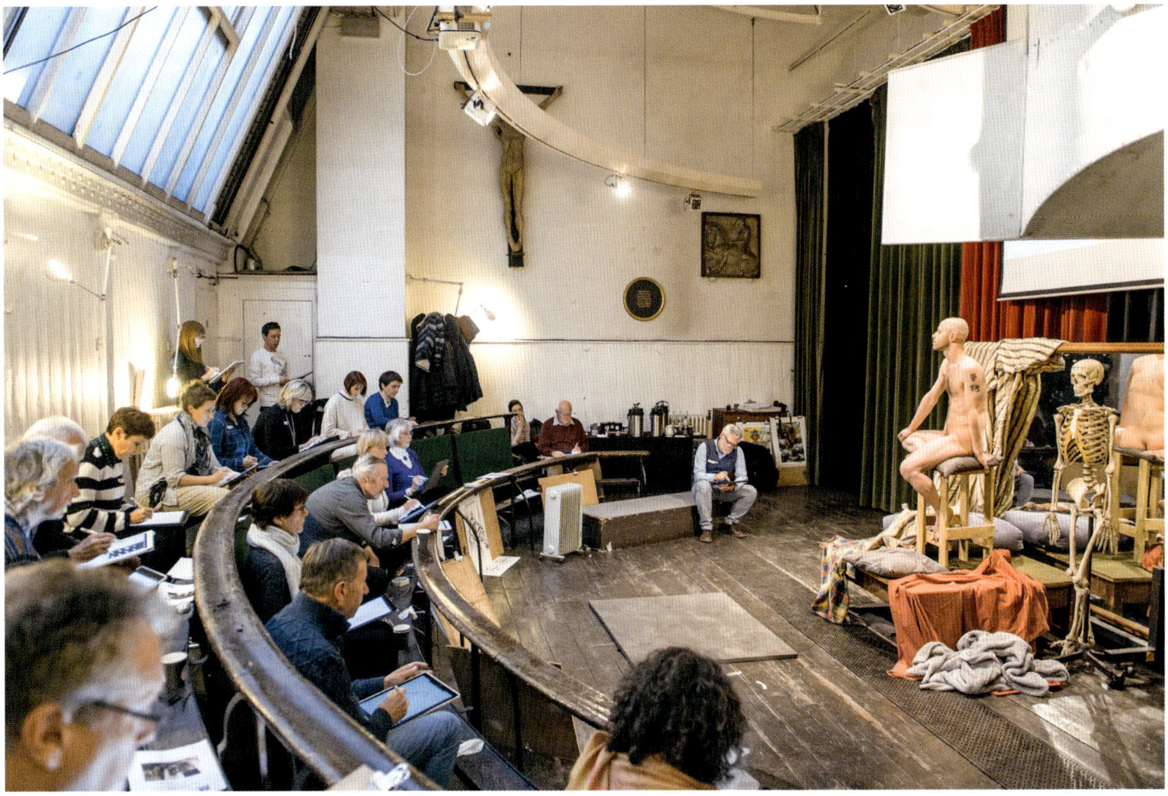

1 Cited by Alison Smith, *Exposed: The Victorian Nude*, exh. cat., Tate Britain, London, 2001, p.207.
2 Cited by Sir Charles Holroyd, *Michael Angelo Buonarroti*, London, 1911, p. 275.
3 'Affairs in France, Italy, and Portugal', *The Scots Magazine*, vol. 26, May 1764, p. 280.
4 Cited by Kathryn Moore Heleniak, *William Mulready*, New Haven and London, 1980, p. 153.
5 David Bindman, *Blake as an Artist*, Oxford, 1977, p. 19, citing Benjamin Heath Malkin. The full text of Malkin's memoir of Blake can be found in G. E. Bentley's *Blake Records*, New Haven and London, 2004, pp. 561–72.
6 Interviewed by Andrew Graham-Dixon, 'Drawing on the Past', *The Independent*, London, 22 January 1991. Also www.andrewgrahamdixon.com/archive/drawing-on-the-past.html (accessed 22 October 2017).
7 Graham-Dixon, 1991.
8 Graham-Dixon, 1991.
9 Henry Moore, in John and Vera Russell, 'Conversations with Henry Moore', *The Sunday Times*, 17 December 1961, cited in *Henry Moore: Writings and Conversations*, Berkeley, p. 47.

A life-drawing class in which participants drew with iPads, in the Life Room of the Royal Academy Schools, 11 February 2017

Overleaf:
Russell Westwood
Students Modelling Figures from Life in the Royal Academy Schools
1953
Photograph from Ilford 100D negative film
6 x 6 cm
Royal Academy of Arts, London

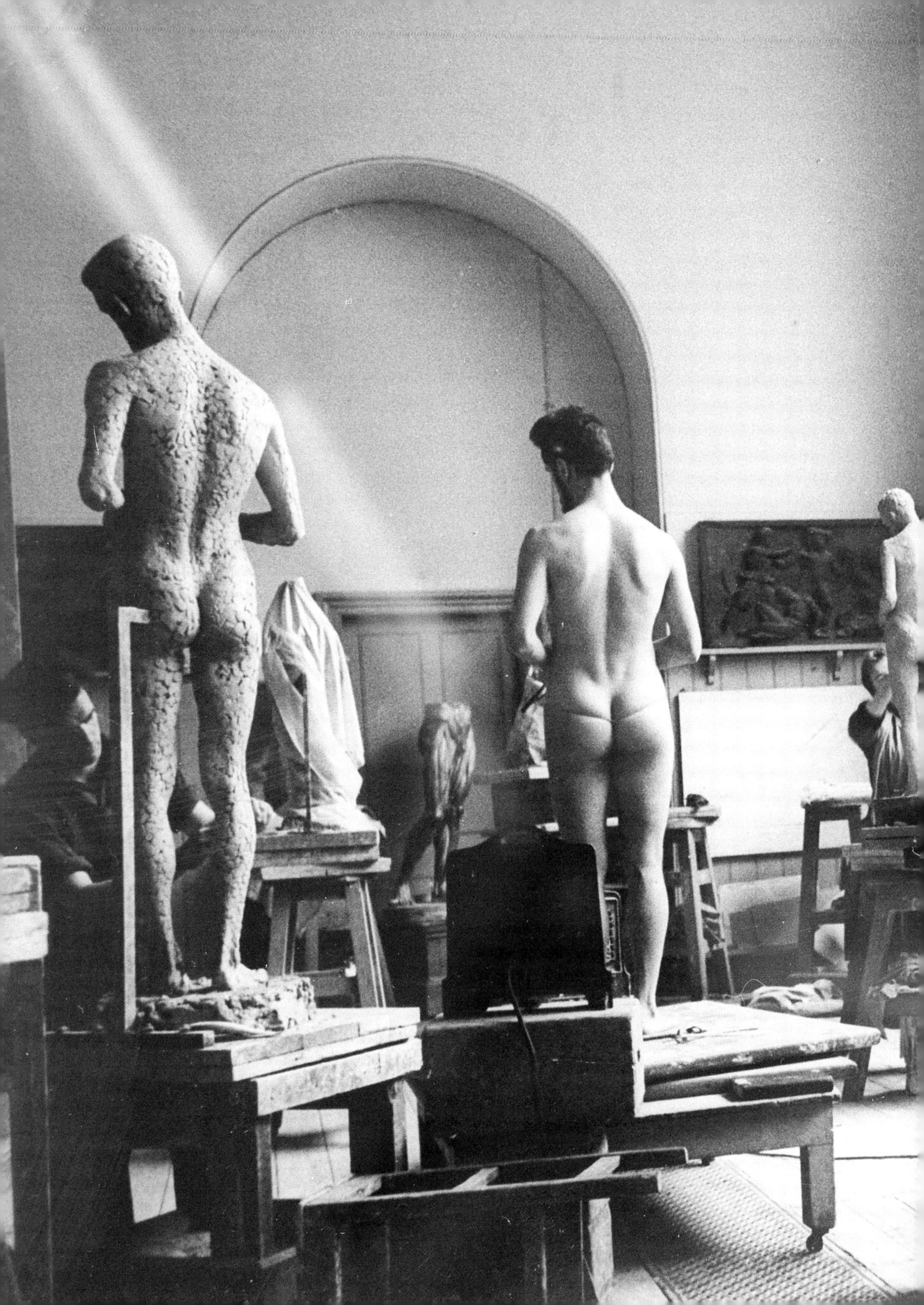

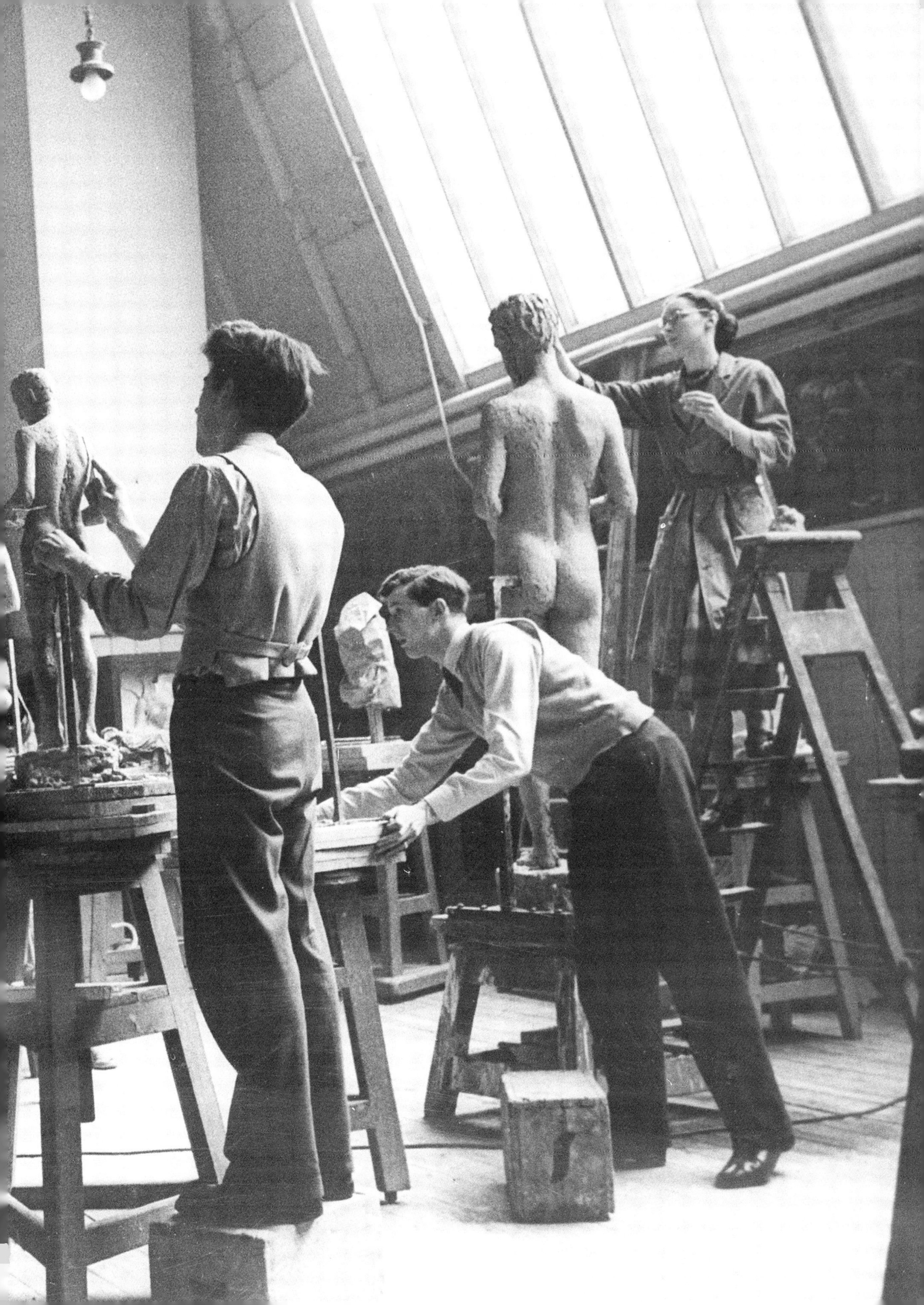

Ellen Altfest

New York-based painter Ellen Altfest (b. 1970) is known for canvases that capture male figures and natural objects in meticulous detail, the result of many hours of careful observation working from life. The artist's paintings of bodies are tightly cropped, focusing on fragments of her male models' forms.

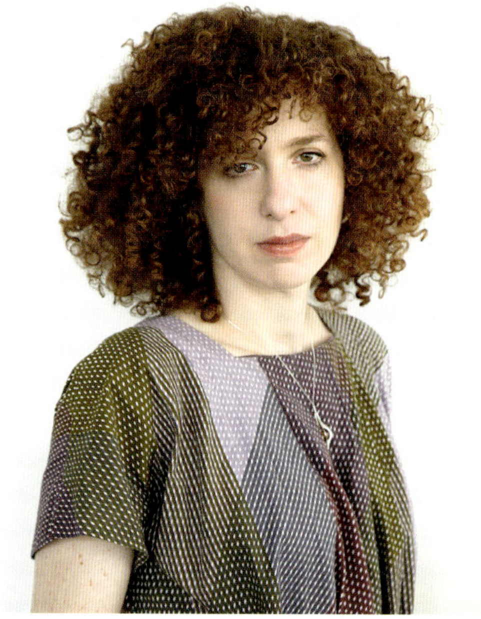

The American painter Ellen Altfest once spent thirteen months in the Connecticut woods working on a single painting; her subject was an A4-size section of the trunk of a fallen tree, which she reproduced to scale on an A4-size canvas. She worked on *Tree* (2012–13; see page 31) in solitude through the winter cold and the summer heat to capture every crease and fold in the bark, every lacy filigree of moss, every variation in the leaves on the forest floor.

Altfest's forensic intensity is also focused on the human body, and if her artistic predecessor for *Tree* was Albrecht Dürer with his *Great Piece of Turf* (1503; Albertina, Vienna), for her paintings of bodies it is perhaps early Lucian Freud or the hyper-realism of Australian sculptor Ron Mueck. As with *Tree*, these paintings do not capture the whole subject, but just an individual part, in isolation. *The Butt* (2007), for example, is just that – a close-up of the lower back and squashed buttocks of a man sitting on a paint-spattered studio stool. There are no legs and no head; this is a slice of a person whose sole distinguishing feature is his hirsute back and the dense cluster of hairs at the cleft of his buttocks. The shape of the sitter suggests that he possesses some heft but Altfest offers no clue as to his looks nor to his identity. He has been deconstructed and turned from something recognisably human into an abstract shape.

In her method Altfest takes the routine of the life class to its extremes. Drawing from life, she says, is 'like all languages, something it is best to learn young.' Although she learnt the traditional way, from plaster heads, from casts of the flayed figure and eventually from the living model, she works only on parts, rather than using that training to treat the whole human body.

Painting the whole figure 'would take me forever', she says. 'I like choosing what the viewer looks at. The full figure can be generic, so I crop it.' Altfest thinks of her pictures in terms of a related group rather than a concerted series: she doesn't need one painting of each constituent part of the body. When she first started painting

The Butt
2007
Oil on canvas
33 x 33 cm

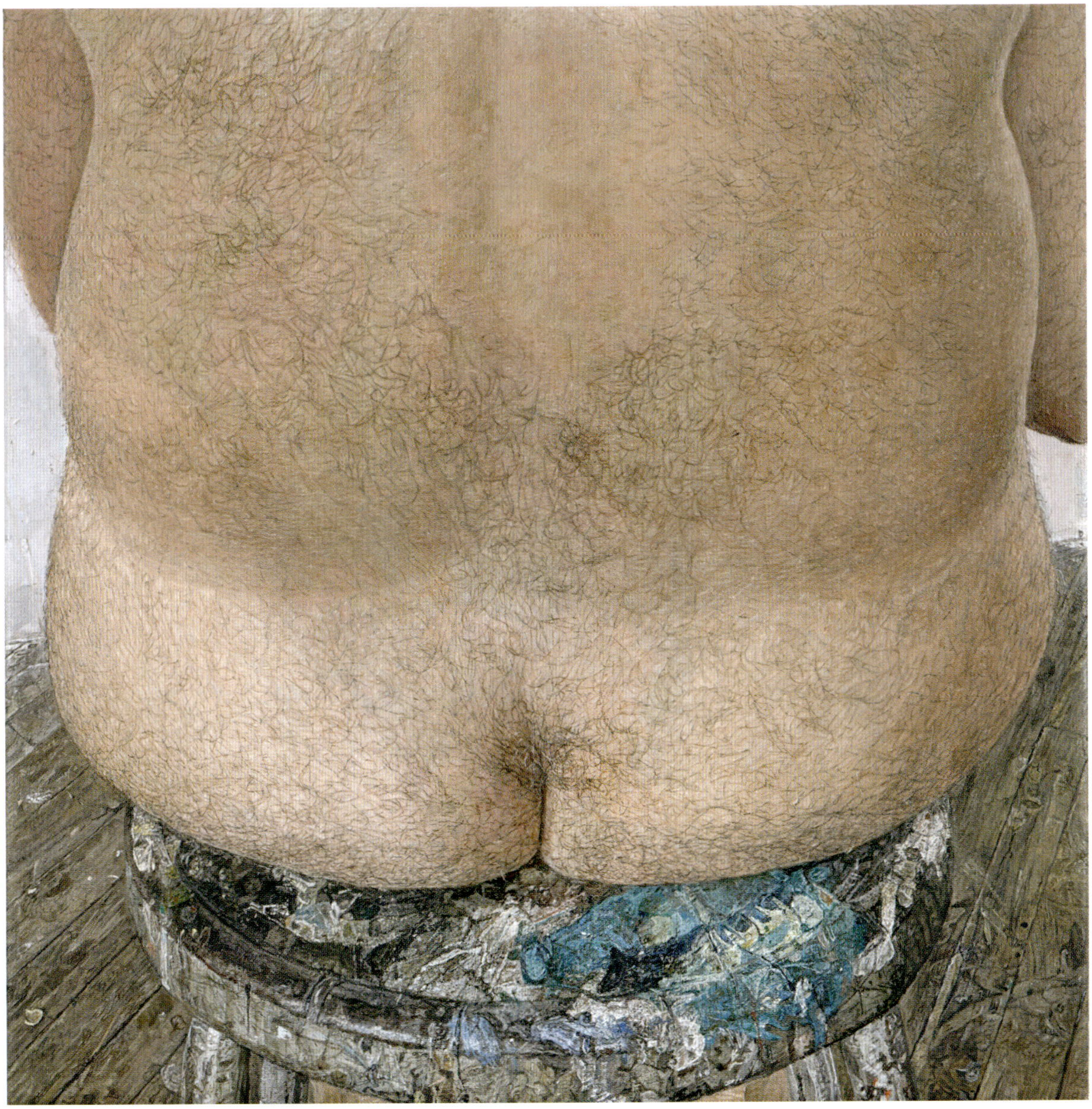

The Bent Leg
2008
Oil on canvas
30.5 x 20.3 cm

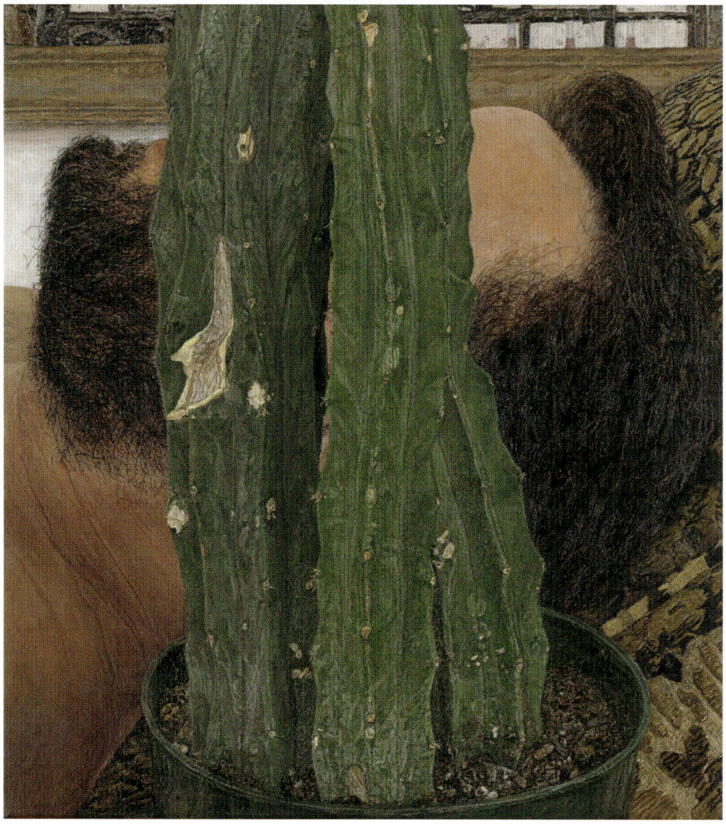

Head and Plant
2009–10
Oil on canvas
27.9 x 25.4 cm

the figure – always male – she started with a close-up of a penis: 'I'm painting man,' she thought, 'so I should start with the most emblematic part.' An armpit, a hand, a section of leg and a bearded head with the features hidden by a cactus followed (a painting that combines her two strands – flora and fauna). 'I forget I'm painting an armpit. I'm very absorbed, involved. I'm trying to push the painting.'

'As a subject the body can overpower the rest of the painting,' she remarks. The owner of the armpit might feel differently; he spent so long holding the pose that he strained his rotator cuff and had to stop posing for several weeks. De-powering the body is also the reason why she doesn't paint faces. 'The face is often the focus of attention in paintings, but I want to make every part of a painting of equal interest.' It means that she has in effect become a still-life painter. The body, for her, offers an extraordinary amount of visual information – every hair, every pore, the blue shadow of veins beneath the skin – so, she asks, 'Why would I leave something out?' This detail is also intended to 'slow down the reading' of her pictures – we are unfamiliar spending so long staring at others' bodies. She uses photography to play around with the composition and test possibilities, but the rest is painstaking observation. 'I'm not anti-technology,' she says, 'but technology hinders my ability to focus.'

Altfest freely admits that her way of working is extremely impractical but then, as she says, 'You wouldn't be an artist if practicality was an issue.' It is the only way she has found to achieve her ultimate aim: 'I want to give a lot to the viewer rather than demand something from them.'

Michael Prodger

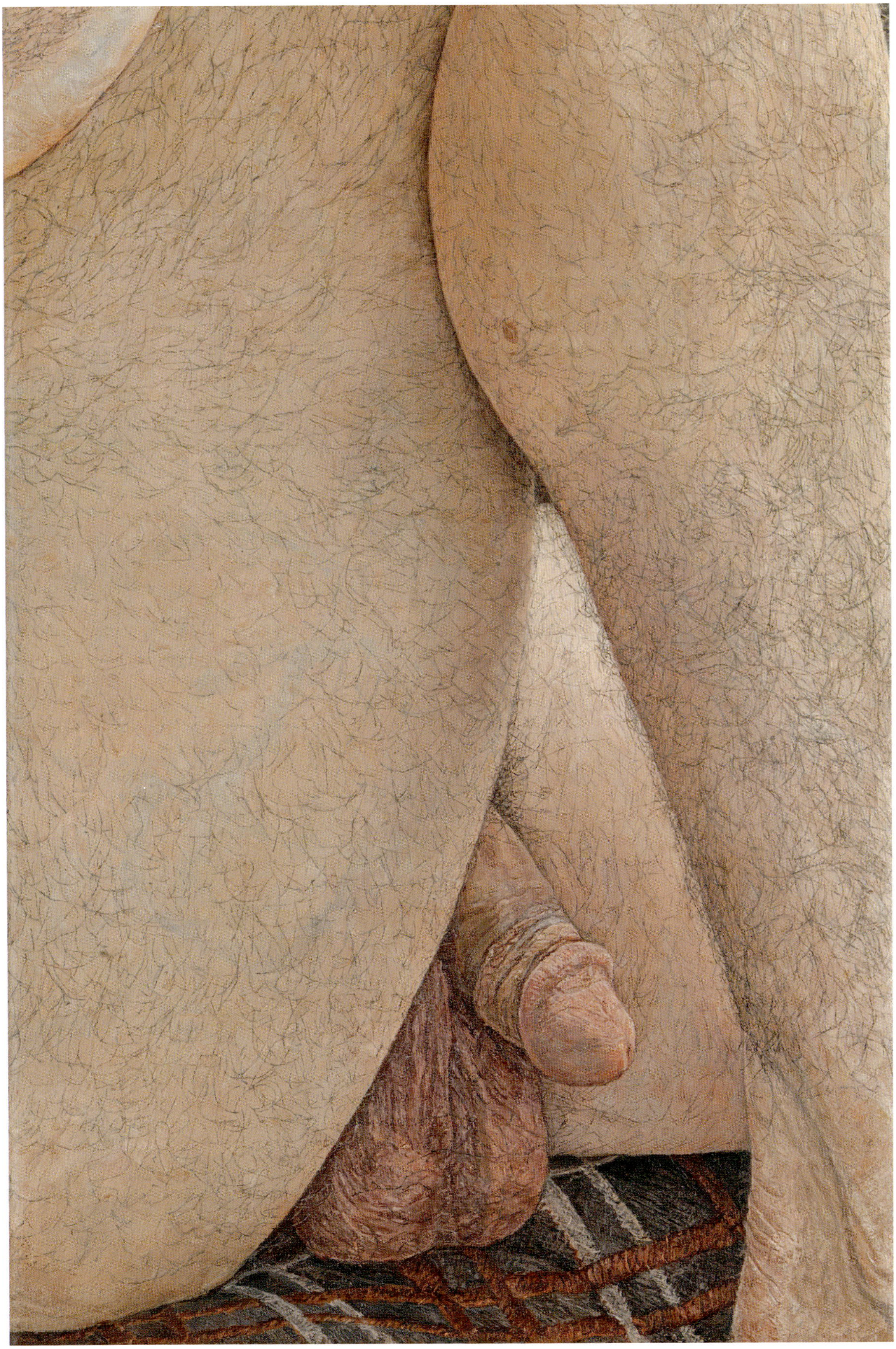

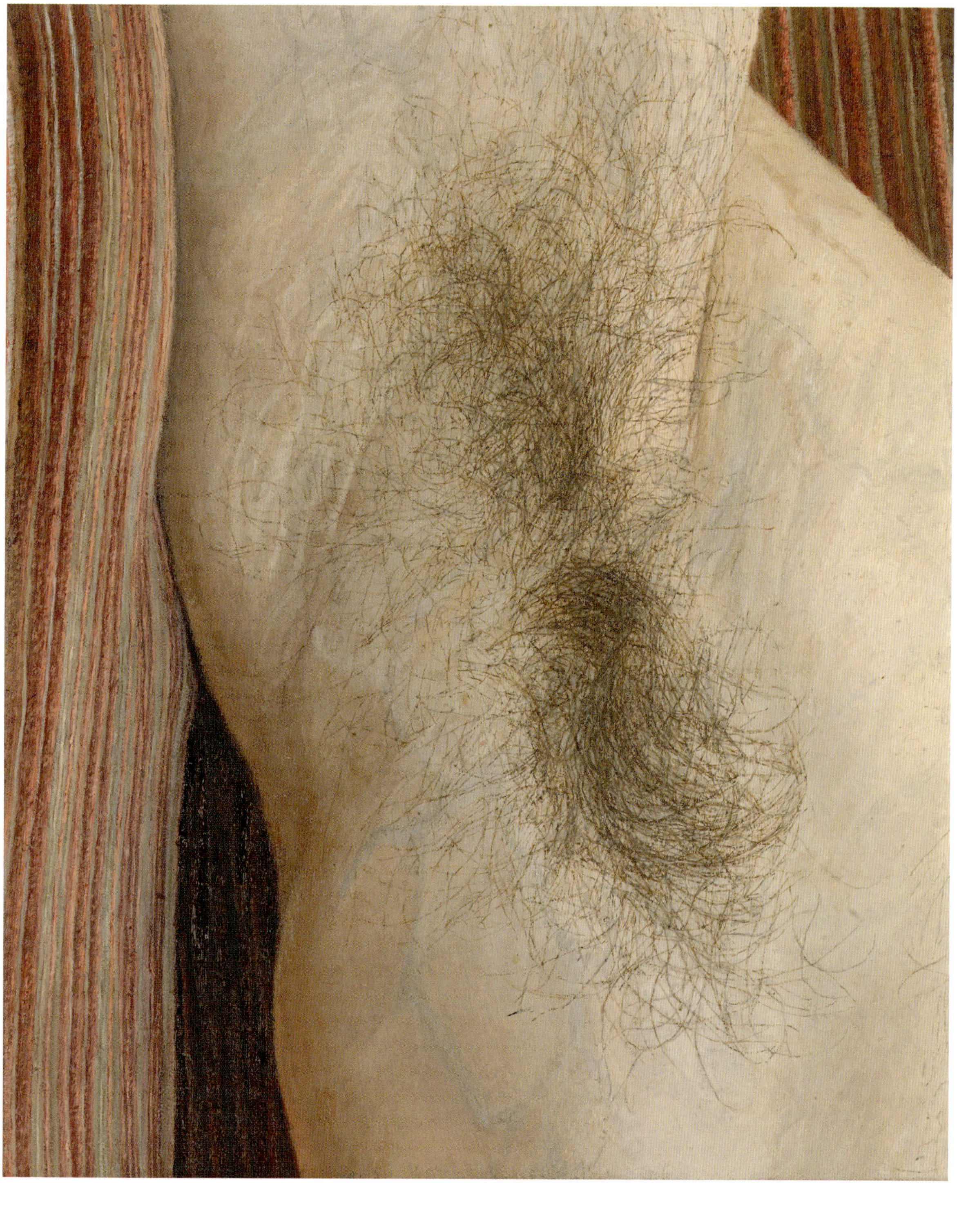

Armpit
2011
Oil on canvas
21.2 x 17.8 cm

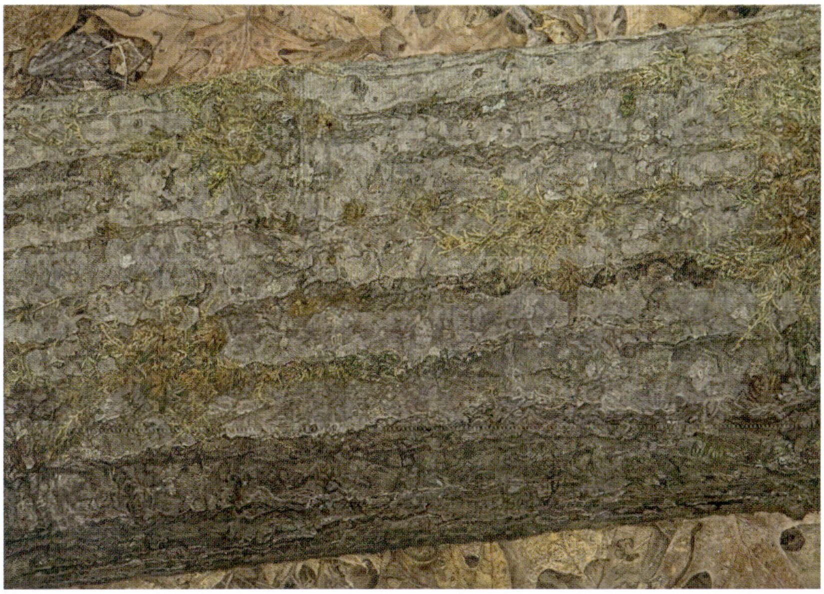

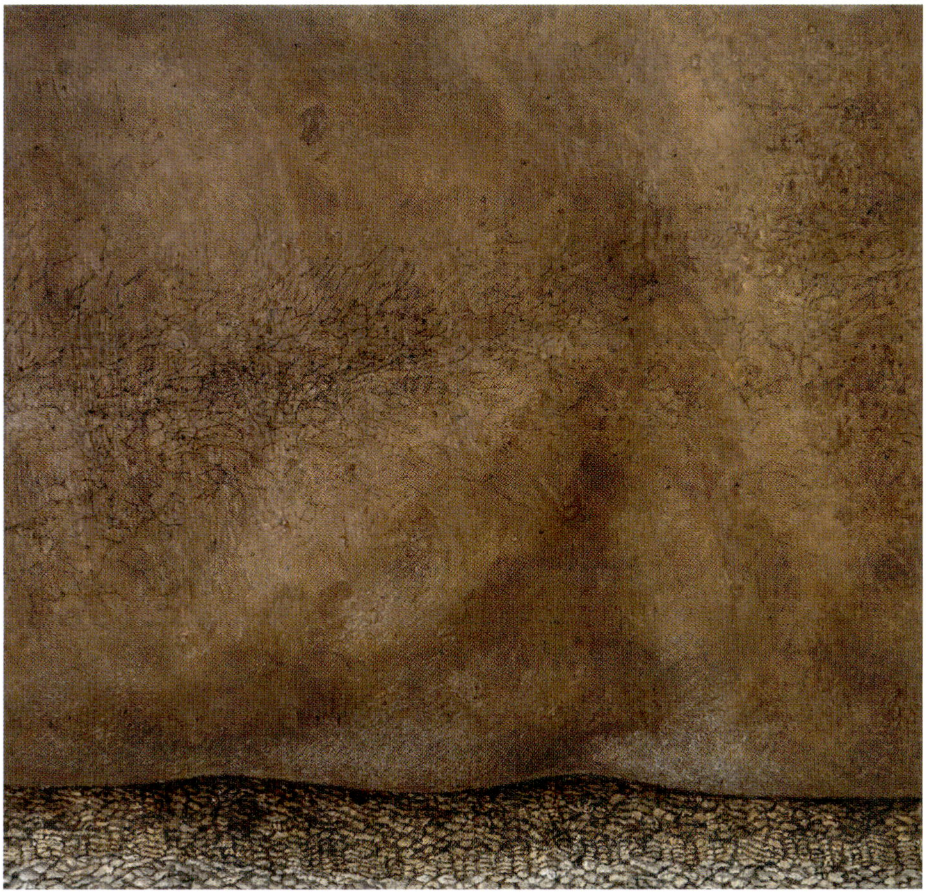

Tree
2013
Oil on canvas
20.6 x 28.6 cm

Abdomen
2014–15
Oil on canvas
23.5 x 25.3 cm

Cai Guo-Qiang

Chinese artist Cai Guo-Qiang (b. 1957) is celebrated for his signature use of gunpowder in drawings, paintings and spectacular events. Trained in stage design at the Shanghai Theatre Academy, Cai also produces mixed-media sculptures, installations and social projects. He is based in New York, where he has been the subject of shows at the Metropolitan Museum of Art (2006) and the Solomon R. Guggenheim Museum (2008).

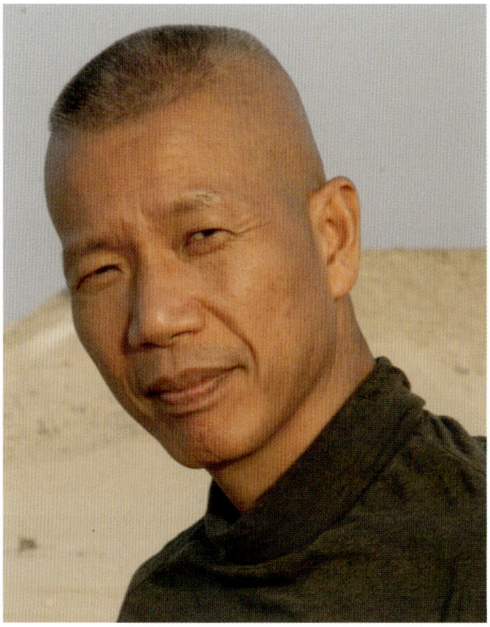

Cai Guo-Qiang is most famous for using gunpowder as his paint and the sky as his canvas. He orchestrates awe-inducing pyrotechnic pieces that, he has said, seek 'a sense of the eternal from the ephemeral'. But like many artists acclaimed today for radical processes, Cai came of age as a young artist while working from life. He began as a teenager, during the 1970s, taking his drawing materials around his home town of Quanzhuo in China, accompanied by his friends and family – his father, Cai Ruiqin, was a gifted traditional brush painter and calligrapher.

'We went to farms and factories to portray the working people,' recalls Cai. These were the years of the Cultural Revolution and Mao Zedong had dictated that art must serve the state by glorifying the proletariat. 'On the rare occasions that I drew from models, I drew myself or other male friends. I only started figure drawings of nude models in college. From this experience of sketching, I learned about the relationship between the artist and subject, and about another person's body, both physically and metaphysically.'

Western artistic processes such as working from life gained a foothold in China during the nineteenth century, as European imperialism exerted cultural influence. In the 1910s and 1920s, after the establishment of the Republic of China (1912–49), a new generation of art educators – many of whom had spent time in Europe – ensured that China's art schools embraced Western techniques. These included making copies from casts of classical sculpture, a process that, in earlier centuries in Europe, had to be mastered before students could progress to living models. Yan Wenliang, for example, who founded the Suzhou Art Academy in 1922, shipped home hundreds of classical casts on his return from France. The practice of working from casts and models persisted through Mao's years, when the state demanded heroic representations of the human form, and it continues to be a central element of Chinese art education today.

Self-portrait: A Subjugated Soul
1985/89
Gunpowder and oil on canvas
167 x 118 cm
Collection of Leo Shih

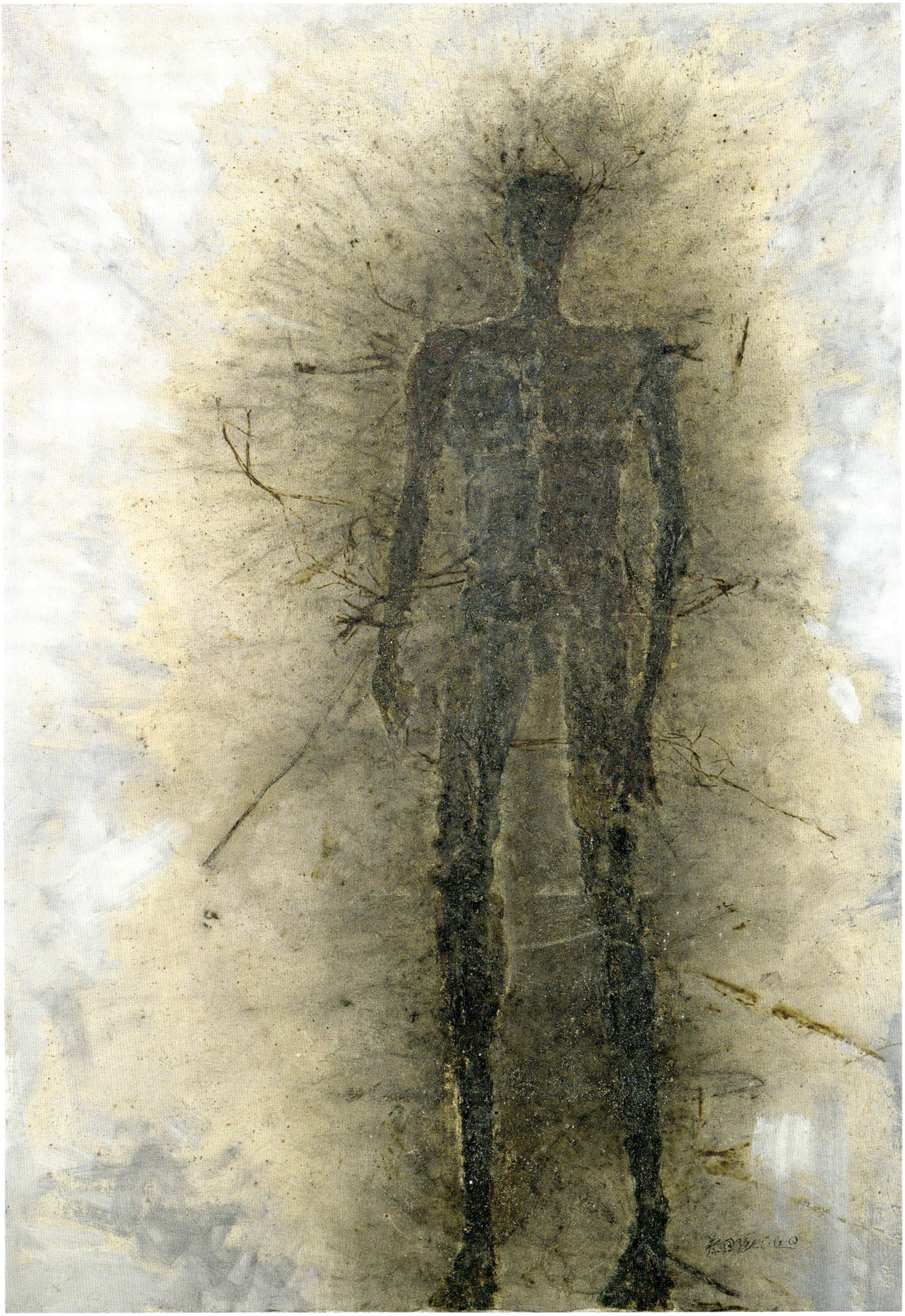

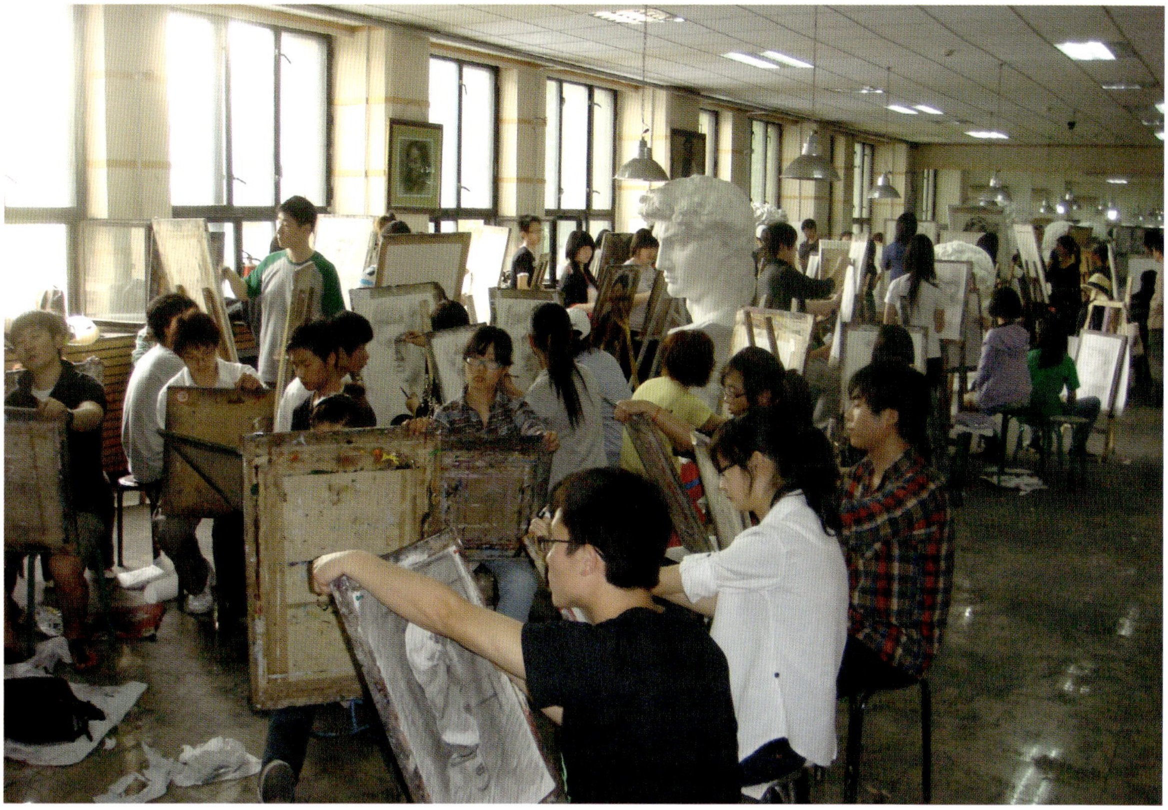

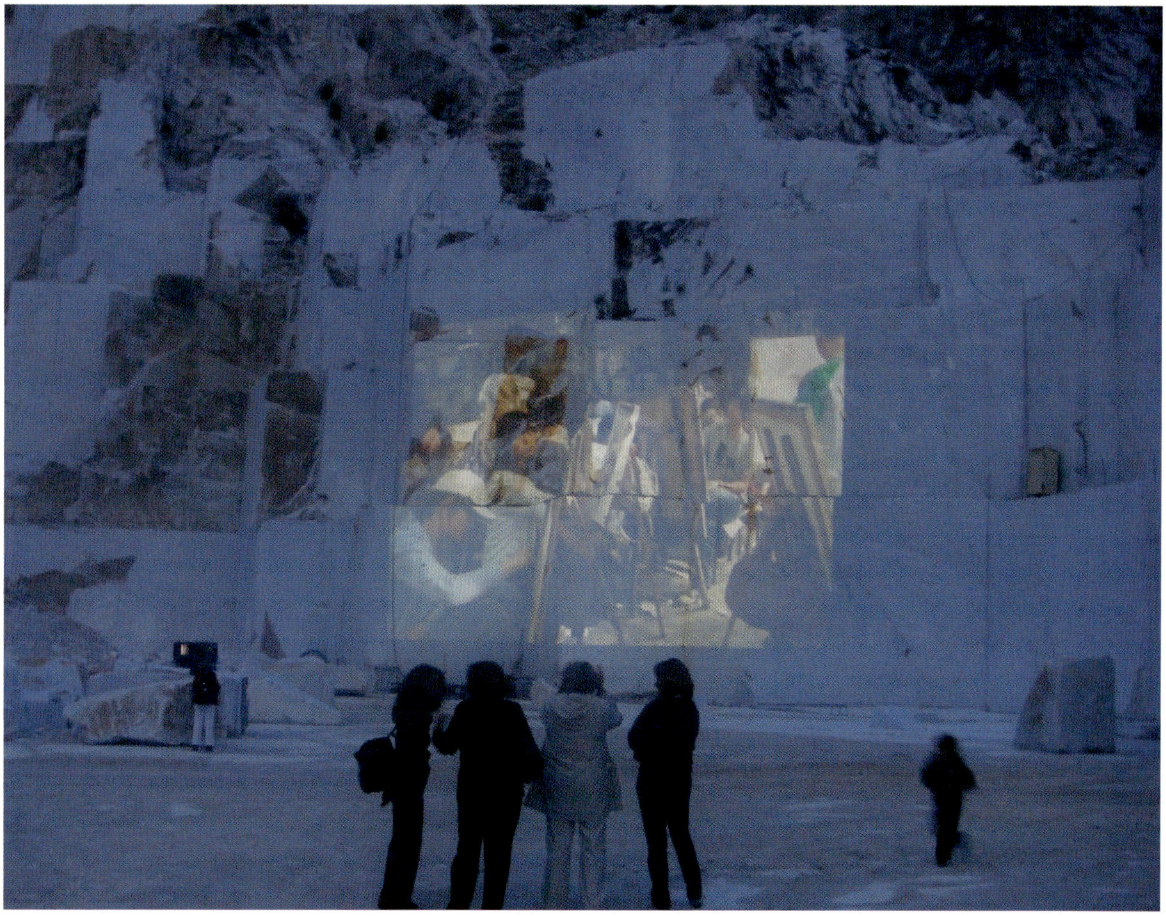

Untitled (David)
1983
Charcoal on paper
123.19 x 88.9 cm
Collection of the artist

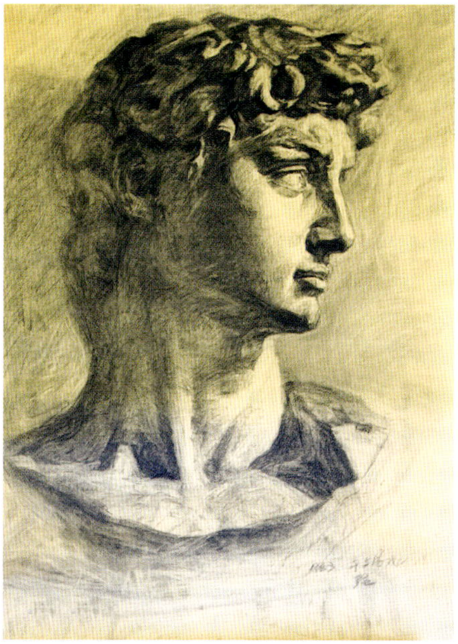

Cai remembers his experience in 1983 of spending days drawing from a portrait-bust copy of Michelangelo's *David* (1501–04; Galleria dell'Accademia, Florence).

'By drawing *David*, I learned to observe the whole while portraying the details, and to look for the relationship between the details and the whole. It taught me to pay attention to form, light and shadow.' It also allowed the young Cai to consider Western influence in new ways, and in particular the abiding impact of the Renaissance. 'Facing the *David* bust was like transcending time and space to confront Western culture,' he says. 'Sketching one detail at a time, I could feel the traces of the sensibility left by the Old Masters.'

Cai's video *One Thousand Youngsters Drawing David*, produced over two decades later in 2010, takes this dissemination of classical Western culture as its subject. Intended for that year's International Sculpture Biennale of Carrara, the work captures hundreds of Beijing students as they sketch monumental plaster reproductions of *David*. At the biennale's opening night, the video was projected onto the façade of one of Carrara's quarries, whose marble had been Michelangelo's material for his original *David* five centuries earlier; the Renaissance masterpiece had returned home in a relay race of replication. 'I was touched by the groups of young boys and girls gathered around *David* busts, drawing with reverence,' says Cai. 'Thousands of Chinese children study and draw *David* at school. Whether that is necessary is a separate matter. As an artist, I feel an overwhelming emotion of pride on Michelangelo's behalf. I also feel a kind of sadness; the education is too uniform and mechanical.'

Copying was also a theme for Cai's installation-performance for the 1999 Venice Biennale, *Venice's Rent Collection Courtyard* (see overleaf), which won the biennale's prestigious Golden Lion award. He invited ten academically trained sculptors to re-create elements of the Socialist-Realist sculptural scene *Rent Collection Courtyard* (1965), a widely replicated work in China that shows a landlord collecting rent from peasants. The Venice audience could encounter the sculptors as they produced the life-size clay figures on site. 'The audience was not only looking at the sculptures; they were looking at artists making sculptures.

Students of Beijing's Black and White Drawing Studio sketching cast busts of Michelangelo's *David* in 2010

One Thousand Youngsters Drawing David
2010
Video performance
Realised in the Cave Michelangelo quarry, Cararra, Italy

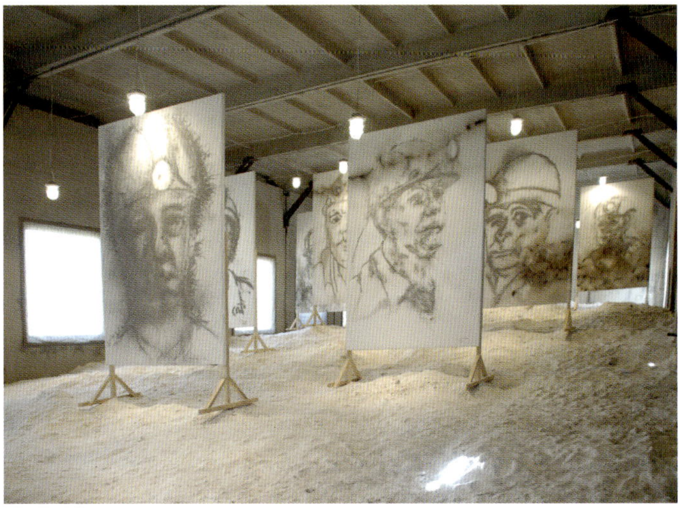

Monuments on Shoulders
2011
Gunpowder on canvas, coal, crystallised salt and mining lamps
Installation view at IZOLYATSIA, Donetsk
Dimensions variable
Collection of the artist

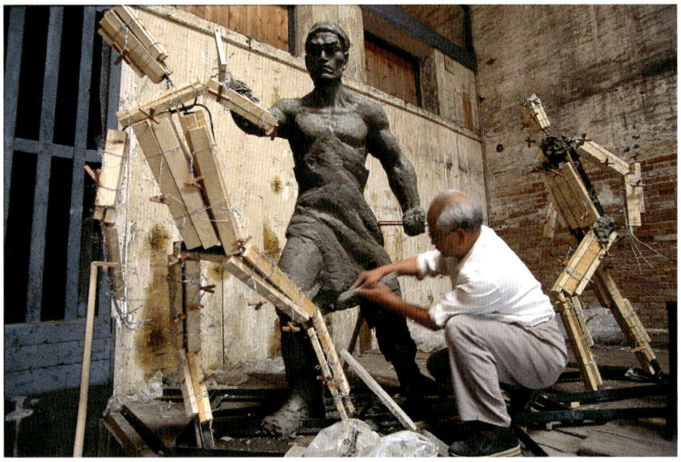

Venice's Rent Collection Courtyard
1999
108 life-size sculptures created on site by Long Xu Li and nine guest artisan sculptors, 60 tons of clay, wire and wood armature
Dimensions variable
Installation view at 48th Venice Biennale

The creators are the subjects of the work, and I presented their fate as a more important concept than the sculptures – the fate of artists in our era.'

He describes his own *David* drawing 'as a relatively poor job ... my approach to drawing is more expressionistic and emotional'. In one of his breakthrough gunpowder paintings, *Self-portrait: A Subjugated Soul* (1985/89; see page 33), he relinquished control of his line, creating his outline by igniting gunpowder on canvas. 'I wasn't overly focused on my actual form. I was trying to portray the characteristics of my time through the explosion of the gunpowder material. That time included destruction and violence, and it was my hope that the work would also carry a certain spiritual idea.' Whereas his gunpowder works tend to draw from nature – landscapes, clouds, flowers, animals – he has continued to ignite the shapes of human figures in works such as *Monuments on Shoulders* (2011), a series of large-scale portraits of Ukrainian miners, and the panorama *Day and Night* (2009), in which a female figure flanked by flowers is constantly transformed in state across 32 metres of paper.

Cai's model for the latter was the Taiwanese dancer Ching-Ying Chien, whose shadows in various positions he traced on paper. 'She determined what I drew. Her emotions in time, the flowers corresponding to her emotions, the shadows of her movements: they were all directed by her. We worked from early in the morning to 9 pm in the evening, and by the end of the day she would become emotional and show loneliness and sadness.' Cai describes working with the model in this process as 'like having mental intercourse'; he has previously described the use of gunpowder on paper or canvas as 'like making love'.

'Using gunpowder is erotic in itself,' he explains. 'This material is violent and eroticism is violent. Gunpowder is difficult to control; it is emotional and there is a lot of chance involved. During the process of making a work, on paper or canvas, I lay the surface and materials on the ground instead of the easel. I drop gunpowder on top, touch and rub the material, draw lines, and place stones on top; this leads to the final ignition – the climax. The hesitation and patience in the process leads to the final release and liberation.'

The process often ends in abstraction, to the artist's delight. 'Photographs can reproduce images of mountains, clouds and flowers, but artists can feel and depict the abstractions within.' But he admits that, whatever shape his work takes today, working from life and from casts is its foundation. 'No matter the material or concept, whenever as an artist you encounter the surface and image, inevitably there is form, which brings you back to your training.'

Sam Phillips

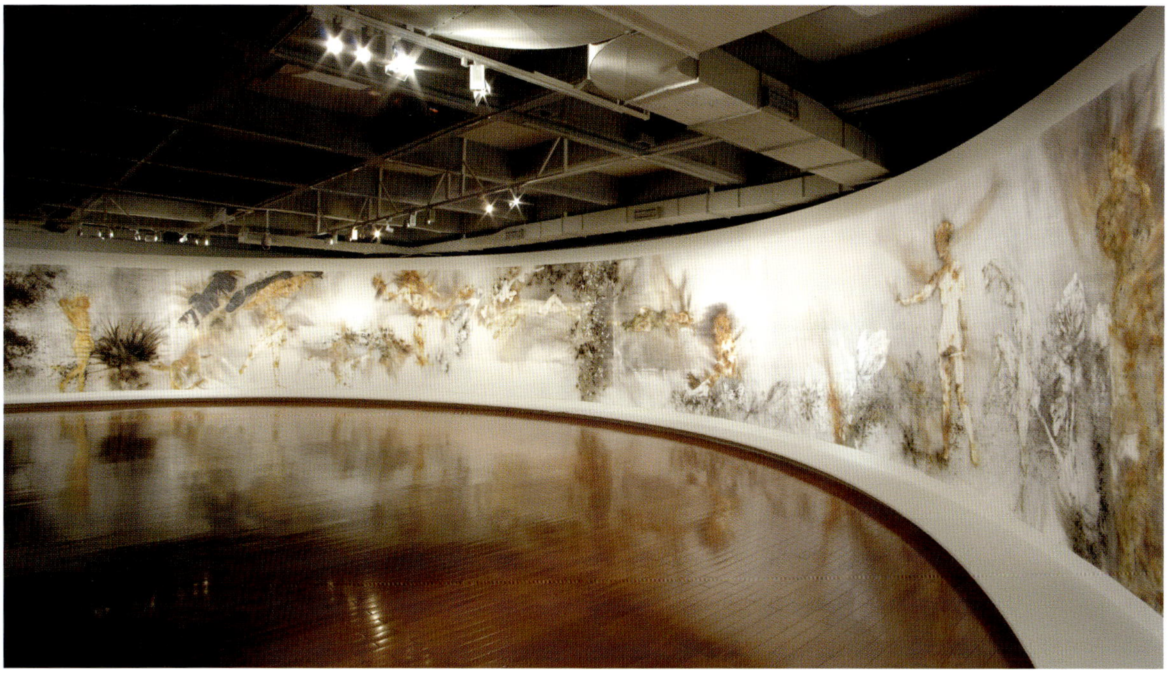

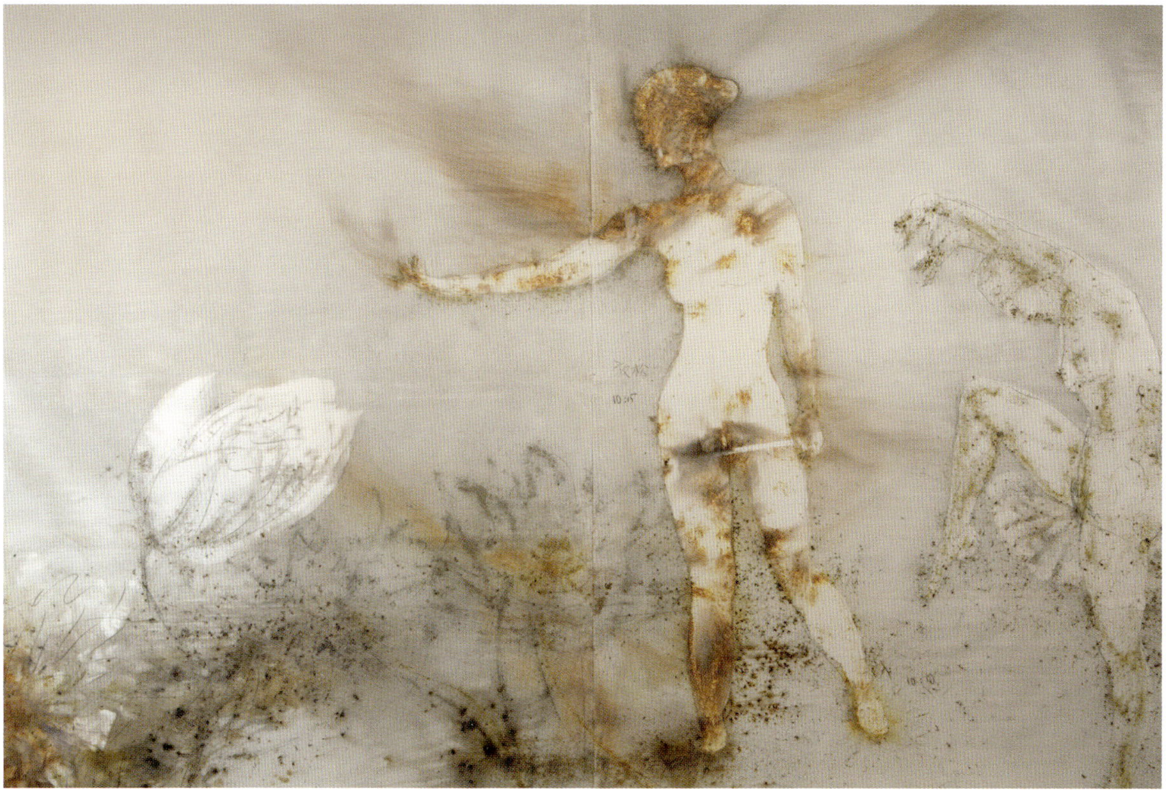

Day and Night
2009
Gunpowder on paper
3 x 32 m
Installation view
at Taipei Fine Arts
Museum; detail below
Collection of the artist

Jeremy Deller

Jeremy Deller (b. 1966) is a British conceptual artist known for orchestrating large-scale collaborative projects, which often result in mixed-media installations and performances. His interest in music has led to several projects, including *Acid Brass* (1997), in which a brass band performed acid house. Winner of the Turner Prize in 2004, Deller lives in London and represented Great Britain at the 55th Venice Biennale in 2013.

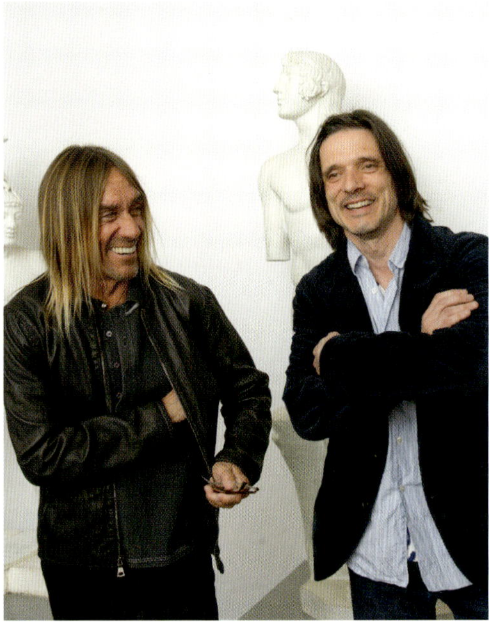

On 21 February 2016 a group of 22 artists arrived at the New York Academy of Art for a life-drawing class. Ranging in age and artistic experience, they settled into their spots, arranged their materials and awaited the model. But there was another artist involved – Jeremy Deller, who had organised the class in collaboration with the Brooklyn Museum. The British conceptual artist had conceived the life class as an artwork in itself. The model was the musician Iggy Pop.

'Most life models are anonymous,' explains Deller, looking back at the work, *Iggy Pop Life Class*, one year later. 'Their identity doesn't interfere with the execution and appreciation of the drawing.' Deller chose Iggy Pop for what his body means in cultural terms. Since the late 1960s, it has been more than flesh and bone; in half-naked form it has leapt, dived, thrashed and writhed on stage in angry performances, making it, in Deller's words, 'emblematic of the art form that is rock music'. By studying this body attentively, representing its every inch on paper, the participants were documenting an aspect of modern culture. Sixty-nine years old at the time of the life class, Iggy Pop has continued his stage theatrics as he has aged, and his still-muscular body remains magnetic and a central part of his on-stage persona. As Deller remarks: 'We've watched that body change over nearly 50 years. At a certain point bodybuilders, wrestlers, boxers and athletes stop showing their body, because it's past its absolute prime, whereas Iggy is quite happy to keep on showing it as it changes.'

The life-drawing class saw Iggy Pop captured in a range of styles, paralleling the diversity of ways in which he is perceived by the public. 'I didn't want just 22 accomplished, realistic drawings of him. We included people in the class who had only been drawing for a week, alongside people who had been drawing all their lives. I wanted a real breadth of interpretations, from the very detailed to an expressionistic vernacular. It was important there were different views of

Iggy Pop Life Class
2016
New York
21 February 2016
Organised by the Brooklyn Museum

Overleaf left:
Dancing Faun
Nineteenth century
Plaster cast after a Roman original by an unknown sculptor
151 cm high
Royal Academy of Arts, London

Overleaf right:
Iggy Pop performing at the Apollo, Manchester, 25 September 1977

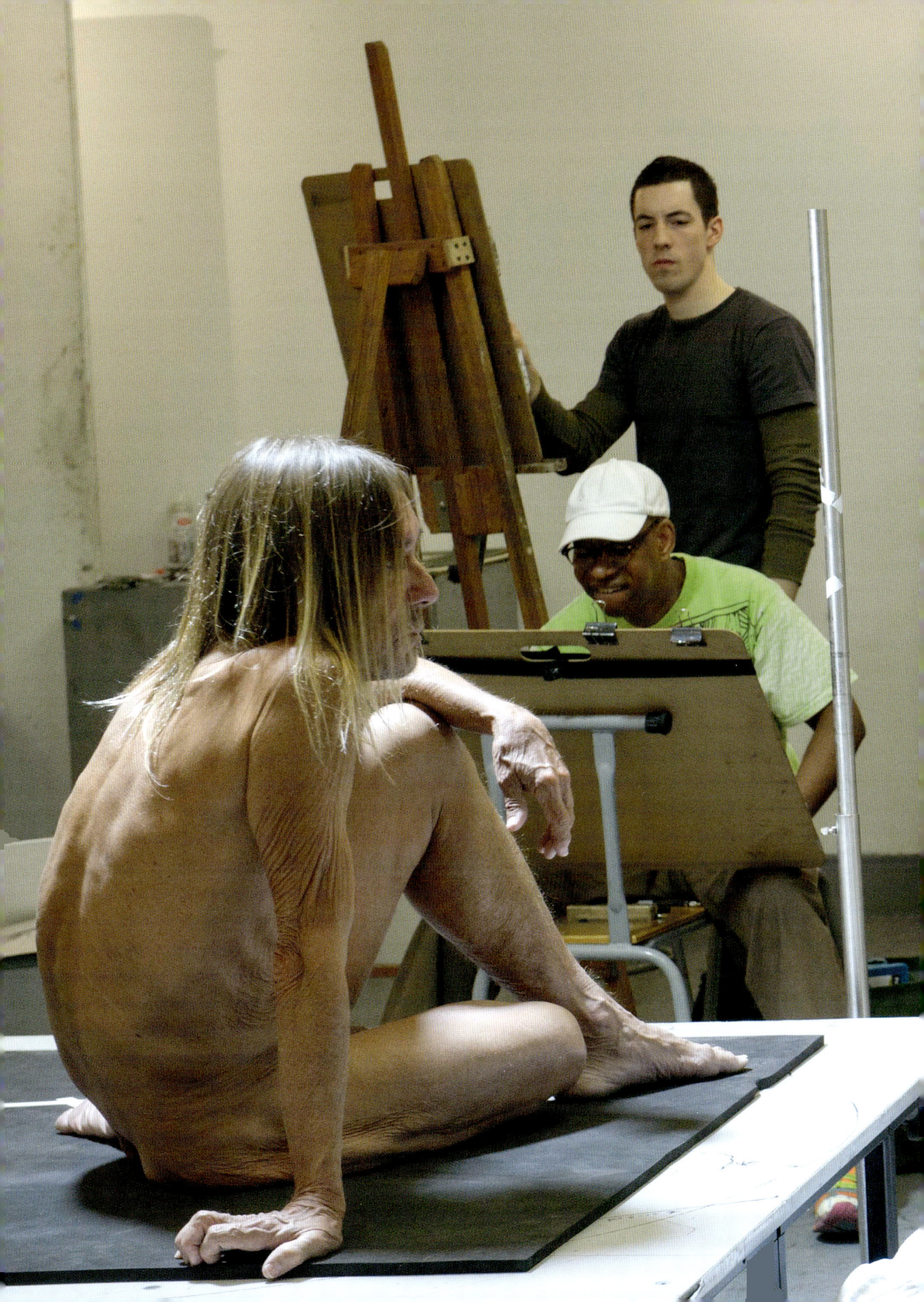

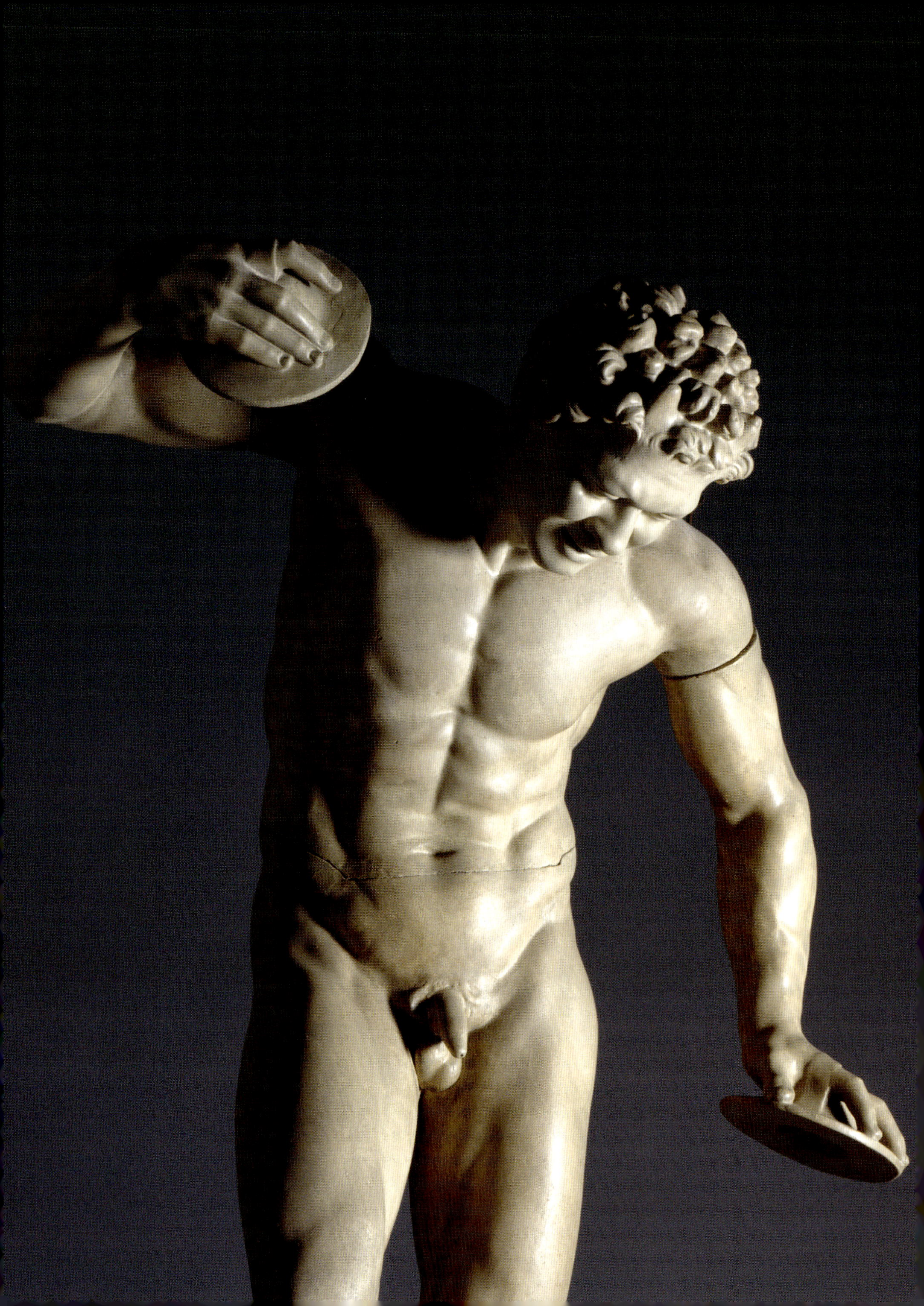

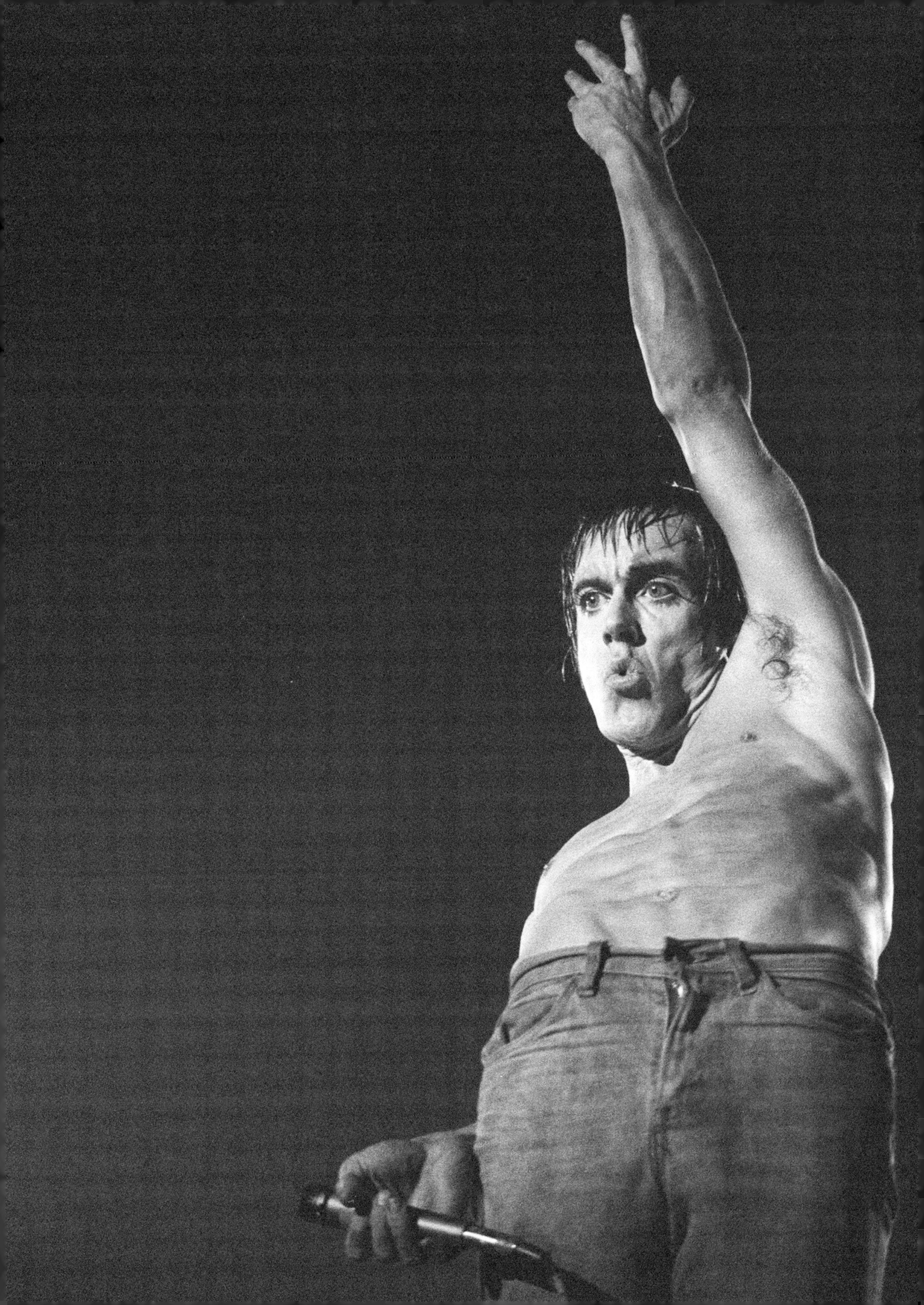

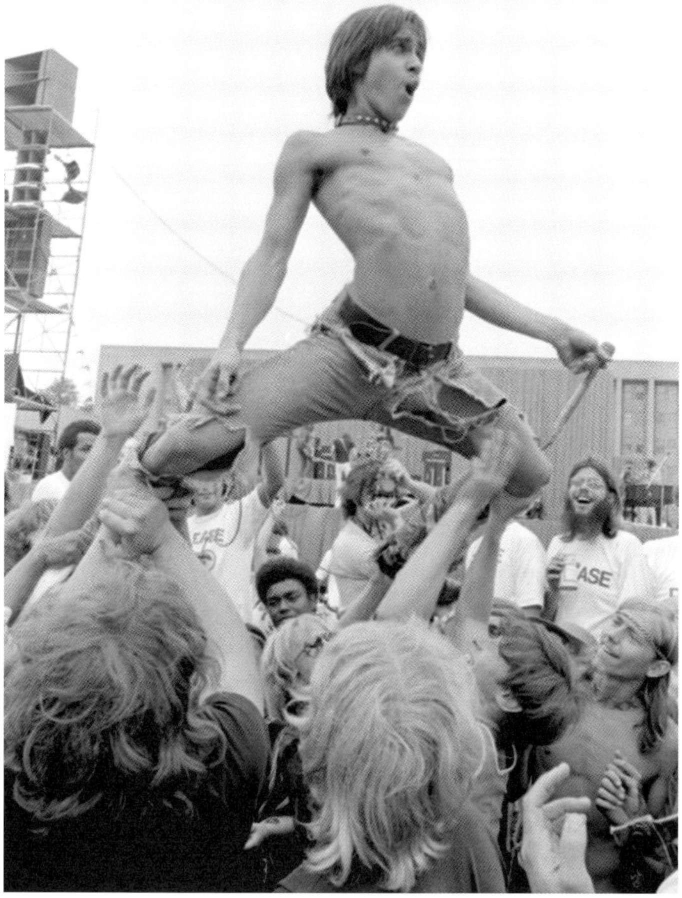

Iggy Pop performing in Soldier Field, Chicago, 18 July 1970

him, to bring out our different ideas of him. For me personally the expressionistic drawings capture his character best.' Iggy Pop admires German Expressionism and he particularly liked the angular style of the drawings by Kallyiah Merilus (see overleaf), a young artist who had begun life classes only two weeks prior. 'Iggy has one leg slightly longer than the other,' says Deller, 'so he walks with a gait and he stands with a gait – she has really captured that with her thick outlines.'

Over 50 drawings were displayed in an exhibition at the Brooklyn Museum that opened later that year. Many captured the short poses in standing and lying positions that Iggy Pop held at the start of the class, before he assumed a seated position, holding a staff. 'It was an intensive four-hour session and the participants were really impressed with how he handled it as a model. He's a performer, and performance takes many forms, not just moving around all the time. We're used to seeing him dance, but when he's stationary his face and body look different, and that's something that took me by surprise.'

Deller studied art history rather than fine art, and does not draw. 'I'd never been in a Life Room before I did this project. It was a place of mystery; I had no idea what the atmosphere was going to be like and how it would feel to be in the presence of a naked person when I was clothed. I was a little nervous, actually, being in the presence of nudity. But you get used to it within seconds – it becomes normal and natural, almost. Even when it's Iggy Pop! There was no diminution in him as a person when he was naked. If anything it was the opposite.'

RA Schools students in the eighteenth and nineteenth centuries would have drawn from casts of antique sculptures before representing living models. 'Now we don't study ancient Greek sculptures, we study the bodies of people in magazines and on the internet,' says Deller. 'Iggy Pop's body is one of the

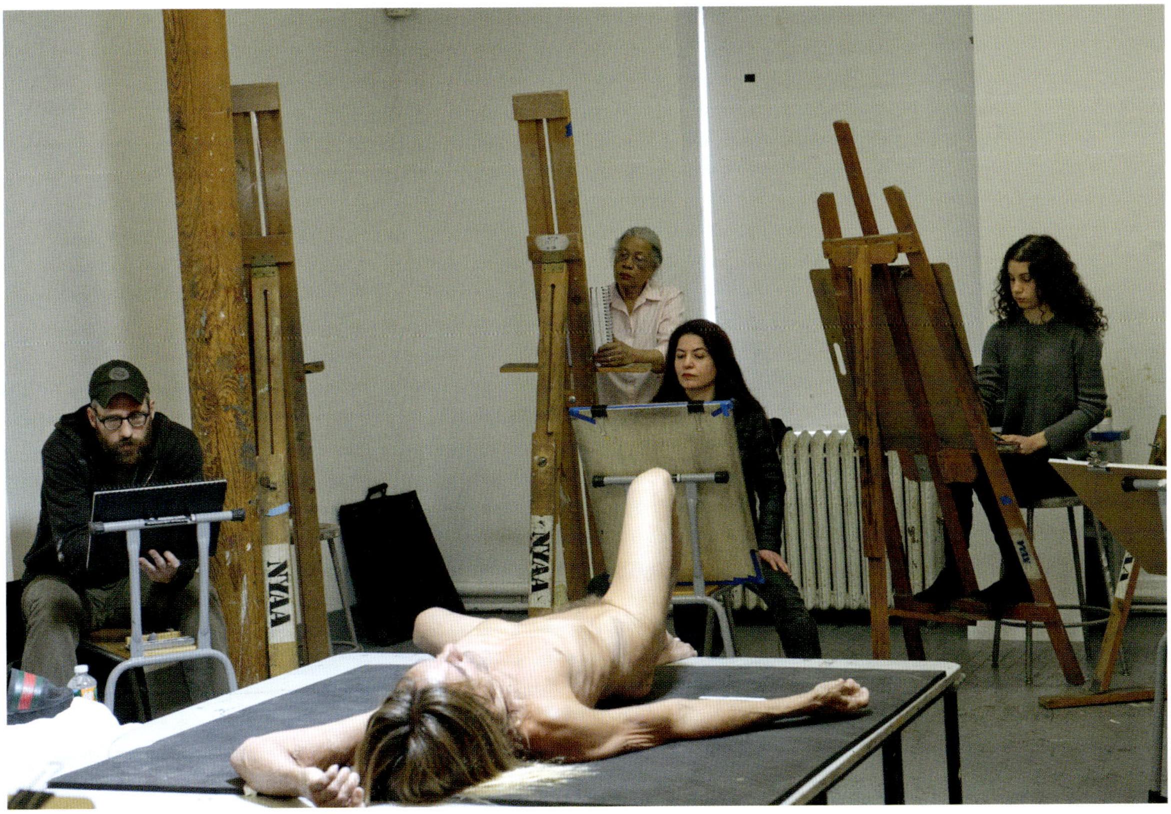

most studied in the world, in a similar way that ancient sculptures were studied and then influenced whole generations of artists.' In mythic terms, Deller sees Iggy Pop as 'a satyr, a mischievous sprite roaming the woods, making music, looking for women and wine, causing mischief'. This Dionysian figure is an archetype that has continued through the ages and 'remains deep within us, understood by us instinctively. It usually takes the form of men who live to extremes and get away with behaviour that would kill mortals.'

Iggy Pop Life Class is also a response to a contemporary phenomenon that Deller hates: the selfie. 'Our whole culture now is about having your photograph taken with a celebrity. Everyone now expects a selfie, and the pressure it must put on celebrities is incredible. So this work is the opposite of a selfie, which basically is a snapshot badly taken on the hoof with someone who doesn't want it to happen. I'd like to think that this work takes a great amount of care to document someone who is there by choice and quite vulnerable. It's a mutual and respectful arrangement.' And for the artist, the work represents a career high, for the clarity of the way it opens up ideas about our culture past and present. 'I think it would be a great work to retire on, because in a sense I can't really do anything much better! I was lucky to have the idea before someone else did, because it's so obvious. It came into my mind suddenly – an image of what the class would look like and what drawings would result – and the project more or less manifested itself in the same way as this image in my mind.'

Sam Phillips

Iggy Pop Life Class
2016
New York
21 February 2016
Organised by the
Brooklyn Museum

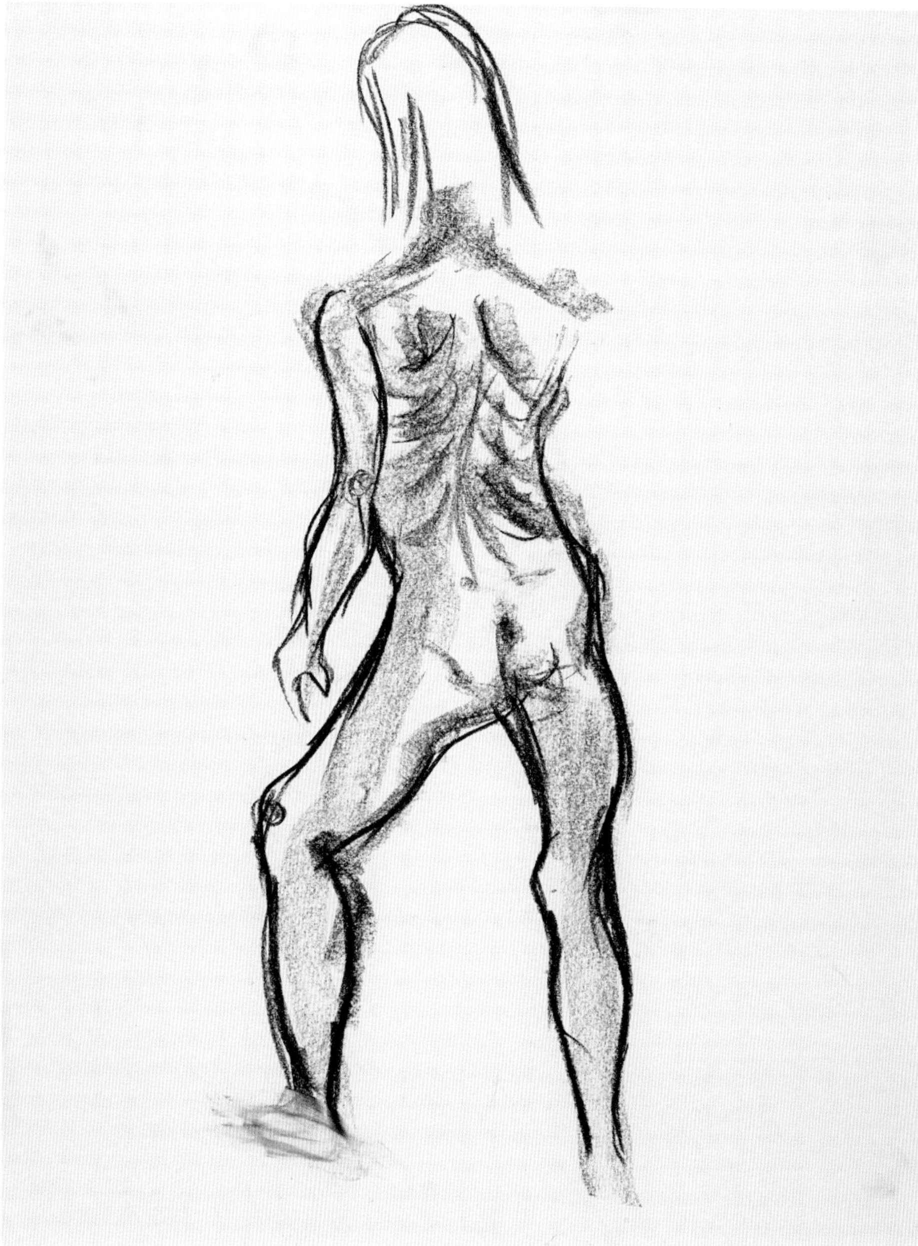

Drawings from
Iggy Pop Life Class
2016
All Brooklyn Museum
Collection, New York

Clockwise from left:

Kallyiah Merilus
Untitled (Standing Pose)
Natural charcoal and
compressed charcoal
with erasing on paper
61.9 x 45.7 cm

Angel Ramirez
Untitled (Seated Pose)
Coloured pencils and
charcoal on paper
62.2 x 45.7 cm

Levan Songulashvili
Untitled (Seated Pose)
Black ink, brushed and
blotted, with scratching
out, with black pencil on
board
55.6 x 47.9 cm

Mauricio Rodriguez
Untitled (Seated Pose)
Graphite pencil with
erasing on paper
43.2 x 35.6 cm

Maureen McAllister
Untitled (Seated Pose)
Natural charcoal and
compressed charcoal
pencil with erasing on
paper
61 x 45.7 cm

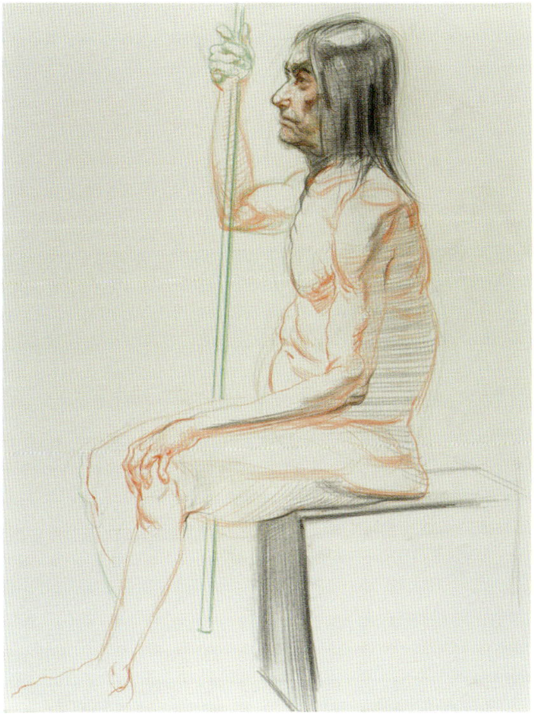
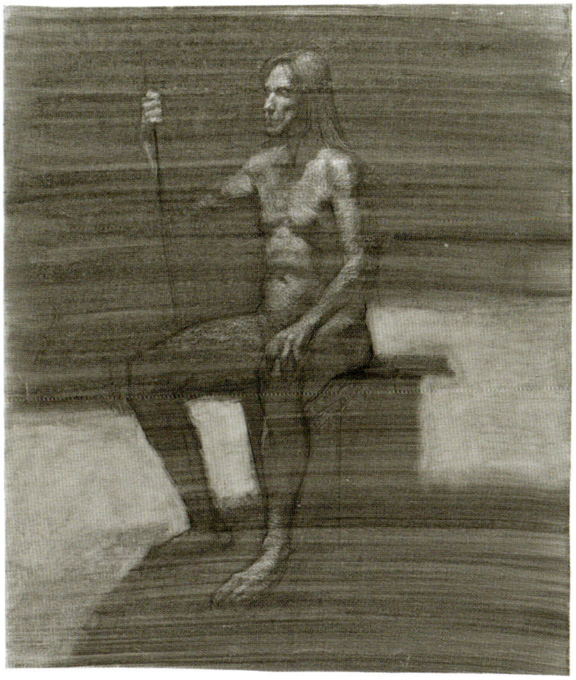
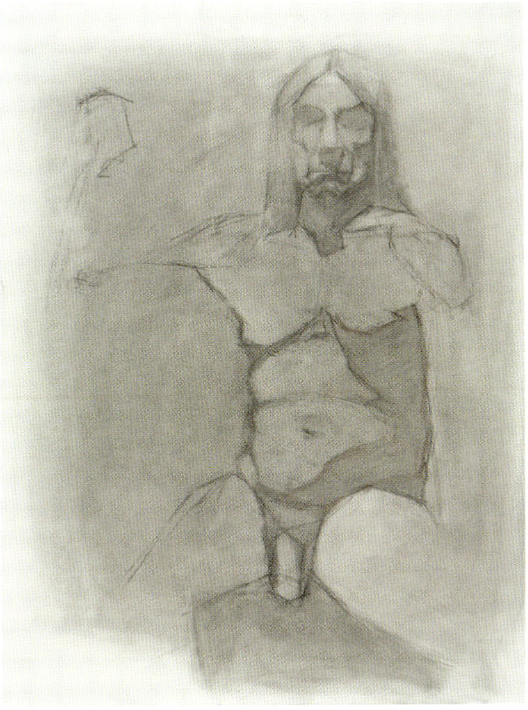
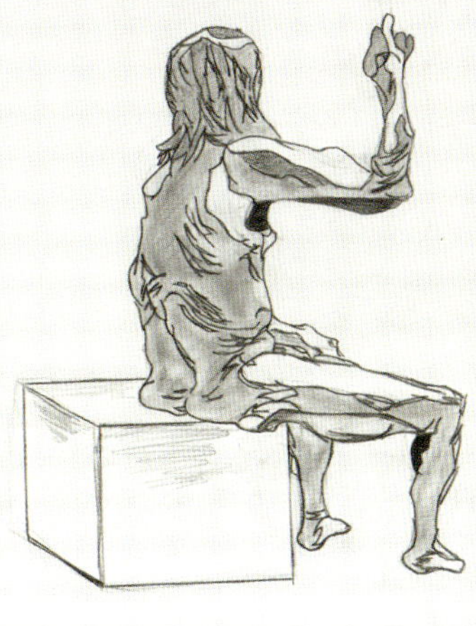

Stephen Farthing

British painter Stephen Farthing RA (b. 1950) currently lives and works in Jordan and London. In research and teaching roles at Oxford's Ruskin School of Drawing and Fine Art (1990–2000), the New York Academy of Art (2000–04) and London's University of the Arts (2004–17), he has explored the processes and functions of drawing.

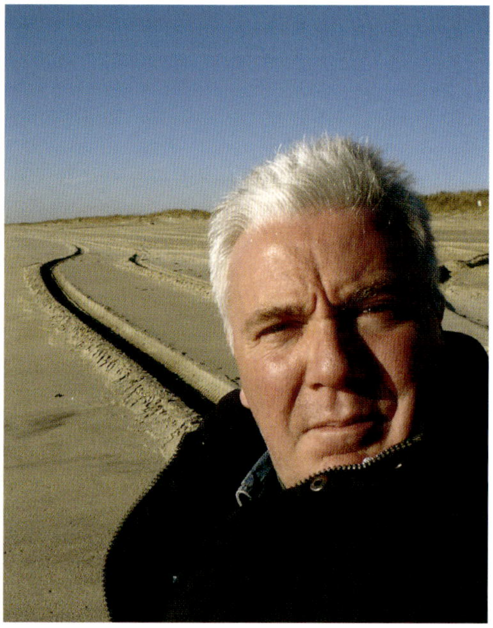

When Stephen Farthing was appointed Ruskin Master at the Ruskin School of Drawing and Fine Art in Oxford, he did some research into the teaching methods of the Victorian artist and critic who founded the institution in 1871. Among other things, he learned that John Ruskin considered life drawing unsuitable for amateur artists and confined his students to drawing from casts. The author of *The Stones of Venice* preferred stone to flesh.

By the time Farthing took up his post in 1990, drawing from life and from casts had both fallen off the curriculum in most art schools in the UK and a digital revolution was transforming the whole concept of drawing. As a first-year student at Saint Martin's School of Art in 1969, Farthing had experienced some of the last formal life classes taught at the school, and he remembers his initial excitement. 'I'd never had a naked person stand in front of me for two and a half hours,' he recalls. 'It was like meeting a Martian.'

These days, as a painter whose work is representational, Farthing rarely has occasion to hire a life model, although he found it useful when working on his 1990s series 'Monarchs', inspired by iconic portraits of royalty. 'As a painter I think in layers and I build my paintings in layers. Starting with a nude makes it easier.' But 'Monarchs', like all Farthing's imagery, was more concerned with the social context than the human figure, and in fact all the figures were missing their heads. In his current series 'Museums of the World' (2015–ongoing), including *Room 3, A Museum of Vernal Pleasure* (2017; see overleaf), an imagined interior of a gallery from the RA Summer Exhibition, the figure is conspicuous by its absence: 'Most of my work has focused on the implied presence of the human figure, the spaces people occupy physically and intellectually.'

Nevertheless, Farthing has continued to draw people throughout his life 'as a sort of rehearsal system, a way of translating the world of three dimensions into two. The naked human form is so much more interesting than any coffee pot I've ever seen.' Farthing worked from life recently

Tattoo
1994
From the series 'Absolute Monarchy'
Oil on canvas
206 x 173 cm
Private collection

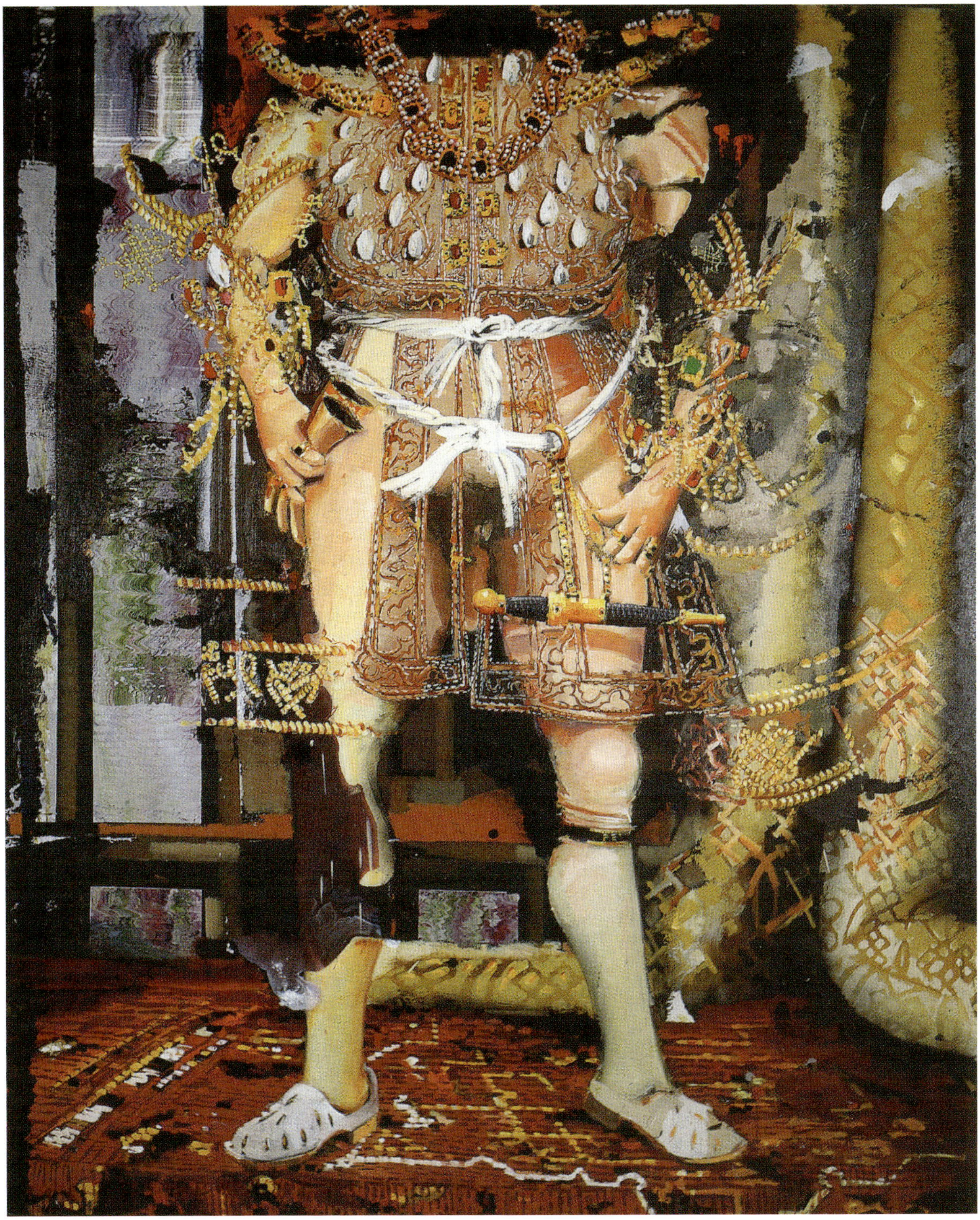

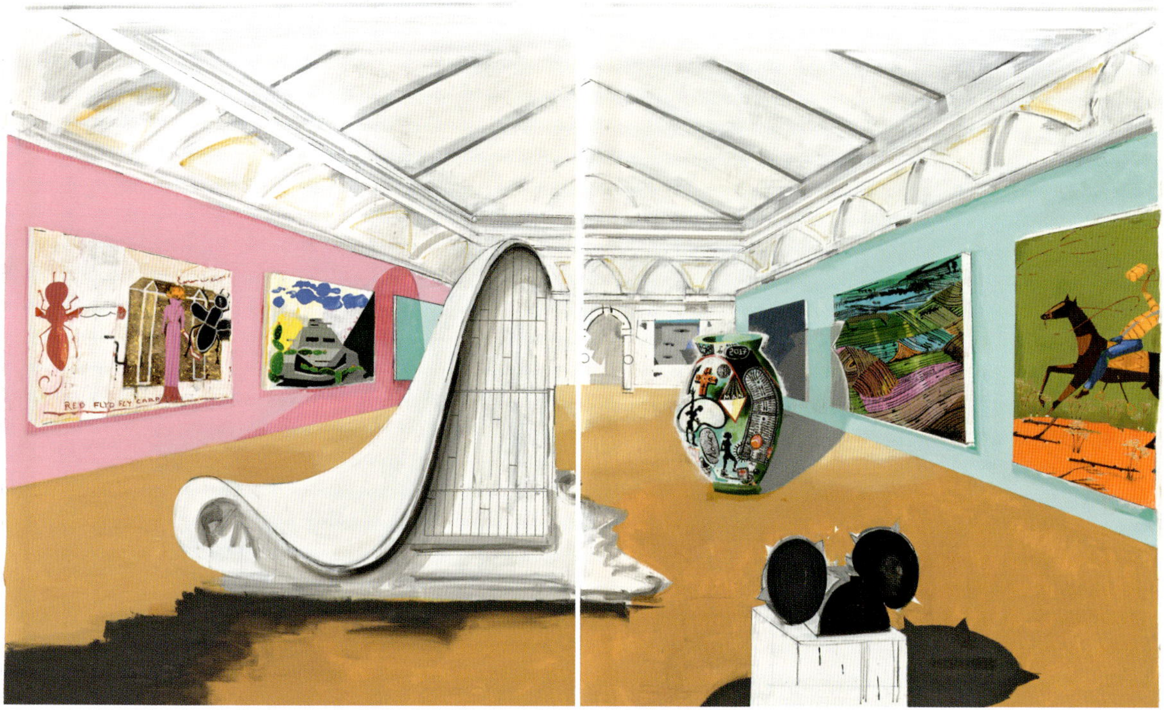

Room 3, A Museum of Vernal Pleasure
2017
Acrylic on canvas
208 x 348 cm
Private collection

when he captured two women drying their hair in *Wash Repeat (after Guercino)* (2017; see overleaf). Life drawing, he points out, is a transferable skill. 'Just because you're learning to draw the human figure doesn't mean you're learning to be a Pre-Raphaelite, as we know from Barnett Newman, Jackson Pollock & Co.'

There's also a human aspect to the Life Room encounter that he feels is missing from contemporary art education. Predictably, perhaps, he is more concerned with the social context than the model. 'I don't think the essence of the Life Room is necessarily the naked figure; it's a social, intellectual, theoretical space.' He believes the life class was 'the soul, heart, pump-house of art education until the late 1960s' and that its replacement in the curriculum with art history and theory has affected the relationship between drawing and thinking. 'If I was going to reinvent the life class I wouldn't be worrying so much about the discipline of drawing but the shared philosophical experience of a bunch of people who want to be visual artists or designers. It's about creating communities rather than individuals running along parallel tracks.'

In 2009 he and artist-curator Donald Smith tested out their ideas in *The Life Room*, an interactive experiment at Chelsea Space in London that combined an art studio with a gym. In a gallery hung with life drawings, sports photographs and plasma screens, and dominated by a large plaster cast of the Venus de Milo, athletes and ballet dancers worked out on state-of-the-art fitness machines while artists captured their movements at the easels and digital drawing pads provided. Initial hopes to re-create the project on a larger scale for the 2012 Cultural Olympiad, the programme of cultural events during the London Olympics, were disappointed: 'People are very conservative.'

Farthing recently decided to adopt a conservative persona himself, teaching

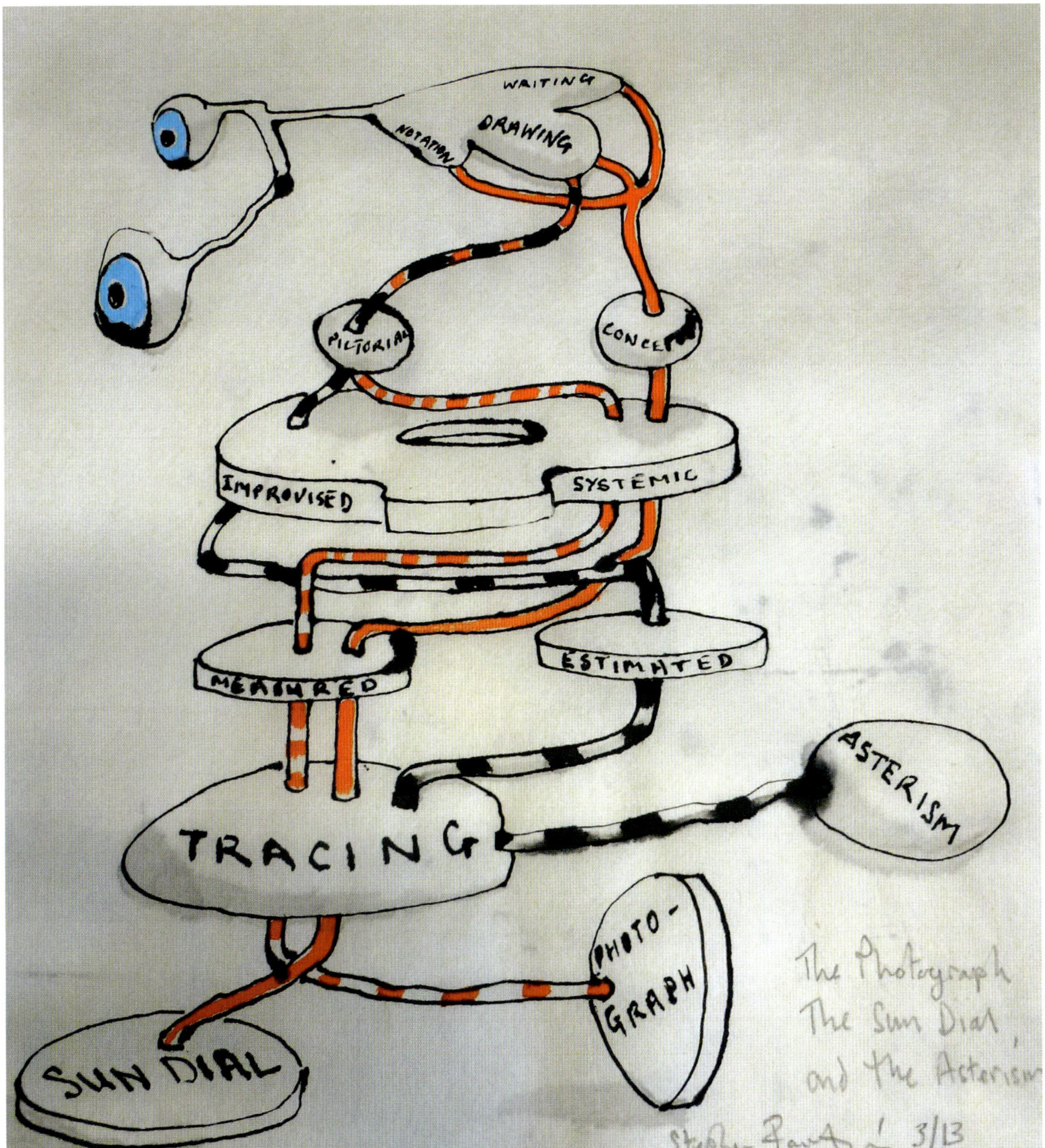

Second Taxonamy of Drawing Showing the Tracing Genus (detail)
2009
Ink and watercolour on paper
40 x 30 cm
Collection of the artist

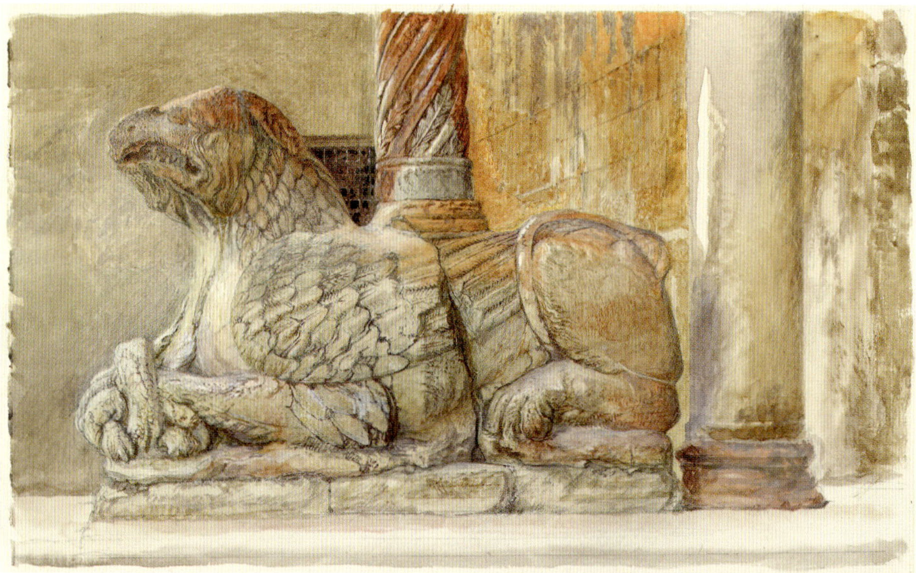

John Ruskin
The Gryphon Bearing the North Shaft of the West Entrance of the Duomo, Verona
1869
Watercolour and bodycolour over graphite on wove paper
22.1 x 35.9 cm
Ashmolean Museum, Oxford

a life-drawing class in the Royal Academy's Life Room in the guise of John Ruskin, to coincide with the RA's 'From Life' exhibition. He planned to wear sub-fusc – the academic dress Ruskin wore at Oxford – and to 'treat the class in a way that would be completely inappropriate today,' being 'extremely strict.' The idea of the class was 'to take people back in time to 1871 to look at how one man thought about life drawing, as a practical history lesson.' Despite his pedagogical differences with Ruskin, he retains a certain respect for the brusque old-school teaching methods he experienced in his youth, which echoed no-nonsense Victorian education. 'A teacher might come out with something like, "This is a life class and your drawings look completely lifeless". That could lead into an interesting discussion of what "lifelike" really is.'

So what, I ask him, is the essential difference between drawing from life and drawing from a cast of the Venus de Milo? 'One is an empty shell that reminds us of the past, the other a living, thinking being that reminds us of now.'

Laura Gascoigne

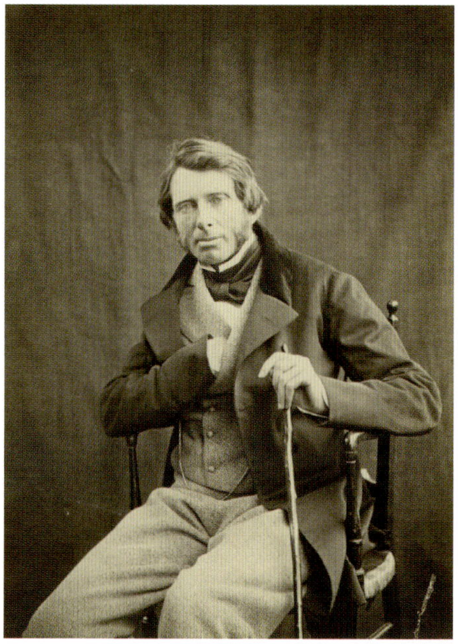

William and Daniel Downey
John Ruskin
1863
Photograph
19.1 x 13.3 cm
Watts Gallery, Compton

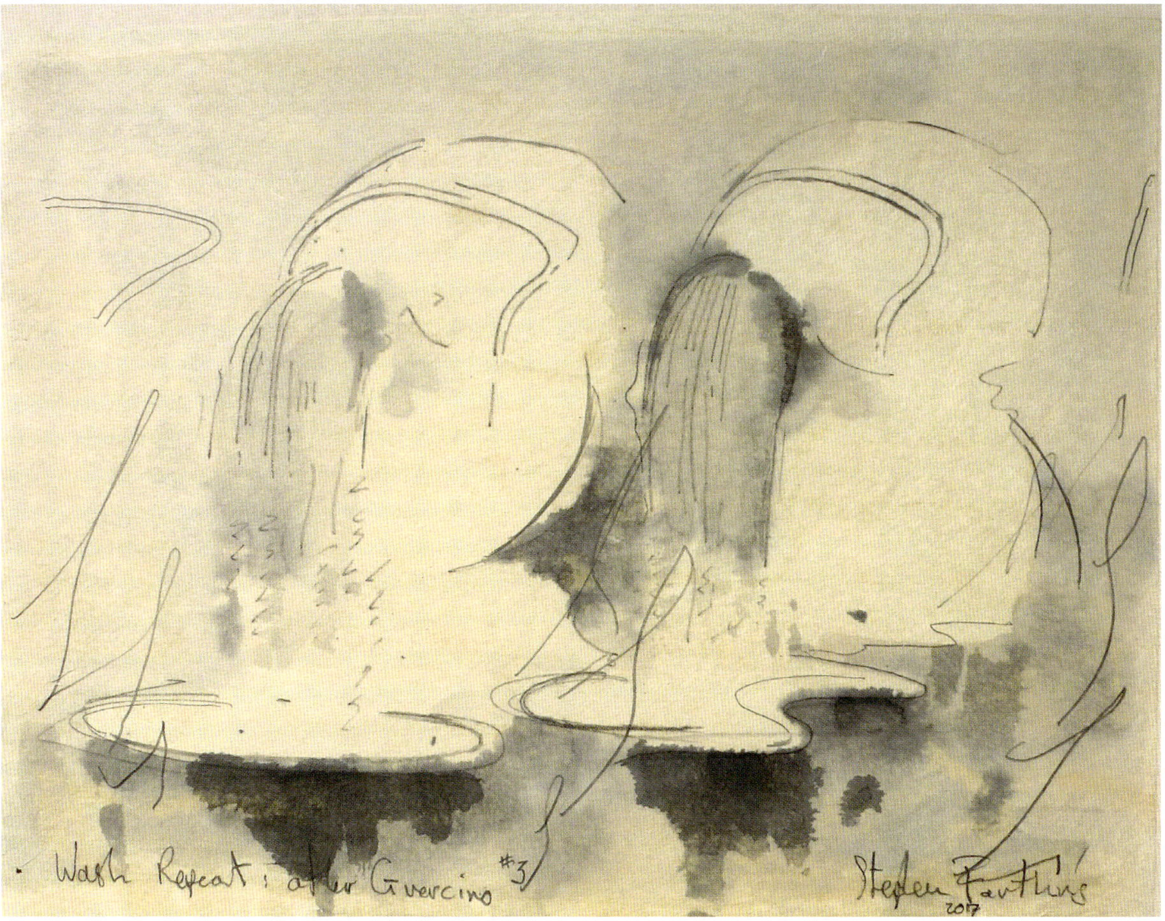

Wash Repeat
(after Guercino)
2017
Graphite and ink wash
on paper
20 x 30 cm
Collection of the artist

Lucian Freud

One of modern Britain's foremost figurative artists, Lucian Freud (1922–2011) was born in Berlin to the youngest son of psychoanalyst Sigmund Freud, moving to England with his family in 1933 to escape the rise of Nazism. The artist became revered for his powerful portraits from life, which required extended sittings from his subjects, mostly friends and family, in his London studio.

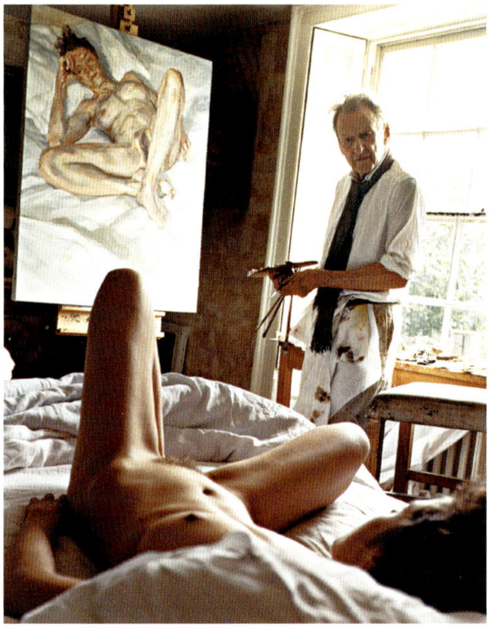

One of Lucian Freud's *obiter dicta* on the subject of drawing was: 'to draw well is the hardest thing – far harder than painting'. He thought that was clearly demonstrated by 'the fact that there are so few great draughtsmen compared to the number of great painters – Ingres, Degas, just a few'.

Freud's assistant for two decades, David Dawson – the person with perhaps the most intimate insight into his mind and art – amplifies that thought. 'Drawing bears out the truth more than any other art form. You can't lie in drawing. Whereas the luxury of paint is that you can cover things up, gloss things over. You can fudge things a bit with paint, with drawing you can't.' A drawing, to Freud, was a distillation of an artist's ability and personality; he once exclaimed, 'I feel you would know whether somebody could draw or not from a footprint!' Freud's own line, in Dawson's opinion, was like the artist himself, lively, never boring. 'His touch was really good. Lucian never deadened the line or made it over-heavy. The volume, space, depth and tension he created with each line were exciting.'

Although as a young man Freud attended life classes at London's Central School of Arts and Crafts, the experience was not suited to his temperament as a mature painter. For one thing, he did not like being watched while he worked; for another, he found professional models were generally 'unsuitable'. One woman who posed for a series of wonderful paintings was, he remembered, at first 'a very bad model, which I never mind, because in a way the last thing I want to do is paint a model. I want it to be, 'My God, you haven't got your clothes on!' Not 'Would you like pose A, B or C?'

To draw a human body, Freud believed, required some understanding of its structure. 'You need a feeling for it,' he said, 'which doesn't necessarily mean medically, but to do with movement and how limbs relate to each other and to the body.' Freud had seen marvellous drawings by Renoir, for example, but he wouldn't place him in the category of great draughtsmen. 'There's a question about them that is not an aesthetic one.

David Dawson
Naked Portrait
2005
Photograph
Private collection

Drawing for Naked Figure
1973–74
Ink on paper
55.8 x 45.1 cm
Private collection

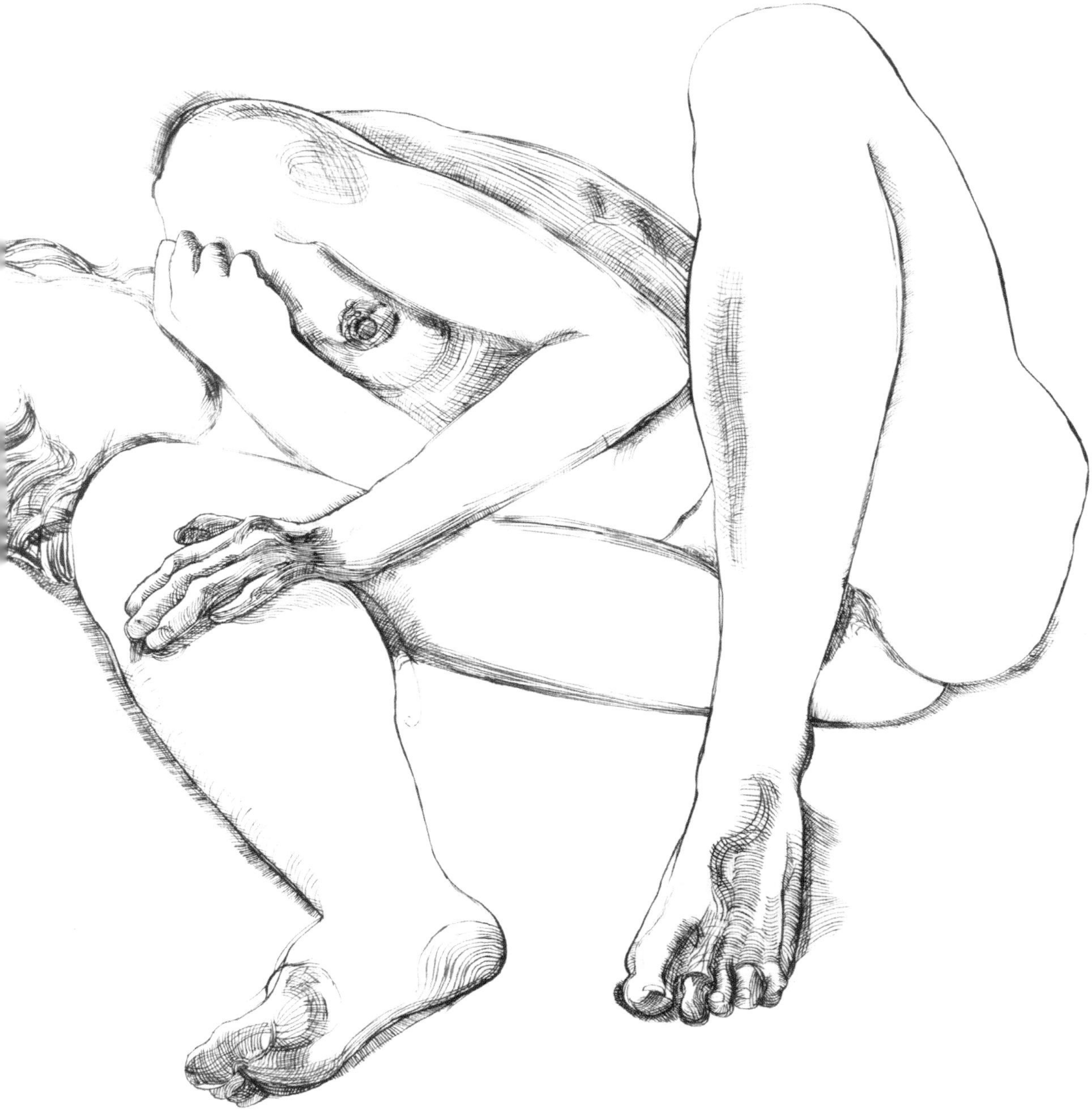

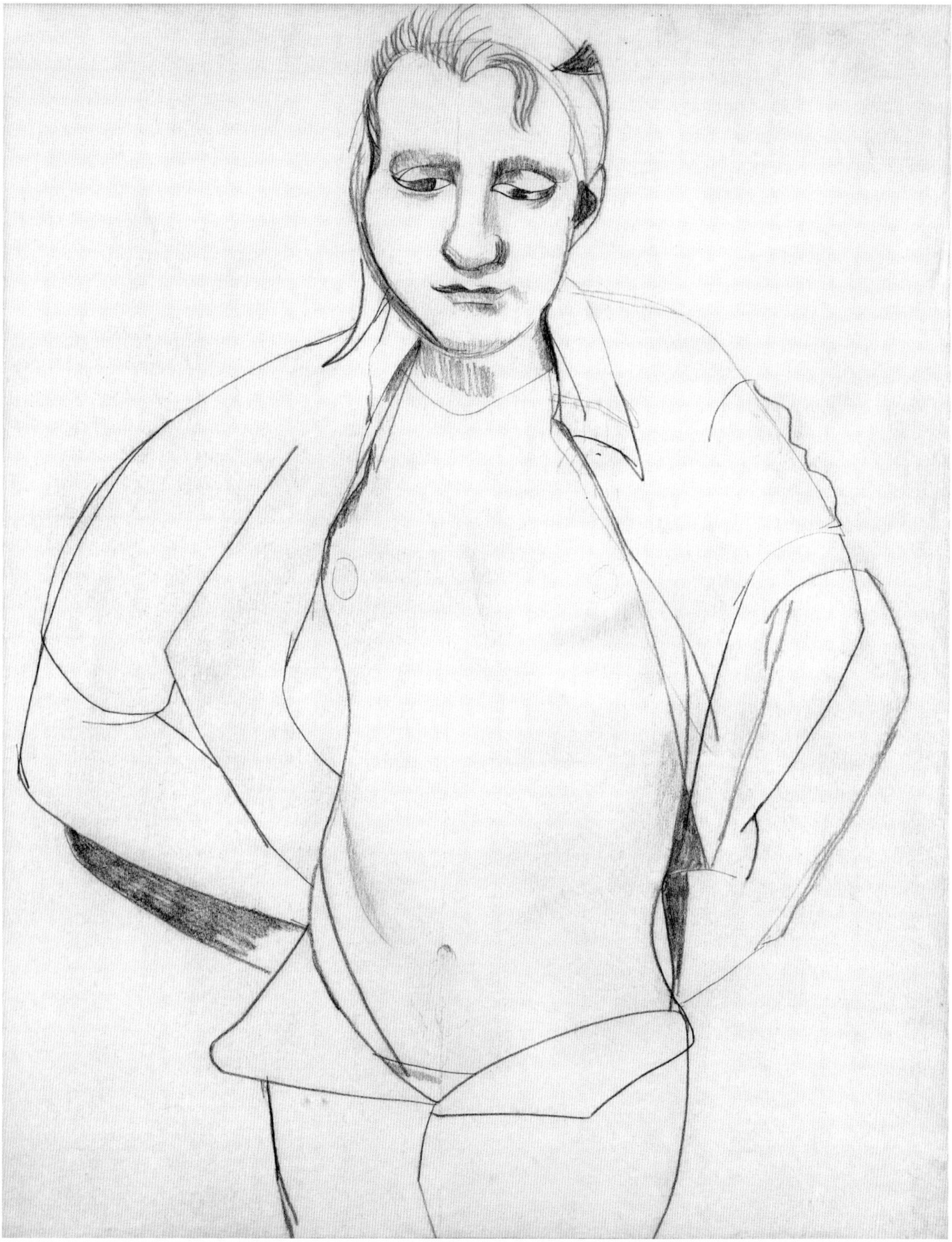

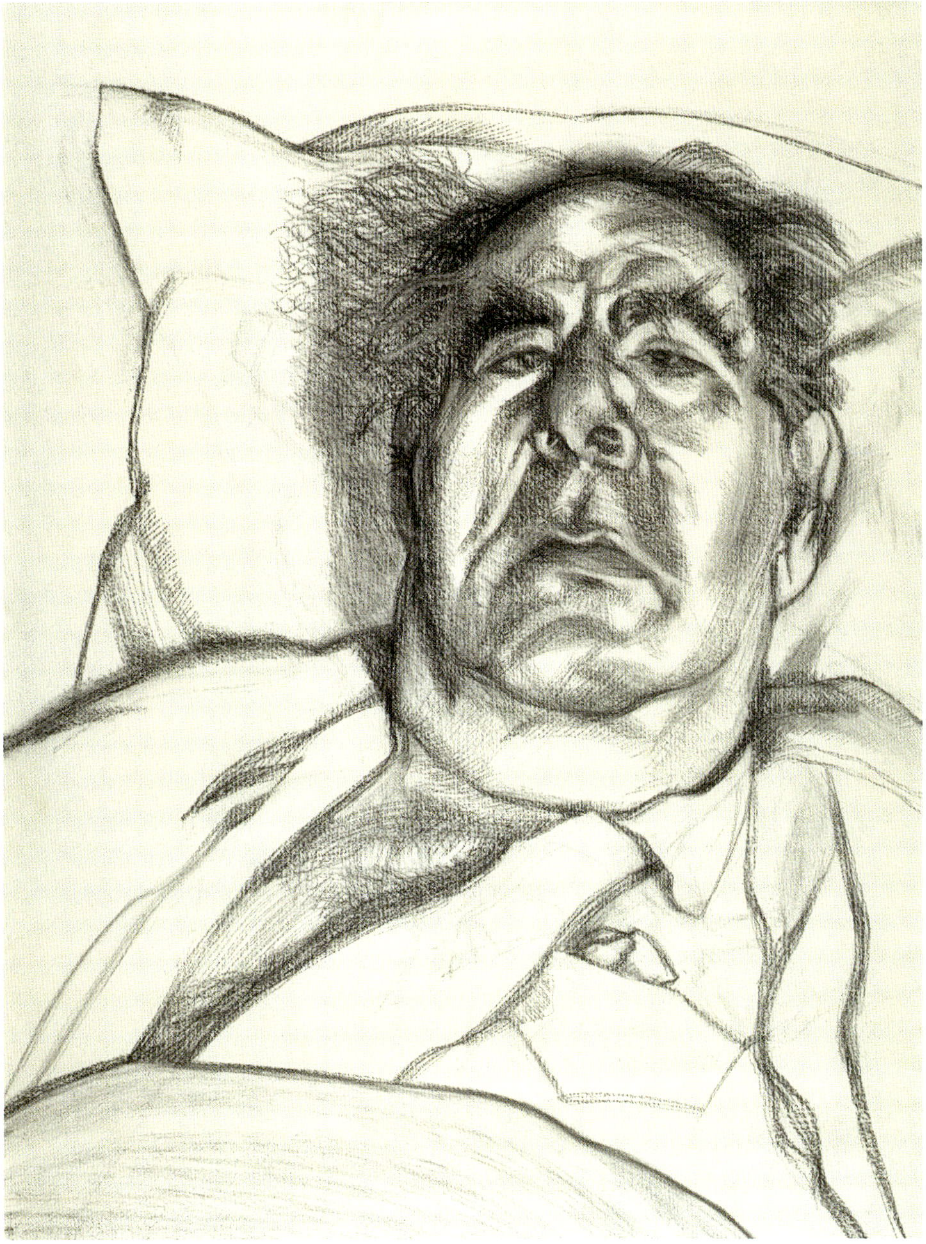

Francis Bacon (III)
1951
Crayon and chalk
on paper
54.7 x 42 cm
Private collection

Lord Goodman
1985
Charcoal on paper
64.3 x 47.8 cm
Private collection

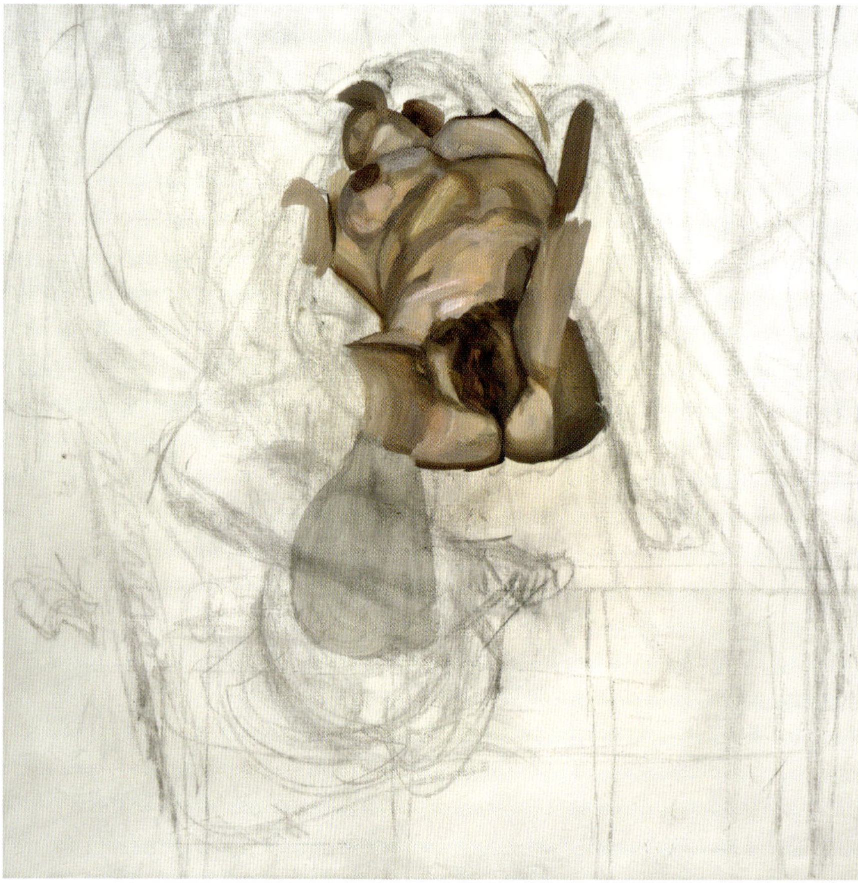

Portrait Fragment
1971
Oil on canvas
61 x 61 cm
Private collection

Naked Man on a Sofa
1986
Etching
56 x 71 cm
Private collection

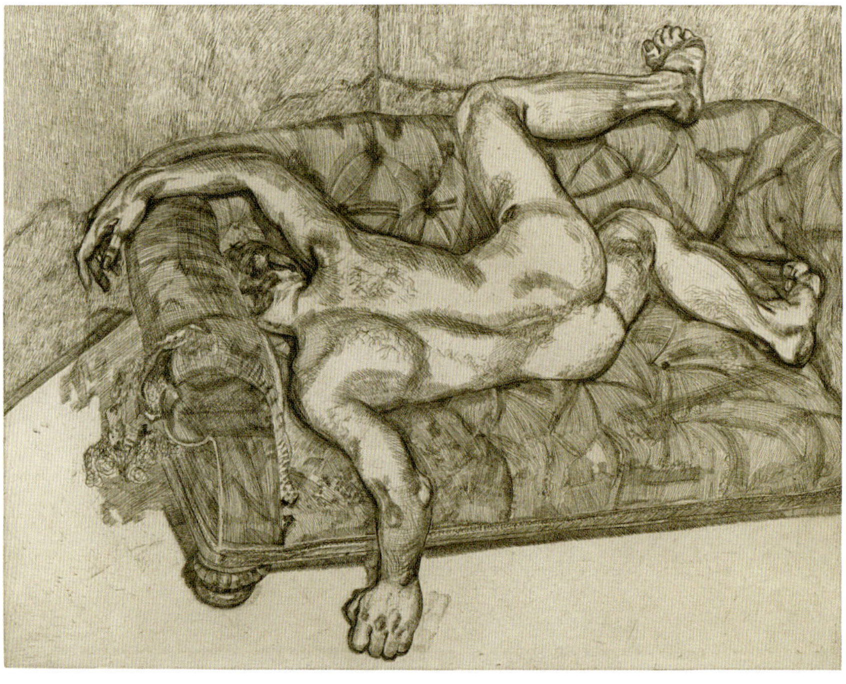

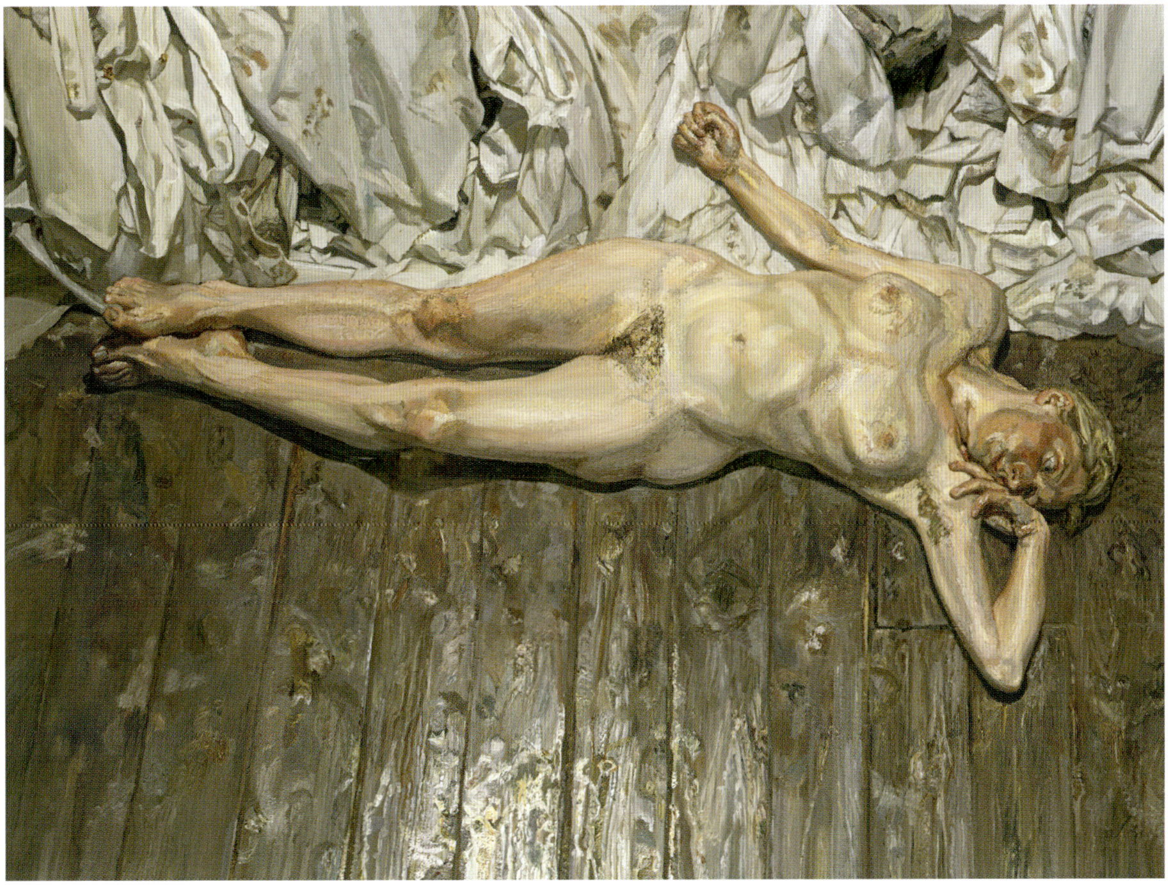

Lying by the Rags
1989–90
Oil on canvas
138.5 x 184 cm
Private collection

His figures' bones aren't quite right, are they, on the whole? Or you wonder if they've got any. Even when they work they can make you wonder about anatomy rather than art. With a good drawing you can see the bones.'

Drawing, quite literally, was the basis of every painting that Freud created. As Dawson explains (and I witnessed myself), 'he started with a drawing in charcoal on canvas, to get the form, scale and feel of the subject. He would then rub it down with cloth so you saw a ghost image. Lucian would start the painting from there.' There was a symbiotic relationship between his painting and his work in graphic media. Freud was clear that he wanted his etchings – the main graphic medium of his last three decades – to 'work like paint'. Dawson watched many of the greatest Freud etchings evolve. 'It was almost as if Lucian were trying to make the lines on the copper behave in the way he used a paintbrush, to give depth and bring life to the picture.'

There were other similarities in the way his etchings and paintings were created. The etching plate was put on an easel as if it were a canvas. In addition, if it was a picture of a person, the sitter had to be present at every moment when Freud was at work – not just when he was depicting their faces or bodies, even when he was concentrating on some aspect of the background (he preferred to call it the 'ground').

In this respect, Freud was an extreme example of an artist working from life. He would work exclusively from real objects, rooms, animals and people, and he would only work when all the contents of a picture were in front of his eyes (just occasionally he would break this rule, as when he made a double portrait of two people who were not on speaking terms). Dawson understands the reasoning that lay behind this apparently tyrannical requirement. 'In one of Lucian's paintings nothing jumps out in relation to anything else.

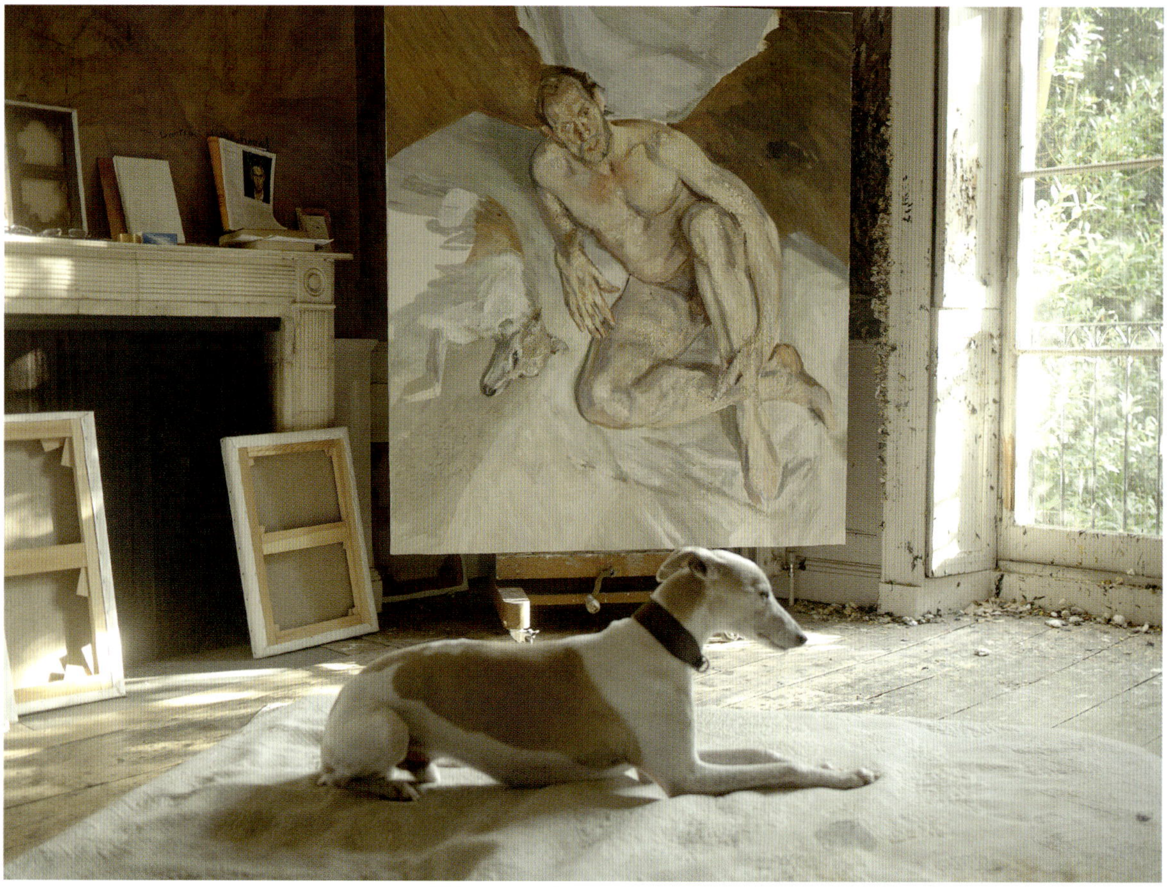

David Dawson
Eli in front of 'Portrait of the Hound'
2011
Photograph
Private collection

If the sitter weren't there and you started painting the floor or the chair, you might over-emphasise it, and unbalance the picture. The sitter had to be there so that the feel of the painting was particular to that person, and so that it wasn't side-tracked into a portrait of a room or floorboards.'

Freud once reflected that he had spent many hours of his life painting floorboards (perhaps almost as long as he had portraying people). But he always observed them closely, saw fresh things in them, found new ways to represent the same old bits of wood, and looked at them in relation to a human being or an animal subject. That's why, as Dawson says, 'there's something incredibly particular about Lucian's pictures that gives them a depth of truth that we, as viewers, pick up on.'

Since Freud's death in 2011, Dawson has been painting in his old studio. Recently he has been working on a series depicting the space itself. For Dawson this is an immensely familiar place. 'I've spent almost every day in it for the last 20 years – and that seemed to me to make it an excellent subject for painting.' Among his other duties, Dawson spent countless hours there posing for numerous oils and etchings by Freud, including his unfinished, moving painting *Portrait of the Hound* (the dog in question being Dawson's pet whippet, Eli).

The floorboards, the radiator, the raw plaster on the studio walls all feature in Freud's pictures, but Dawson paints them with a difference. In *Absence Fills the Room* (2017) pale sunlight slants through the window as it does into the empty interiors of the late nineteenth-century Danish master, Vilhelm Hammershøi. Dawson acknowledges the work is about 'change, time passing, losing Lucian – but that's in the background. It's also about the enveloping stillness of the studio. It's such a lovely room to be in.'

Martin Gayford

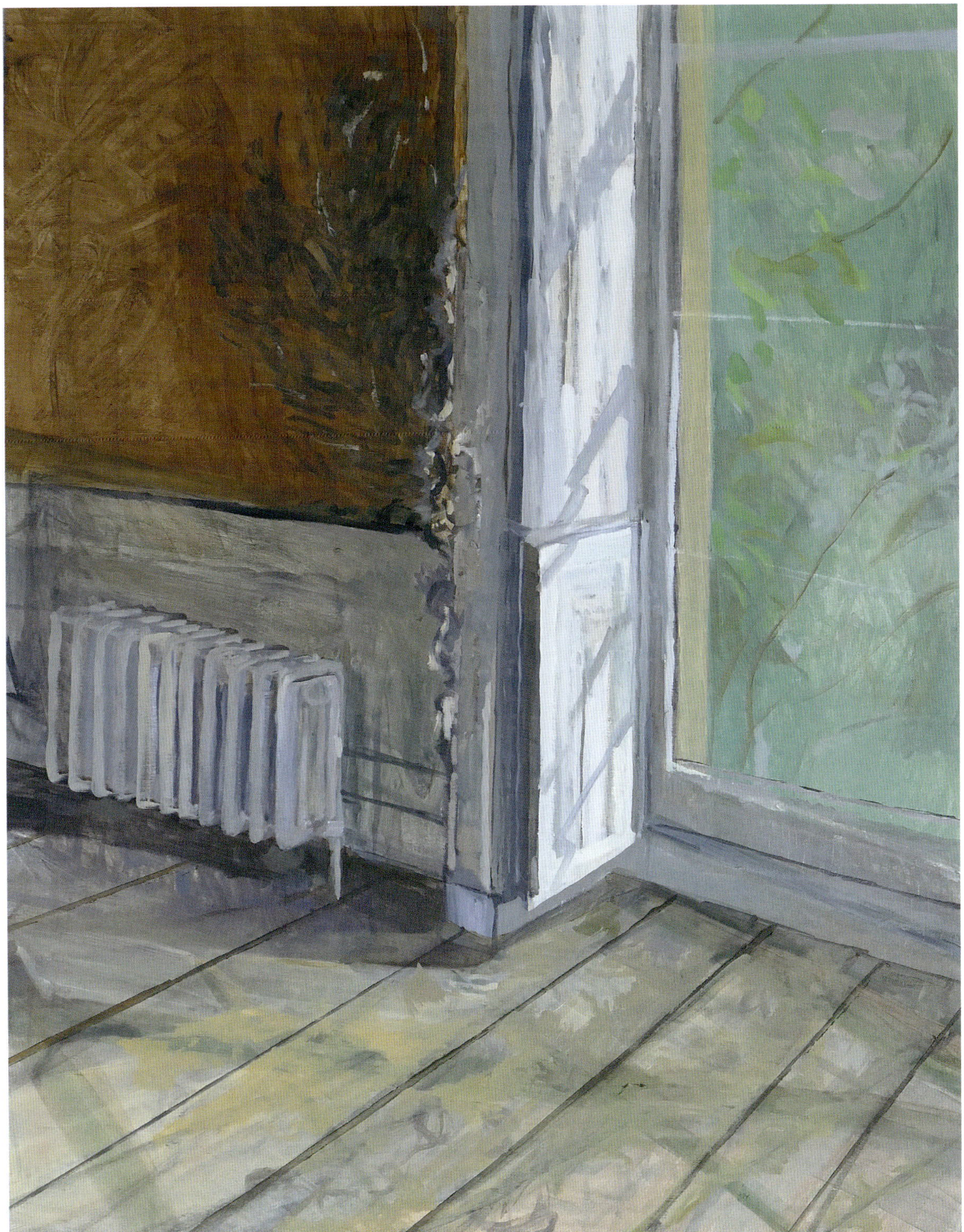

David Dawson
Absence Fills the Room
2017
Oil on linen
71.5 x 56.2 cm
Private collection

Antony Gormley

Sculptor Sir Antony Gormley OBE RA (b. 1950) creates wide-ranging figurative works whose basis is his own body. Winner of the Turner Prize in 1994, the London-based artist is celebrated for his public sculpture, which includes the 20-metre-high winged figure *Angel of the North* (1998) in Gateshead and *Another Place* (2007), comprising 100 cast-iron figures facing towards the sea from a Merseyside beach.

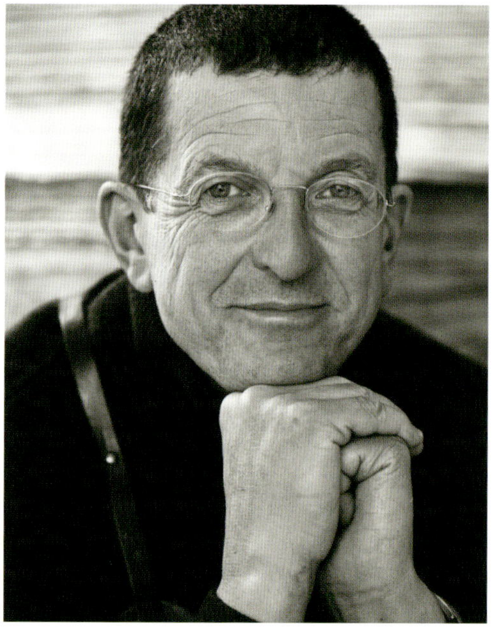

Antony Gormley has always been inclined to think that the Western tradition of working from life misses something essential: namely, life.

'At art school, I had a really uncomfortable feeling during life-drawing classes that we were ignoring the main subject, which was the *sensation of living*. The Life Room was denying the most interesting thing. My memory of the Life Room is of a strange place where a real body was turned into a landscape – or, more to the point, an object. People were supposed to reproduce it dispassionately in two dimensions.'

So Gormley looked for ways of making art that was true to life. 'From the late 1970s and early 1980s, by treating my own existence as subject, instrument and material, I tried to make the most accurate account I could of a moment of being. I was more interested in living inside a body than making a reproduction of what it looked like from the outside. In other words, I wanted to ask what it felt like to be alive and to see if there were ways of notating the answer. I felt that there were a number of ways that you could make the subject – the body – your tool.' He tried some of these out as a teacher of art at Maidstone, then Brighton. 'In classes I would lead exercises in which I would get one student to stand behind another and draw all over his or her body with a finger. Then the subject was supposed to replicate the feeling of the mark of the finger on his or her body on a piece of paper.' Alternatively, he would ask the students 'to do internal mapping, to feel the Earth pushing up against their feet and to try and follow that load-path.'

These exercises were ways of recognising, in the artist's words, 'what it *feels* like to inhabit a body'. This became a major theme in Gormley's own art as it developed, as he began moulding his own body, the procedure by which much of his work was made in the 1980s and 1990s. 'In my earlier work the moulds were empty, void and often sealed,' Gormley recalls. 'Then I went on to making massive solids from the inside of the moulds.'

INTO THE LIGHT
1986–87
Lead, fibreglass, plaster and air
193 x 50 x 38 cm

Overleaf left:
SCAFFOLD VII
2016
4 mm square section stainless steel bar
193.2 x 36.2 x 46.7 cm

Overleaf right:
GAZE III
2015
Cast iron
193.4 x 49 x 35.5 cm

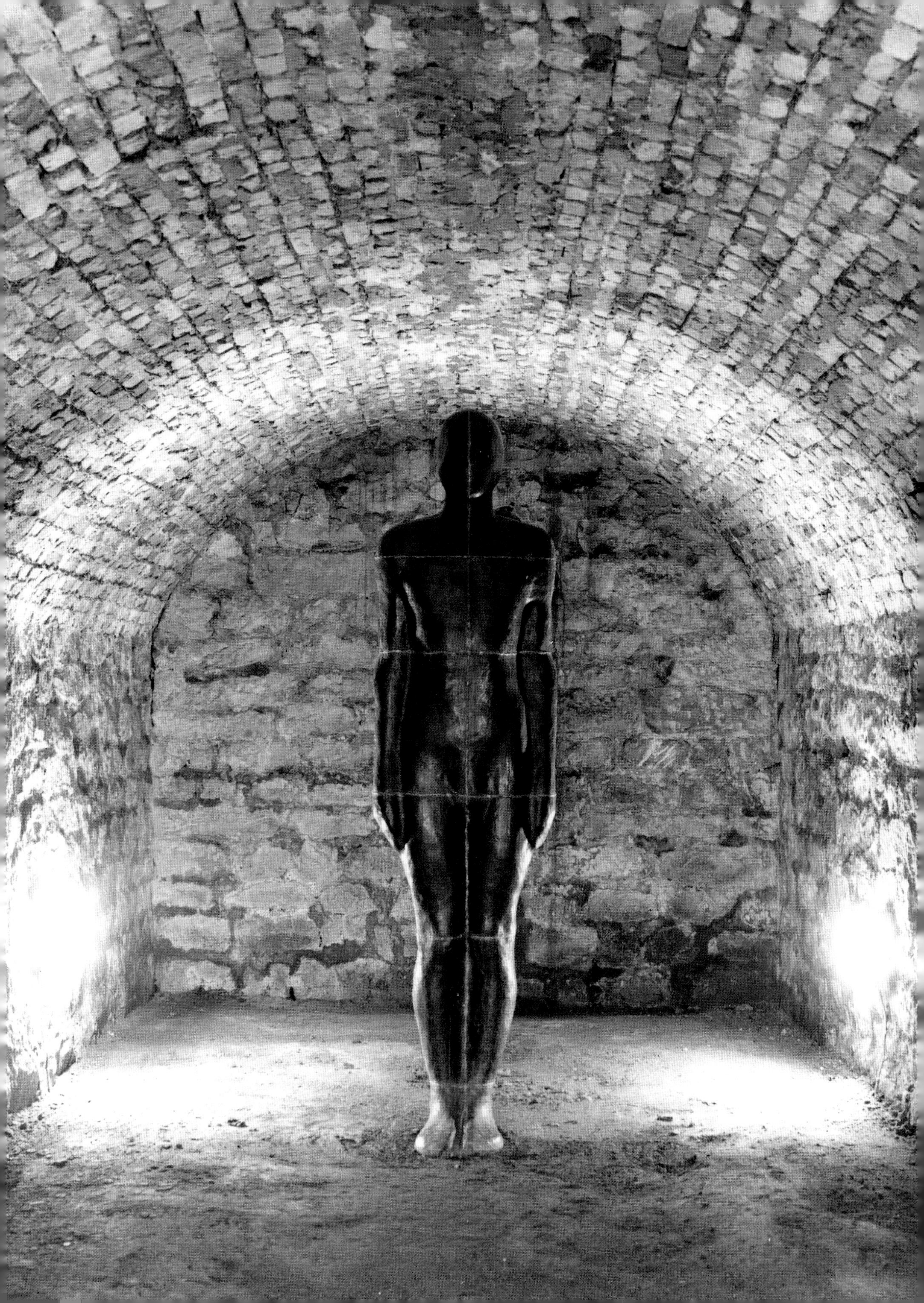

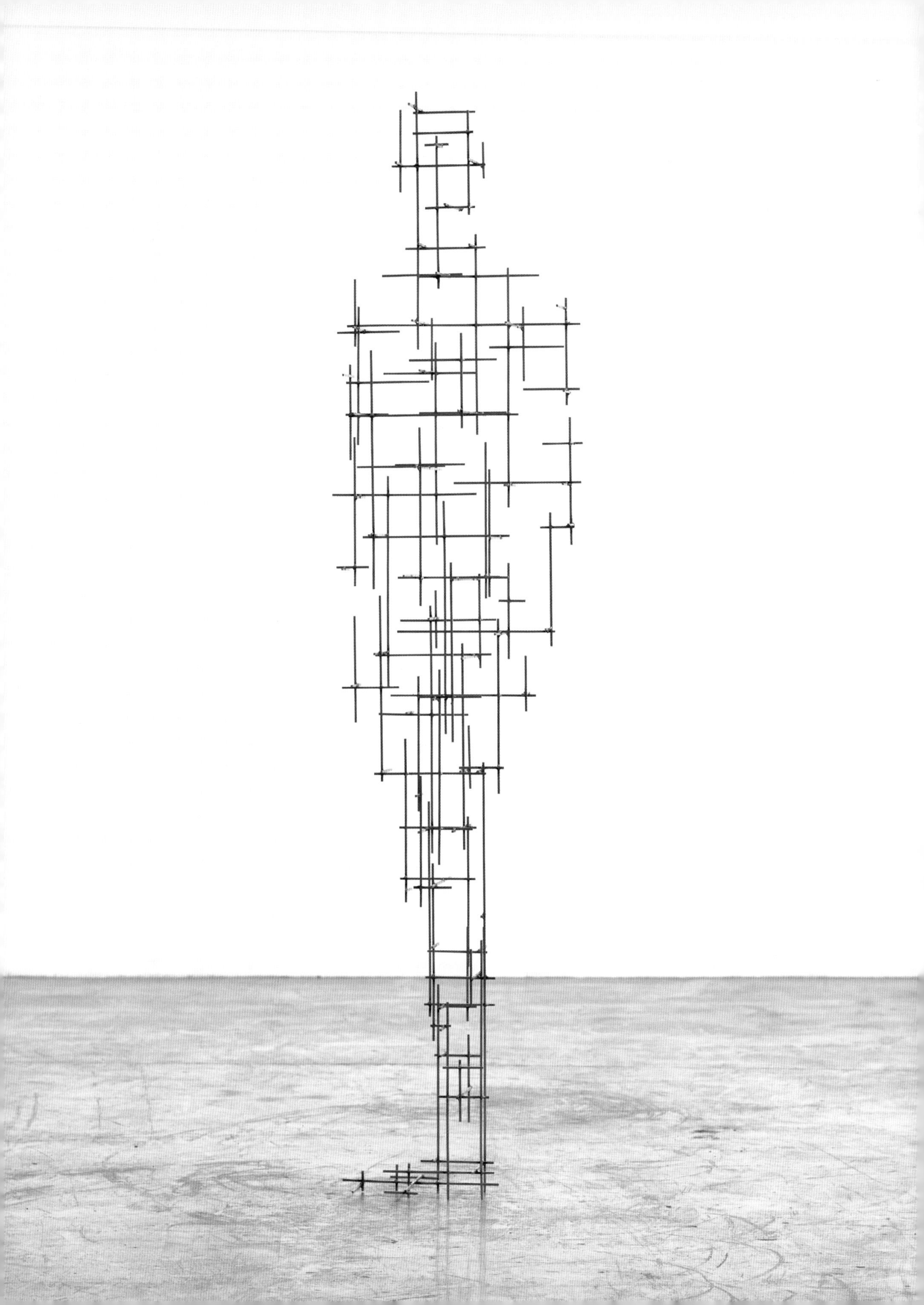

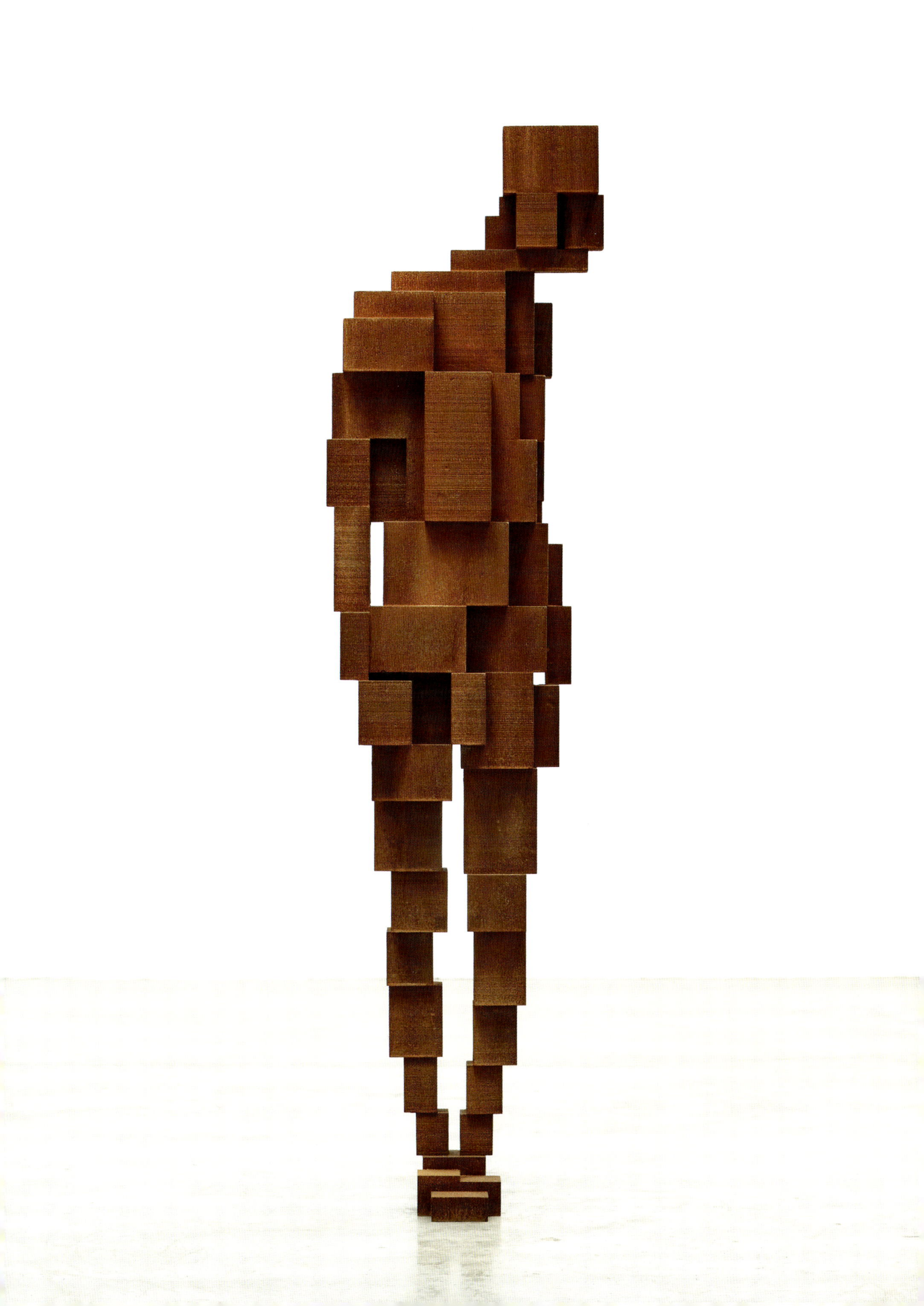

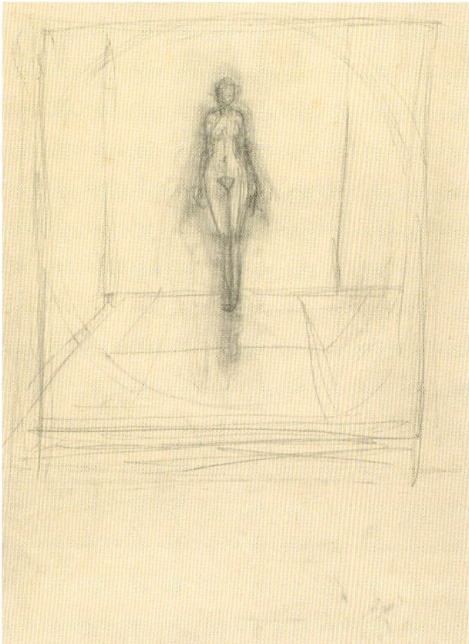

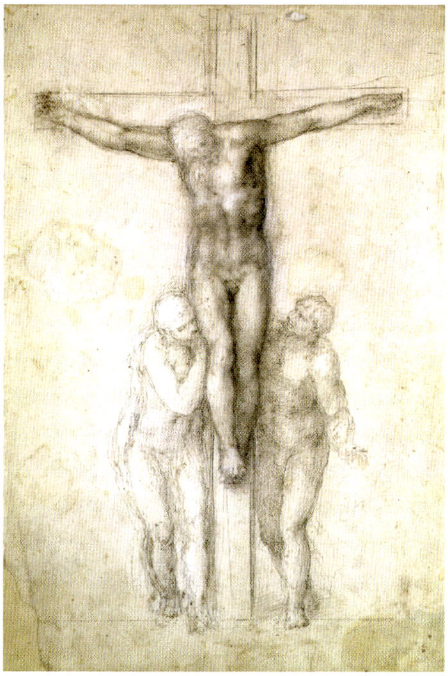

Alberto Giacometti
Standing Nude Circled and Framed
c. 1942
Pencil on paper
33.2 x 24.5 cm
Collection Fondation Alberto & Annette Giacometti, Paris

Michelangelo Buonarroti
Study of Christ on the Cross between the Virgin and St John the Evangelist (recto)
c. 1555–64
Black chalk on paper
41 x 27.8 cm
The British Museum, London

For Gormley, moulding 'was a way of saying, "Why use another body as a model when you have one already?"' As a result, he short-circuited the old distinction between artist and model.

Gormley points out that Giacometti's work takes this distinction to an extreme. 'It's all about the distance between the viewer and the viewed, and making that tunnel-vision part of the account. The body in question – Giacometti's sitter – is only seen in relation to the space that separates the artist from his model.' In a way, Giacometti's deepest theme is the impossibility of bridging this gulf. His numerous versions of *Standing Woman* were based on a memory of seeing a woman, with whom he was in love, one evening in the far distance on the Boulevard Saint-Michel: Giacometti was trying, in other words, to sculpt an experience of remoteness.

On the other hand, some of the greatest art is informed by exactly the kind of information Gormley is talking about: the sort that comes not from looking at a body from a distance, but from having one yourself. 'You always feel with Michelangelo that he is inhabiting the figure he is drawing. It's the opposite of Giacometti. Michelangelo is not trying to fix this image in space, he's actually *in* the image. And it got more and more powerful as he got older. That's why I love his late drawings of the Crucifixion, because you feel that he's there.'

Gormley describes his own drawing as 'a form of meditation, less about image and more about states of being'. A case in point is his series 'Body and Light' from the early 1990s, small sheets drawn with a black wash of pigment. 'The drawings are very loose and fluid. They came from watching things happen. Observing this often-dark world emerge was more important for me than the captured or the exactly represented.'

More recently, body moulding has been replaced by body scanning, but these are different methods of doing the same job. 'A mould is an analogue map and a scan is a digital map but they both do the same thing: they tell you about

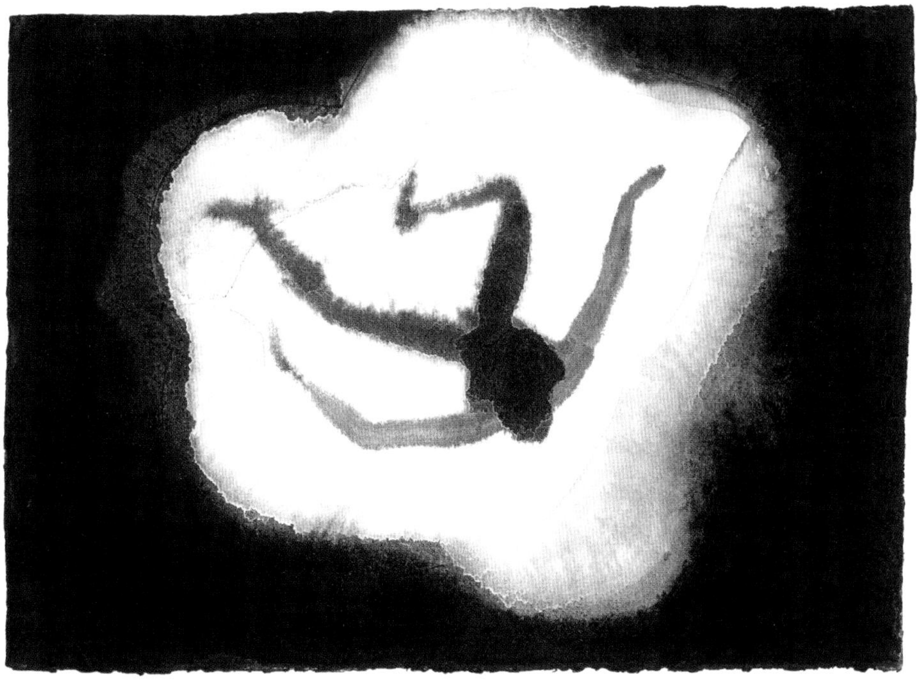

EARTH
1994
Carbon and casein on paper
14 x 19.5 cm
The British Museum, London

the bounding condition of a body in a particular moment of time.' Both moulding and scanning have been ways of gathering information about the subject, its contours, posture and position in space – in the same way, you might say, as looking and drawing are ways of gathering information from a model in the Life Room.

Reproduced here is the negative of a person, so to speak: half of a cast of Gormley's body (see overleaf). This is a relic of the creative process: a sculpture consisting of hundreds of steel balls was made from the cast, leaving its interior dramatically blackened. Though very unalike in appearance, a digital scan (also overleaf) presents similar information: an analogue of the outer surfaces of a human body. In this case, the anatomy is mapped not by a hollow shape in plaster but by thousands of infrared dots – a miniature galaxy adding up to a man. Gormley describes the effect of such a scan – beautiful and mysterious in itself – as 'a rotating web of points of light'.

These are two different ways of harvesting data about a body. 'The challenge,' Gormley says, 'has always been how to *translate* this information, whether from a mould or scan.' This is why his sculptures take such diverse forms, ranging from figures analysed into cubic geometry to bodies consisting of a criss-cross of girders like the structure of a bridge. *GAZE III* (2015; see page 63) comes from the 'Blockworks' series, which are the result of what Gormley calls a 'physical pixellation'. The anatomical forms have been schematised into large and small rectangular metal shapes.

As the physicist Werner Heisenberg noted, 'What we observe is not nature itself, but nature exposed to our method of questioning.' Gormley agrees, 'Information is the basis for making something. But there is always interpretation in that information already.' He wants to demonstrate that making works from life, however it is accomplished, 'is not a logical process. How we translate information into a place for feeling is the core task of art.'

Martin Gayford

Overleaf:
A plaster mould, 2000, and Scan 360, 2014, used for the production of sculptures

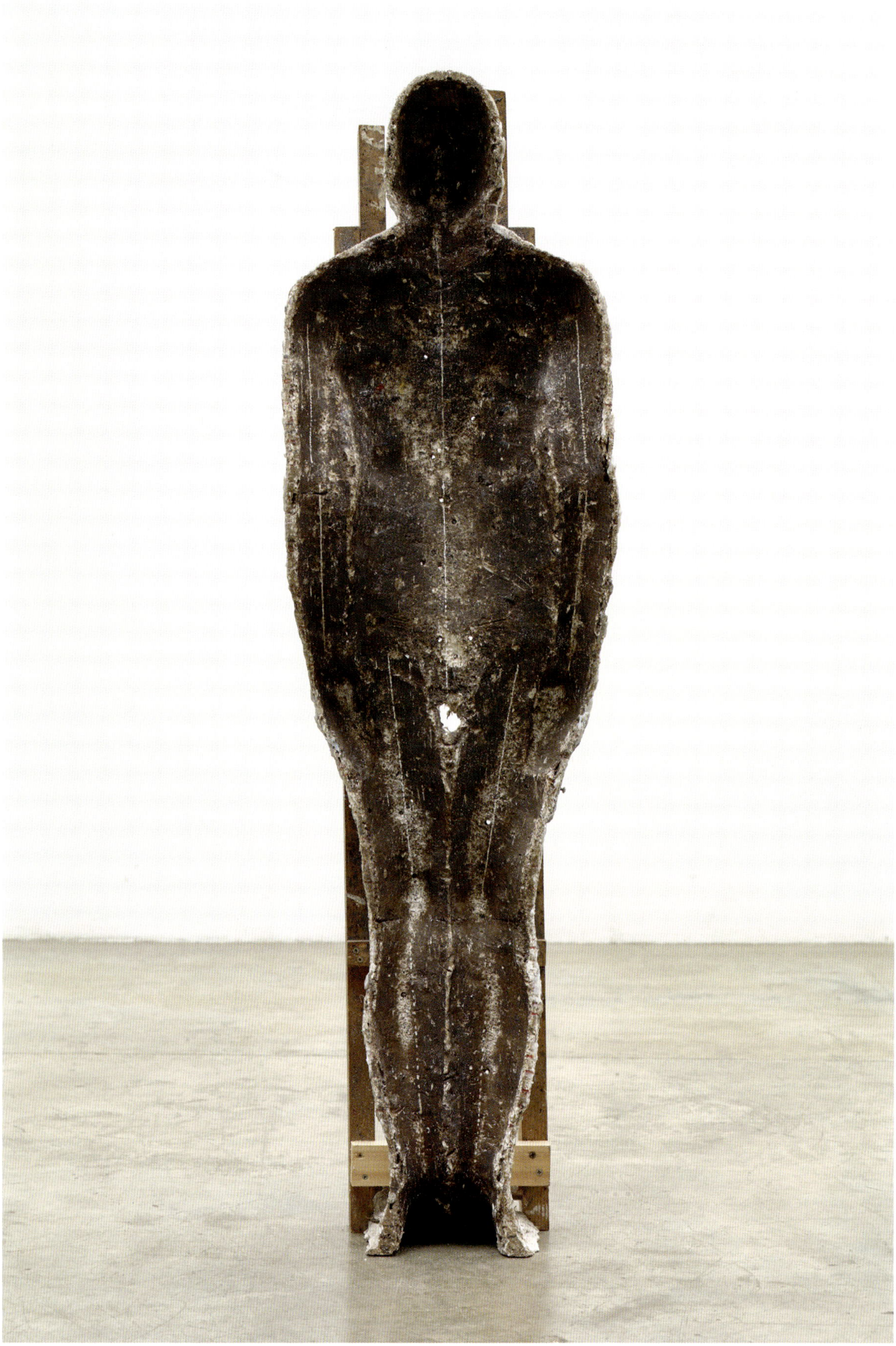

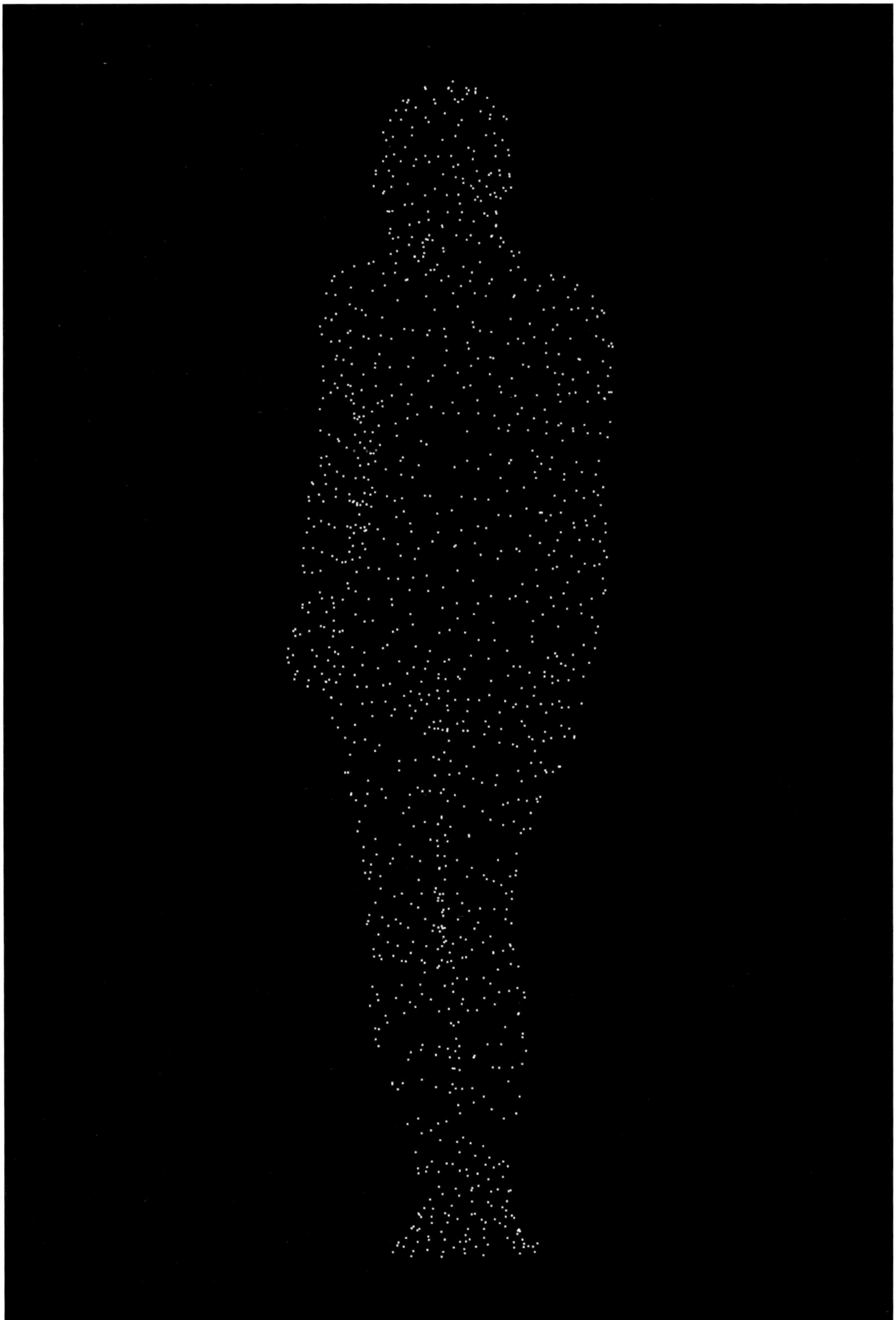

David Hockney

For over seven decades, David Hockney OM CH RA (b. 1937) has dedicated himself to representing life – the people, places and objects around him – in paintings, prints, photographs and drawings. An authority on the history of images, and a proponent of the importance of drawing, the Los Angeles-based artist embraces new technology, most recently drawing portraits, still-lifes and landscapes on his iPad.

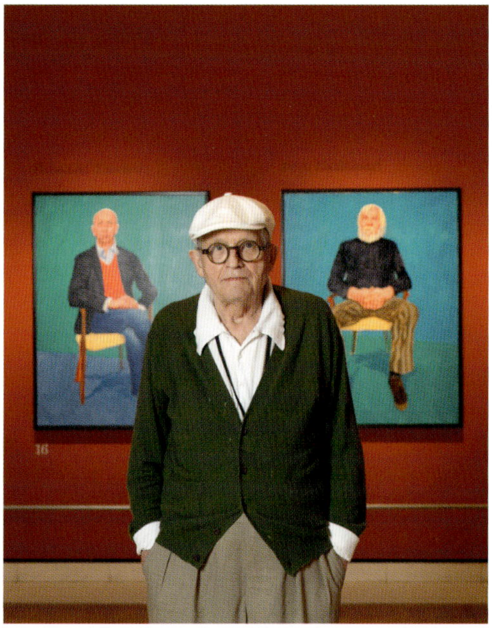

For David Hockney, drawing is a pleasure. 'I happen to like drawing. I draw all the time. Wasn't it Degas who said, "I'm just a man who likes to draw"? That's me!' Of course, Hockney's not alone. Many people like to draw, but to do so well requires, as he says, 'a bit of practice'.

'You need things pointed out to you: how to see in a clearer way. The teaching of drawing is training in mark-making and also the teaching of *looking*. It teaches us to look *hard* at things.' There are, it is true, limitations to this training. 'You can't teach someone to draw like Rembrandt, but you can teach them to draw quite competently. In other words, you can teach the craft; the poetry you can't teach.'

Mastering drawing comes down, Hockney believes, to something like the 10,000 hours of practice the writer Malcolm Gladwell famously claimed were necessary to learn any demanding skill. Hockney himself put in that time, and more, at Bradford School of Art. 'I went there when I was 16, and I drew every day for four years. Well, at the end of four years you've got quite good at drawing. The way they used to teach drawing was that the model would pose, then you'd start. After half an hour the teacher would come round and then he'd start drawing, say, a shoulder. And as he drew you would think, "Well, he's seeing more. I'm not *looking* hard enough." You could just see it – he drew much better. Afterwards, you'd draw better. And you would look at the next-year students, someone who had been drawing longer. You'd follow them a bit. When they had a rest, you'd be looking at their pictures, noticing what they did.'

This was, of course, drawing from life, the core of old-fashioned, academic art education, and a discipline that began to be swept away – over the protests of Hockney, among others – in the 1970s. 'At one meeting I went to they said, "Oh, I see, it's back to the Life Room is it, Hockney?" So I said, "No, it's *forward* to the Life Room!"'

There were reasons why the exercise of attempting to draw or paint another human being naked had persisted for so many years. 'The most complicated thing

Self-portrait, 20 March 2012 (1219)
2012
iPad drawing printed on paper, mounted on Dibond
81.3 x 61 cm

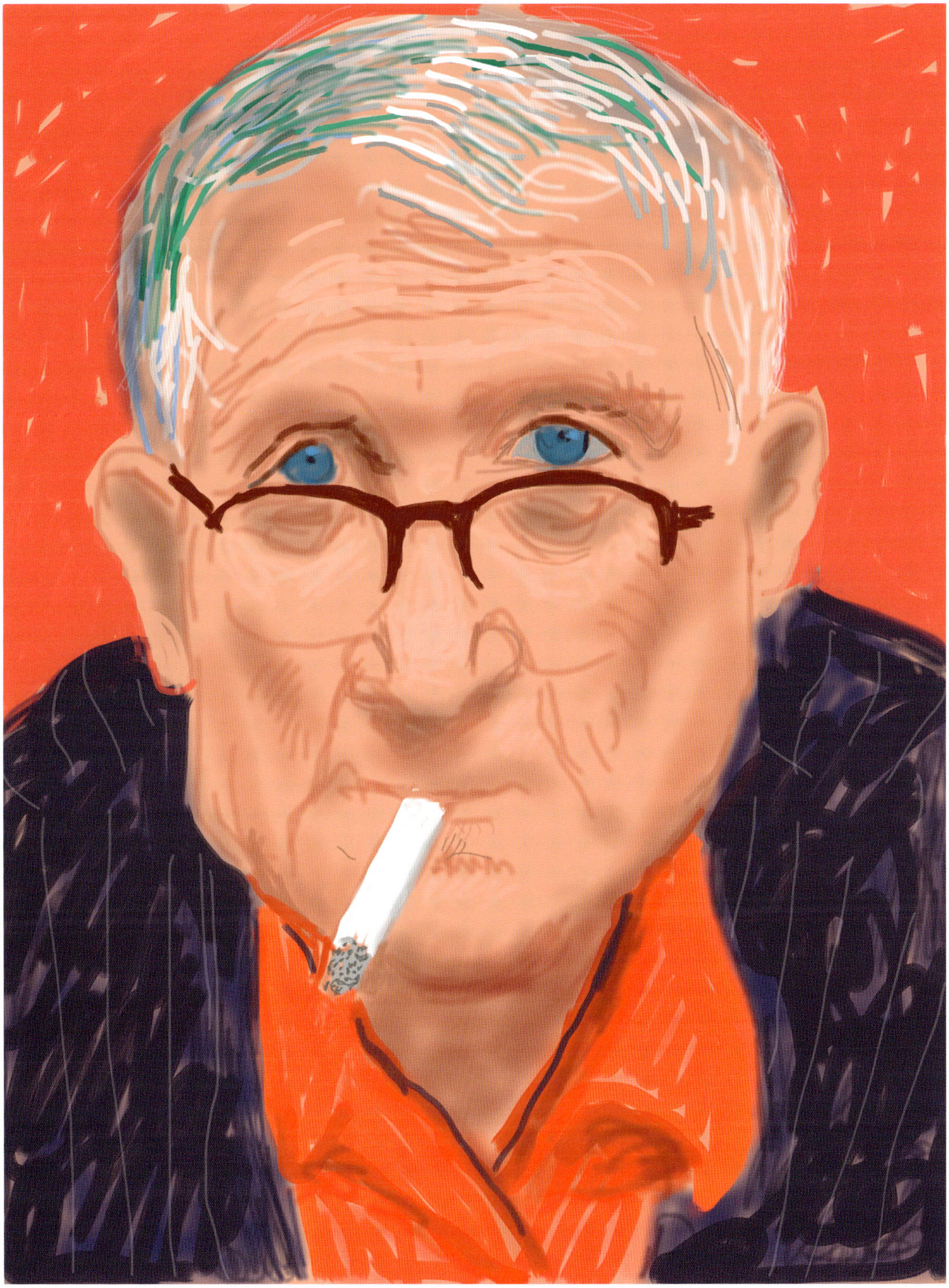

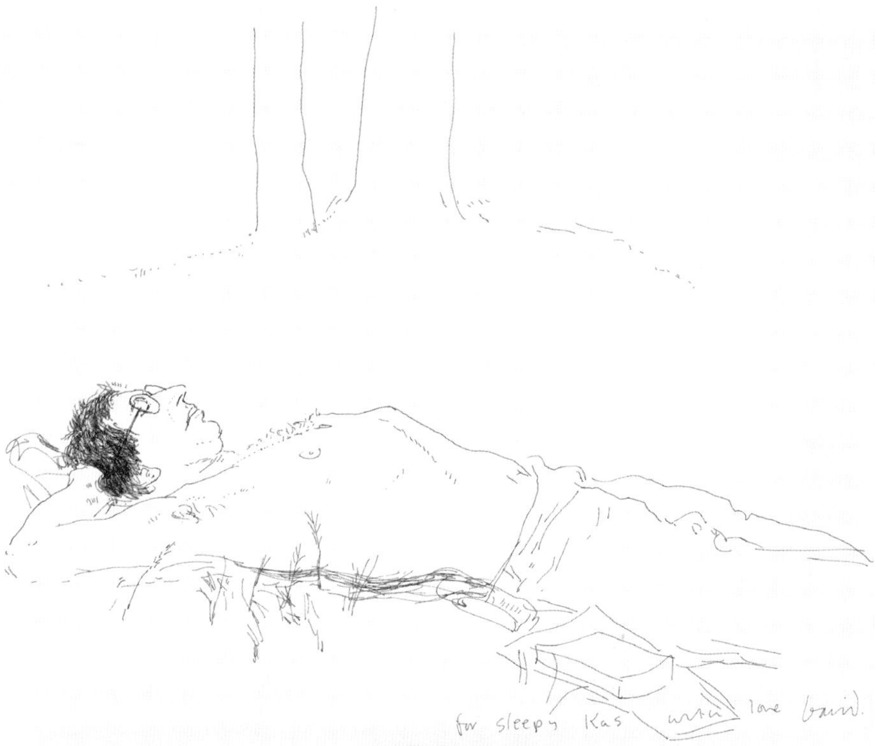

For Sleepy Kas
1967
Ink on paper
50 x 64 cm

we look at – and the most interesting thing – is another human being, so that is the hardest thing to draw. Most people can draw a tree because we don't care that much if a branch is a bit wrong. But if an arm is a bit wrong, *everybody* notices.'

This is not to say that that nudes and portraits are the only subjects that respond to the discipline of looking. Hockney's contention is that the human eye can see more, and the hand can make a more interesting picture of what it sees, than any camera lens. 'When I work on a still-life such as a vase of flowers, I get very excited because I realise there are a thousand things here I can see! Which will I choose? These simple little subjects are unbelievably rich.' This is partly because, as Hockney likes to emphasise, the eye is connected to the mind. Consequently, we see with memory, emotion and imagination.

One of Hockney's insights is that all pictures include a certain quantum of time. It takes time to make them, and it takes time to look at them. One of the problems with a photograph, in his view, is that it takes very little time to make – often less than a hundredth of a second; a painting or drawing, in contrast, requires a much longer period of observation and concentration. 'You have to take time even just to look at the figure.' Without drawing and painting, Hockney declares, the only way of making pictures would be photography, 'and that's not good enough!'

One of the strangest and least-noted aspects of recent technological innovations – digital photo-editing, for example, and most computer games – is that their creation, perhaps counter-intuitively, requires a lot of drawing. 'It's actually photography that's changing, and it's painting and drawing that are altering it, because the computer is being used to change photographs. If you can draw well, of course, you can do that *better*. People try anything to get round drawing, but we are drawing with smartphones now. It's always back to the drawing board!'

Martin Gayford

Portrait of the Artist's Mother, Mrs Laura Hockney, Bradford
1972
Ink on paper
43.2 x 35.3 cm
Tate, London

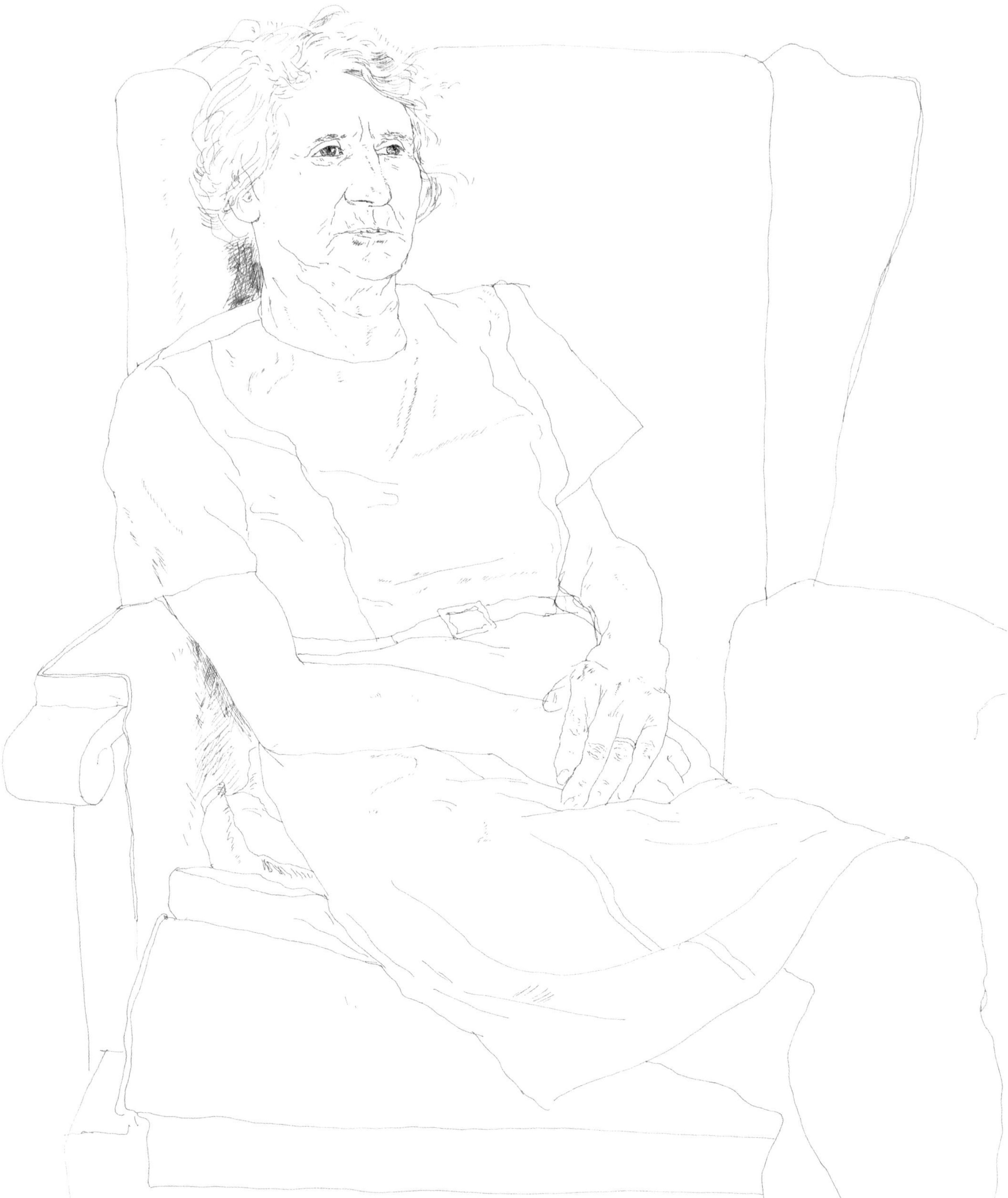
DH Bradford Aug 2nd 1972

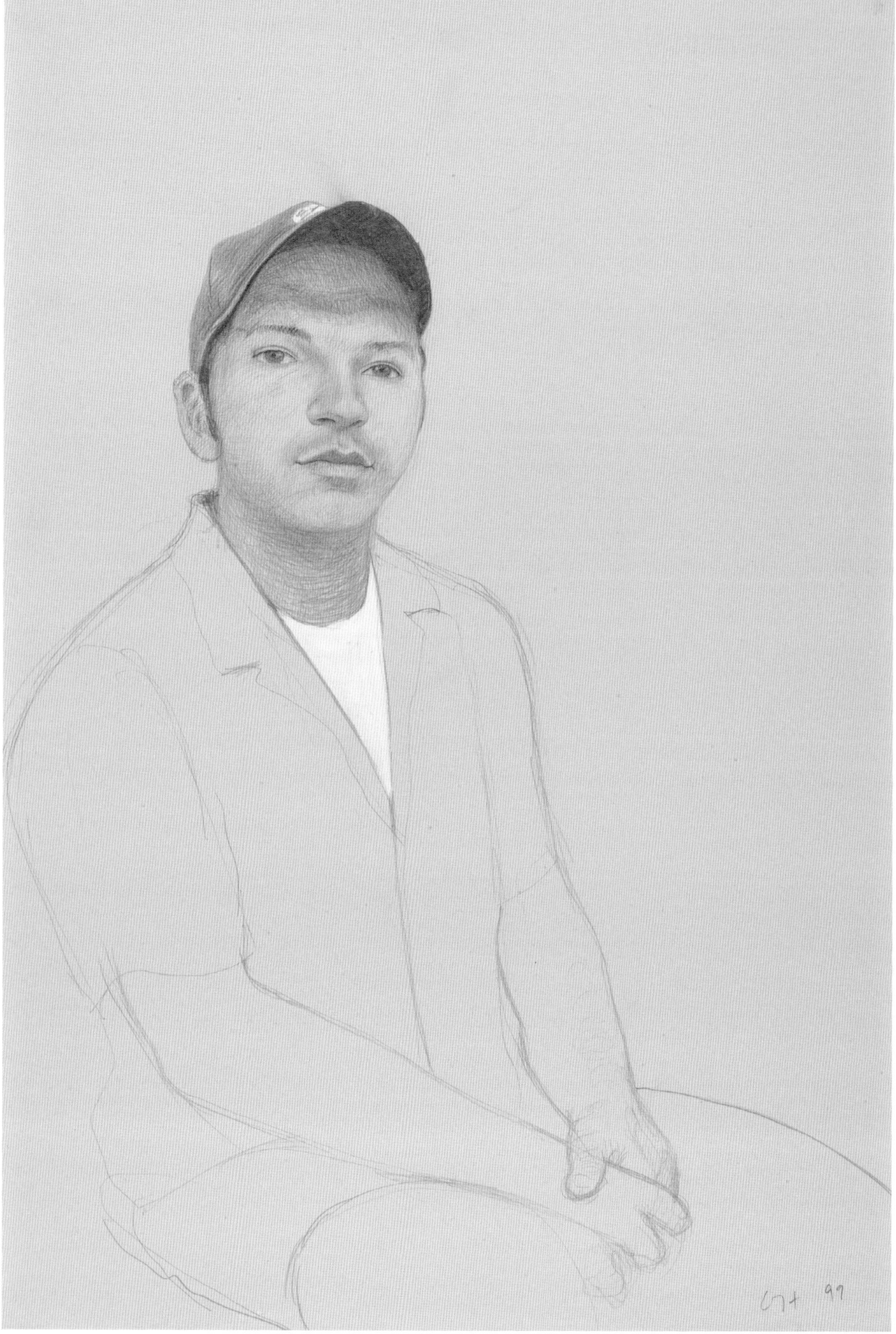

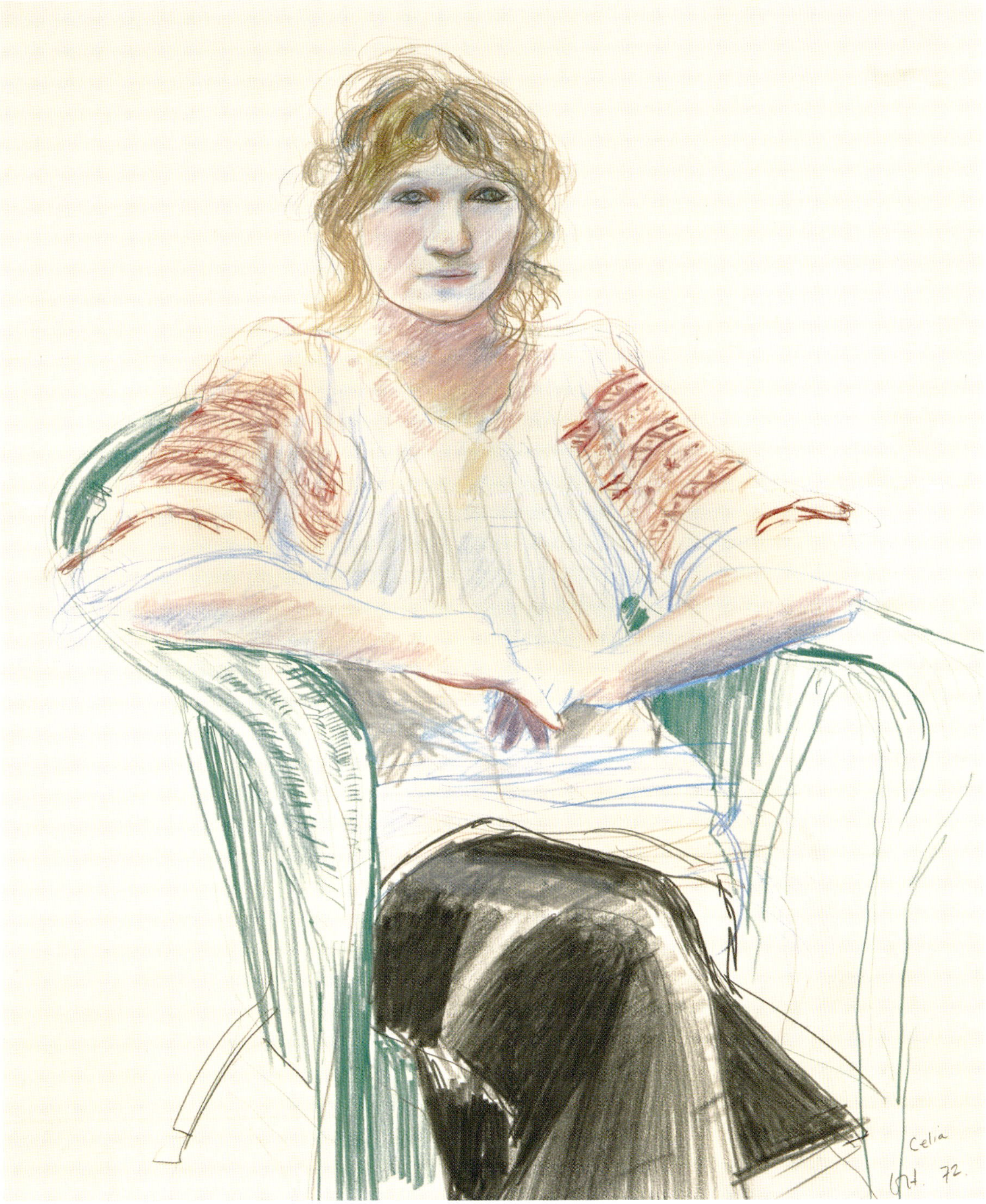

David Morales. Los Angeles. 23 August 1999
1999
Pencil and coloured pencil on paper, drawn using a camera lucida
56.2 x 38.1 cm
Collection The David Hockney Foundation

Celia
1972
Graphite, charcoal and coloured pencil on paper
43 x 35.5 cm

Overleaf:
Margaret and Ken, Bridlington
2002
Ink on paper
31.1 x 41.3 cm
Collection The David Hockney Foundation

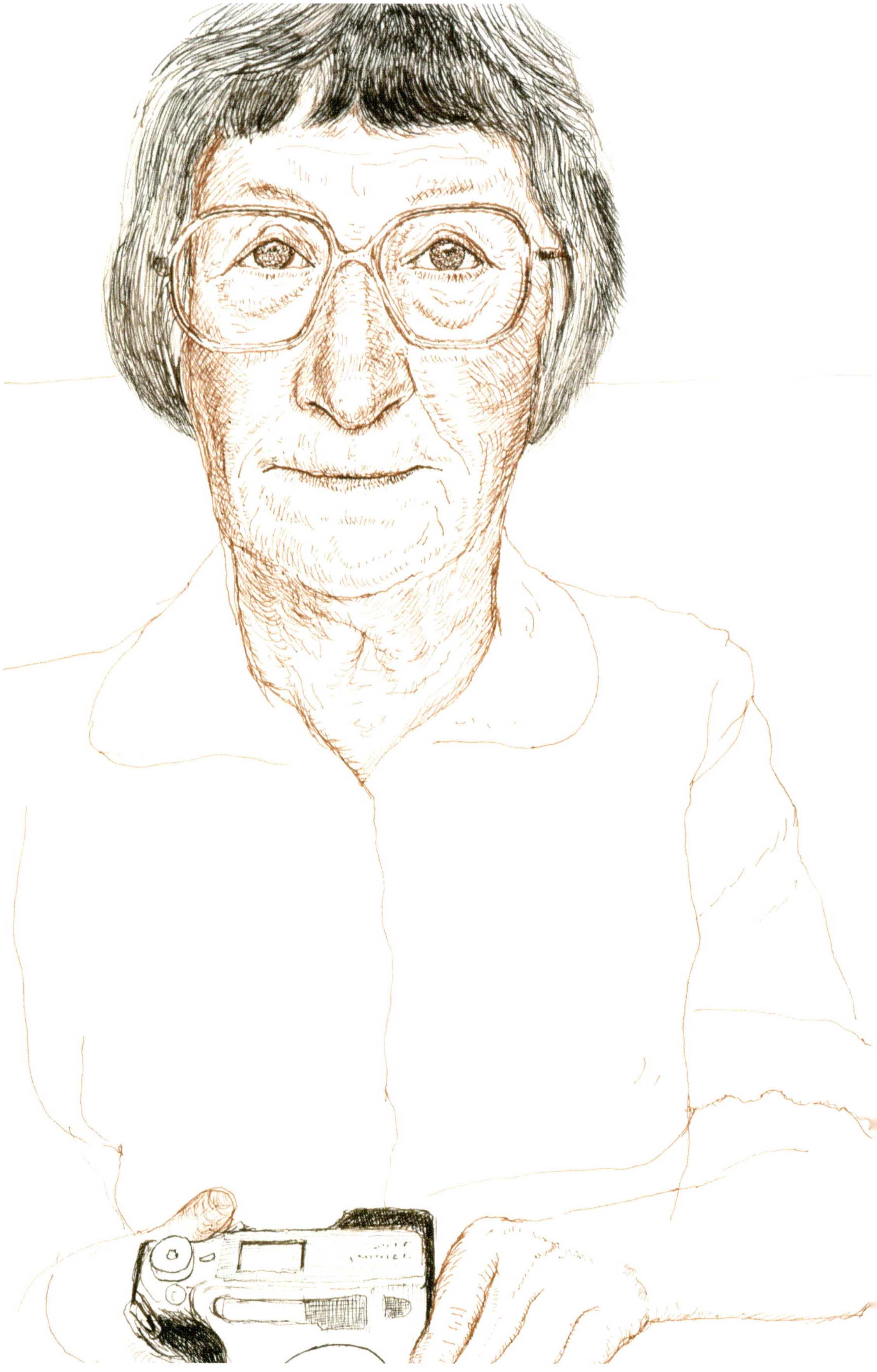

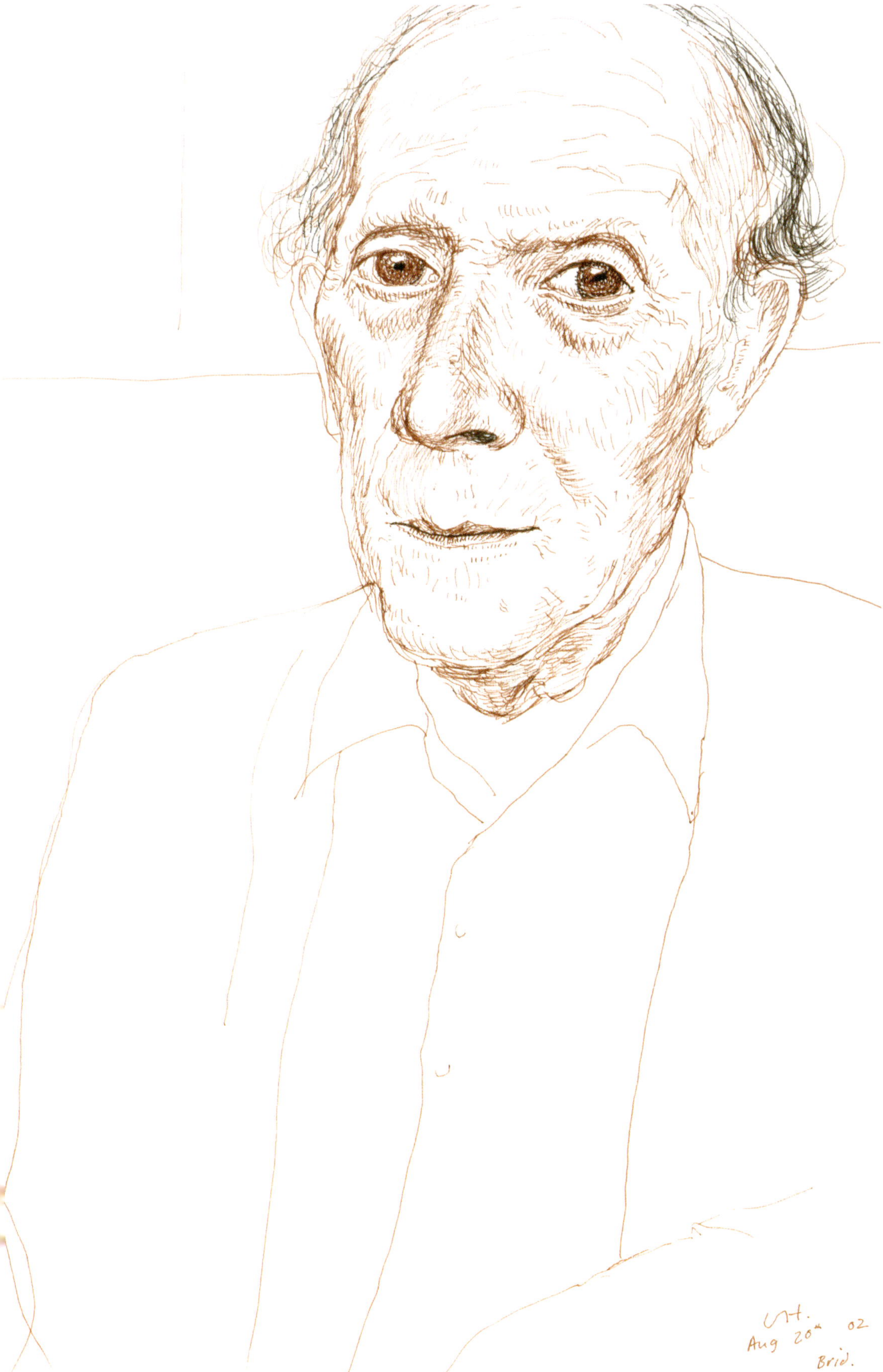
Aug 20th 02
Brid.

Chantal Joffe

Painter Chantal Joffe RA (b. 1969) is acclaimed for expressionistic works that capture figures in strong colour and fluid, forceful brush strokes. The London-based artist's subjects include friends, family members and herself. Joffe's early paintings used the pages of pornographic magazines as source material, and she continues to work from photographs as well as in person.

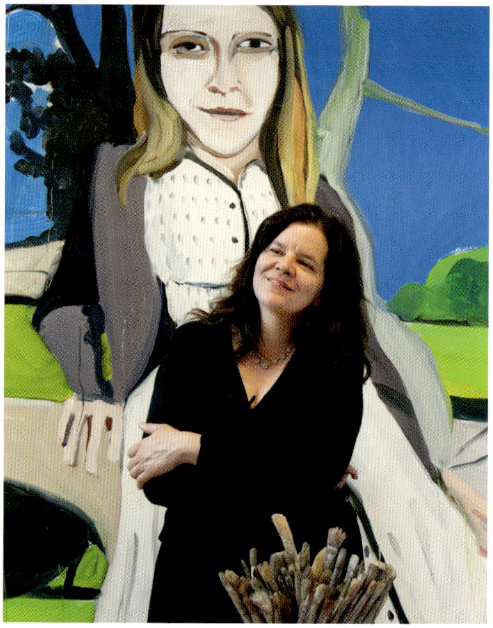

Chantal Joffe RA's work is about people, particularly those close to her: portraits of her partner Dan Coombs, her daughter Esme, her close friend Ishbel Myerscough, as well as a significant number of self-portraits, painted from a mirror or from photographs taken of her by Coombs. The self-portraits are therapeutic. 'When things are hard in my life I will paint myself,' Joffe explains. 'It is a way of saying I am okay. If I can paint that then I can deal with it. It's a way of owning it, of holding onto a moment. Painting is the absolute present tense of a moment.'

Working from life in this way, in Joffe's words, 'records one's own journey through life – this is what I saw, my view, my history'. She recalls how she once gave a talk at a college in which she arranged a chronological sequence of self-portraits: 'I did that for myself. I loved it. You could see all my obsessions. They stirred my emotions when I looked at them. Self-portraits are as close as I can get to writing a memoir.' Besides, she adds, 'you can do anything you want to yourself. Enlarge yourself, shrink yourself.'

Combined with her love for reading, particularly memoirs, as well as photography, the practice of working from life has made Joffe into an avid observer, forever looking at the world around her. This attention can be intense. She confesses: 'I swim to clear my head, although the swimming pool is a hard place for me – it's like a feast.' Likewise New York, a city she describes as 'full of magic, the casualness of weirdness'. The challenge for someone who observes life as much as Joffe is to separate what she has seen from what she is looking at when she is painting – to clear her mind and focus on the subject in front of her.

Her appetite for observation is evident in her painting and pastels, where the energy and speed of her brushwork and drawing, the need to capture the intensity of the moment, are palpable. 'I like speed – through speed things happen that you don't anticipate,' she says, although, she adds, 'I have to

Self-portrait at Night
2015
Oil on board
45.5 x 38.4 cm

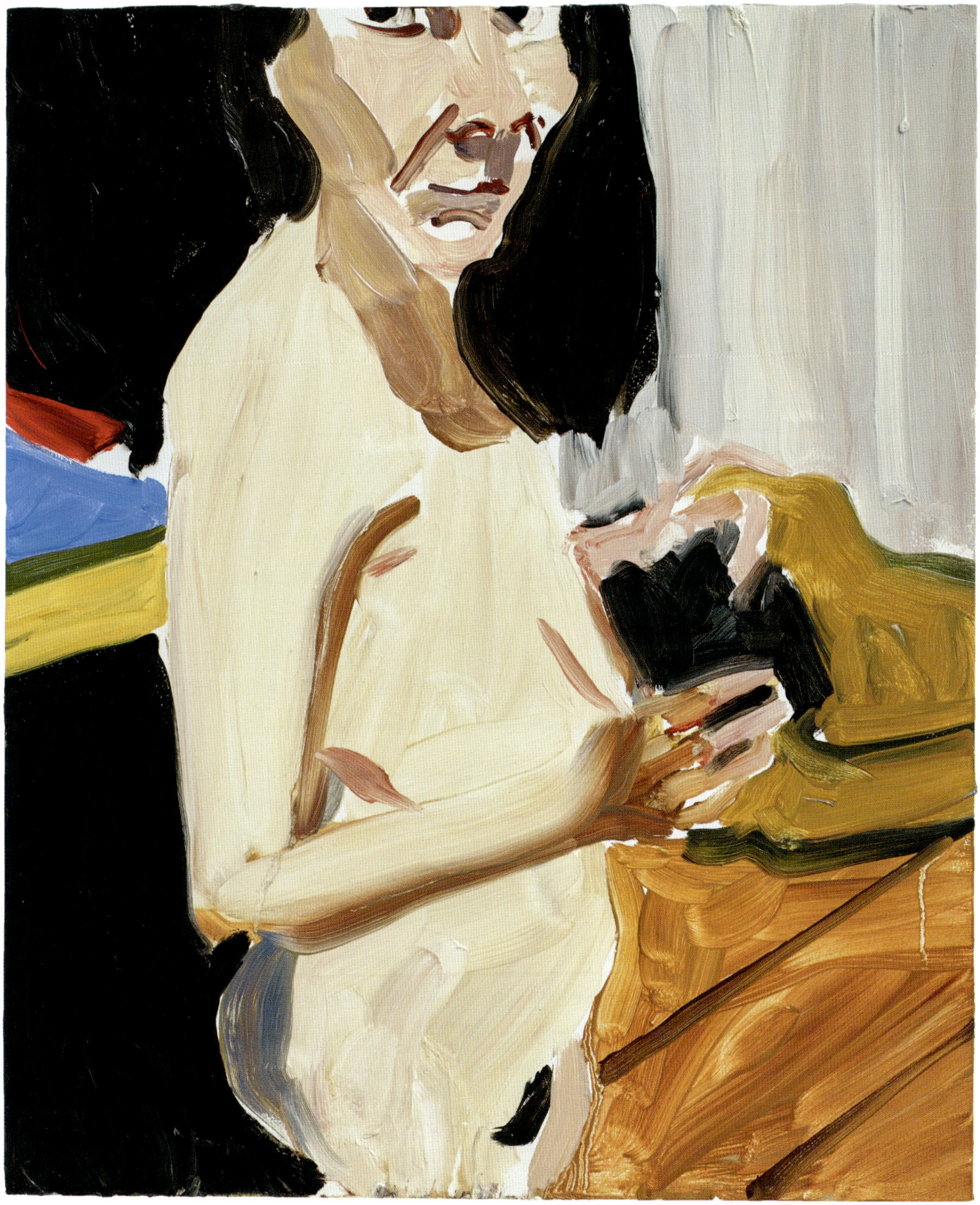

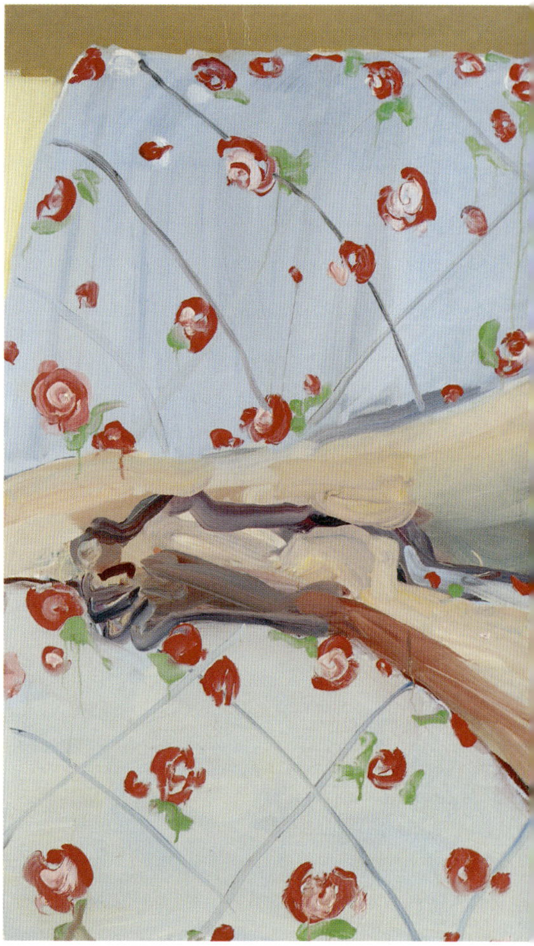

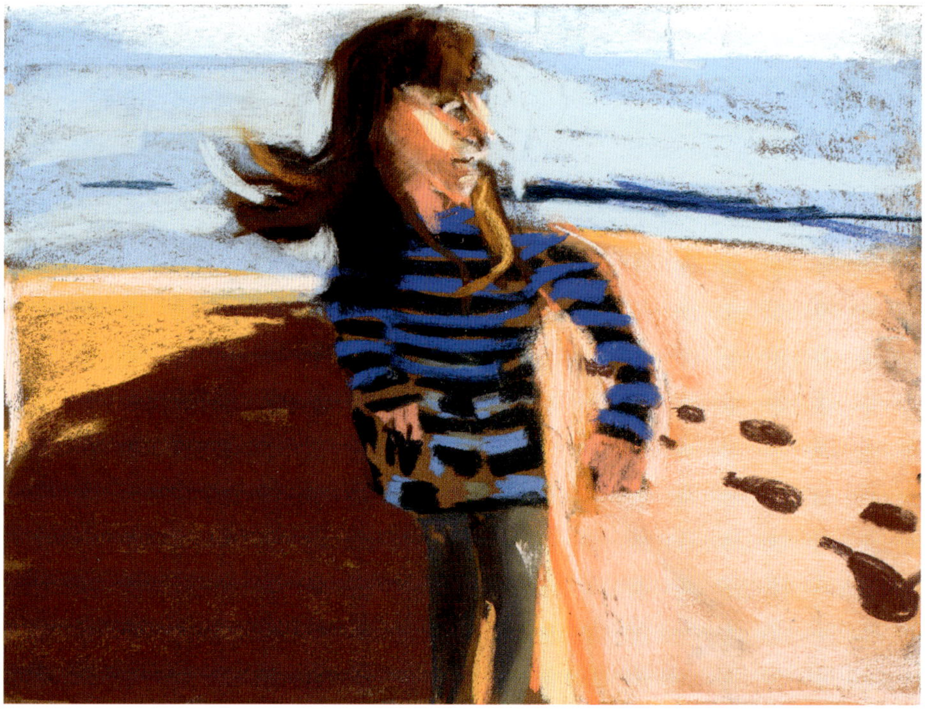

Esme in St Leonards
2015
Pastel on paper board
37.8 x 47.6 cm
Collection of Rena and
Scott Hoffman, USA

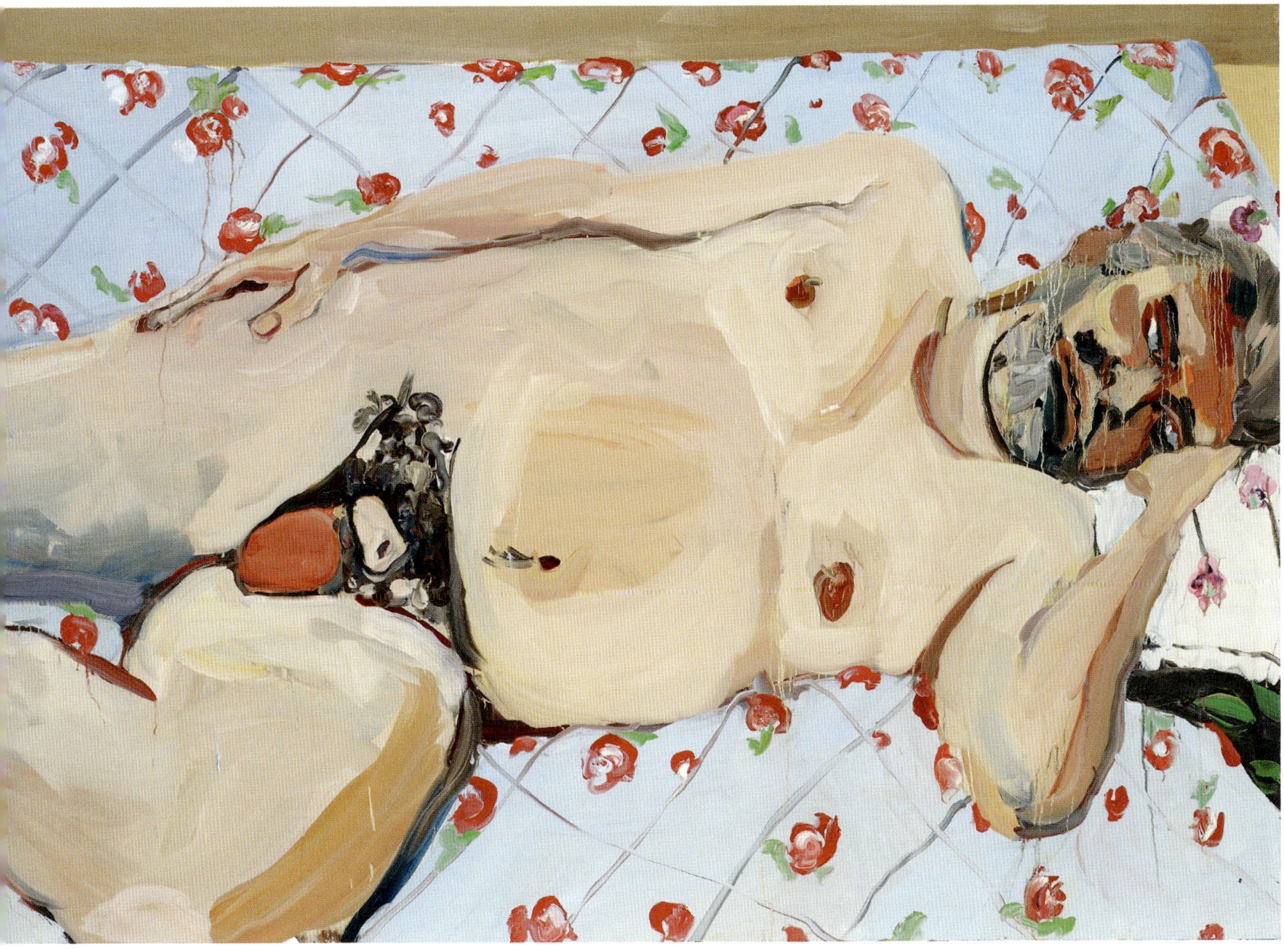

Naked Dan
2010
Oil on board
152 x 304 cm

slow myself down, so that I'm not done before I'm started.' Joffe gauges the pace at which she works, in order not to lose the vital essence of the subject by working too quickly.

'Nobody talks about the energy you need to paint, to be so in the moment and to paint fast, physically,' she continues. 'It is such an introspective activity. You are on your own most of the time. To find a place to actually paint, and the energy, to harness it all, to hold on to the discipline and balance, is hard. You need to paint with a level of anxiety, of truth.'

Joffe is conscious of the distinct challenges that confront women artists and admires pioneering female painters who worked from life, such as the French Impressionist Berthe Morisot, the German Expressionist Paula Modersohn-Becker and Alice Neel, the American portrait painter, acknowledging how courageous they were. 'Being a female artist is exciting. You don't have the luxury of just saying I am an artist in the same way as men, historically. Maybe it is harder, but more interesting because of how hard it is. I have to believe in all the good that comes with it.'

Pastel is 'a perfect medium' for the artist. 'You can go really hard with it,' she explains. 'Very immediate. Very fast.' *Self-portrait Naked in the Garden* (2016; see overleaf) and her series 'Self-portrait in the Garden at Night' (2016) are pastels inspired by Turkish novelist Sabahattin Ali's *Madonna in a Fur Coat* (1943), the story of a doomed relationship between a Turkish man and an artist in 1920s Berlin. 'These pastels capture figures at night. Flesh at night. How you lose a lot of colour. The pallor of the flesh. Me seated on a garden chair. There is something about flesh near metal. Pure geometry against my own fleshiness.' She worked from photographs rather than a mirror. The contrast between the darkness of the background and the luminosity of her figure, intensified by the flash of the camera operated by Coombs, gives the works a slightly illicit feel. For Joffe, photography was the only way to capture

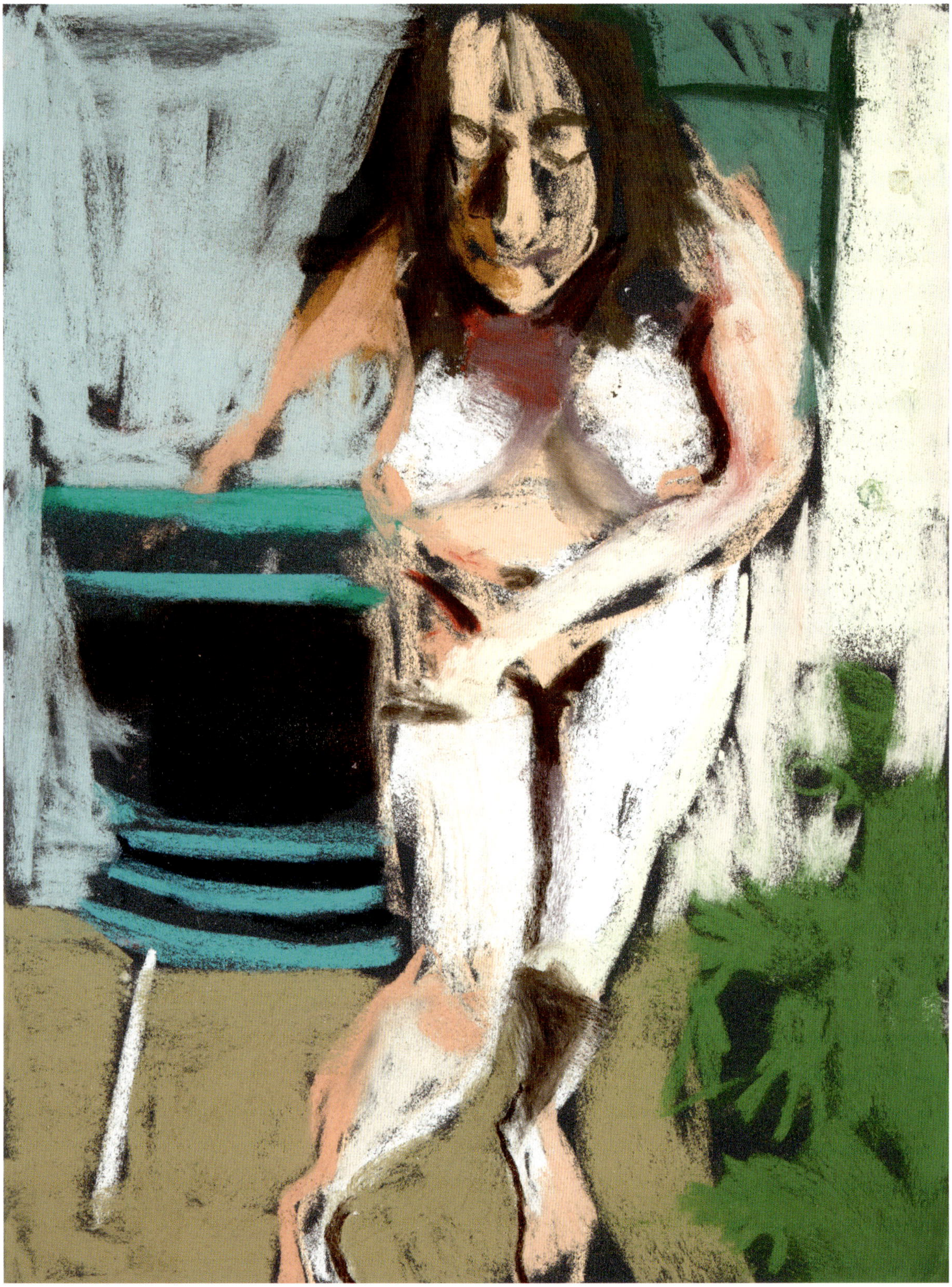

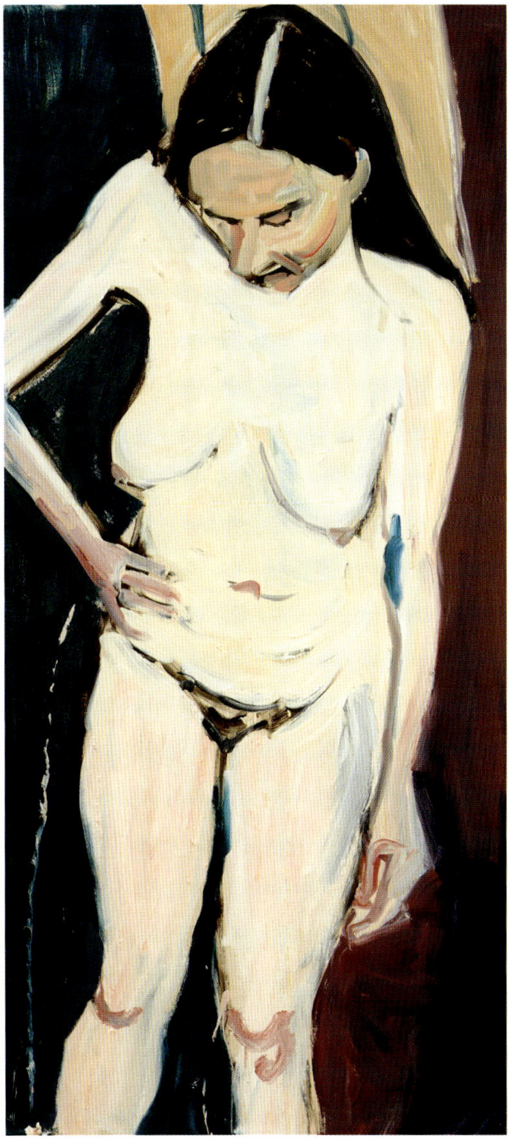

Self-portrait with Hand on Hip
2016
Oil on board
201.6 x 90 cm

the potency of the moment; working from photographs in this way, for Joffe, is working from life.

For some of her oil paintings, such as *Self-portrait with Hand on Hip* (2016), Joffe prepares panels in advance with homemade gesso, which is a laborious process. 'It is difficult and time-consuming to do, but it makes the most incredible surface, like human skin. Really intoxicating. Two weeks just to prime the panels. It is actually painted fast, but the gesso absorbs the mark and slows you down.' The painting reflects Joffe's fascination with the American artist Willem de Kooning, in particular his 'Door Cycle' series of female figures (1964–66), which he painted on the surface of hollow-core doors that had been previously installed in his studio; Joffe's painting is exactly the same size as those in his series. She started by making a sequence of 'blind' drawings, also inspired by De Kooning, who, in 1966, made 24 charcoal drawings of figures with his eyes closed. Doing this was part of her process of leading up to the painting – in her words 'thinking your way into De Kooning'.

Working with her eyes closed also allowed her to realise 'how little one thinks' when one draws or paints. Such intuition is evident in Joffe's art, although that which appears so immediate and instinctive masks the deep thought, research and consideration that prefaces each body of her work.

Adrian Locke

Self-portrait Naked in Garden
2016
Pastel on paper
47.6 x 37.8 cm

Michael Landy

Michael Landy RA (b. 1963) produces installations that explore social issues, such as consumerism and the commodification of art. The London-based artist also maintains a diverse drawing practice, which has included portraits and botanical drawings. He was Eranda Professor of Drawing at the Royal Academy Schools between 2014 and 2016.

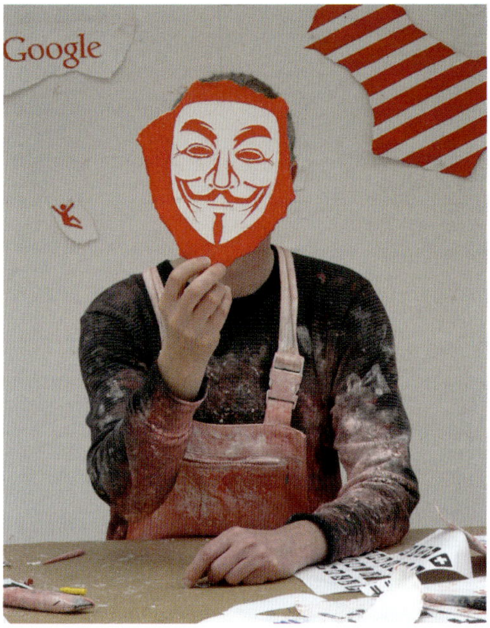

Michael Landy's art oscillates between extremes – gigantic and minute, performative and private – but everything he has done to date is underpinned by close observation from life.

One of the generation of Young British Artists (YBAs), Landy initially became known for his large-scale installations, most famously *Break Down* (2001), in which he systematically destroyed all his possessions over a period of fourteen days in an empty C&A department store on Oxford Street. Yet it was his love of drawing that ignited his artistic career. As a child he would copy things from books as well as the patterned wallpaper in the family home. Later, at Loughton College of Further Education, he spent hours working from live models. 'Between the ages of 16 and 18 I did a lot of life drawing on my foundation course,' he recalls. 'I loved it. The teachers taught lots of techniques, but as time went on I taught myself how to look. I spent most of my time just observing.'

Despite this early passion for life drawing, the artist drew nothing during his BA degree course at Goldsmiths in London. It was only later, after *Break Down*, that he took up drawing again in earnest, adopting the same graphic, linear style with minimal modelling that he had developed as a teenager, and which has remained constant for his entire career. This time his chosen subjects were weeds, and he drew directly onto the etching plate. 'It was about having empathy for little plants that grow in cracks in the street. The plant is alive still – it's flowering, it's shooting seeds.'

Weeds are forgotten, undervalued things considered by most to be blots on the landscape. Landy is interested in imperfection, fragility and decay, and his portrayals of the human body are never idealised. In 2004 he tenderly recorded his disabled father's hands, feet and face, documenting every last detail of puckered skin, wrinkle and vein. A year later, he drew the aftermath of his own operation to remove a cancerous testicle, turning

Landy Family. Gillian
2007
Graphite on paper
70 x 50 cm
Trinity Fine Art, London

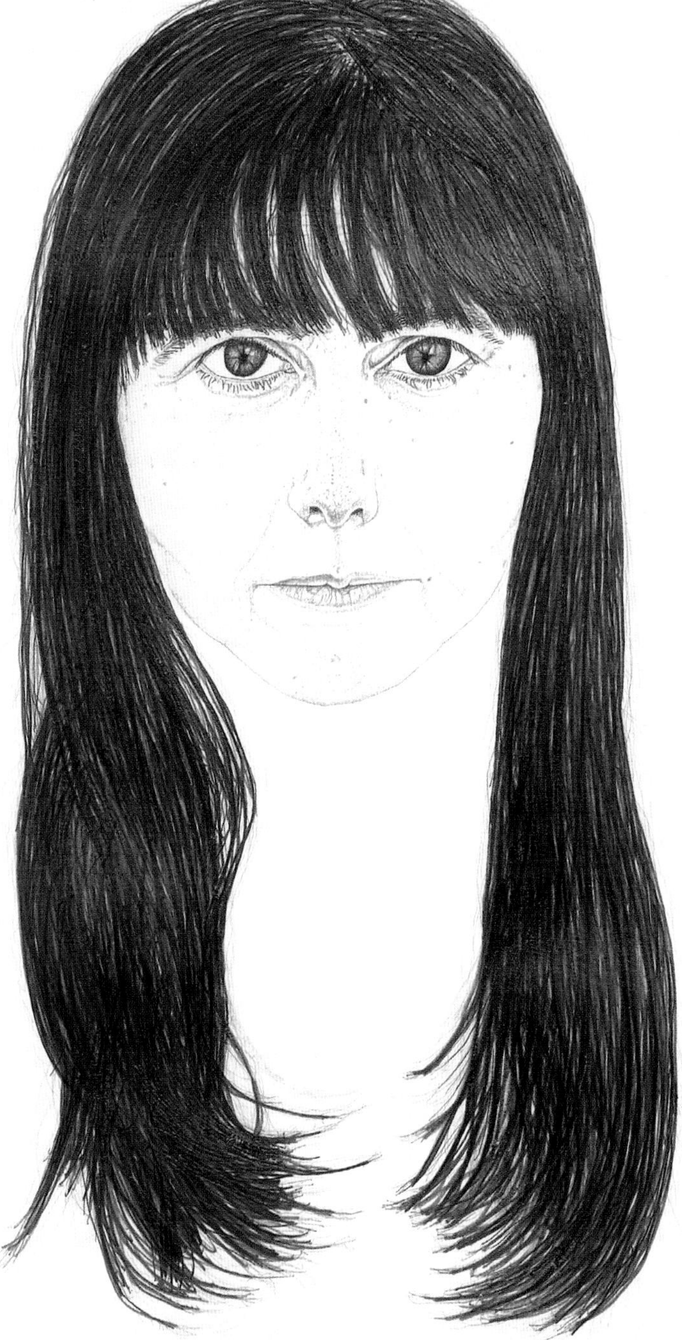

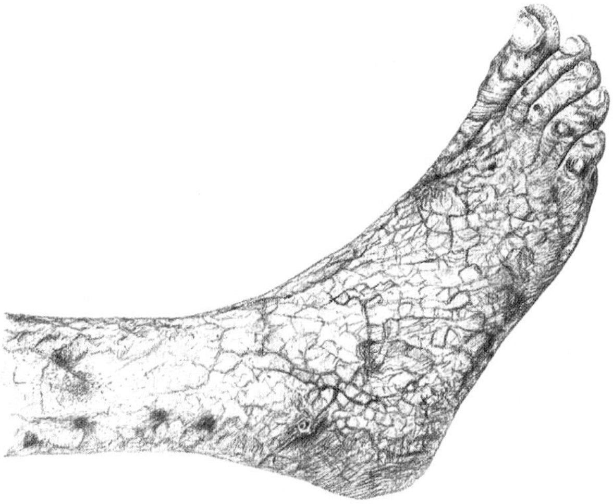

Claudication
2004
Pencil on paper
42.2 x 59.7 cm
MoMA, New York

himself into the subject of his own life class. All these drawings record physical suffering or trauma, and they focus on parts of the body rather than its entirety. 'Even when I was doing life drawing at 18 I would leave bits out,' says Landy. 'I wouldn't necessarily fill in the whole face ... I wouldn't finish off the bottom of the feet. Things have always just hovered on the page.'

In the series of 80 meticulous pencil portraits of family and friends he made between 2007 and 2008, the faces are shown in the middle of the page with no neck or torso to anchor them, nor background to fix them in space. Landy did not vary his style to suit each sitter, but adopted the same approach throughout the series. 'The portraits are all on the same piece of paper, all in HB pencil,' he says. 'I didn't give myself rules, but I might as well have done.' Each drawing took two days to complete, and Landy's portrait of his partner, the artist Gillian Wearing, is a typical example (page 83). Gillian's neutral expression is captured in relatively few lines; her dark eyes and hair stand out against her pale skin and the empty background, giving her an

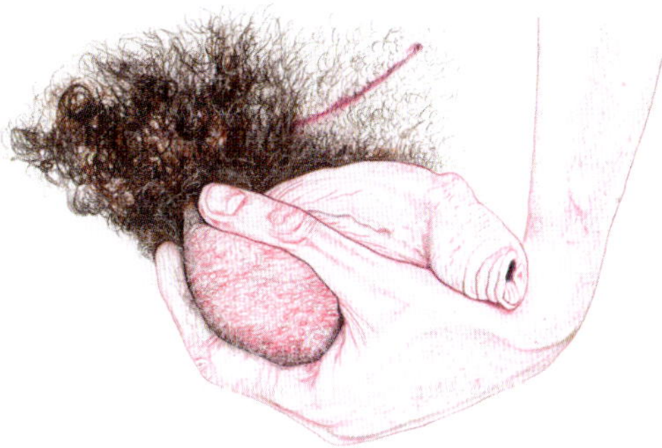

Radical Orchidectomy for a Solid Mass in the Upper Pole of the Left Testis
2005
Coloured pencil on paper
57 x 78 cm
Collection of Marc Vlessing and Suzanna Taverne

unreal, almost spectral appearance. 'I just like looking into people's faces,' he muses. 'They have to look me in the eye at the beginning. I spend less time looking on the page, especially at the beginning. Looking at the subject is fundamental.' This practice of close scrutiny has spilled over into his daily life and can be unnerving for strangers. 'Since that project I find myself looking at people a lot more. On the Tube when I'm in close proximity to people I start looking at their features. They get freaked out.'

Landy's obsession with the fragmented and suffering body came to the fore in his exhibition 'Saints Alive' in 2013, produced at the end of his residency at the National Gallery. Fascinated by the martyred saints in the gallery's collection, he mixed up and reassembled photographs of their body parts to create humorous kinetic sculptures. These were inspired by Jean Tinguely's apparently purposeless sculptural machines, and, like the Swiss artist's self-destructive kinetic sculpture *Homage to New York* (1960), they contain the seeds of their own destruction. Landy's fibreglass saints gradually degrade over time: St Jerome abrades his chest with a rock (see overleaf); St Apollonia scars her face while extracting her tooth; and doubting Thomas's finger leaves a mark on Christ's torso each time he jabs it.

Appropriating or copying figures by other artists extends the practice of working from life, and it also forms part of Landy's current body of work, 'Breaking News' (2014–ongoing). He has gone back to drawing, but the latest works in this series are on a massive scale. Using oil sticks, he has produced a number of images of gigantic graffiti-like or cartoon figures borrowed from the painters Philip Guston and Jean Dubuffet (see overleaf). Other works represent a move away from the figure, including two large pieces that are purely abstract. For an artist who has always portrayed what he sees or perceives in the real world, it's a departure. 'I just decided to see what it's like drawing without anything in front of me. I've normally got something in front of me, whether it's copied or a person or a plant, and I thought, "What if I freestyle?"'

Caroline Bugler

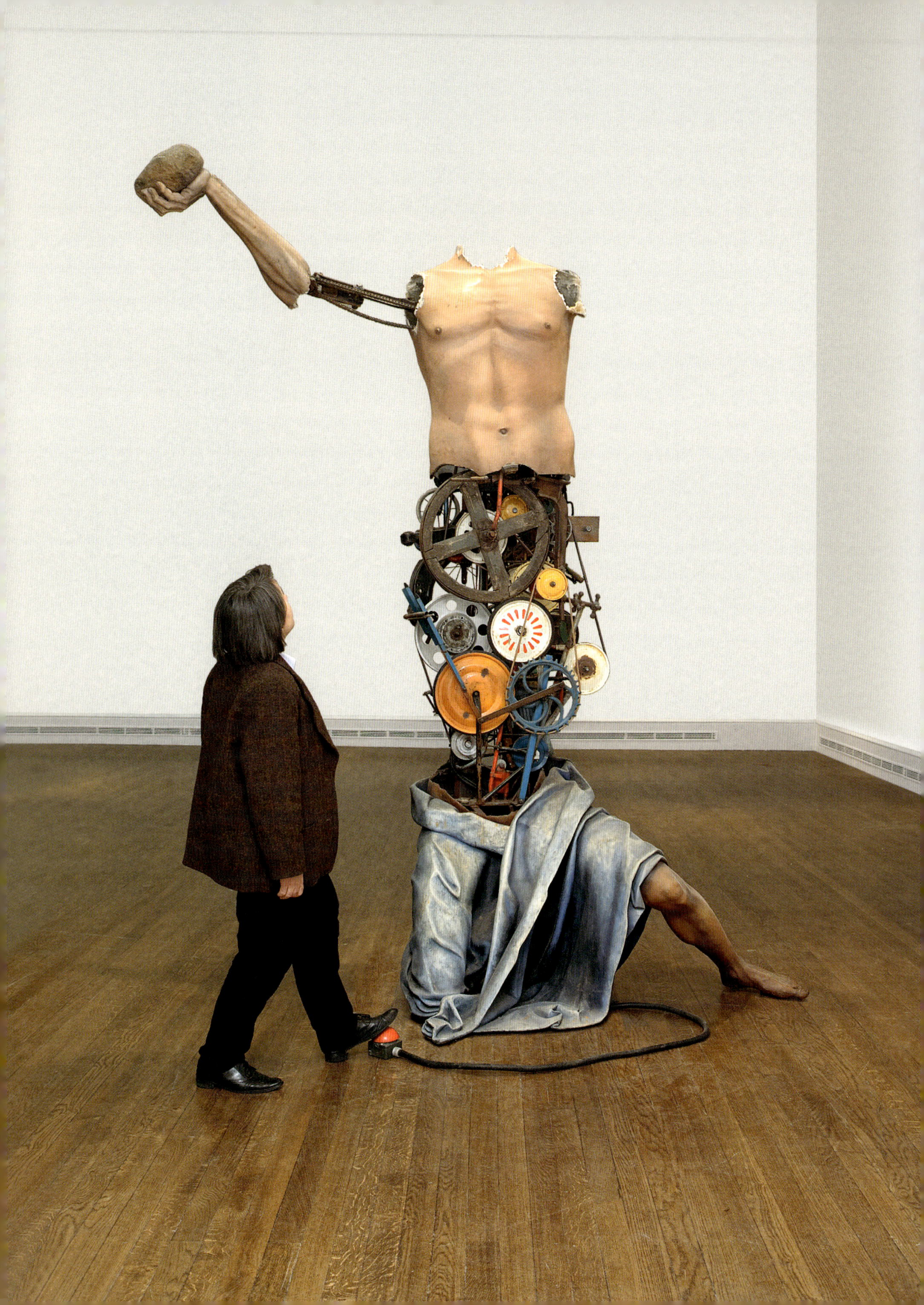

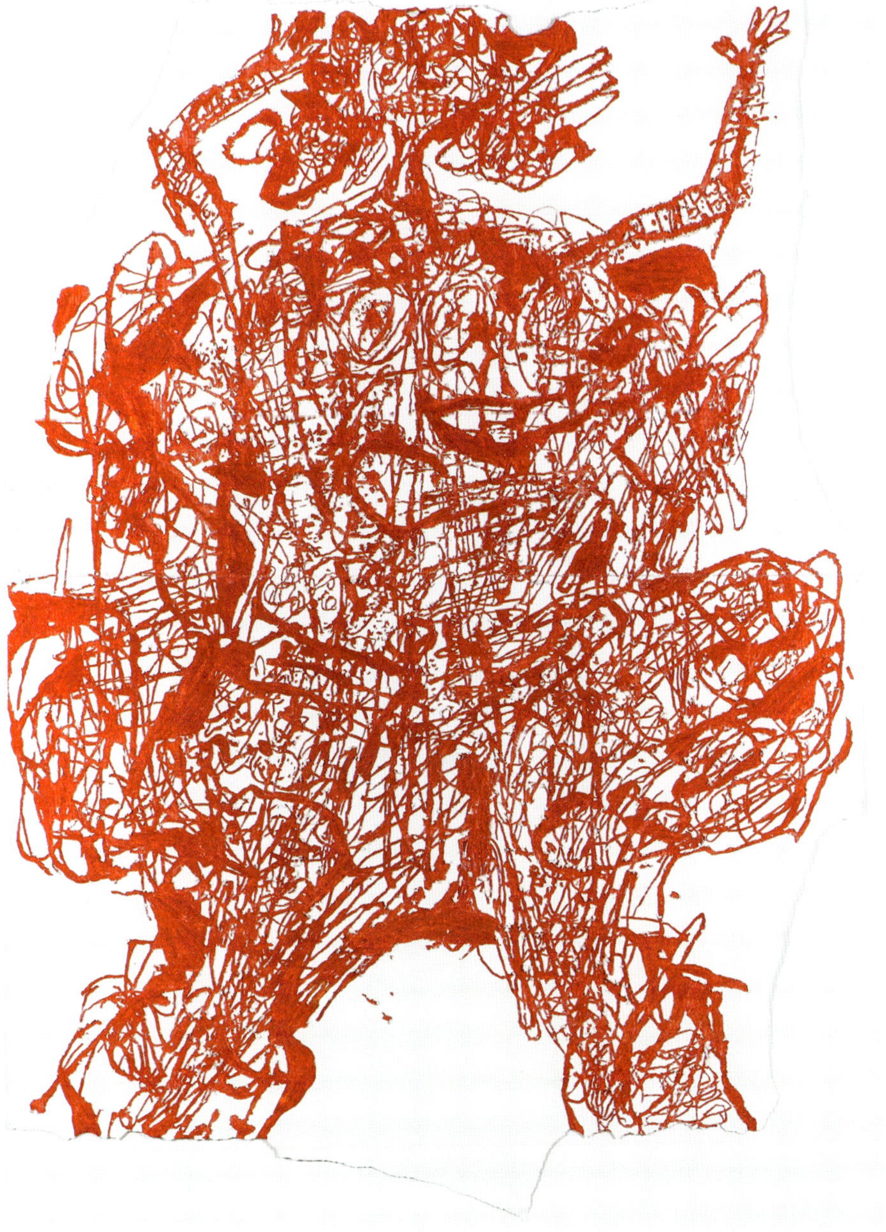

Saint Jerome
2012
Mixed media
310 x 245 x 106 cm
Duerckheim Collection

Dubuffet
2016
Oil stick on paper
229.8 x 152.2 cm

Liane Lang

Liane Lang (b. 1973) studied at the Royal Academy Schools between 2003 and 2006. Born in Munich, she now lives and works in London. Her photographs and videos examine the verisimilitude of figurative sculptures, and include works in response to the écorchés and casts of antique statues in the RA's Life Room.

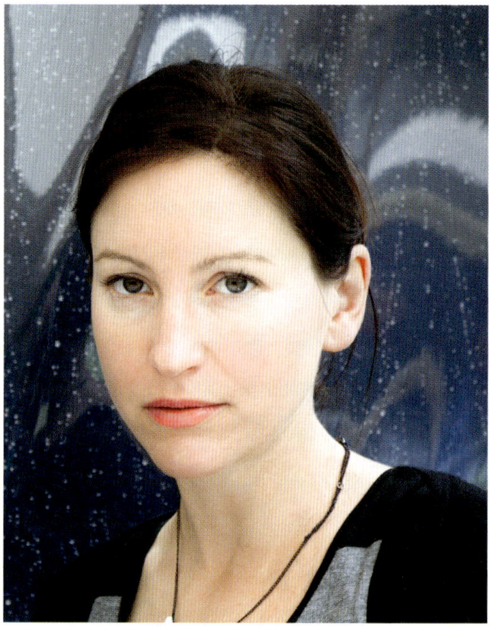

'Animacy' is not a word in common usage, but it is one Liane Lang often uses. In the study of cognitive linguistics, it refers to our measures of how sentient, alive or animate any subject is. While distinctions of animacy are grasped by babies as young as six months, animacy as a concept is far from simple: it can be perceived as a hierarchical scale, with human beings at one end and concrete objects at the other, and dolls seemingly somewhere in between.

Lang is fascinated by what she calls this 'register of aliveness' and how it relates to the sculpted figure. The German artist made her first puppet from a cast of her own face at the age of 16, around the time she began attending life-drawing sessions in a painter's studio. Had she gone on to study fine art at a German academy, life drawing would probably have been a key part of her training, but she chose to study for her Foundation Diploma at the National College of Art and Design in Dublin – where life drawing was administered 'like a punishment if they considered you hadn't properly progressed in your project' – and her BA in Fine Art at Goldsmiths in London, 'where if you wanted to do life drawing you were looked at as a reactionary'. The only way she could pursue her interest in figuration was by making animations with clay figures.

It was while studying for a Postgraduate Diploma at the Royal Academy Schools that she found a new way of playing with ideas of animacy. For her photographic series *Casts* (2006–08), she created uncannily lifelike latex dolls of young women from body casts and photographed them in the RA's Life Room interacting with the plaster casts and écorchés from which generations of students had learned to draw. In *Life Room* (see overleaf), a nude doll, overlooked by classical statues, reclines with her head and legs wrapped in a velvet curtain on an old couch covered in Morris & Co. fabric, which has been 'host to thousands of nude models over the centuries'; in *The Encroacher*, a doll dressed only in rubber gloves and

Ars Equina
2006
C-type analogue hand print on aluminium
150 x 120 cm
Private collection

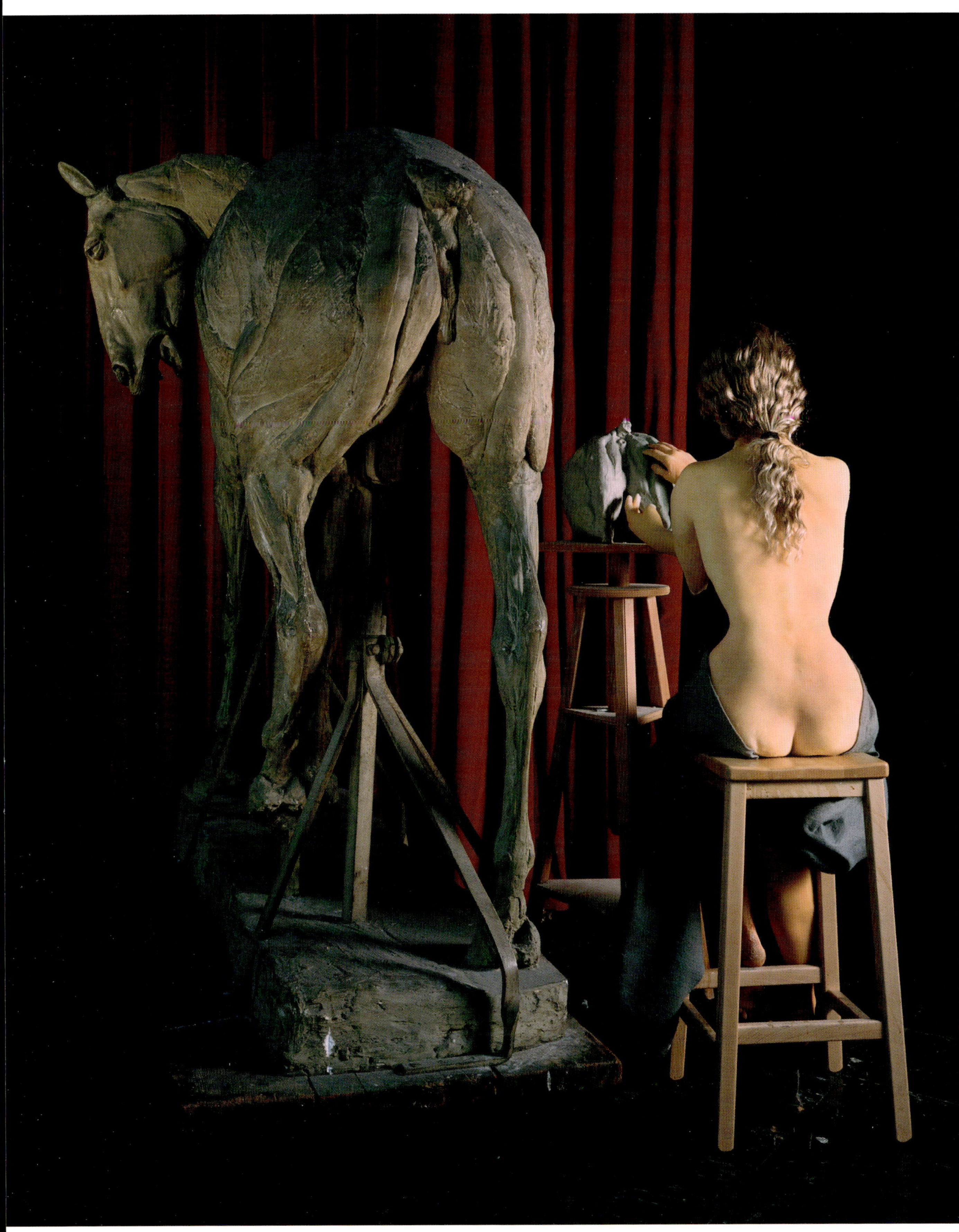

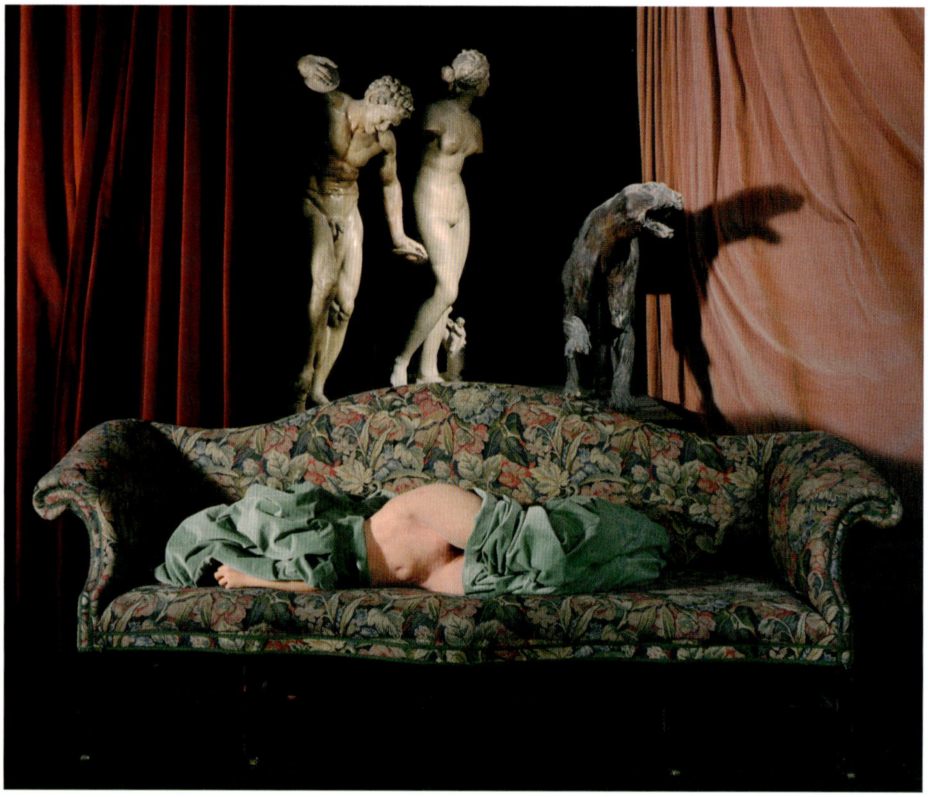

The Life Room
2006
C-type analogue hand print on aluminium
120 x 150 cm
Private collection

The Encroacher
2007
Durst Lambda print on aluminium
120 x 150 cm
Private collection

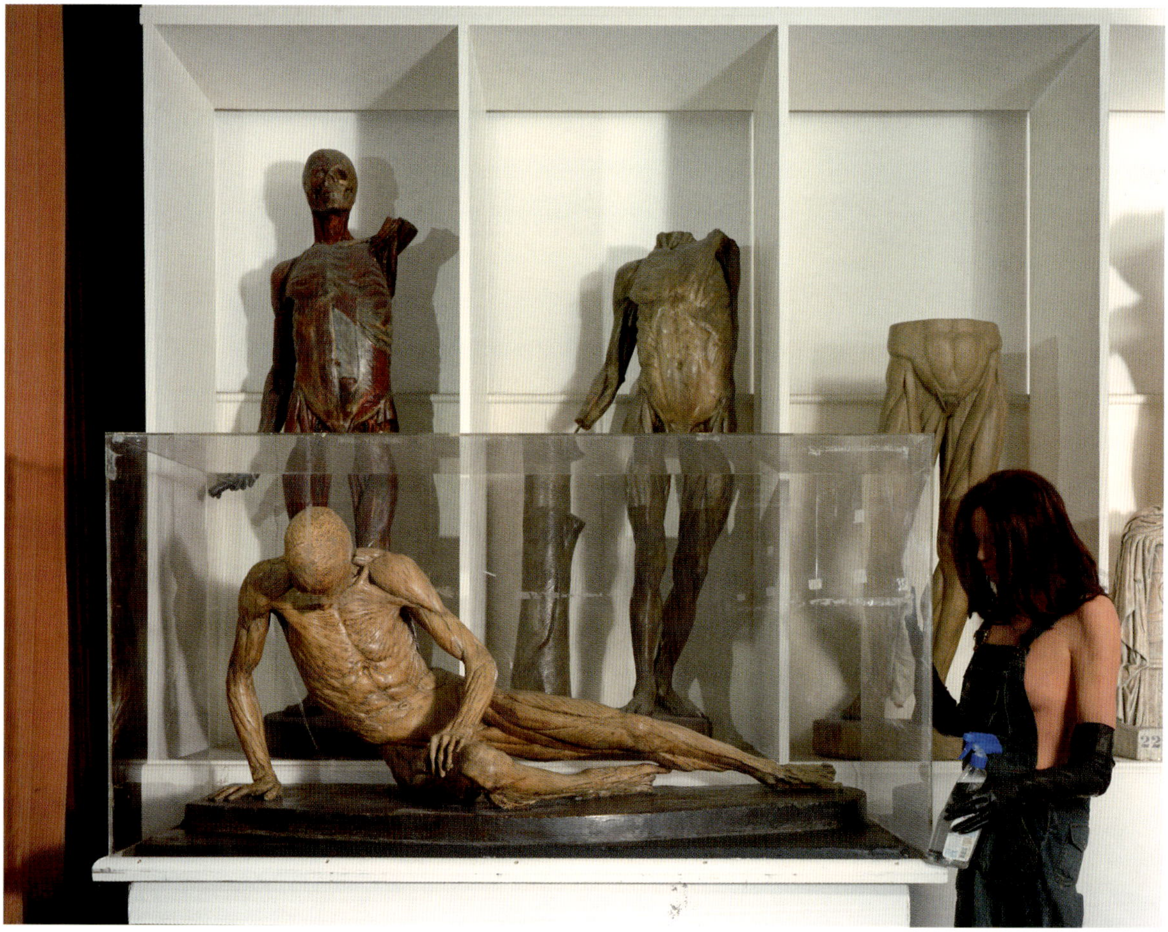

dungarees inspects a famous Academy écorché nicknamed *Smugglerius*. 'When I was a student at the Royal Academy Schools, those things were subtly lingering,' she says, leaving it unclear whether she means the écorchés or the attitudes to the female body that her work explores. 'I am interested in the weird in-between space between being an active agent and a nude model. My dolls are somewhere in between.'

Lang's dolls have since appeared in other sculptural contexts. In her photographic series 'Monumental Misconceptions' (2015), set in Memento Park, a graveyard for Soviet-era statuary in Budapest, apparently living women dangle from the giant bronze arms of former dictators or are crushed beneath their monumental boots – female 'interlopers' in a sculptural narrative dominated by men. Lang's next body of work will focus on the relatively few sculpted monuments to historical women; more melancholic than iconoclastic, this series will be called 'Glorious Oblivion'. 'I'm interested in conveying a kind of haunted presence. The figure in sculpture has a presence, a life of its own that no other kind of object has.'

Although she has taught life classes, Lang doesn't draw from life – 'I wouldn't pay someone to sit in my studio and take their clothes off' – but she recognises the contribution made by models: 'Life models are much underappreciated. The work is both physically demanding and often quite creative, and they're very interested in what they generate with their different poses. It's a performance art.' The models who pose for her casts, usually friends, bring something personal to the encounter: 'They have an impact on what I do and their physical peculiarities give me ideas; it's the interaction with the living body, I suppose.' In *Ursula and Her Virgins*, from the series 'Saints' (2015; see overleaf), it's the physical peculiarities of the latex legs seen beneath the table – the knobbly knees and the wonky toes – that make them so lifelike.

The casting process is very intimate – 'you have to slather a lot of alginate over the models' – but the poses are for short periods, as the seaweed compound sets in just eight minutes. The short time only allows for moulds of separate body parts rather than full-body casts. 'My figures are in pieces and I compose them in constellations,' Lang explains. The models' poses are worked out beforehand in rough pencil drawings. 'The fact that the mark is not accurate has its own generative qualities. Sometimes the drawing instructs me to devise a more interesting pose.' Unlike the ideal of classical perfection embodied by the casts in the RA's Life Room, Lang's disturbingly lifelike dolls owe their animacy to their imperfections.

Laura Gascoigne

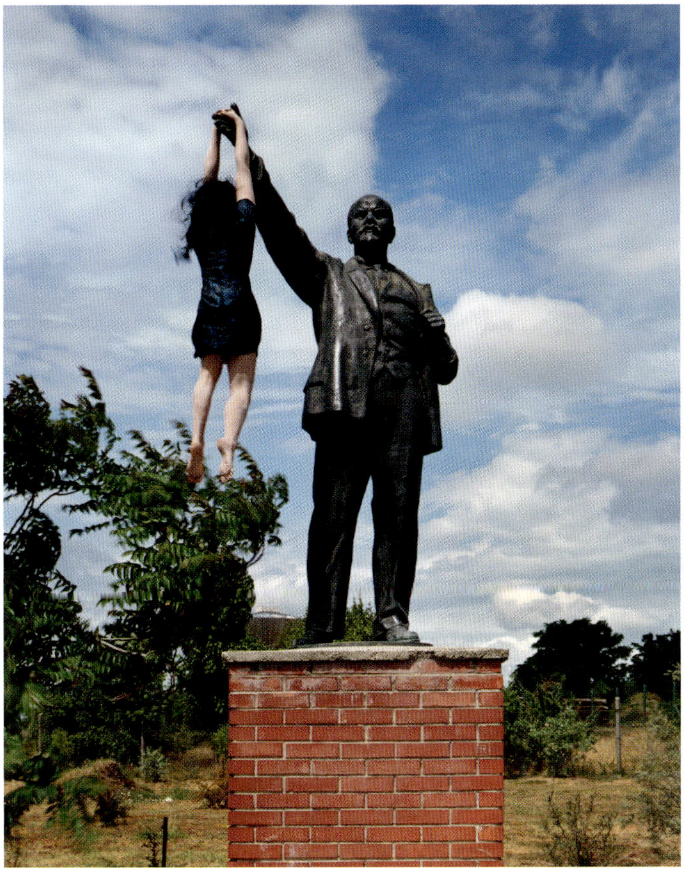

Grand Gestures
2010
C-type analogue hand print on aluminium
150 x 120 cm
Private collection

Overleaf:
Ursula and Her Virgins
2015
C-type print
80 x 120 cm
Private collection

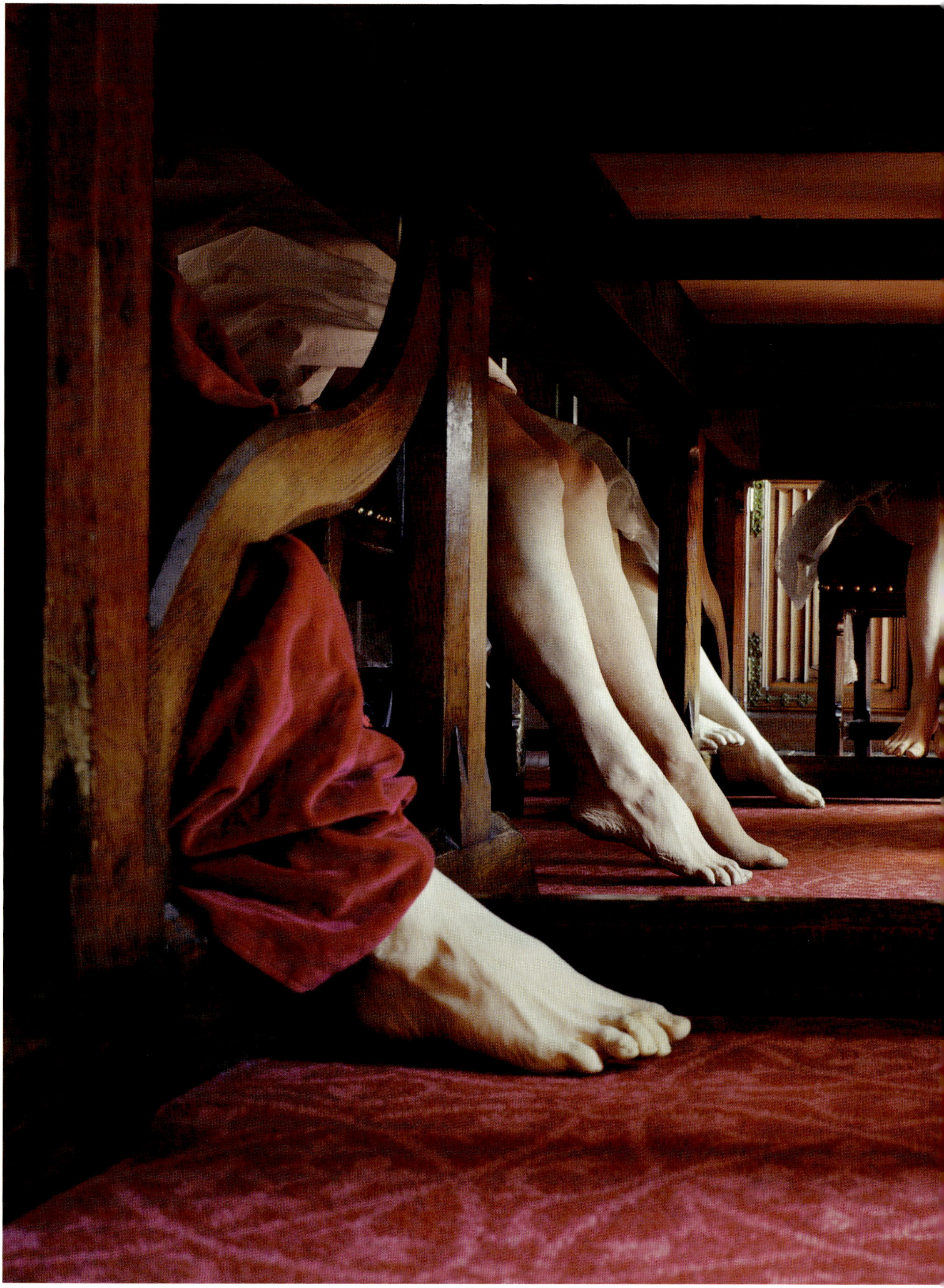

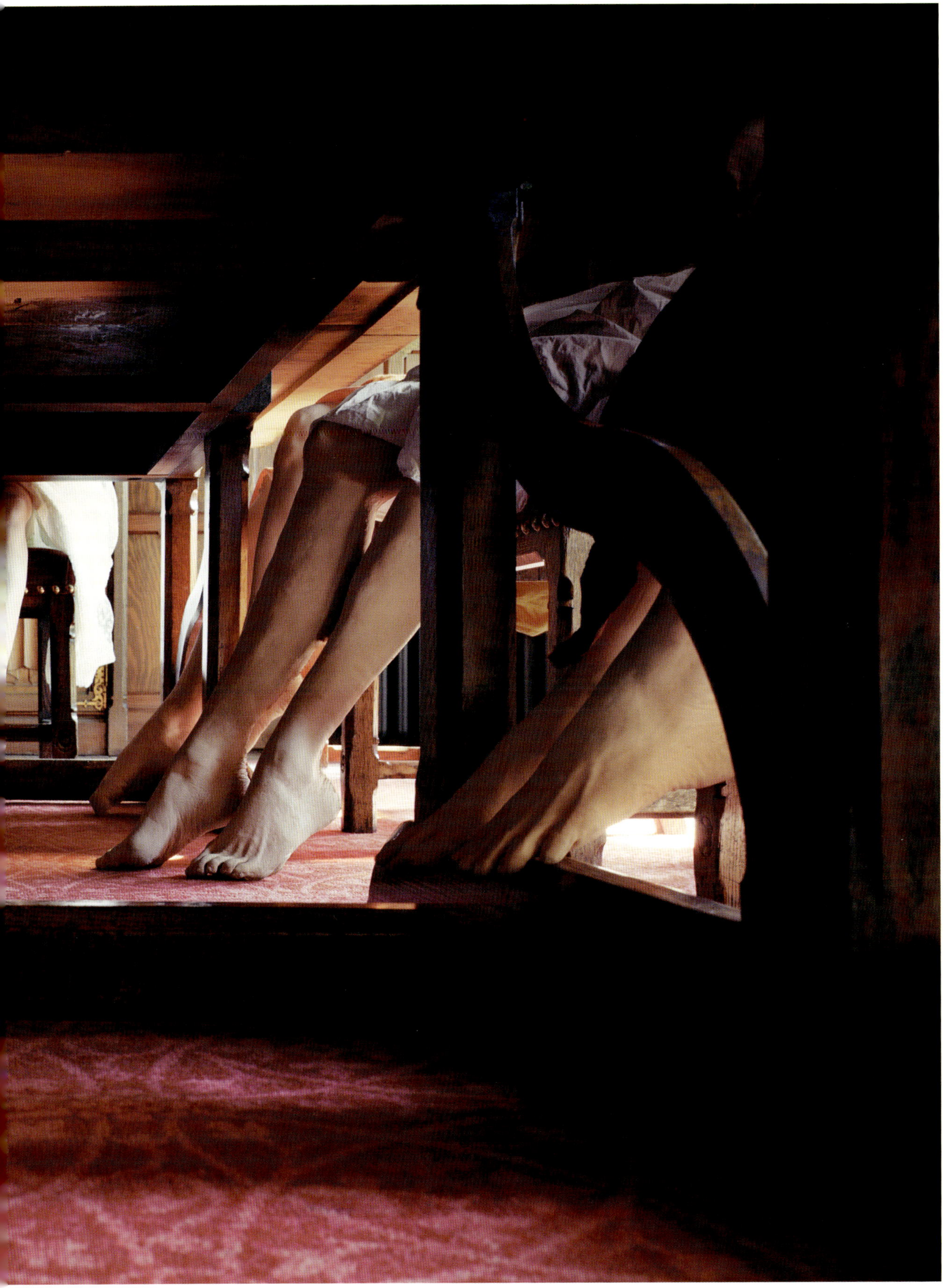

Farshid Moussavi

Farshid Moussavi RA (b. 1965) is an internationally acclaimed architect and Professor in Practice of Architecture at the Harvard University Graduate School of Design. Her London-based practice has completed buildings that include the Museum of Contemporary Art Cleveland (2012), the Victoria Beckham Flagship Store in London (2014), La Folie Divine, Montpellier (2017), and the Îlot 19 residential complex in the La Défense district of Paris (2017).

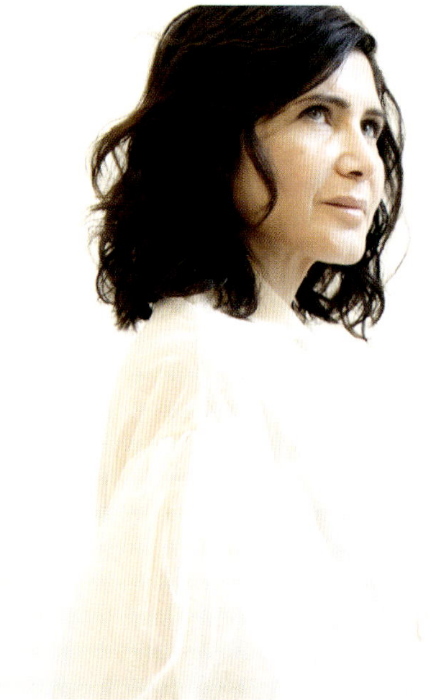

What does working from life mean to an architect? 'Architecture has everything to do with life; architecture is *about* everyday life,' says Farshid Moussavi. 'Working from life is something some artists may do and others may not do, but for architects it is just degree zero. Architecture cannot escape everyday life.'

Farshid Moussavi is one of the UK's leading architects and, indeed, thinkers about architecture. She rose to prominence with Foreign Office Architects (FOA), a practice founded with her former husband Alejandro Zaera Polo, and started Farshid Moussavi Architecture (FMA) in 2011. With the two practices, she has been involved with some remarkable buildings and masterplans. They include the award-winning ferry terminal in Yokohama (with FOA), completed in 2002, a wonderfully organic, undulating structure with a revolutionary porosity of interior and exterior and a rich array of materials and textures; and the Museum of Contemporary Art Cleveland (MOCA) (with FMA), a building clad in shimmering mirror-finish black stainless steel, rising from a hexagonal base to a square summit (see pages 100–01).

Moussavi has been experimenting with virtual reality (VR), intrigued by the prospect of 'trying to connect gaming technology with the subject of drawing from life', she says. 'We can do that with architecture. We can treat existing buildings as animate objects that we draw from, and draw ideas from, just like a model who sits in front of you. That's because great buildings embody ideas that are virtual, ideas that transcend their structures – the actual building is only one way that those ideas can be actualised. We can approach the 'virtual' in the way philosophers, such as Henri Bergson or Gilles Deleuze, understood it: that the virtual is not the opposite of the real, but the potentiality for the real, and the actual is just one manifestation of that potentiality.'

Moussavi and her team have created a VR space in which viewers can take two masterpieces of ecclesiastical

Steel-folded structural roof of the Yokohama International Passenger Cruise Terminal, Japan, 1995–2002

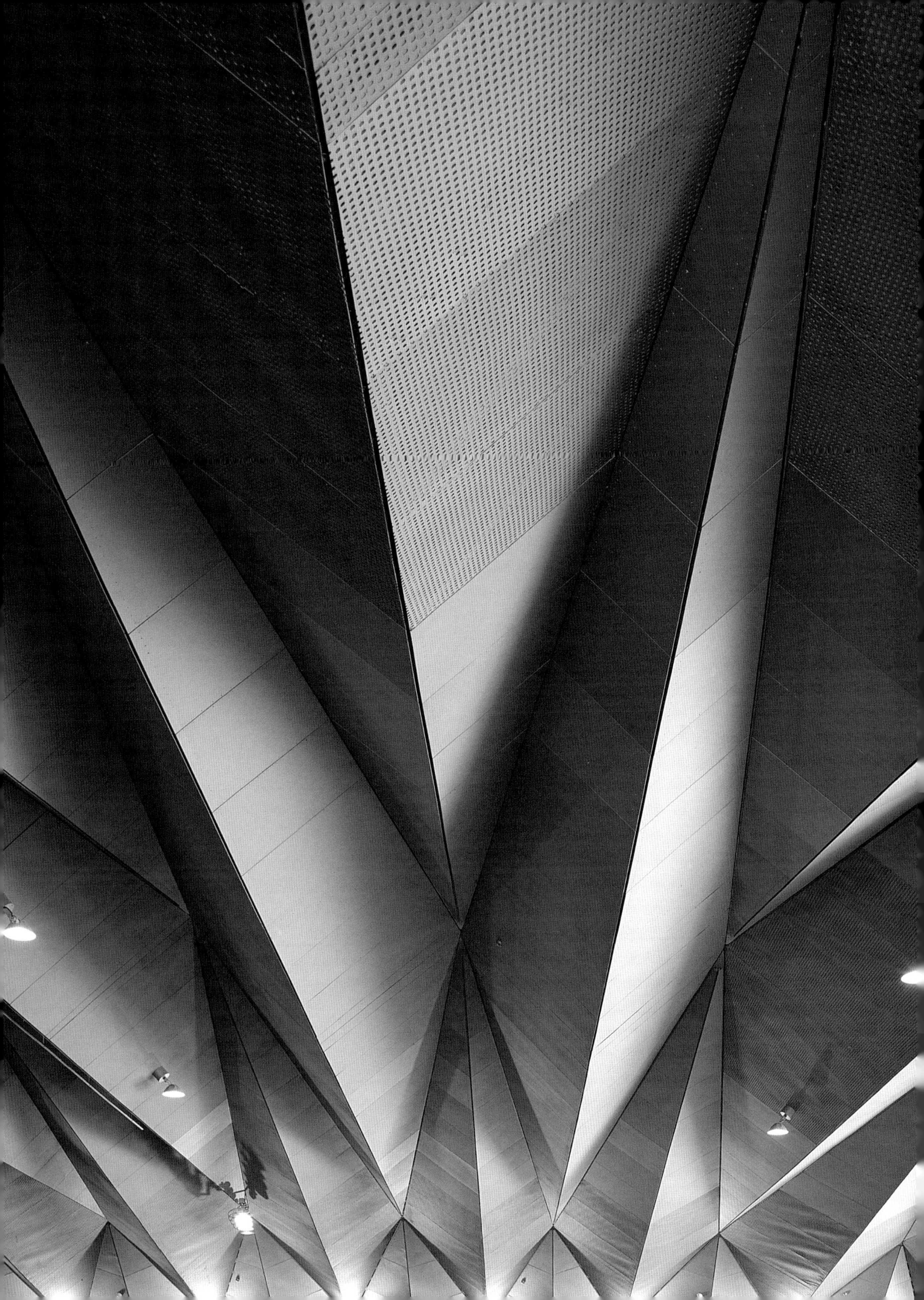

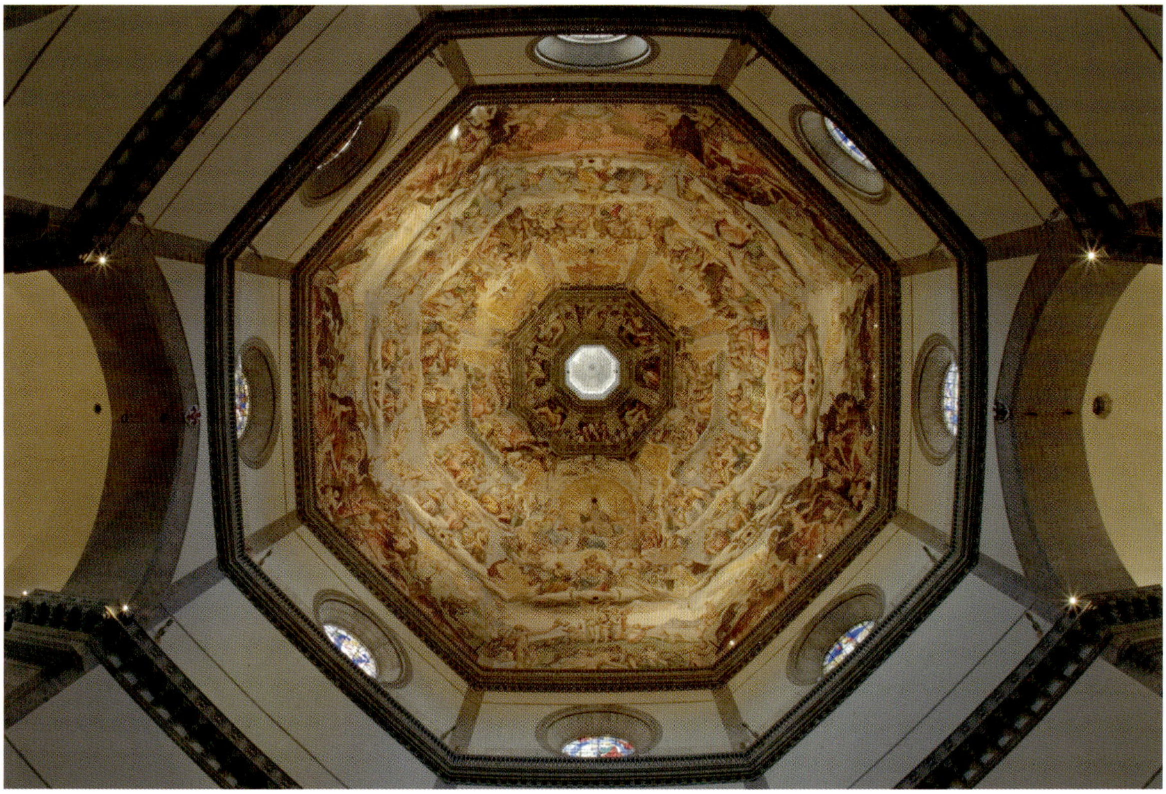

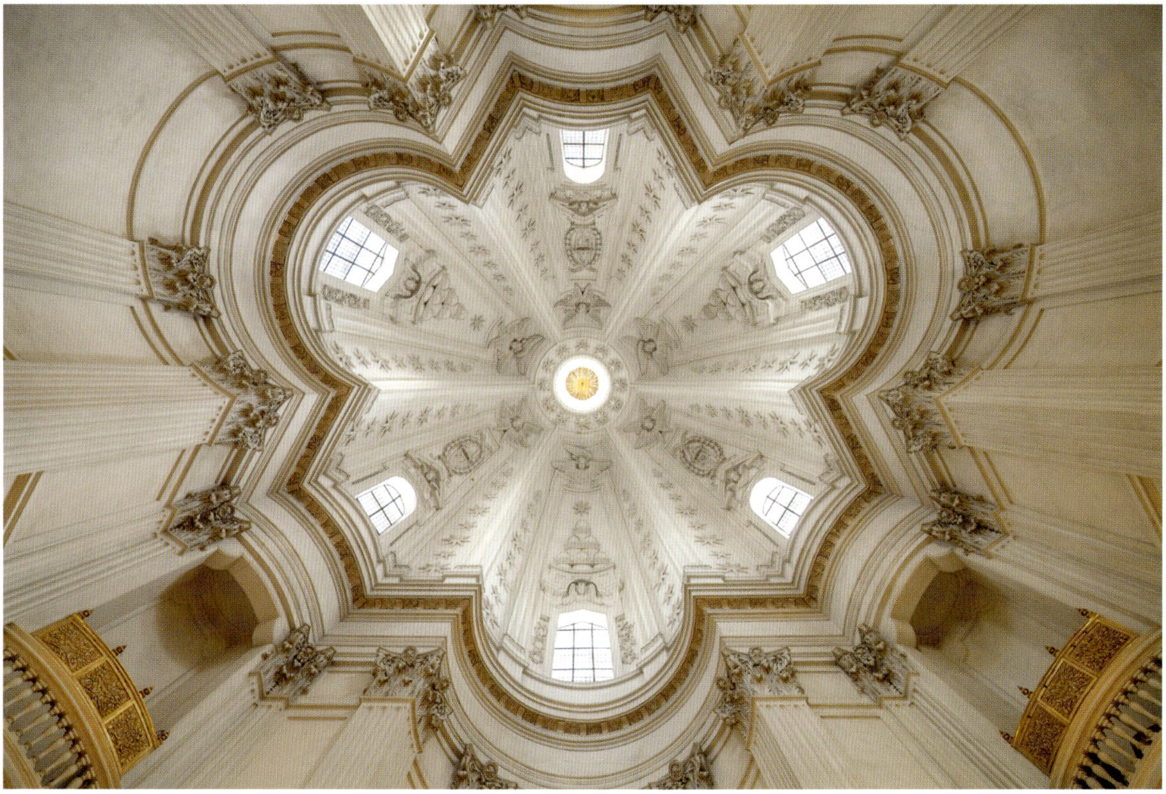

Above:
Filippo Brunelleschi
Dome of Santa Maria
del Fiore, Florence,
1420–36

Below:
Francesco Borromini
Dome of Sant'Ivo
alla Sapienza,
Rome, 1632–60

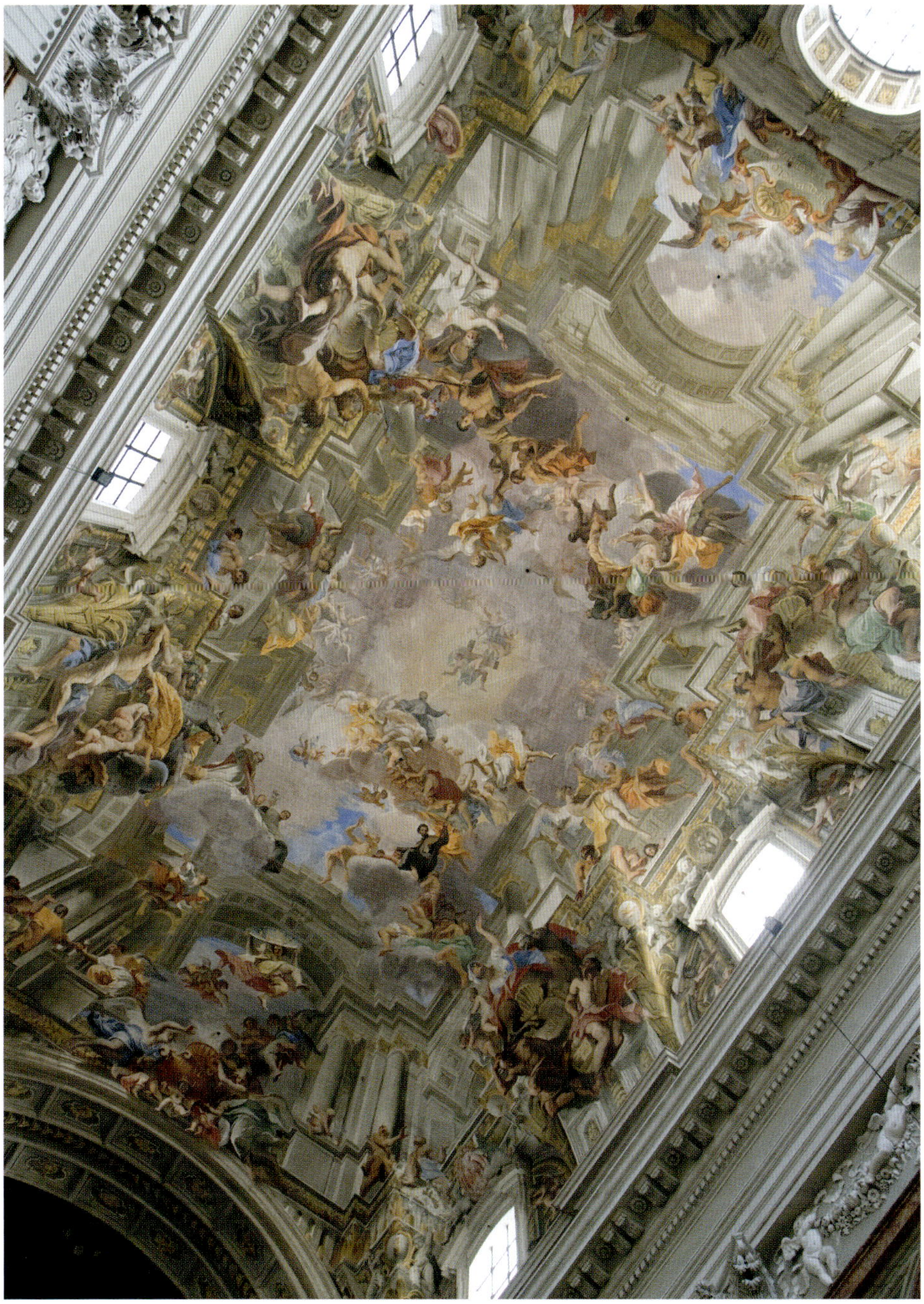

Andrea Pozzo
Illusory frescoes on the ceiling and clerestory of Sant'Ignazio, Rome, 1685–94

architecture – Brunelleschi's dome for the Duomo in Florence (1420–36) and Borromini's for his Church of Sant'Ivo alla Sapienza (1632–60) in Rome – and adjust various parameters to create their own domed architectural spaces. 'They both have ribbed domes,' Moussavi explains. 'The two buildings are united by this, and they both actualise the idea of the ribbed dome in different ways.' With a HTC Vive headset on and a wireless controller in their grasp, users can change each structure before their very eyes, so that the domes can 'have different numbers of ribs, or different surfaces, or their oculi can be varied in size or closed completely'.

'The virtual or virtuality is something that is not limited to twenty-first-century digital technology,' Moussavi continues. 'It goes back centuries. In architecture, we can look at the dioramas that were created in the nineteenth century, or Baroque ceilings that were painted to give you the illusion of virtual space.' While these phenomena encouraged visual interaction, they were inevitably limited by physical restraints, however evocative that illusionism or ingenious

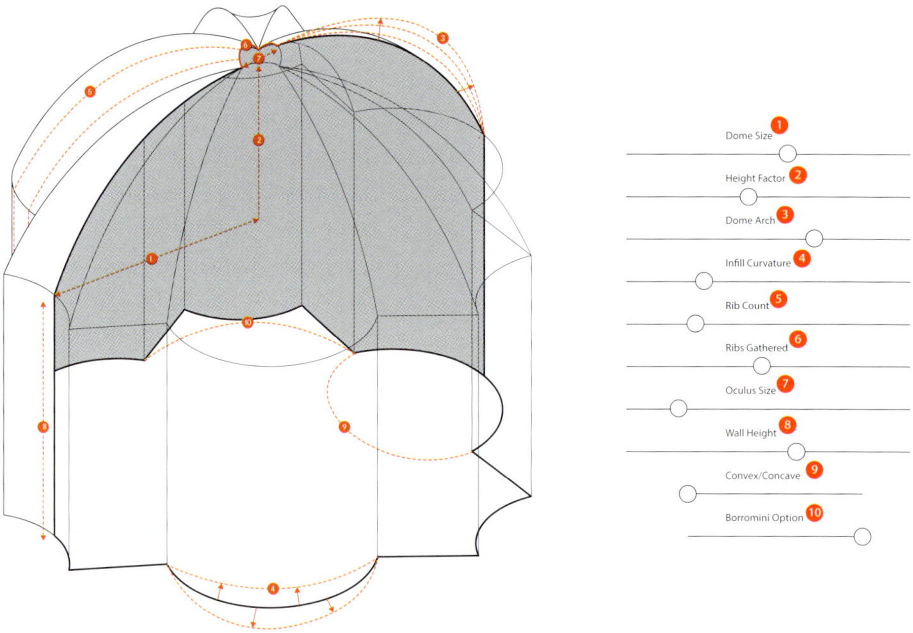

Diagram of the user interface for Moussavi's virtual-reality project, in which different aspects of domes are reconfigured by the user

Visualisation of a user's view through the virtual-reality headset

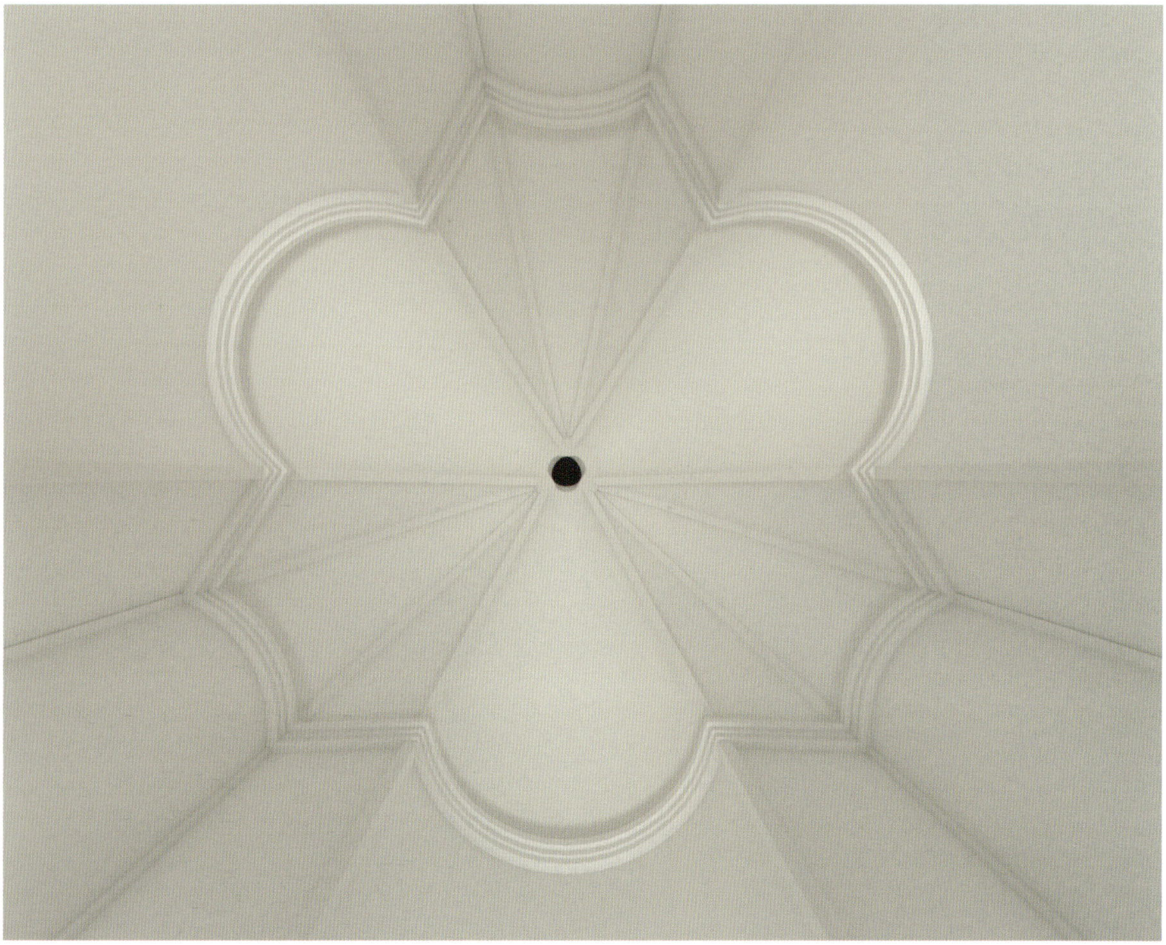

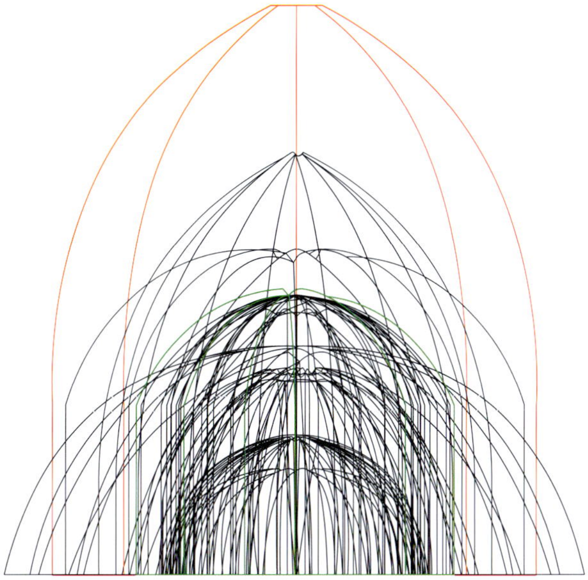

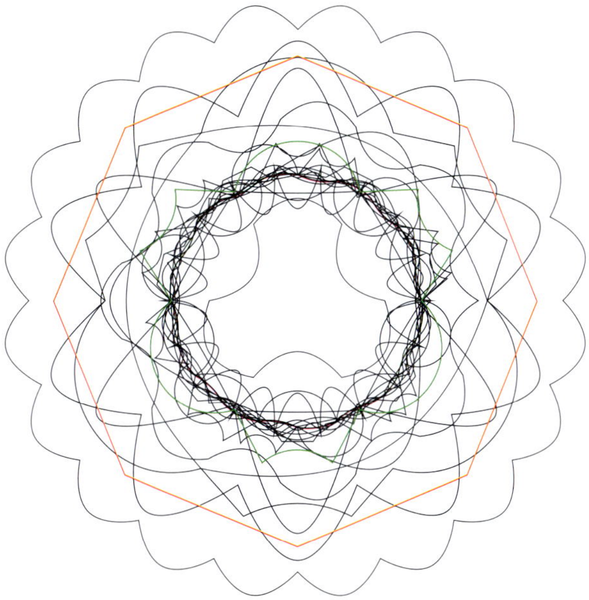

Drawings showing different domes that can be created by the user in Moussavi's virtual-reality project, each with different height (above), and plan size and shape (below)

the artists' and architects' perspectival tricks. As Moussavi says, 'people could visually project themselves, but they could not modify the space in any way, so it was a closed virtual reality.' The VR space strips away these constraints.

Although her VR work is purely experimental at this stage, Moussavi suggests that if gaming technology 'were ever to become complex enough', she could use it 'as a way to involve collaborators and end users of a building in the process of design'. It suits FMA's approach: the practice is 'specifically very interested in not fixing a project from the start but evolving it through time', she says. 'If we fix the design at the beginning it means that the extra intelligence that can come in – should come in – later on is suppressed.' Very often, she explains, 'people outside our own design team bring great ideas, sometimes without knowing it – they come at the project from a different angle. And I am very interested in that openness or space of unpredictability that working with other people brings us.' She gives the example of the Cleveland museum: the building was originally to be

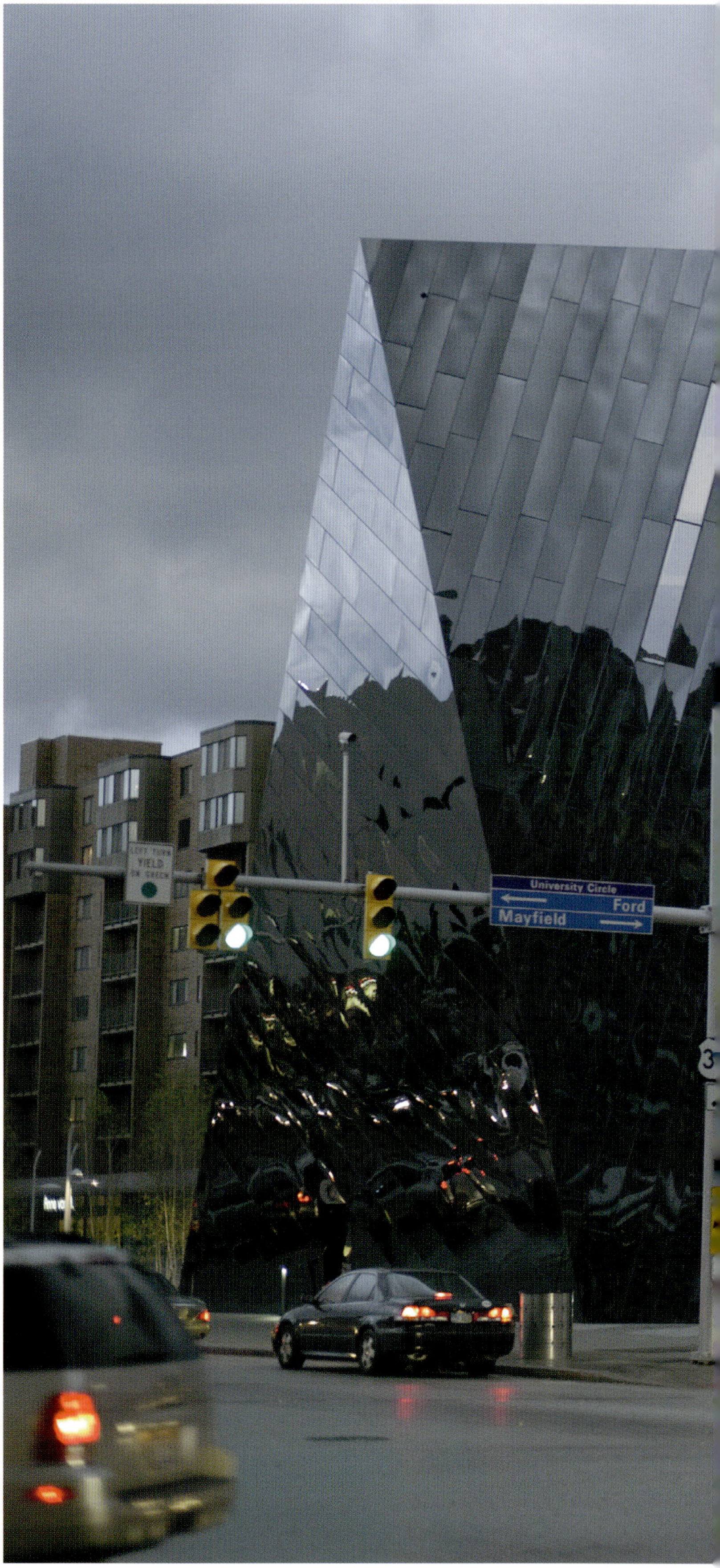

The exterior of MOCA Cleveland, clad in mirror-finish black stainless steel, 2008–12

clad in gold aluminium, but the reservations of a potential donor prompted a rethink and the eventual use of mirror-finish black stainless steel. 'We realised that, actually, when used for a building whose different faces were either tilting towards the sky or the ground, the steel would generate dynamics that we hadn't anticipated. I think it made the project so much better.'

Even the most sophisticated digital representations are, in her mind, 'much cruder than the real design process', which is the challenge of negotiating the constantly changing parameters involved in any architectural project. 'Ultimately, we end up looking at our designs on a computer screen, which is not the real-life scale that the building will be.' But working with VR has led to new considerations for Moussavi. 'If we can have these VR environments set up when we present a project at each of its various stages, we can involve end users in the process and understand better the possible actualisation of an architectural idea at its life-size scale.'

Ben Luke

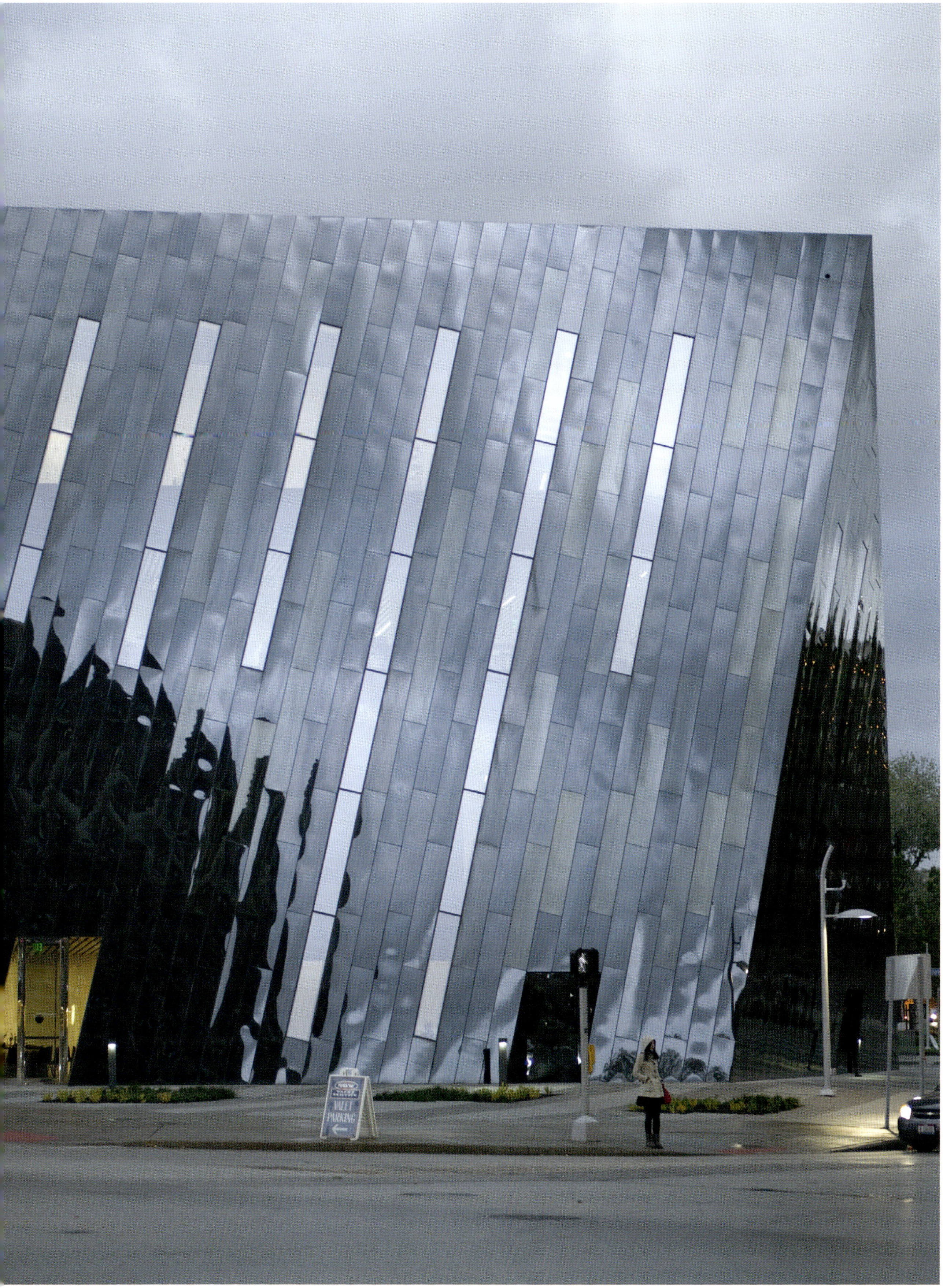
VALET
PARKING

Humphrey Ocean

Humphrey Ocean RA (b. 1951) paints pictures of people, landscapes and objects, including everyday things we overlook, such as radios and road signs. His portraits of sitters including Tony Benn and Paul McCartney are part of the collection of London's National Portrait Gallery, where Ocean was the subject of a major retrospective in 2012. He lives and works in London.

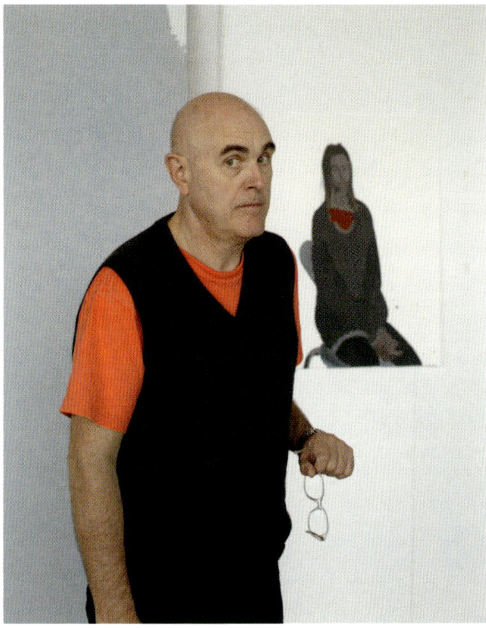

Humphrey Ocean describes himself as an artist who 'lives chiefly by the eye'. But he recognises the subjectivity in that eye. 'The great difficulty is almost summed up by Magritte's painting of a pipe, which he inscribed, "This is not a pipe". A painting is not the thing that it depicts, it's something else; it's me, and by that I mean the generic me, the artist who made it.'

So the series of gouache portraits Ocean has made since the mid-2000s, painted in an hour or less, are portraits both of a sitter and the personal response of the artist. They capture the immediacy of an interaction with family and friends, art-world acquaintances, writers and poets. 'I produce a colour likeness, and it's remarkable if there's any mimetic likeness – that's almost a bonus,' he says. 'If you make something 'like' a particular element of the subject, then all sorts of other likenesses will come into play. But you must never try too hard.' Ocean recognises that there is subjectivity not only in the artist's depiction, but in the painting's reception. 'No one will ever think what you're thinking, looking at the same picture,' he suggests. 'And there are certain things you can't set out in paint: if people say, "to paint a portrait you must paint the soul", that is for the birds, really. If you paint what is there, the portrait might have soul, but that is another thing.'

Ocean contrasts his one-hour pictures with the more formal portraits he has been commissioned to make. 'I have realised that the gouaches are response rather than research. I have done what I call research portraits, for which I have read up. When I was painting Philip Larkin 30 years ago [for the National Portrait Gallery], of course I knew his work, but I wanted to read more, and I spent quite a long time with the man.' The Larkin portrait (see overleaf) differs from the gouache portraits in its careful rendering of detail in the sitter and background, capturing Larkin in his attic in Hull with a view to a mock-Tudor house beyond; the gouaches are not concerned with background, only with essentials in the sitter's head and body. He likens the quick

Clockwise, from top left:

Hugo
2016
Gouache on paper
77 x 56 cm

Alice
2016
Gouache on paper
77 x 56 cm
Private collection

Christopher
2016
Gouache on paper
77 x 56 cm

Lily
2012
Gouache on paper
77 x 56 cm
Private collection

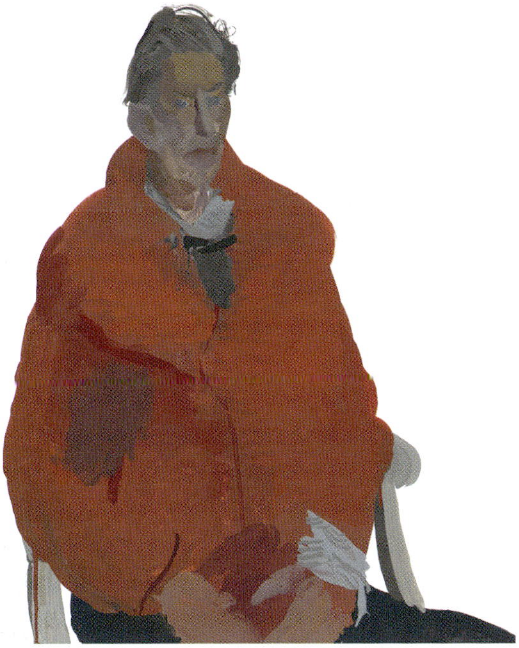
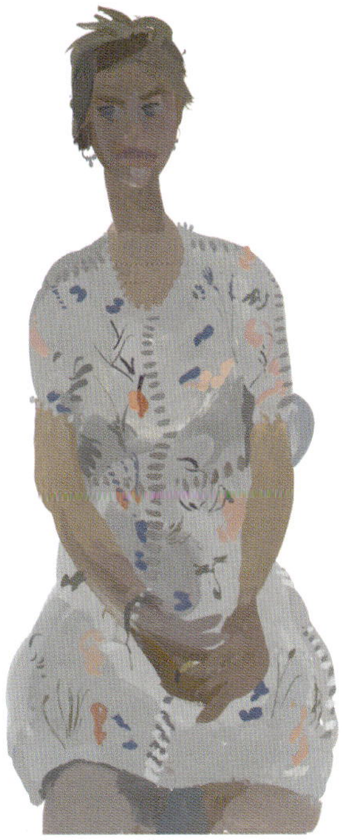
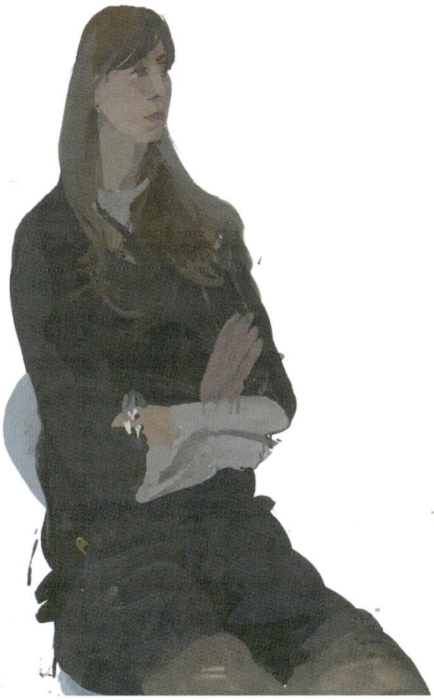
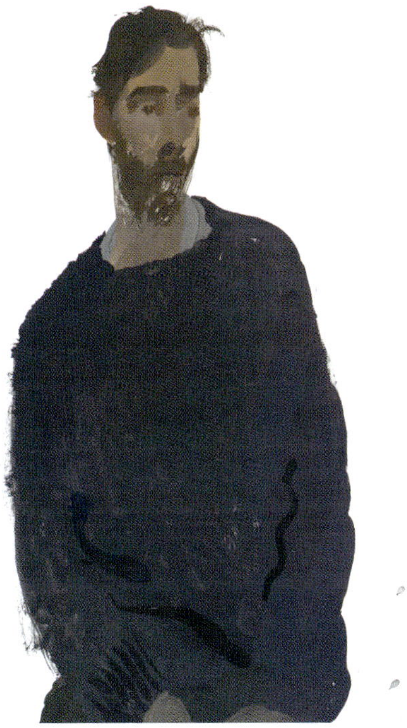

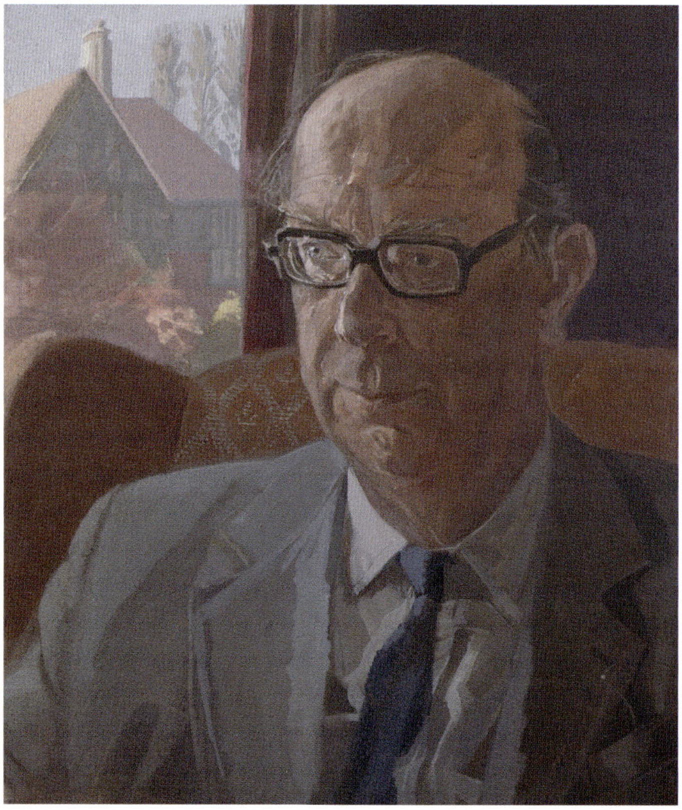

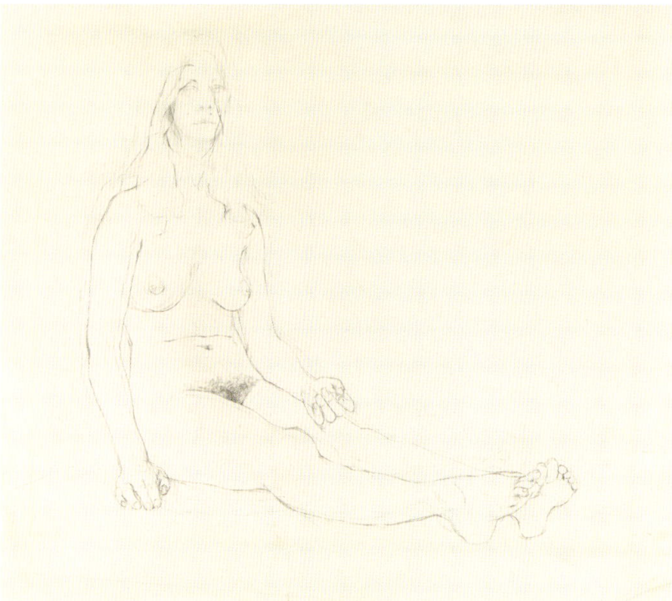

Philip Larkin
1984
Acrylic on canvas
52.3 x 44.8 cm
National Portrait Gallery, London

Life Drawing
1971
Pencil on paper
50.5 x 58.7 cm

portraits to 'a click of a shutter, but it's an extended click and it's a human lens'. Crucially, Ocean does not over-theorise the experience: he relies on instinct. 'I'm not being coy when I say that I do not know what I am doing when I am doing them – I can't quite describe it, I am just in it.' He is modest about the results. 'And at the end I'm exhausted, and I look at it: it mostly looks like a mess to me, a very odd equivalent to the actual person.'

The biggest lessons Ocean learned when drawing from life occurred while he was studying at Canterbury College of Art under Ian Dury, who later went on to become an enormously successful musician (indeed, Ocean was in Dury's band, Kilburn and the High Roads, for a period). A pencil drawing from a four-day life-drawing session in 1971 survives and is illustrated here. During that intense class, Dury noted that the positioning of elements of the figure in relation to one another in Ocean's drawing was wrong: 'You've put a line down, and then you've put another line down and you've told a lie – and then you've had to compound that lie.' Ocean says he learned in those four days about proportion and harmony, formerly 'abstract notions' to him, he says. He learned to resist the brain's need to 'straighten out things and symmetrise things'. But it was not a prescriptive approach. 'It's not to do with defining a drawing style: Van Gogh painted accurate Van Goghs; accuracy is crucial.'

Ocean applies the same scrutiny to inanimate objects: cars and chairs have been particular preoccupations, but they, too, are in essence part of his investigation of the human body. 'We have designed a world in our image – everything we make,' he says. Chairs are the most corporeal of manmade things: they have arms, legs and a back, after all. Ocean's series of chair pictures began inauspiciously in 2004 in a hospital waiting room, when he was confronted with an armchair that evoked 'old-fashioned aunties and *Songs of Praise*'. The paintings he made from that fusty chair have an elegance and lightness the original could never have possessed. He finds cars 'endlessly fascinating' as a metaphor for modern life.

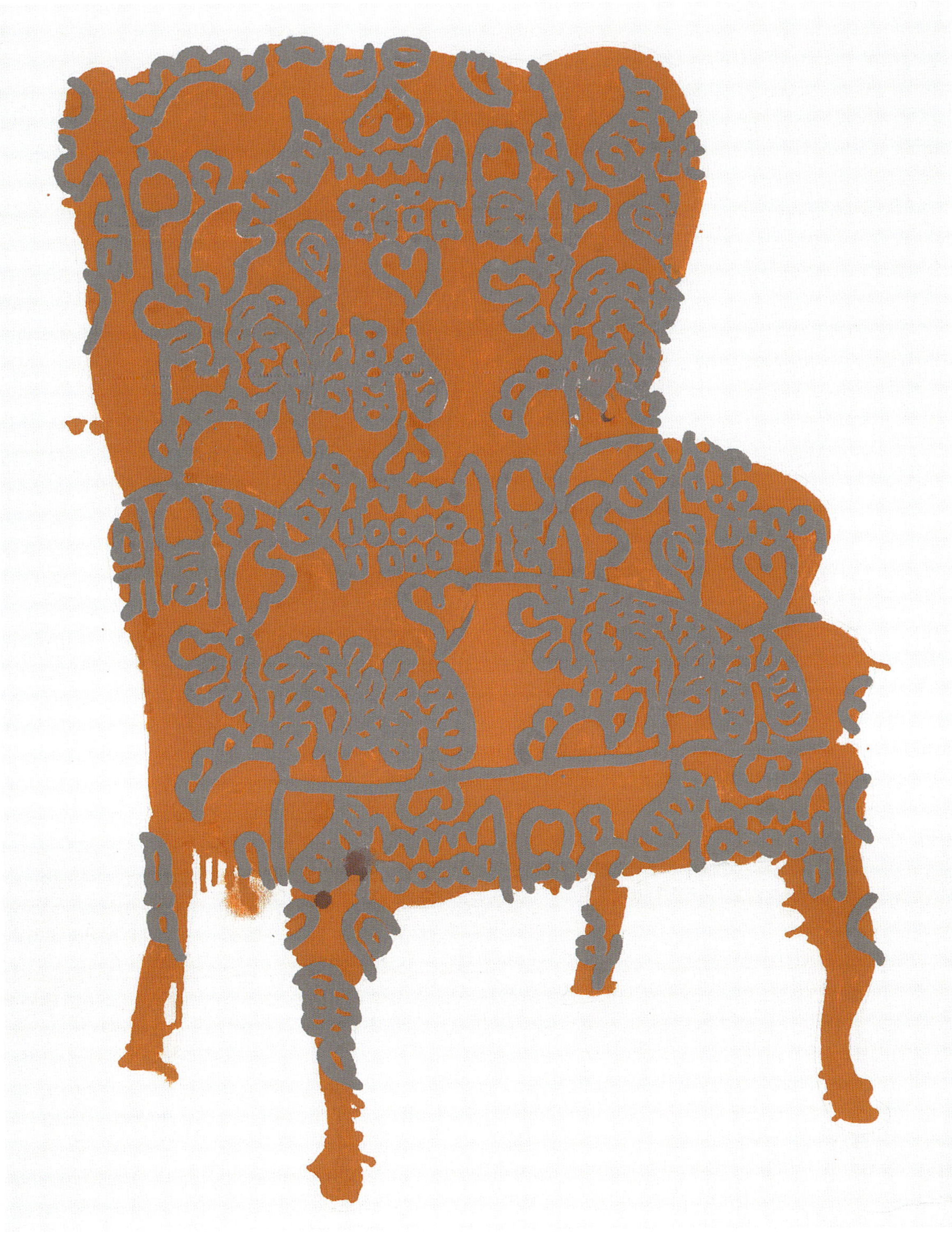

Orange
2009
Oil on canvas
92 x 73 cm

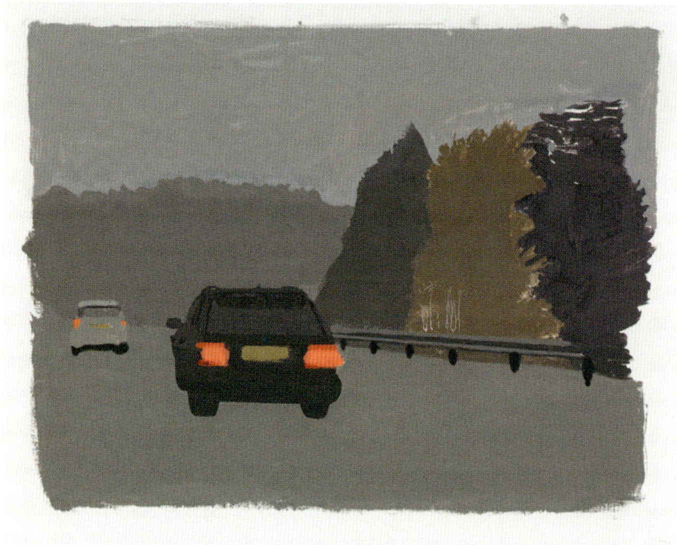

Afternoon
2007
Oil on canvas
73 x 92 cm

'If it doesn't sound fatuous, I think we're in a slow-motion car crash at the moment,' he says. 'Every time I get into that lethal object, that could be it – yet I'm comfy as if I were in my front room. Like the chair, it is utterly designed for me, it fits me like a glove.'

Ocean connects his love of chairs and cars in a new sculpture of a chair. It is being designed within virtual reality (VR), using HTC Vive hardware and Google's Tilt Brush and MakeVR Pro software, before being made into a physical object with a mix of wood and resin. The sculpture reflects the elegant VR design, yet also expresses a potential danger that Ocean articulates, a sense that, despite his wonder at the automobile, 'we are all car-crunched ... cars are changing the way we think and very few people seem to be talking about that.' Ominously, his sculpture features a variation on crash-test dummy legs.

Ocean liked the experience of working with VR – 'I am enjoying drawing in mid-air,' he says – and adds that the new medium suits his fast drawing speed. He carries with him into the VR space his experience of looking at designed objects and the human body, and improvises forms using the new medium. But working in virtual space also reinforces his feeling for his principal medium, a sense that 'paint is ahead of the curve' as a technology. Paint, he says, is 'nothing, it comes out of the ground under our feet', yet it has the miraculous ability to represent the physical qualities, and the ineffable vitality, of people and the things designed around them.

Ben Luke

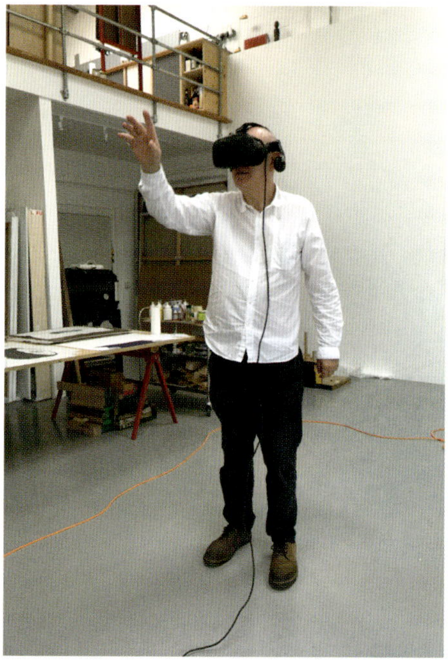

Humphrey Ocean at work on his virtual reality designs in his London studio

Chair Legs
2017
Pen and crayon on paper
29.6 x 21 cm

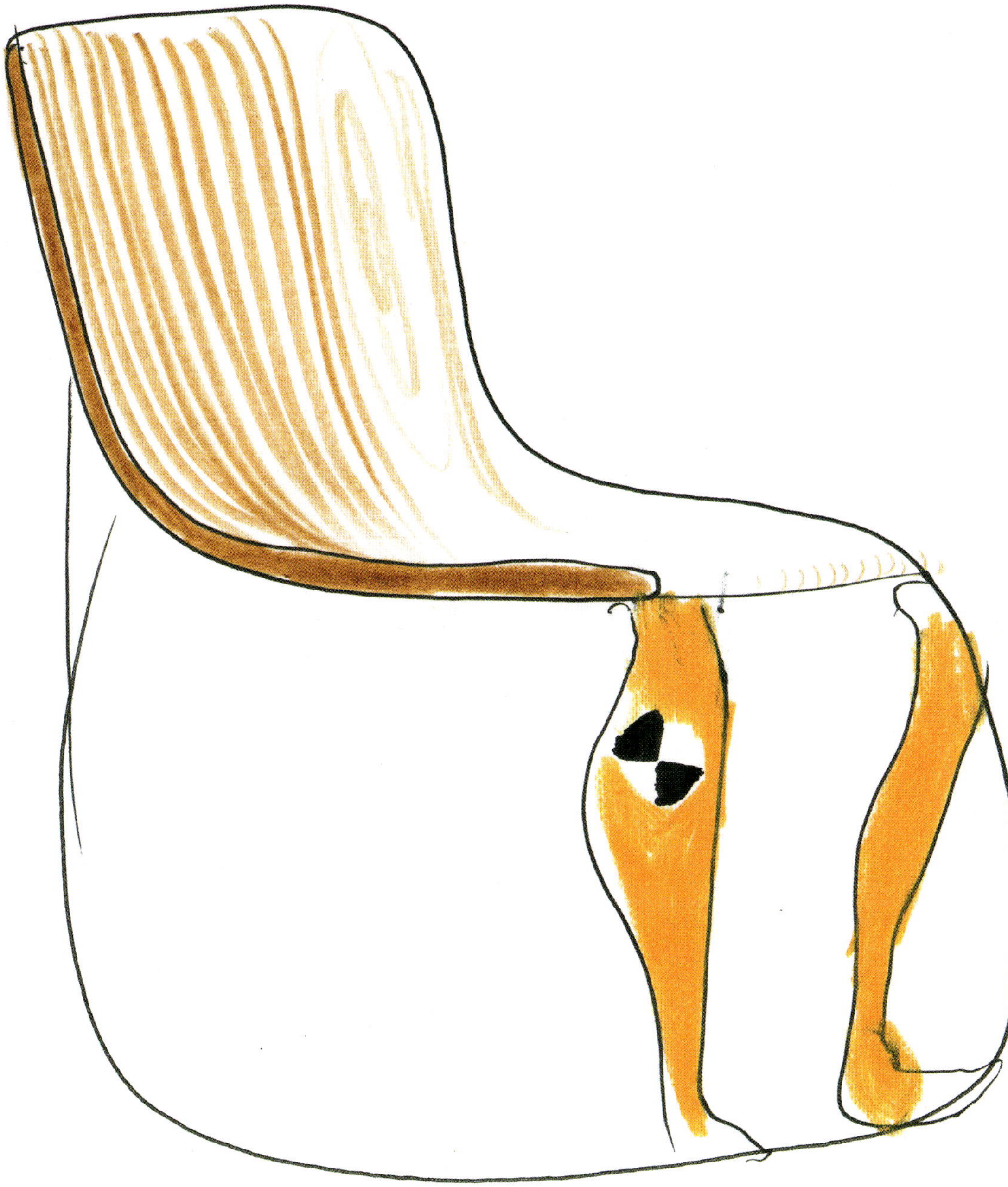

Eddie Peake

British artist Eddie Peake (b. 1981) came to public prominence for the multi-media works he made while completing his postgraduate course at the Royal Academy Schools (2011–13). His live art events, installations, sculptures, paintings and photographs are concerned with how we attribute meaning, in particular to the naked body. He lives and works in London, where he was the subject of an exhibition at the Barbican Art Gallery (2015-16).

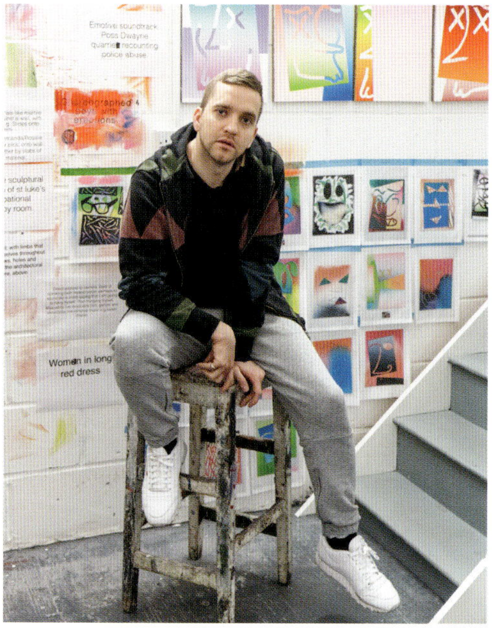

Eddie Peake participated in a life-drawing class during his three-year postgraduate course at the Royal Academy Schools – as a model. 'I was short on money so I did bits and bobs for work, and then a modelling session in the Life Room came up. It was fine, really. I don't have a problem being nude, as I guess you can tell from my work.' The 36-year-old makes art across multiple media, including photography, painting, sculpture and installation, but he is best known for choreographing inventive, collaborative performance-art pieces involving nude bodies, sometimes including his own. Instead of drawing naked forms, he orchestrates them before our eyes.

In his second year at the Schools, he staged *Touch* (2012), a naked five-a-side football match in one of the Academy's Burlington Gardens galleries. A metaphor for the homoeroticism of sport, the performance also showed how unerotic nudity could be: after a few minutes watching the game, the audience became accustomed to the sweating, naked bodies. His two-part performance *Amidst A Sea Of Flailing High Heels And Cooking Utensils* (2012; see overleaf) was, in contrast, a more sexual spectacle, with naked dancers, some of them painted gold, at points writhing together on the floor. His exhibitions of spray-paintings and strange sculpted objects at White Cube Bermondsey in London (2013) and the City's Barbican (2015–16) were animated by bodies naked and clothed, including some on roller skates.

'The nude body is integral to both the Life Room and the Cast Corridor at the Royal Academy,' Peake continues. 'In a sense, the nude form is normalised in both those contexts. And yet the nude is anything but normalised in our society.' The European art academies revered the naked body, whether in flesh or plaster, but it elicits embarrassment, shame, anxiety and anger in everyday life today. 'Before I started at the Royal Academy I was living in Rome, where the nude figure as a classical, archetypal, aesthetic phenomenon is extremely prevalent.

Touch
2012
Performed by Dave Anderson, Dan Borg, Alex Chase White, Sonke Faltien, Richard Gasper, Will Joys, Stevie McGarrity-Alderdice, Oliver Osborne, Eddie Peake, Paul Schneider and Jake Schneider
Royal Academy of Arts, London, 1 March 2012

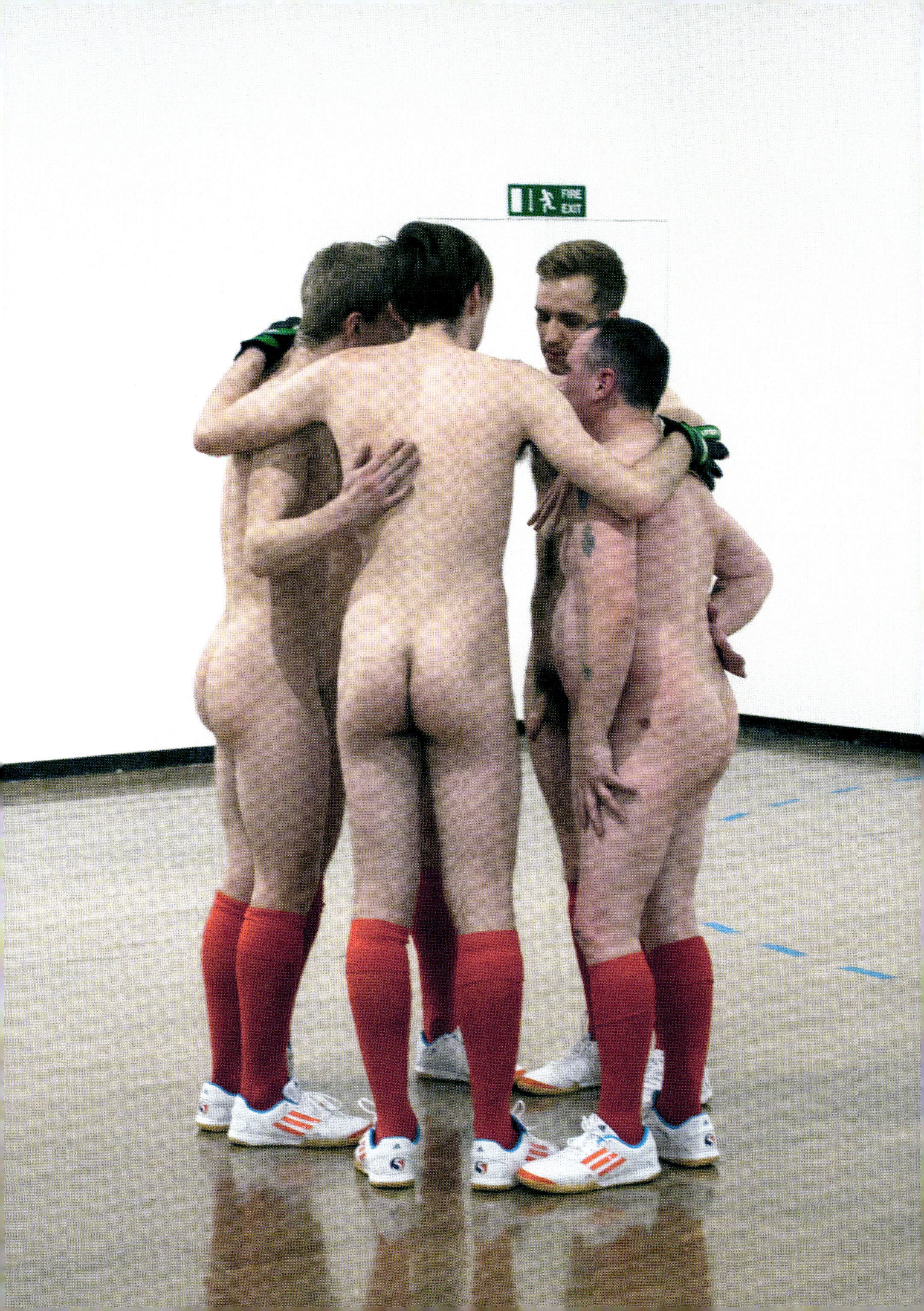
FIRE
EXIT

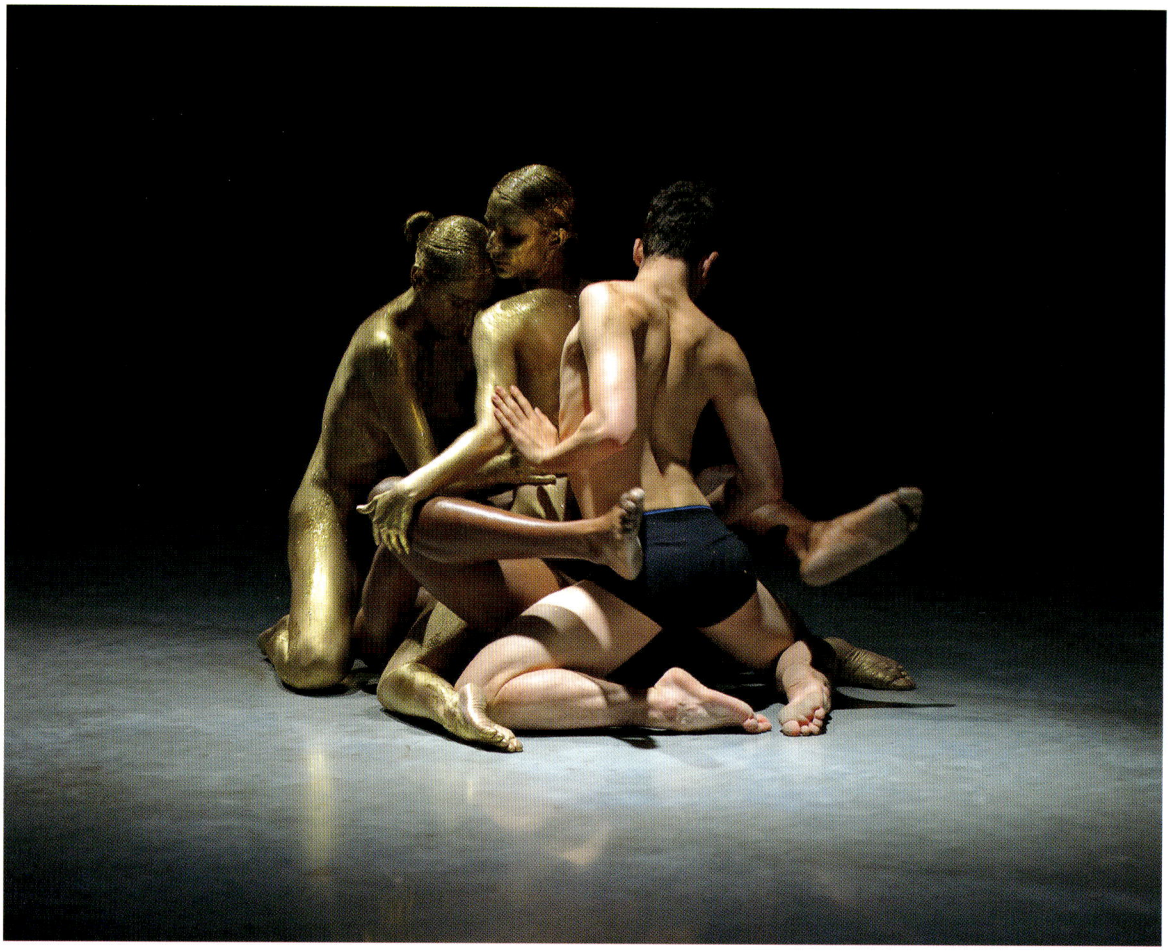

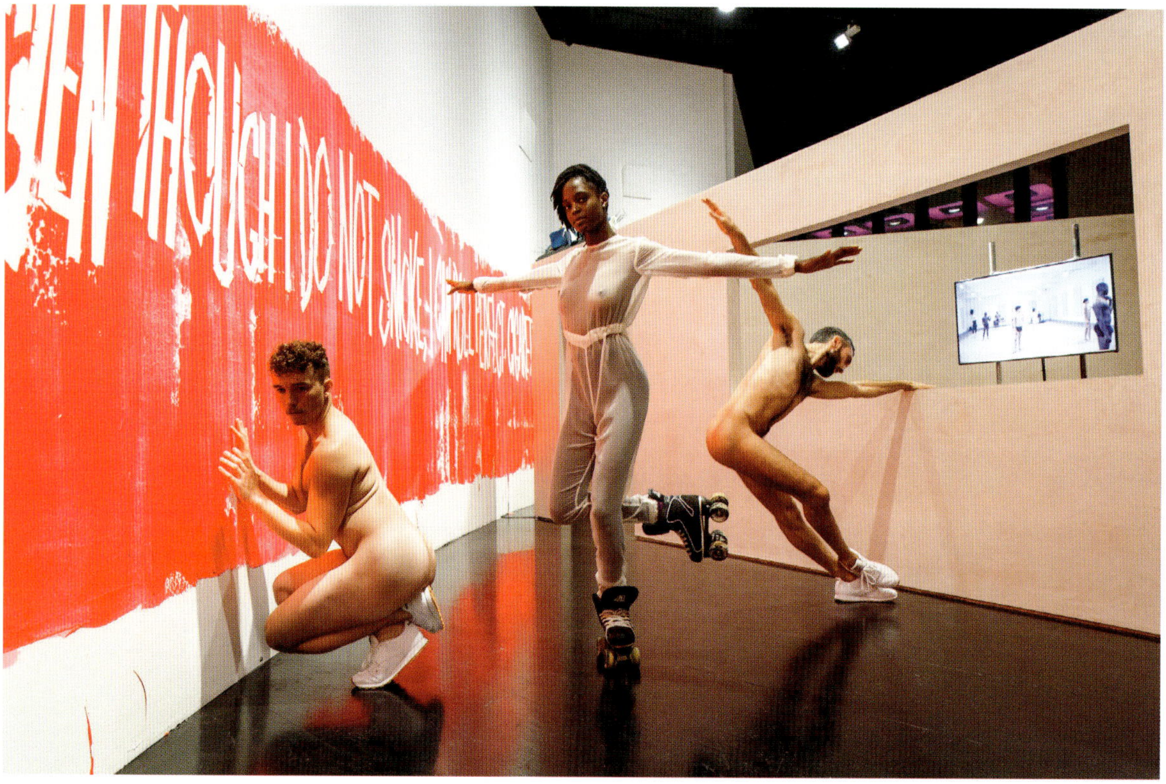
THOUGH I DO NOT SMOKE

Amidst A Sea Of Flailing High Heels And Cooking Utensils, Part 1
2012
Performed by Bruce Aguilar-Rohan, Fiona Burns, Dapo Coker, Kieram Corrin Mitchell, Sean Moon, Fernanda Muñoz-Newsome, Amanda Prince-Lubawy and Luke Wilson
The Tanks, Tate Modern, London, 21 July 2012

The Forever Loop
2015
Performed by Gareth Mole, Fattima Mahdi and Paolo Rosini
Barbican Art Gallery, London, October 2015

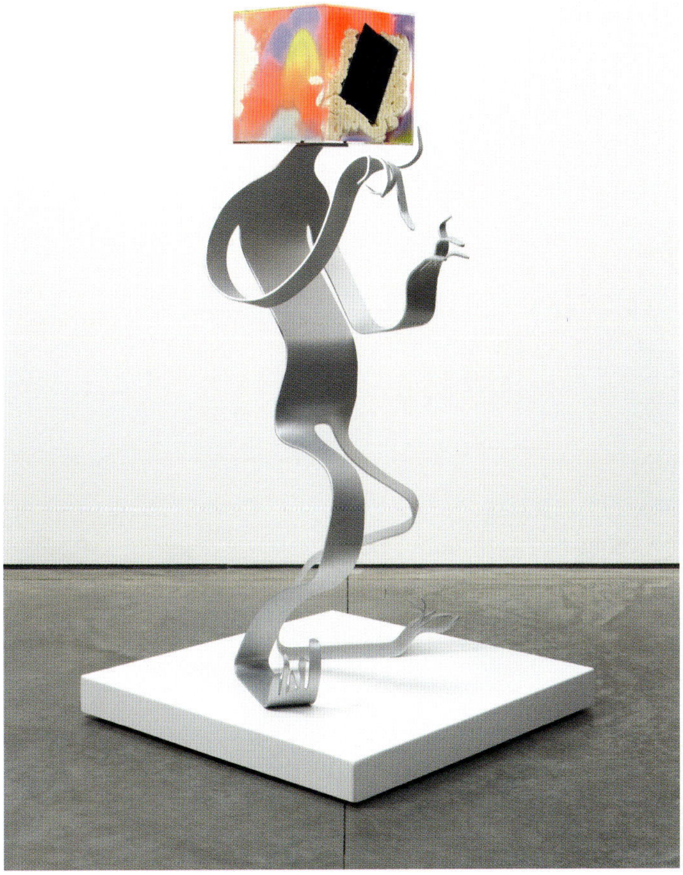

Devastatingly Insecure And Socially Inept Jpeg
2014
Painted rolled steel, acrylic, spray paint, expanding foam, diary and shoe
190 x 100 x 100 cm

But when it's presented in a contemporary context, the nude is suddenly not acceptable, even though everywhere you turn there's a naked statue.'

It is our sensitivity towards the body, rather than the body itself, that preoccupies Peake. 'I'm not interested, frankly, in the body, or the nude form, for its own sake – for me, it's just a means to an end. It brings up certain fascinating things to me, such as our innate inclination to apply meanings. We readily allow ourselves to give meaning to bodies, meanings about gender, race, sexuality, culture and class. The body is a battleground for those meanings. But the body is just a form, it doesn't have essential meanings, so the meanings that we apply to it are cultural and societal, and they raise issues and problems that are much broader than the body itself.'

Peake says the meanings that his works suggest to his audiences are not his 'conscious choice'. Instead he sees the body in his work 'functioning like a mirror – like a bendy mirror, like the ones in a funfair, where you see a distorted reflection of yourself and your own ideas about identity and culture.' *Devastatingly Insecure And Socially Inept Jpeg* (2014), his wibbly-wobbly sculptural figure in curved reflective steel, appears to anthropomorphise that idea (Peake calls him his 'bendy man' and uses reflective metal often elsewhere, as a ground for his spray-paintings). Can we ever see the body as neutral? 'I can't imagine someone working with the body in a way that feels truly free of association or meaning,' he answers. 'I would love to see that, but I don't think it's possible really. I think you need to work with that tyranny of associations – you just need to accept and embrace them.'

Peake's wall-based works often pair words with photographs or sprayed forms of naked bodies. Language and bodies act in almost opposite ways for the artist. Peake says he hates language for the way it closes down possible meaning, reducing things he wants to express. Bodies, on the other hand, constantly open up meanings

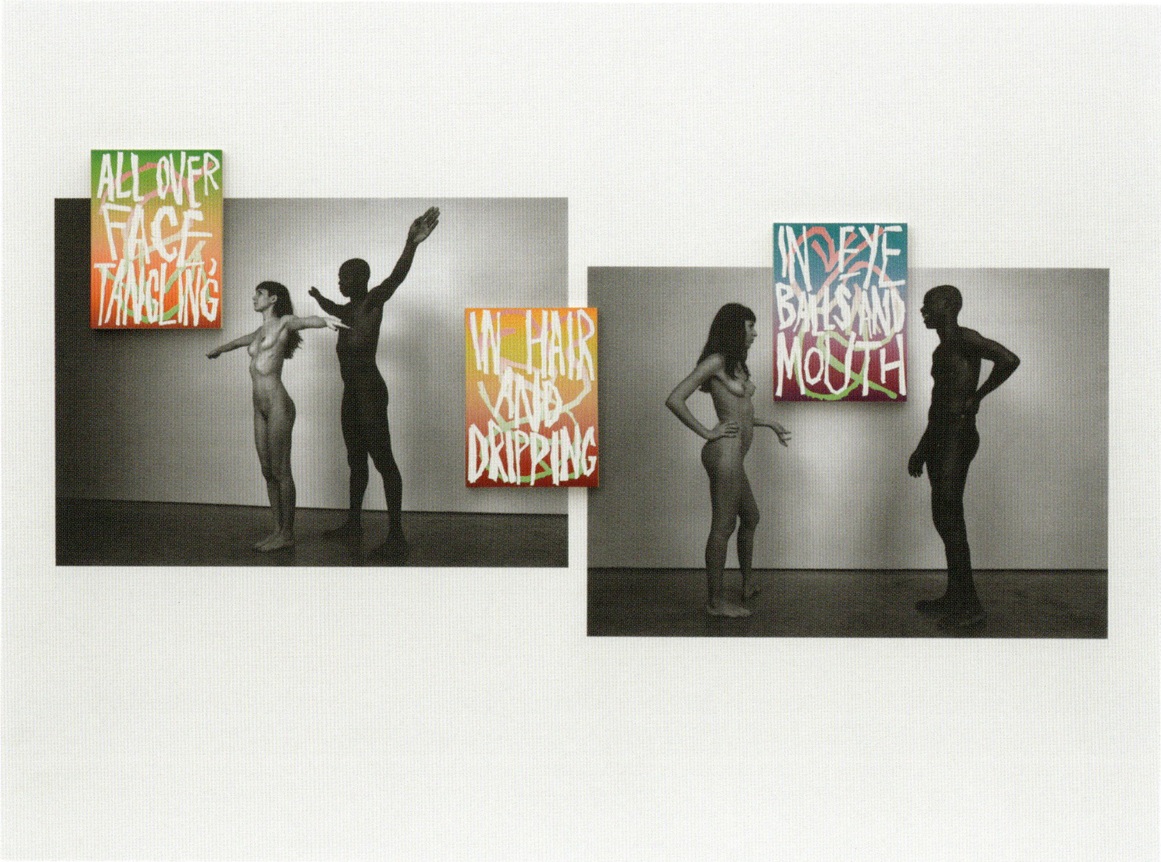

that can never be fixed. 'I think the body is something innately transcendent of language, whereas words can never escape themselves. The body is like a cultural blank canvas that we're desperate to chuck meaning at, and that fascinates me, but I also hate it, because I hate having to describe the body with words. Words are clumsy and clunky. They fail. And yet why have we not found an alternative? In art, in particular, we're always faced with that problem.'

Infinite Disparity (2013), his White Cube performance, took place in a sculptural installation inspired by the modernist penguin pool at London Zoo, designed by architect Berthold Lubetkin in 1934. 'Lubetkin imposed this very dramatic narrative upon the penguins with his design. I liked the idea of imposing a narrative on the bodies in the performance by the presence of a similar structure.' He sees a parallel in the architecture of the Life Room. 'A classic Life Room, like the one at the Royal Academy, has the same amphitheatrical form. As the viewer of the body, the person drawing from it, you can't help but be in a dramatic relationship to the body in such a space – it's almost like a film set.'

Interestingly, Peake says, a repeat visitor to *Infinite Disparity* used the space as his own Life Room, sitting down with charcoal and drawing the performances. But art galleries are often formal spaces in which his audiences can become awkward when faced with nudity. 'When you're looking at performers who are naked, enacting movements, interactions, exchanges or dialogues that are quite sexualised, the experience is very different to, say, being alone with a lover in a bedroom, where you're allowed to let your body just respond as it does to that naked form. The situation of an art gallery is a very unnatural one, where we are expected to control our bodily, emotional and psychological responses. It's an inhuman environment, but I like it for that reason.'

Sam Phillips

Tangling In Hair
2013
Two black-and-white posters and three oil-on-wood paintings
109 x 343.5 x 2.5 cm

Infinite Disparity
2013
Performed by Greg Dodd, Ben Esser, Gwilym Gold, Alex Hemsley, Kieram Corrin Mitchell, Fernada Muñoz-Newsome, Alexandrina Nuñez and Amanda Prince-Lubawy
White Cube, Bermondsey, London
April 2013

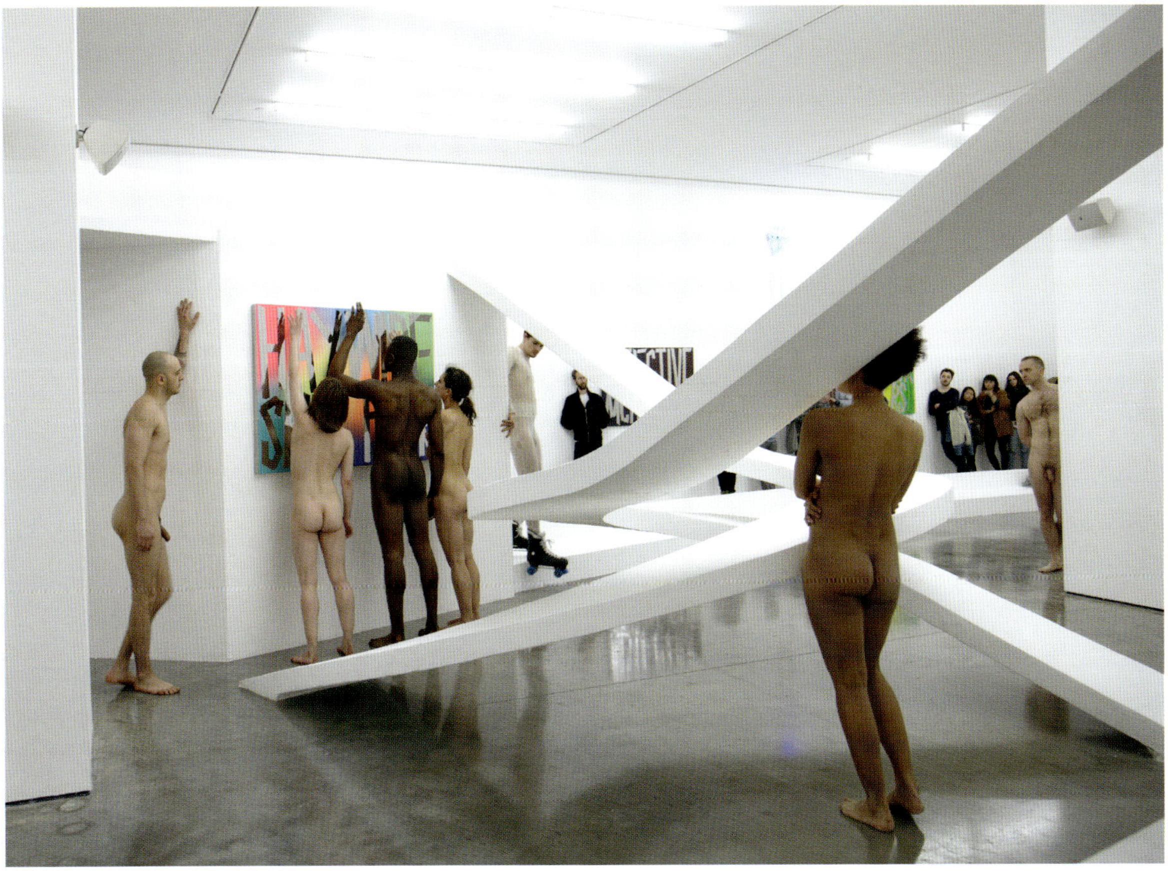

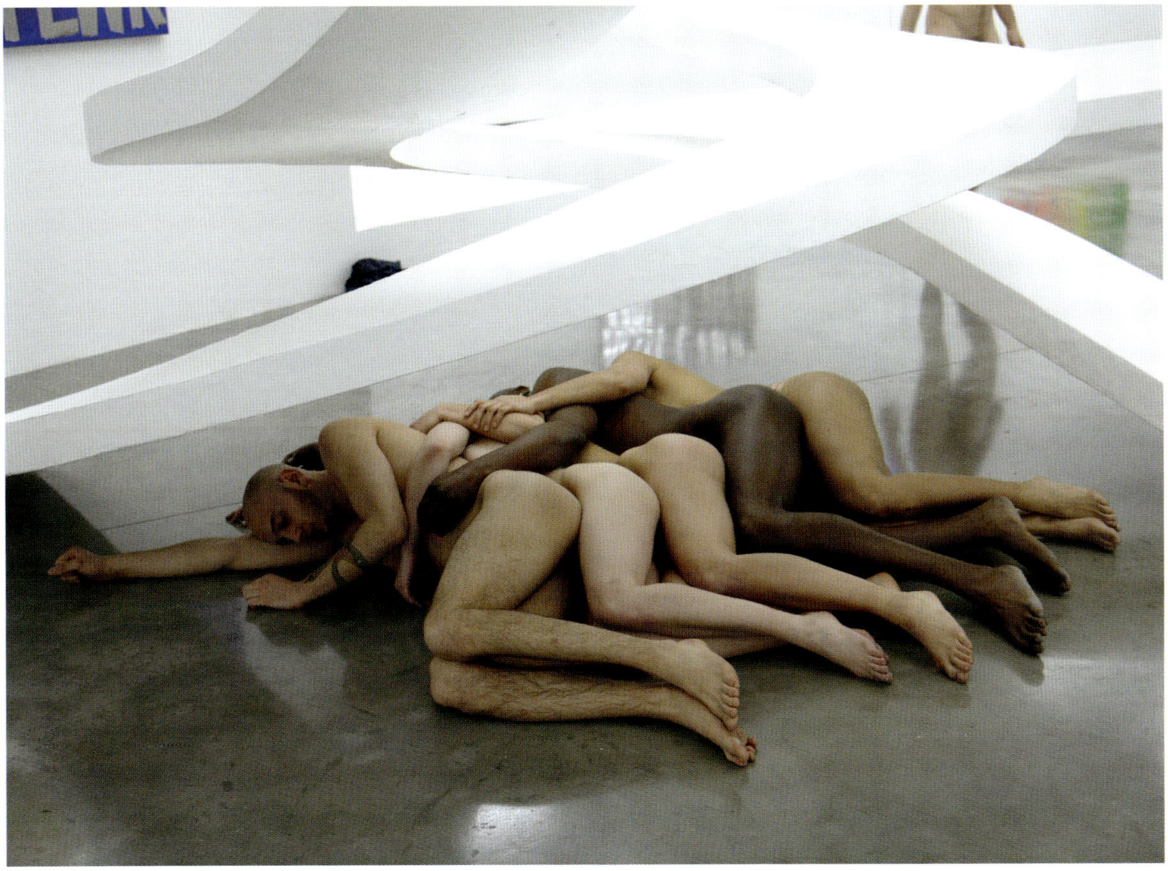

Cathie Pilkington

Cathie Pilkington RA (b. 1968) is a London-based sculptor. Her ambiguous figurative works are created through a wide range of processes, ranging from plaster casting, stone carving and clay modelling to the assemblage of found materials. Pilkington was elected Professor of Sculpture at the Royal Academy in 2015.

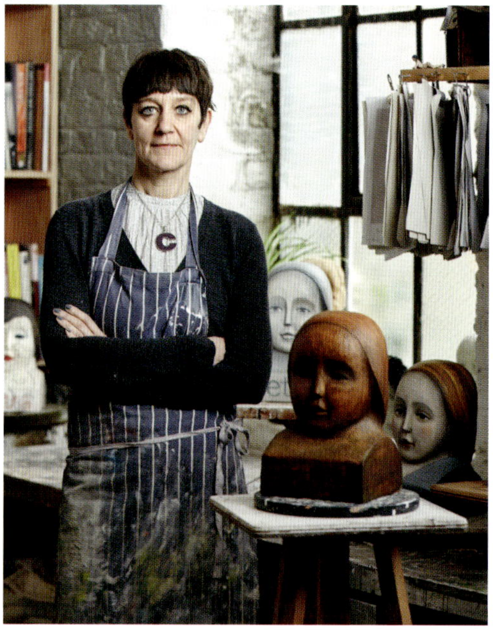

It is January 1769. Sir Joshua Reynolds, President of the newly founded Royal Academy of Arts, is giving a lecture in which he refers to the discipline of working from the 'living model'. He speaks disparagingly of those artists who 'change the form according to their vague and uncertain ideas of beauty, and make a drawing rather of what they think the figure ought to be than of what it appears', and who, by 'curiously trifling endeavour ... give the gloss of stuffs so as to appear real...'.

Now picture an art installation in the Life Room of the Royal Academy Schools nearly 250 years later, in 2017, that flies in the face of this erudition. It's by Royal College of Art-trained artist and Royal Academician Cathie Pilkington. On Pilkington's appointment as RA Professor of Sculpture, Eileen Cooper RA, then Keeper of the Royal Academy – the artist responsible for the Schools – asked her what she would most like to do. The exhibition that ensued, 'Anatomy of a Doll', was remarkable for its wrong turns and beguiling impressions.

At the centre of the Life Room, Pilkington placed five Degas-inspired ballet-dancer girls, seemingly in the process of being sculpted by her. But the little dancers had busily taken on characteristics that they surely shouldn't have: one had preposterous arms, another was hugely pregnant; all were off-kilter, sexed-up and lushly coiffured.

Ranged all around the Life Room were human figures and figure-like objects of different sizes. Some were the classical plaster figures that RA students formerly drew for weeks and months, now on permanent display. But, as Pilkington explains: 'The RA plaster figures were so dominant in the space that I had to take ownership by covering them with fabric, transforming them from important men into stuffed dolls and soft, morphed, formal shapes – turning them into my own objects.' A great many other objects were Pilkington's direct creations. 'Installing my work felt like moving in, colonising the space, making the Life Room my own personal studio space.'

Dummies in a Landscape
2017
Painted resin, woollen blankets, tree roots, antique casts and mixed fabrics
Dimensions variable

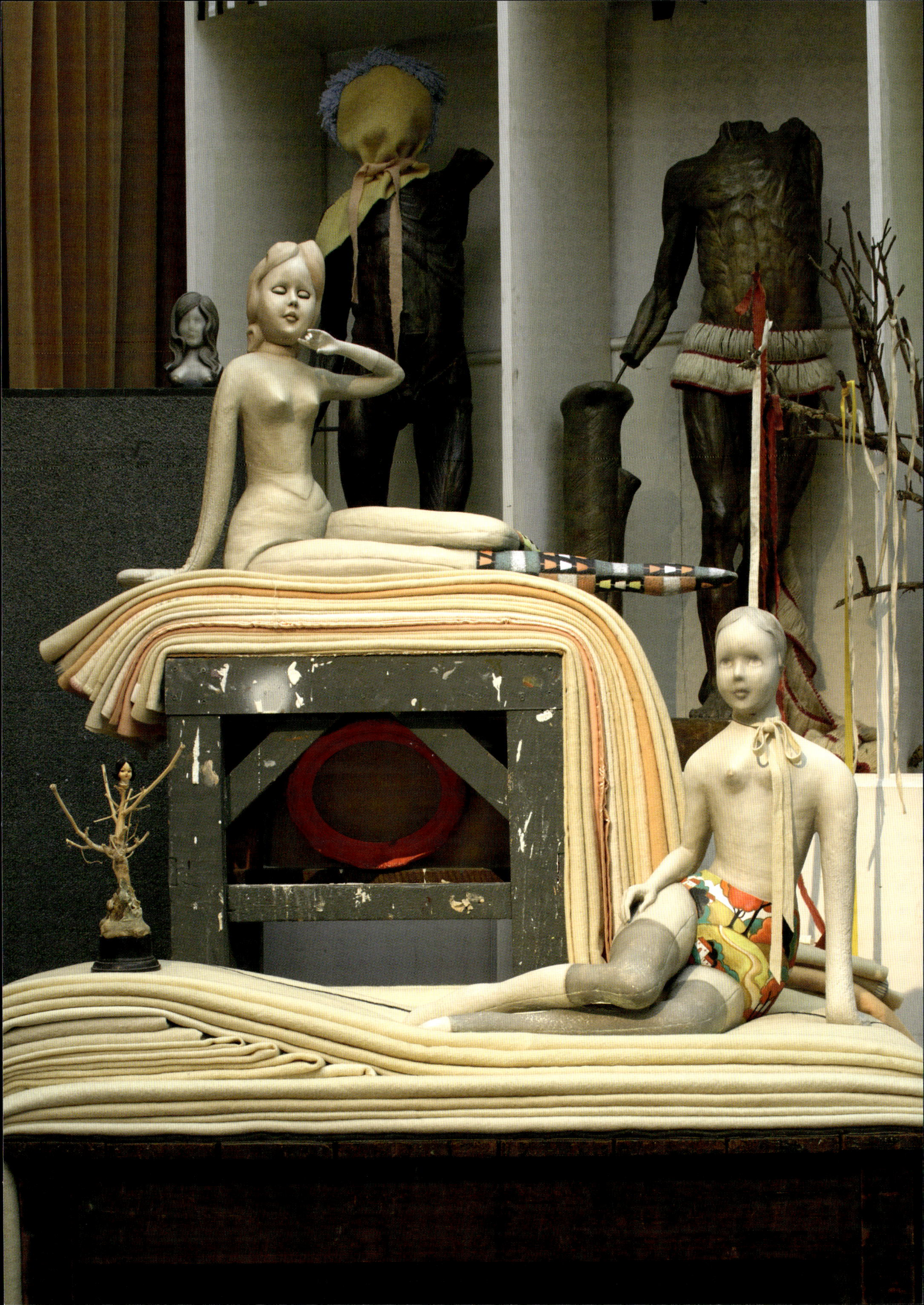

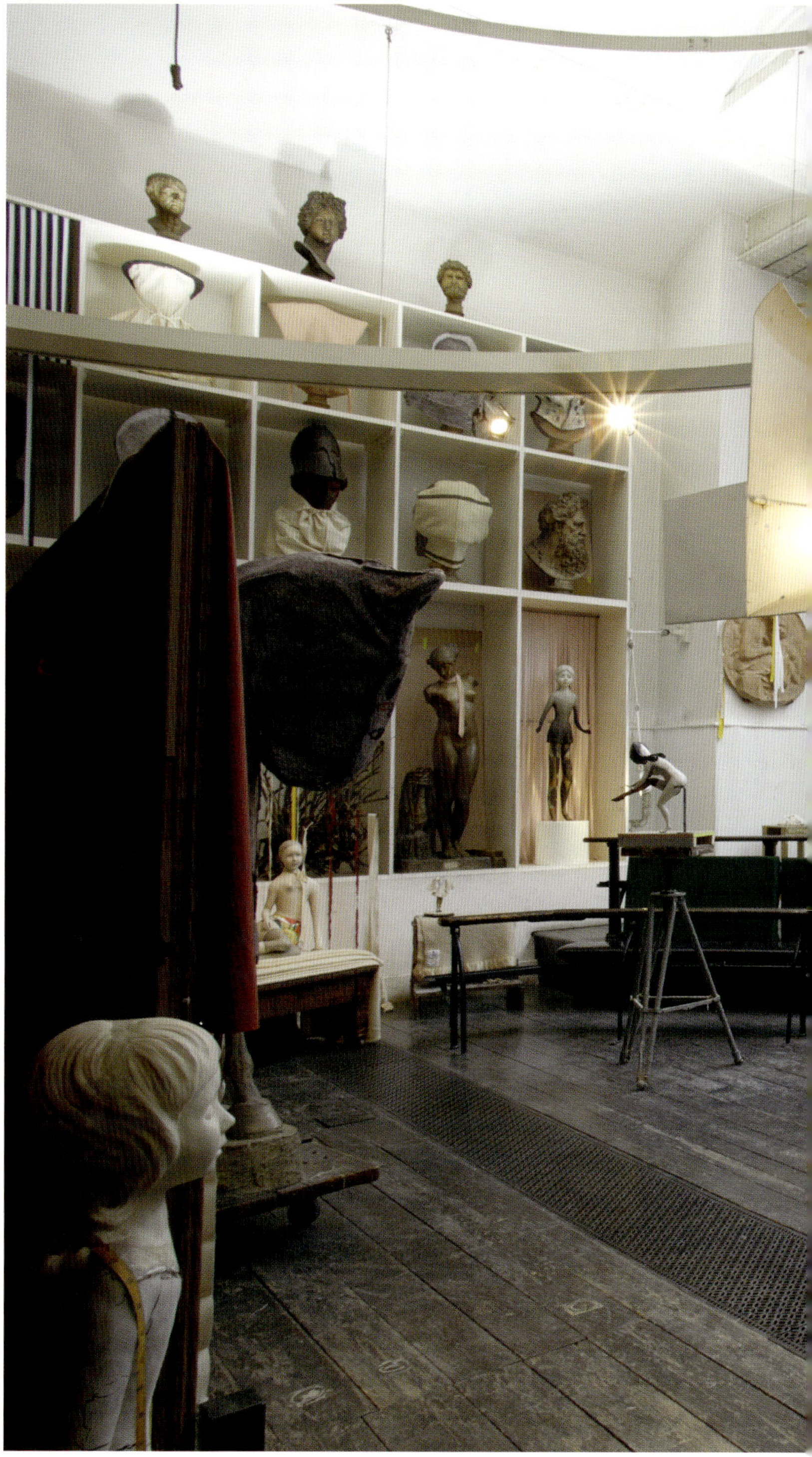

Most of Pilkington's sculptures were of women and girls, and almost all were doll-like. In the case of *Dummies in a Landscape* (see page 115), one figure had the stitched and stuffed legs of a soft doll, cover-girl hips, a Barbie-doll hand and a child-doll head. Her posture, with extended leg, pointed toe and the backs of her fingers about to rest against her mouth, could not have been more mannered. She was, precisely, 'the gloss of stuffs', to borrow Reynolds's phrase. So utterly out of place was this artifice in the sombre RA Life Room that it seemed positively exuberant.

Her figures also evoked shop-window dummies or even mantelpiece ornaments, as gloriously excessive expressions of (to quote Reynolds again) 'vague and uncertain ideas of beauty' and 'what they think the figure ought to be than of what it appears'. Pilkington seemed to point out that our responses to doll, mannequin, ornament and sculpture are essentially the same: we see a certain human presence in them all. 'I like riffing on

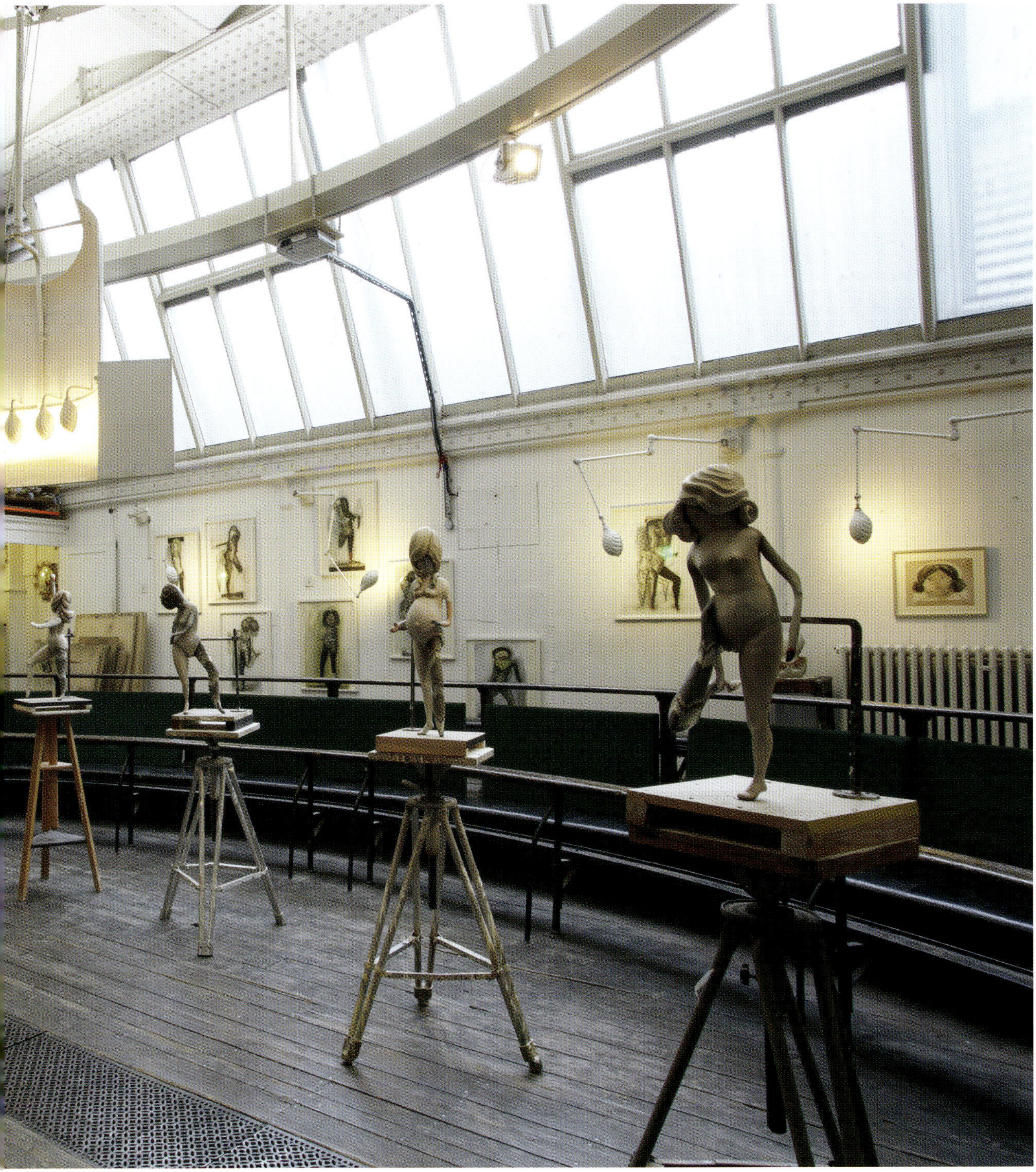

Life Room: Anatomy of a Doll
2017
Wool blanket, steel, wood, paint, resin, paper, plaster, clay and mixed fabrics
Dimensions variable

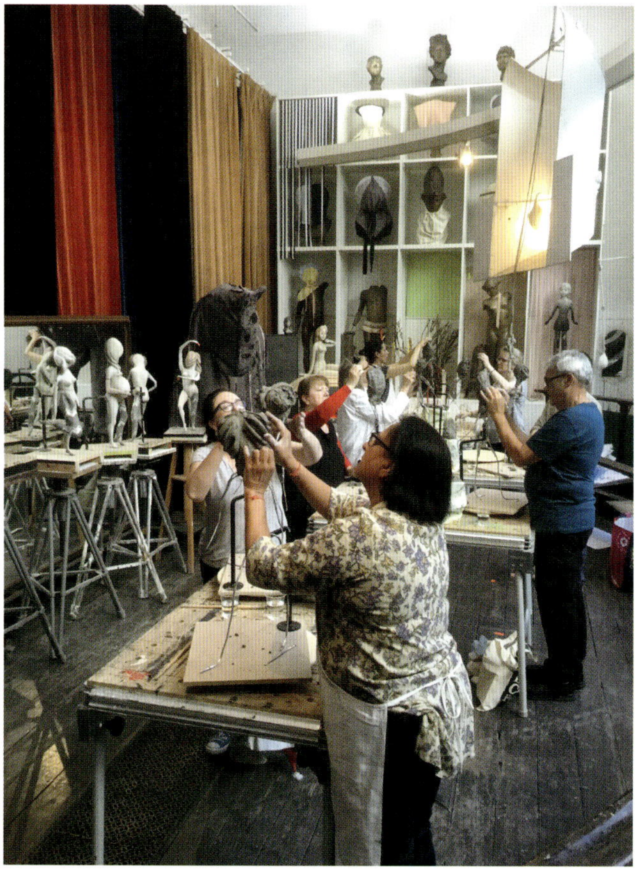

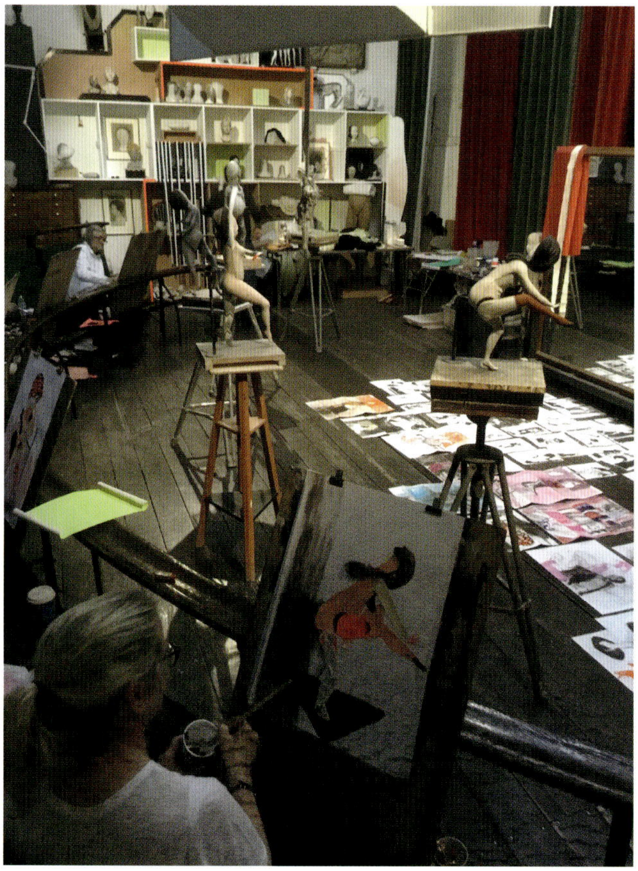

Participants produce work as part of the course 'Exquisite Corpse: A Masterclass with Cathie Pilkington RA' in the RA Schools Life Room in April 2017

connections,' she explains, 'especially if it's a way of pricking bubbles and cutting things down to size.' For her, it's about 'the pull of the ordinary versus the elite, the democratising of forms'.

It is the wider, messy, complicated life *as lived*, and especially the condition of being female, that Pilkington brought to the Life Room. 'With the help of Surrealist thinking, it's possible to go beyond that feeling of being simply the "wrong sex",' she asserts. 'I am consciously joining in with the objectification of the female form, but on my own terms and with glee. As a sculptor I am more interested in making form than anything else, and I am always looking for a wooden awkwardness in combination with moments of utter believability.'

Remember, too, that the Degas-inspired dancers were works in progress: in Pilkington's words, the Life Room is a 'making space'. In keeping with this, during her exhibition she taught a number of lively classes within the space, in which participants worked from the plaster figures, Pilkington's sculptures and a living model. Moreover, Pilkington's sense of her artwork is as 'a playful combination of the figure and doll that can be a starting point for inventing unexpected forms and objects'. She saw her exhibition as 'a venue for participants to join in with this idea'. And so visitors, as they moved about the space and encountered her figures – and also what they thought about and their own imaginative leaps – were part and parcel of Pilkington's concept of enlivening the RA Life Room.

Although Pilkington is accomplished in working from life, her only formal training in the practice, on her foundation course at North Cheshire College in Northwich, ended in frustration. 'As a nineteen-year-old I was terrified by life drawing. I couldn't find a way in. I had a real block. I used to storm out of the life-drawing room and play truant.' It was ten years later that she began to teach herself anatomical modelling skills in clay.

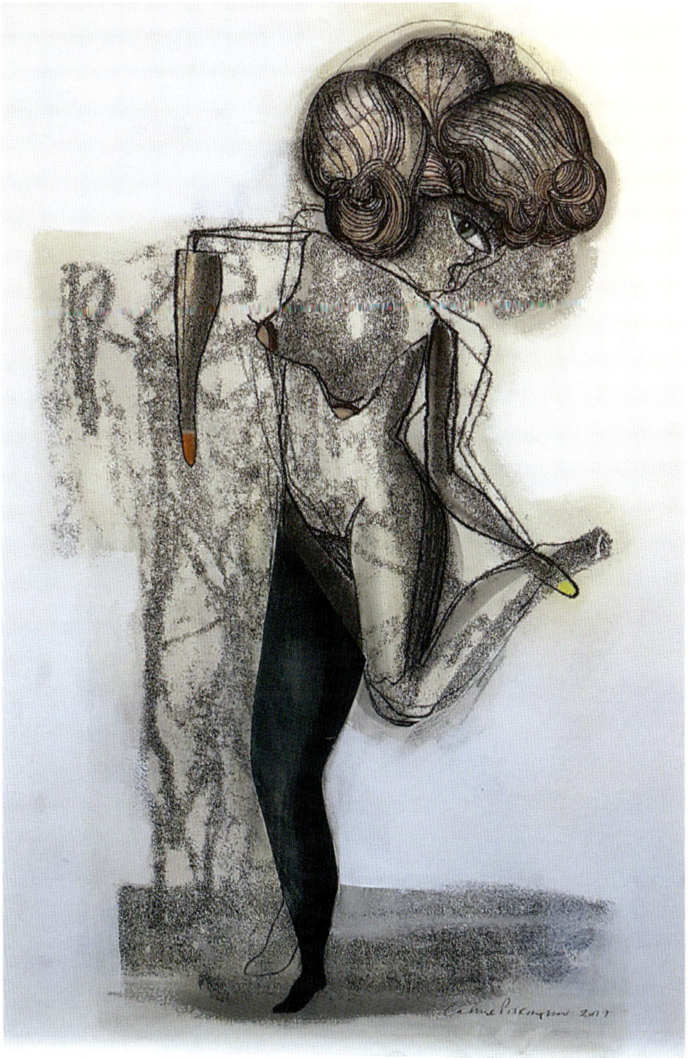

Life Room Doll 6
2017
Ink, oil paint and collage
on paper
62 x 43 cm

'I saw then that these skills would give me the freedom to make whatever I wanted in whatever way I chose. And I was excited about applying these traditional skills to a contemporary situation – being able to use them without getting hung up or tripped up by them.'

So Pilkington's takeover of the once-feared Life Room was on her own terms; it was perhaps even, as one RA student visitor expressed it, 'the revenge of her competence'. She is nowadays more likely to model from a doll than from a living being, and is curious about how she 'makes a lot of work from un-life' in her quest 'paradoxically to inject life into un-life'.

Pilkington's fierce way of looking at dolls, supercharged with adult insight, finds its way into her sculptures via the craft skills she has honed for decades. There is an extraordinary kickback from the doll-sculptures she makes: bloodless, oppressive, magnificent. In 'Anatomy of a Doll', Pilkington moved between the animate and inanimate, and between anger and rapture. It was an exhibition that brought life to the Life Room and the denied into the light.

Angela Kingston

Overleaf left:
Degas Dolls 5
2017
Painted resin, steel
and wood
60 x 60 x 50 cm

Overleaf right:
Degas Dolls 3
2017
Painted resin, steel
and wood
70 x 50 x 45 cm

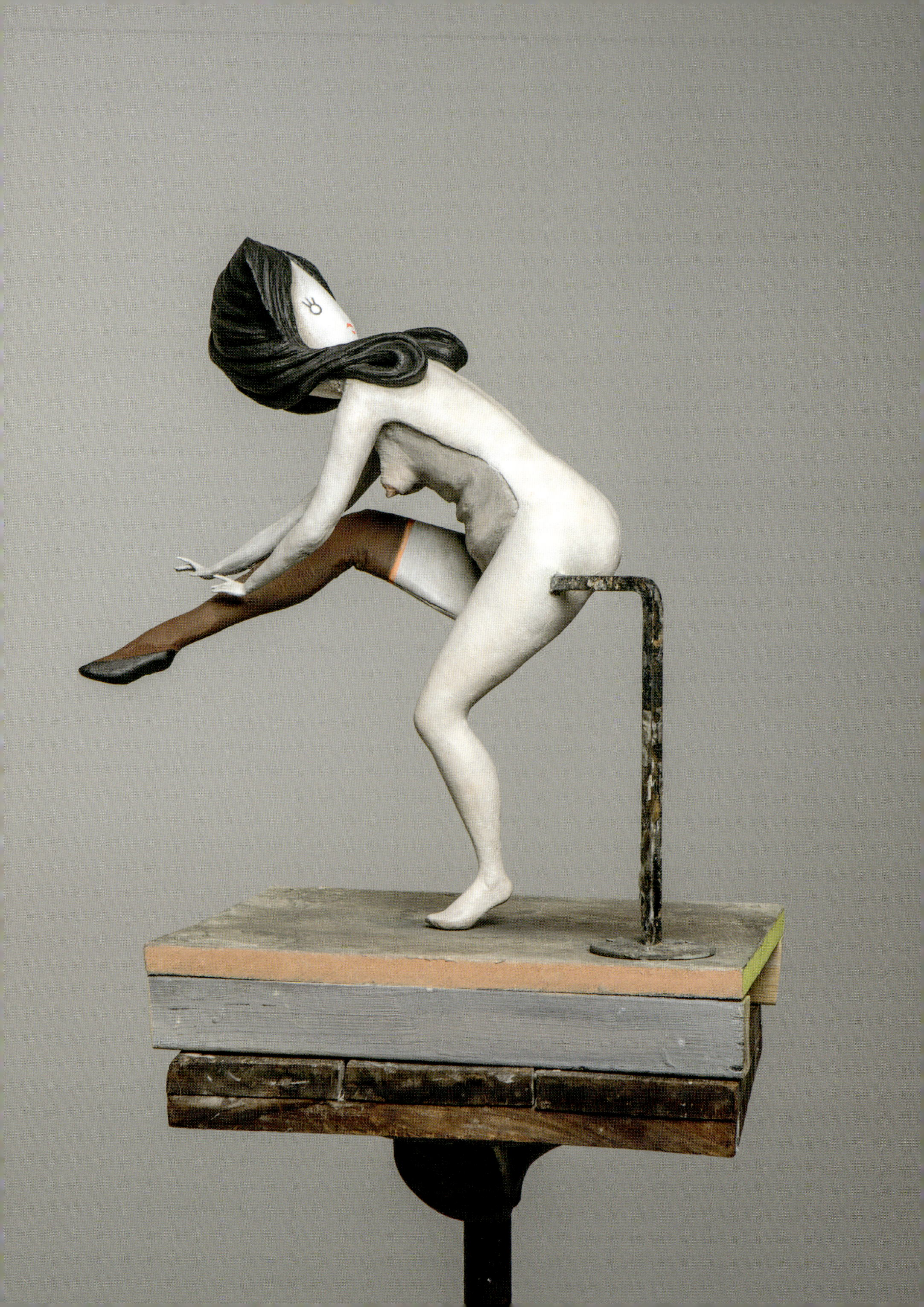

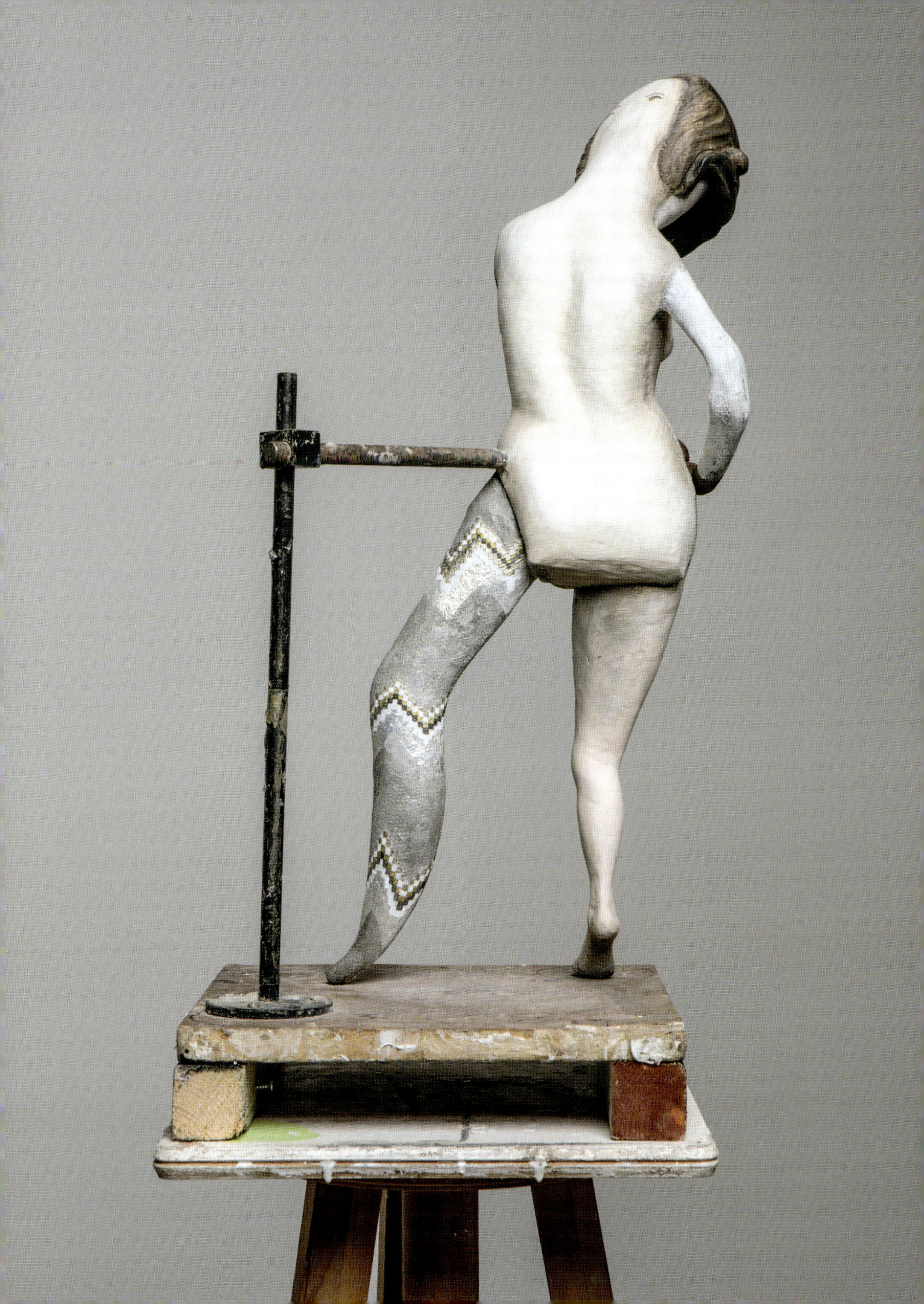

Bridget Riley

One of Britain's most significant living artists, Bridget Riley CH CBE (b. 1931) has explored the interaction of form and colour since the early 1960s, when she first began developing her dynamic geometric works that trigger optical sensations of vibration and movement. In 2010 the National Portrait Gallery in London – the city where she lives and works – presented 'Bridget Riley: From Life', an exhibition of her little-known life drawings.

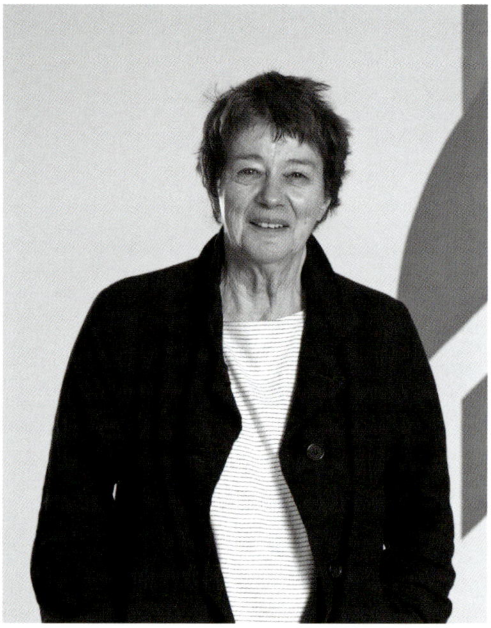

Like most younger people thinking of a career as a painter, an eighteen-year-old Bridget Riley began by going to art school. She arrived at Goldsmiths in London in 1949. 'Very slowly I began to find out what I didn't know, what I could find out, and whom I could find to teach me, which is always a difficult thing.'

She counts herself fortunate that her drawing master, Sam Rabin, was an exponent of draughtsmanship in the tradition of Henry Tonks (1862–1937). The latter, a plastic surgeon during the First World War and later a teacher at London's Slade School of Fine Art for many years, had taught earlier generations of British artists, David Bomberg, Paul Nash, Stanley Spencer RA and Gwen John among them. And what did he impart? Riley sums it up as 'French classical drawing' – in other words, a tradition that flowed back through Degas and Ingres to Raphael and the Florentine Renaissance.

Looking back, Riley recalls that she realised that life drawing was 'a firm and solid discipline', and she was thankful to practise it. This might seem surprising, since her mature work is superficially very different from that of, say, Bomberg or Spencer. For one thing, it is abstract. But, she emphasises, the most important lessons she learnt were not about naturalism. 'The way Sam Rabin taught drawing was not an approach to realism. It was not about verisimilitude. It was about re-creating a visual experience that had taken place in three dimensions on a two-dimensional surface. So it was actually very abstract.'

Like many teachers imparting the elements of drawing, Rabin taught only by demonstration. 'Words wouldn't come into it,' she reflects, 'but it was still a process of thought.' For the young Riley, those life classes constituted 'a most important piece of structural thinking'. Rabin posed questions rather than giving instructions. 'For instance, he would say, "What is the model doing?" You would think it was quite obvious, because you were both looking at her. He was hoping for an answer such as "She's standing" or

Young Girl
Early 1950s
Sepia Conté crayon on paper
56.5 x 38.5 cm

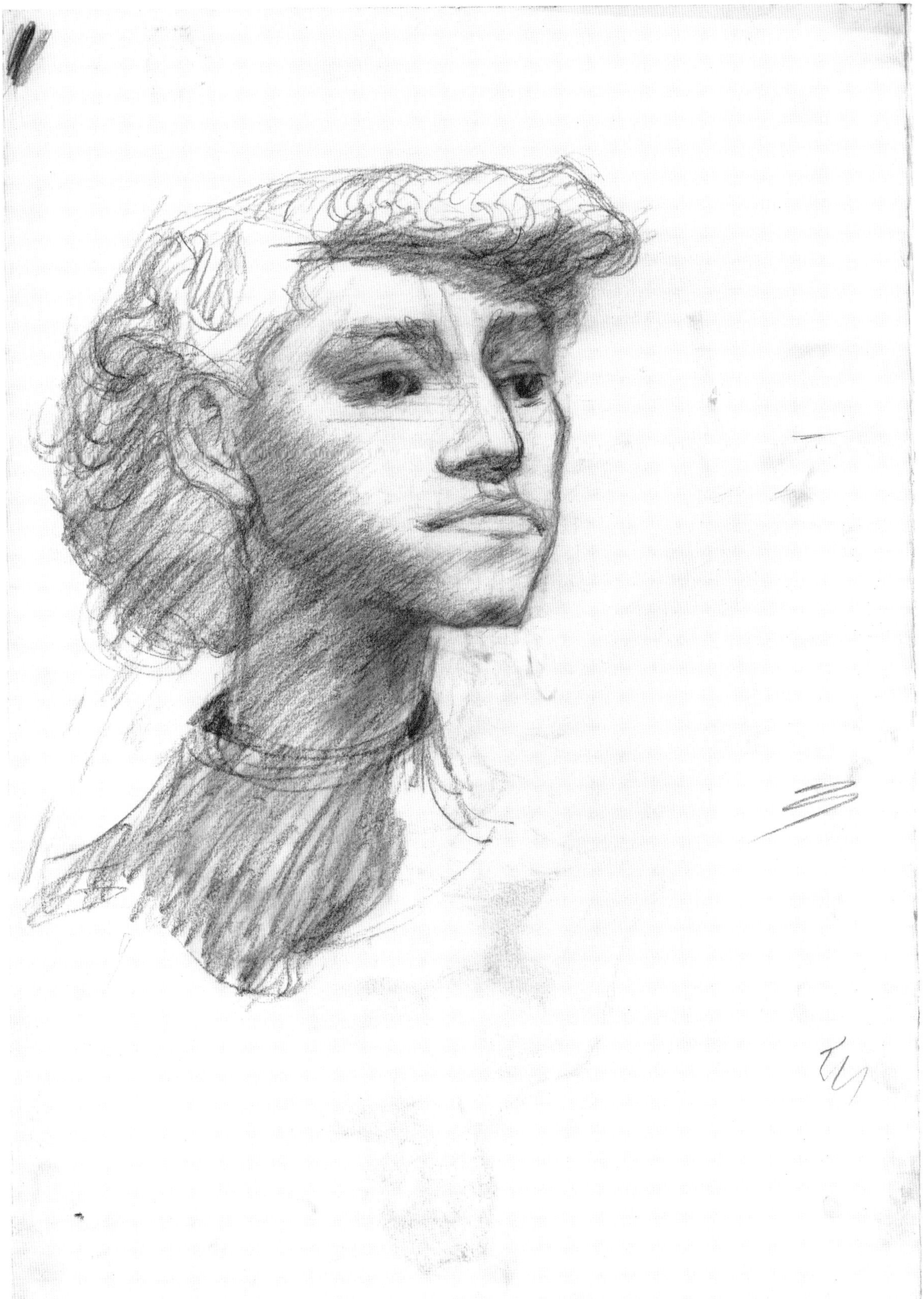

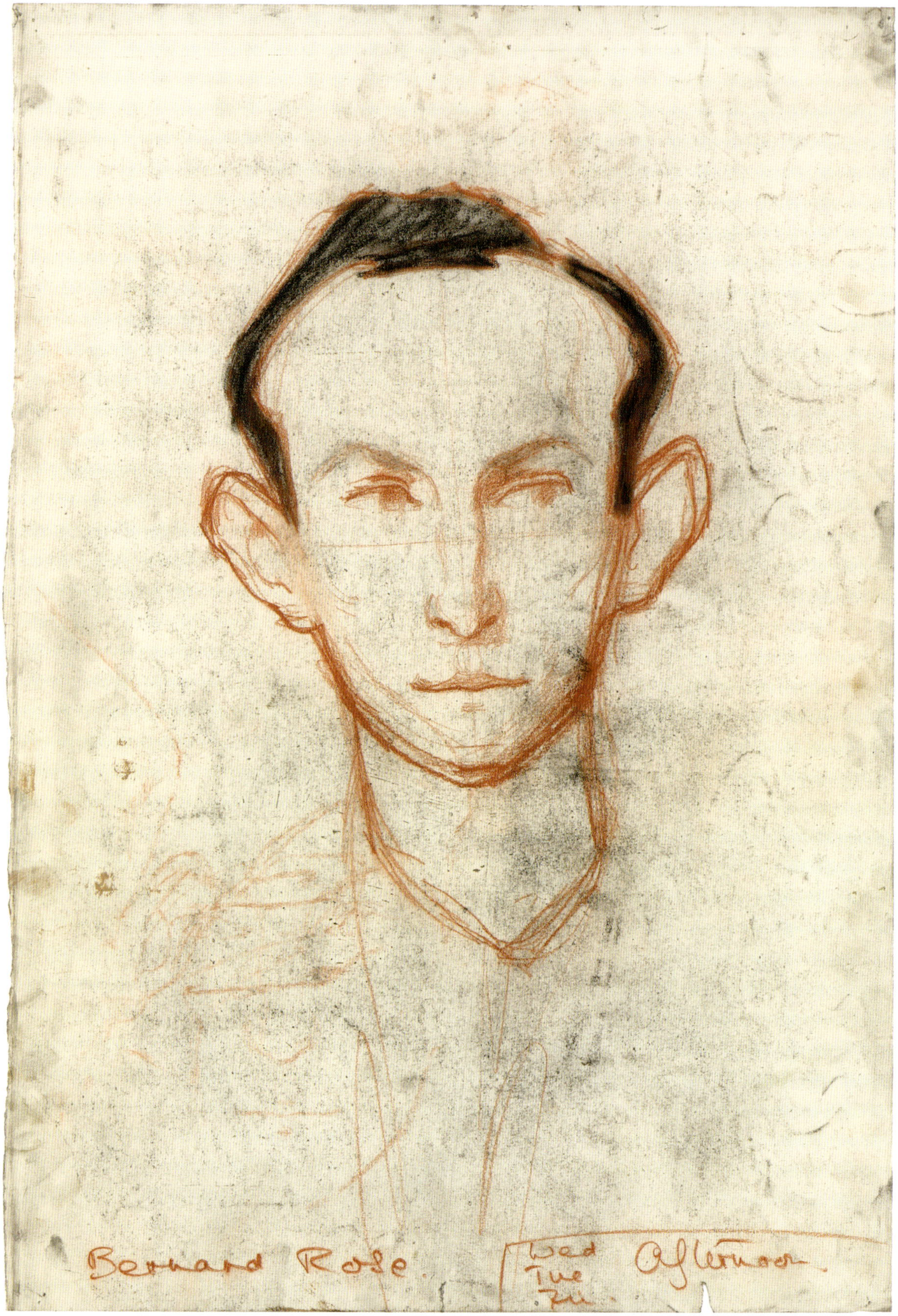
Bernard Rose
Wed
Tue
Fri
Afternoon

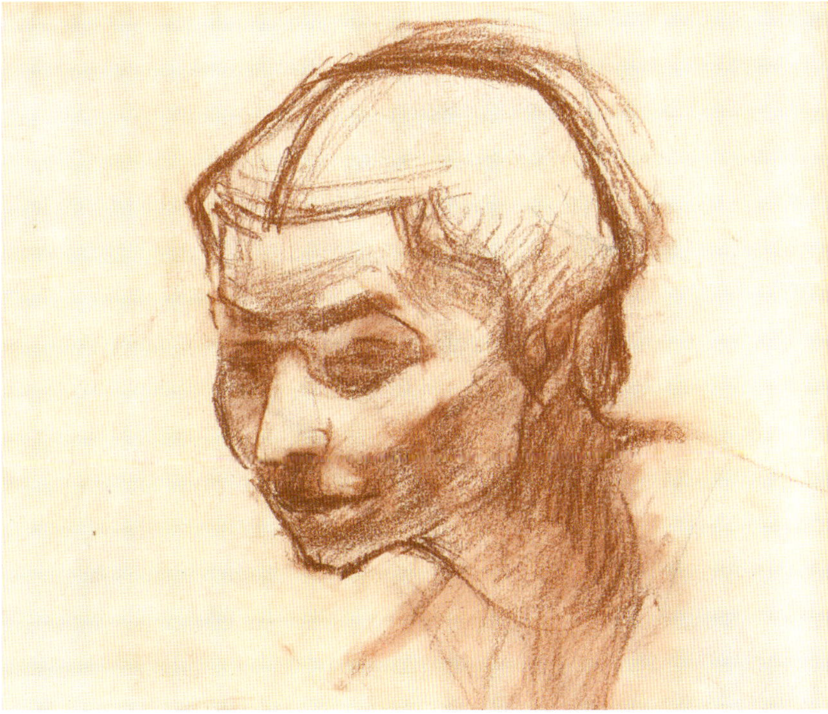

"She's sitting". Then he would say, "And is your drawing standing?" He meant, "Is the balance and structure and weight articulated there?" He would say, "What is the lightest part of what you are looking at?" You might say that the light is falling on her legs and shoulders and the rest of her is in shadow. And he would say, "What is happening on your paper?" That started you thinking in terms of relationships in a different way – tonally, which was an approach to colour. It was an absorbing study.'

With this in mind, when one looks at a Riley painting from the 1960s or later, after she developed her individual style and approach, one sees that the canvas – although nothing like a naked model on a throne – has those very qualities of balance, rhythm and structure that she describes.

This is Riley's conclusion about her early education in life drawing: 'I think – and there is evidence enough from other artists – that this kind of discipline is useful even when you are not actually drawing. It creates a kind of thinking that feeds right through into picture-making. It lays an intellectual foundation.'

This foundation can be invaluable to a student, even if he or she does not eventually become a figurative artist. Riley is aware that 'there are a number of students these days who don't want to do any life drawing and they argue that they can get a more realistic image through a photograph'. Of course, Riley acknowledges that a camera image has its own possibilities. However, she believes that a photograph cannot give an artist an internalised understanding of how a body stands and sits, its equilibrium or otherwise in space, the shifting patterns of light and shade it generates, the ways those might translate into a range of colour – everything Riley sums up as 'analysis of structure'. For that, there is no substitute for learning to draw. She recalls Boudin's advice to young Monet, 'learn to draw, learn to see.'

Martin Gayford

Bernard Rose. Study for Painting
1952
Red and black Conté crayon on paper
55.9 x 38.7 cm

Louise
1956
Red and black Conté crayon on paper
20.3 x 24.3 cm

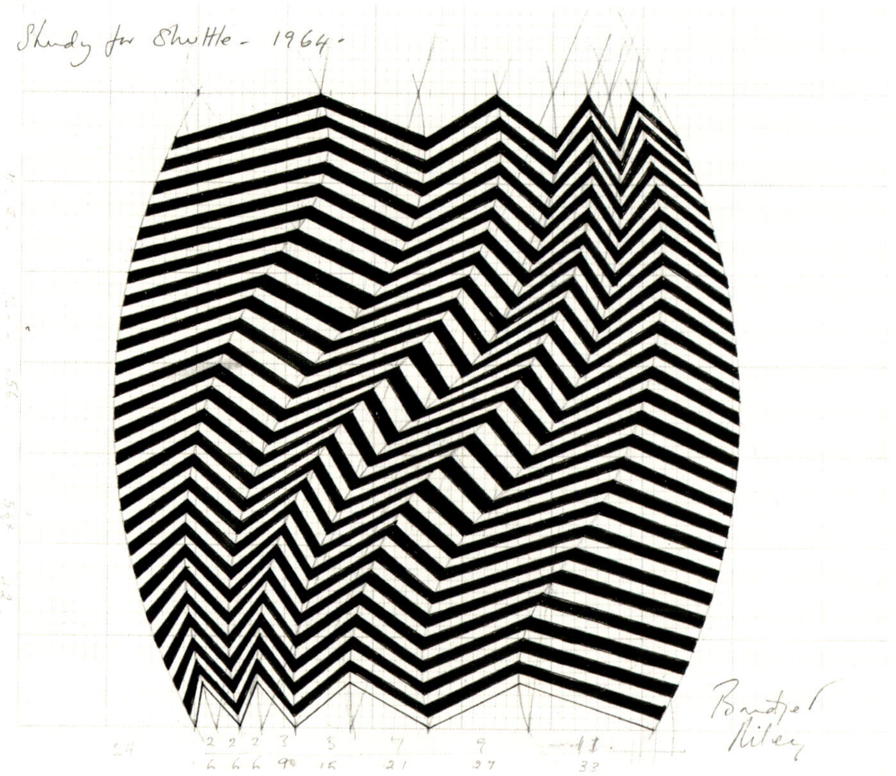
Study for Shuttle - 1964 -
Bridget Riley

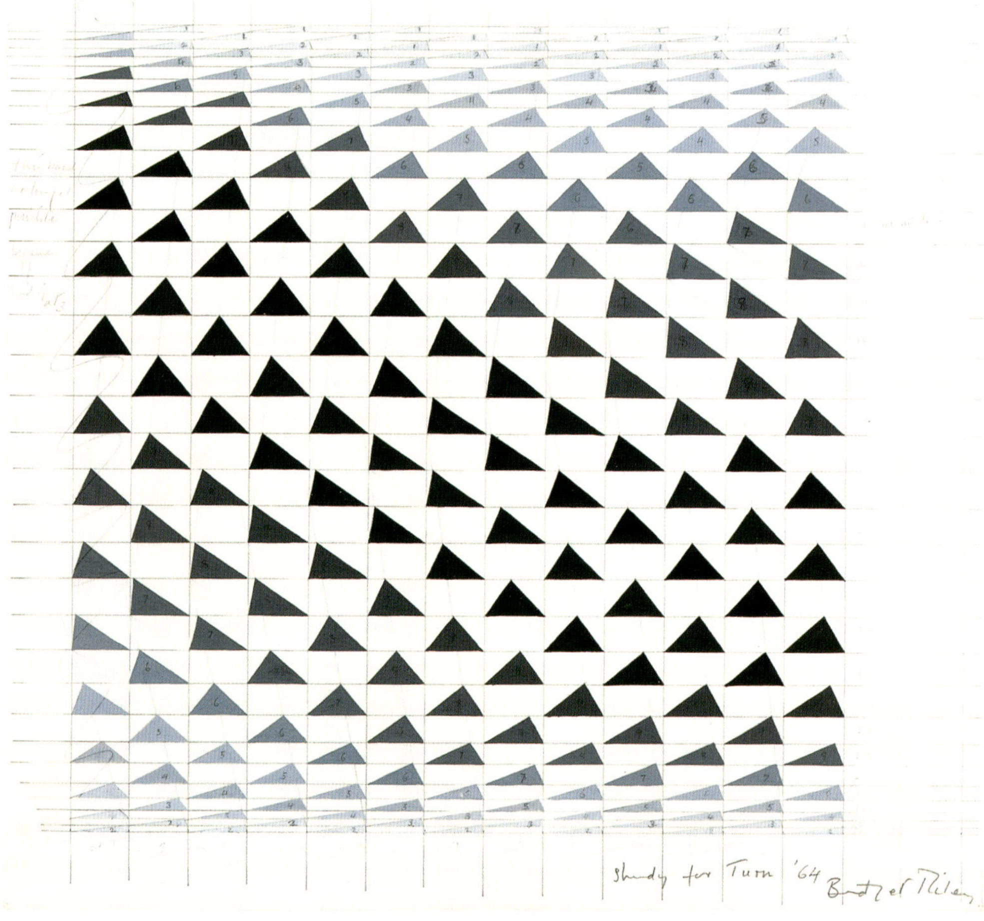
Study for Turn '64 Bridget Riley

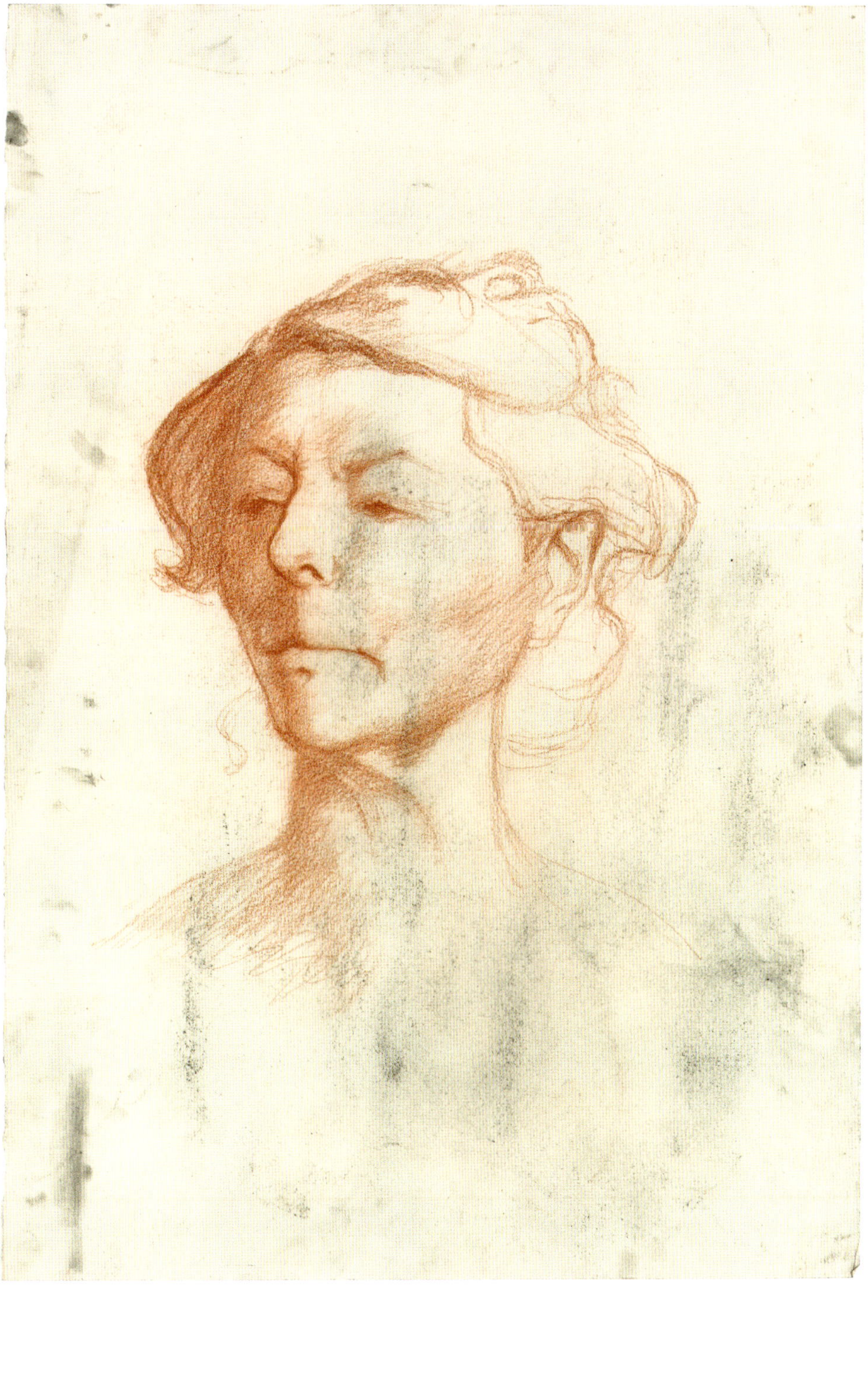

Study for Shuttle
1964
Pencil and gouache
on graph paper
21.6 x 26 cm

Study for Turn
1964
Gouache and pencil
on paper
34.4 x 37 cm

Woman Looking Ahead
Mid-1950s
Red Conté crayon
on paper
56 x 38.1 cm

Jenny Saville

Jenny Saville RA (b. 1970) is one of the foremost painters of her generation, celebrated for large-scale oil paintings of naked female figures. Her work is renowned for its rich handling of paint, which makes the flesh of her subjects palpable. The British artist lives and works in Oxford, where she was the subject of a survey at Modern Art Oxford (2012).

Jenny Saville's massive oil paintings of fleshy, female nudes catapulted her into public view in the early 1990s, when she was in her early twenties. In 1992 her graduate show caught the eye of the collector Charles Saatchi, leading to a two-year commission to create work for his London gallery, and enabling her to continue along her path of exploring the human body in all its complexity, quirkiness and imperfection. She has spent hours observing and recording the work of a plastic surgeon in New York; she has focused on her own body, subjecting her face, torso and limbs to merciless scrutiny and distortion; she has painted sexually ambiguous and transgender figures, as well as victims of trauma, such as in *Entry* (2004–05), in which a female face is disfigured with what appears to be a massive wound. Seen from extreme angles in exaggerated foreshortening, her bulky figures with their scarred and mottled flesh are deliberately challenging, and can generate a profound sense of unease.

The artist's fascination with the human form began early. She was only a child when her art-historian uncle, Paul Saville, taught her to draw from life, and she continued the practice while she was a student at Glasgow School of Art. 'I was lucky that my art school had a permanent life-painting room as well as life-drawing classes,' she recalls. 'You could join the life-painting room for several weeks at a time, and there were life-drawing classes between 7 pm and 9 pm in the evenings.'

Everything she does is underpinned by the habit of intensive observation of individual bodies, but these days she rarely paints from a live model. 'I work with models for four or five hours over several sessions, taking photographs of them sitting and moving, and I make drawings. I also use images from medical books, magazines and prints from the internet.' She finds it difficult to capture 'life' with a model lying or sitting in front of her, because 'they usually stay still in positions they would never normally hold without moving and it looks false to my eye.'

Entry
2004–05
Oil on canvas
240 x 191 cm
ISelf Collection

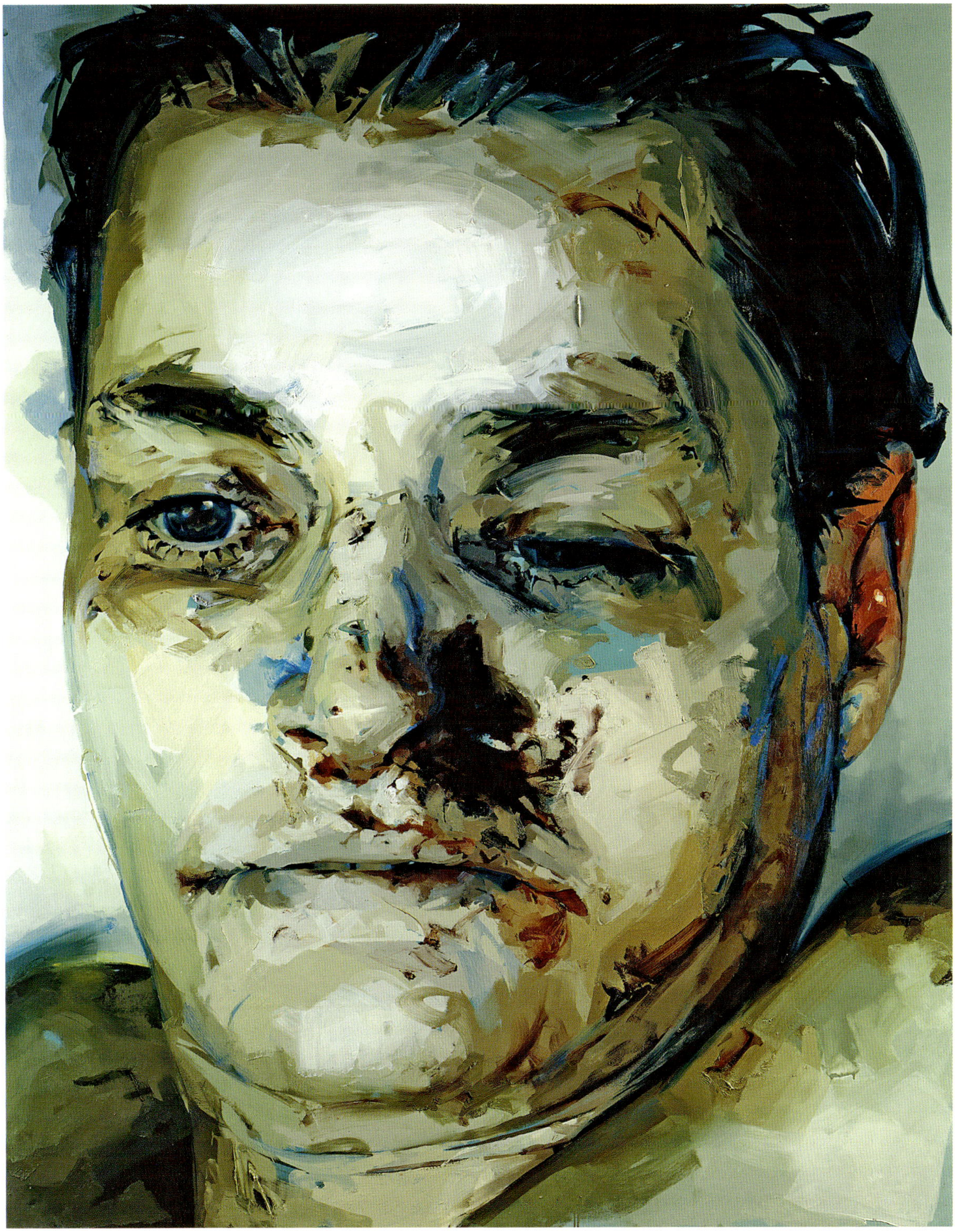

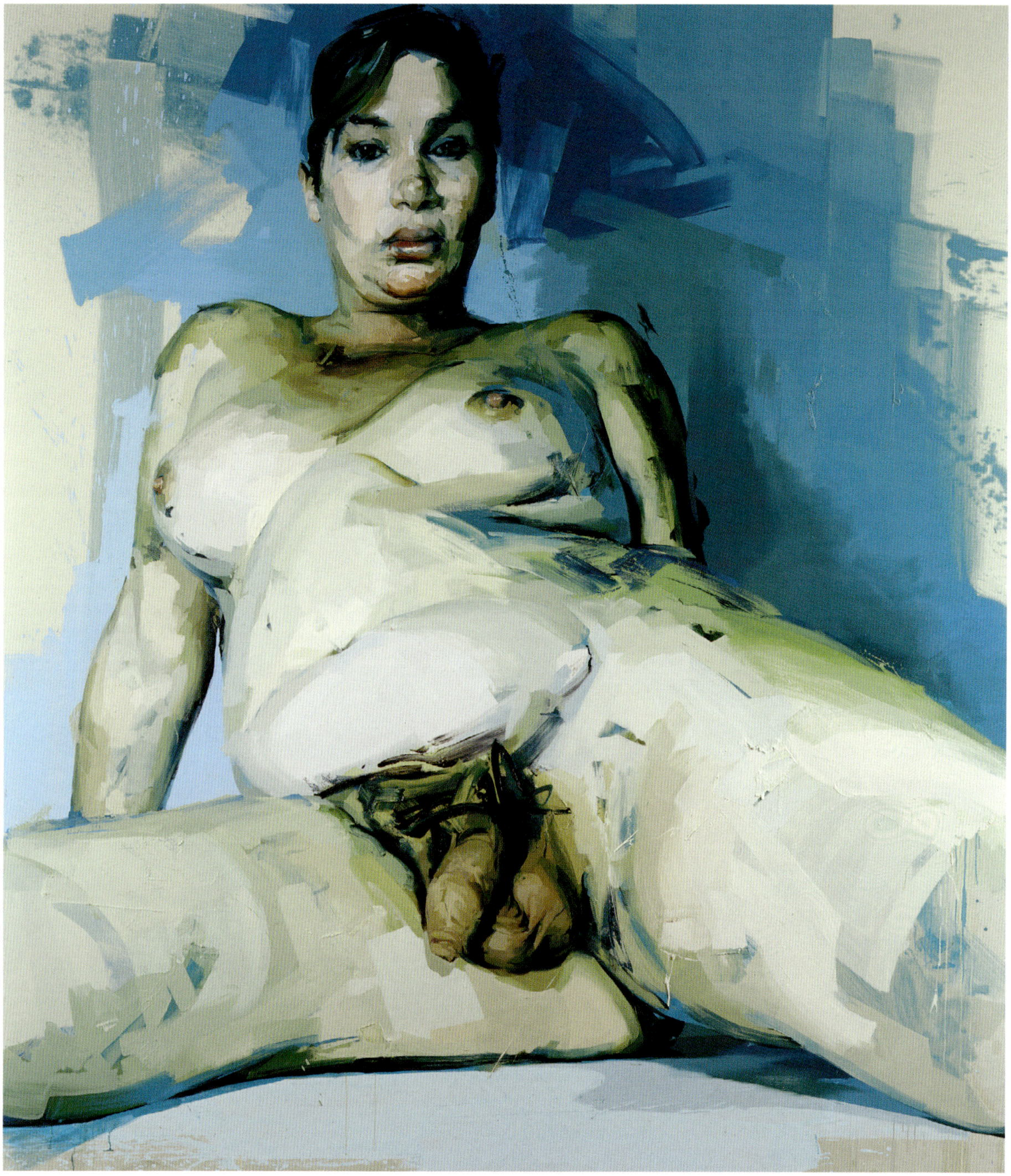

Passage
2004
Oil on canvas
336 x 290 cm

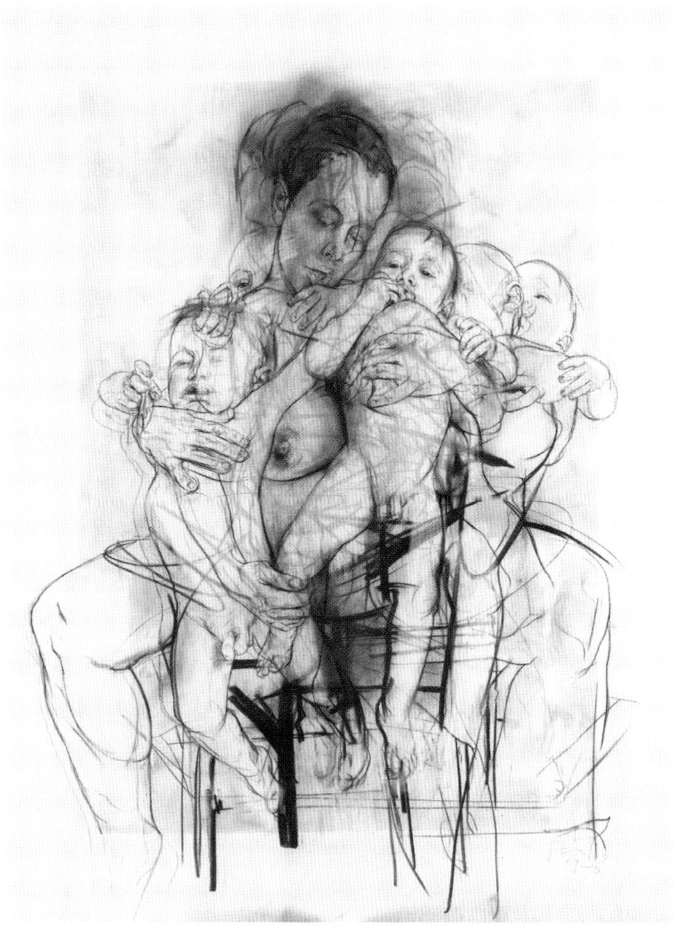

Reproduction Drawing I (after the Leonardo Cartoon)
2009–10
Pencil on paper
226.3 x 176.5 cm

Photography helps to capture movement and enables her to create a greater sense of reality: 'I use a camera like sketching – picking out details, compositions, rhythms of bodies and so on just like the Old Masters did on paper. It provides me with an armature to draw and paint from.' But, she adds, 'maybe I couldn't do that without the academic Life Room background that I had'.

Although much of Saville's work appears to confront traditional images of idealised femininity, it also connects in subtle ways to figures painted by the giants of Western art, including Leonardo, Rubens, Titian, Rembrandt, Schiele, De Kooning, Picasso, Bacon and Lucian Freud. Because she often works near the Ashmolean Museum in Oxford, she can also go there to look at Michelangelo and Raphael drawings at close quarters. 'The problems experienced in realising a figure haven't changed much for artists – moving a hand, getting a figure to sit on the ground of the paper, smudging the back of a shoulder so it sits in space.'

Like the Old Masters she admires, she has also been attracted to the immediacy of working in pencil and charcoal. Drawing – for her 'a timeless and experimental discipline' – seemed the best way to capture the constant movement and rapidly changing bodies of her own children. Having children also brought about a shift in her feelings about her own body that had an impact on her art: 'I experienced a profound sense of life being cyclic through growing a body inside my body. The children have helped me accept beauty and love in a way I didn't have in my work before they were born.' One senses that affirmation of life in *Umbilical (Study)* (2009; see page 4), the study she made of her howling baby emerging from her body, still attached by the cord.

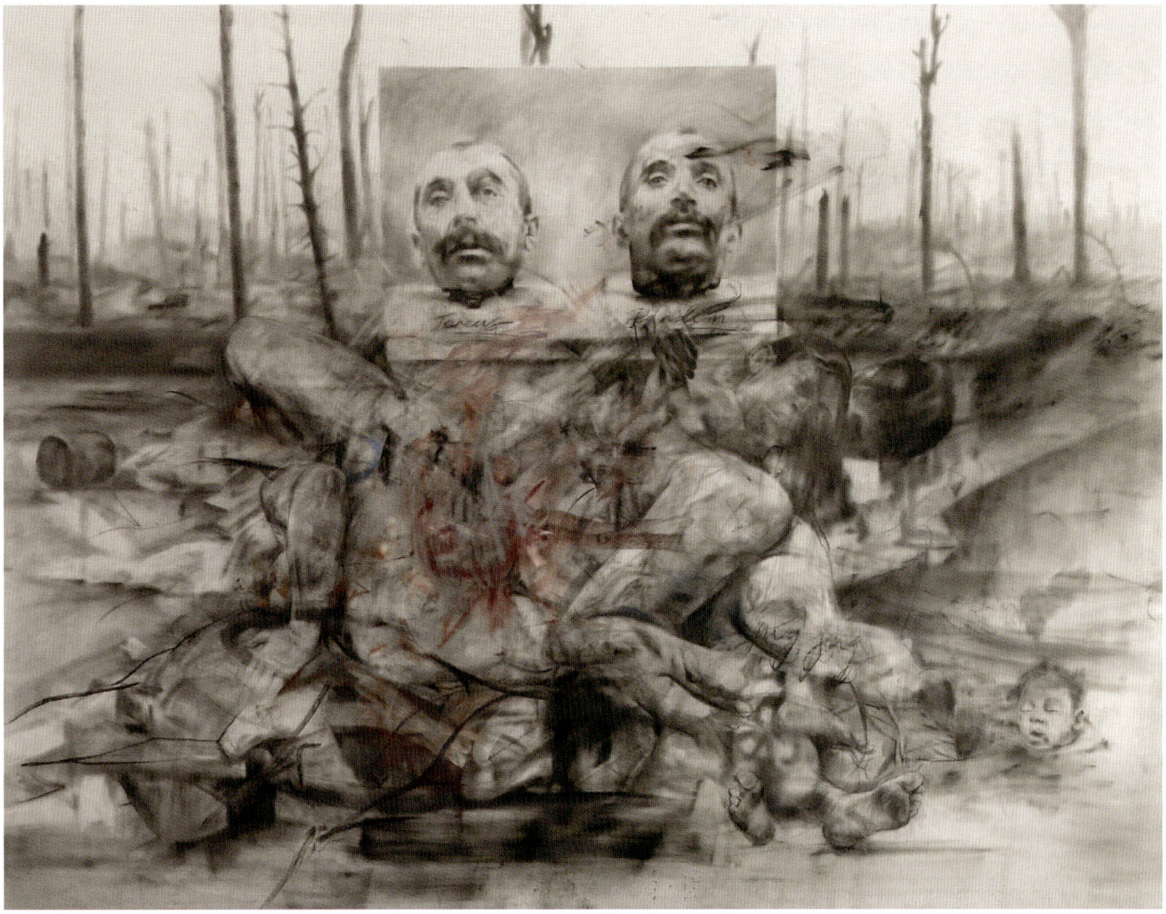

Voice of the Shuttle (Philomela)
2014–15
Pastel and charcoal on canvas
280 x 360 cm

Reflective Flesh Study (Red)
2015
Charcoal and pastel on paper mounted on board
200 x 152 cm

Overleaf:
One Out of Two (Symposium)
2016
Charcoal and pastel on canvas
152 x 225 cm

She continues to paint in a very fleshy way – 'I'm naturally drawn to the sensual possibilities of oil paint' – but what has changed is her deepening knowledge of the way bodies have been depicted throughout history. 'Spending a lot of time in the ancient Mediterranean world of Sicily, Spain and Greece, I have worked more with ancient sculpture and myths, and that's expanded my perception of what's possible.' Seeing 'sculptural bodies entangled and fractured' in the archaeological museum in Athens was pivotal. A painting she produced in response to Rubens, *Voice of the Shuttle (Philomela)* (2014–15), portrays a Greek myth of rape and murder in a jumble of nude bodies surmounted by two decapitated heads. These overlapping figures blend into each other, evoking flux and impermanence and a sense that several different moments are being depicted simultaneously.

The artist is producing paintings for a forthcoming show that are similarly multi-layered. 'I've been working with identical twin models. They are fascinating as they move together in unison, as they have strong physical bodies that interlock so effortlessly. Their skin tones are the same too, so they create one human mass.' Saville sees this current venture as a development from the works she made for her 2016 London drawing show, 'Erota', in which bodies overlaid with restless lines and patches of oil stain and pastel appear to be in a continuous state of movement. 'This is an expansion of the way I started working in those pieces, with layered-up marks that become submerged in paint. It's almost an abstract approach to painting but I don't want to get rid of the figure. I'm convinced I can chase this image in my mind of simultaneous realities. Perhaps I'm just a dog chasing its tail.'

Caroline Bugler

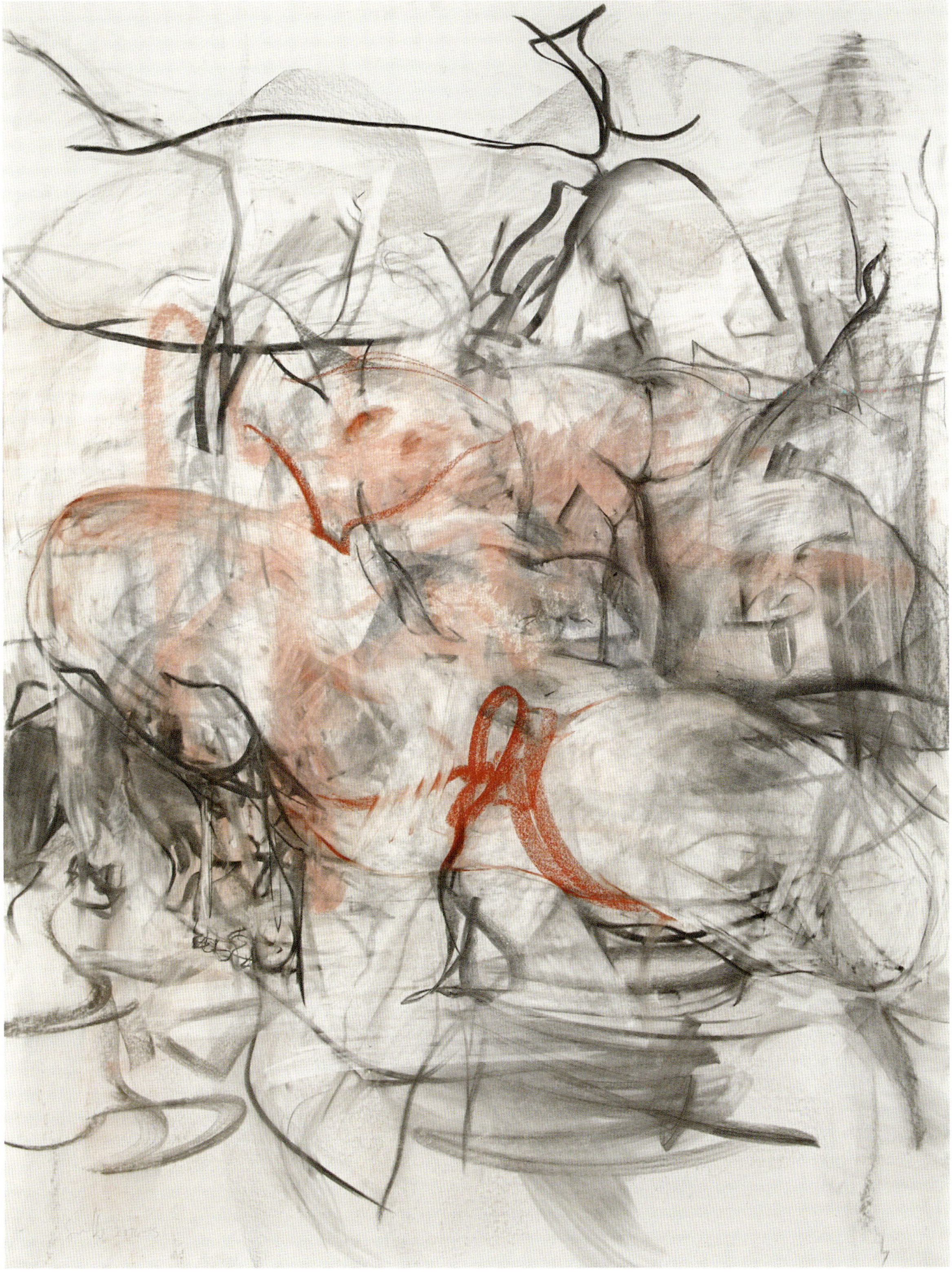

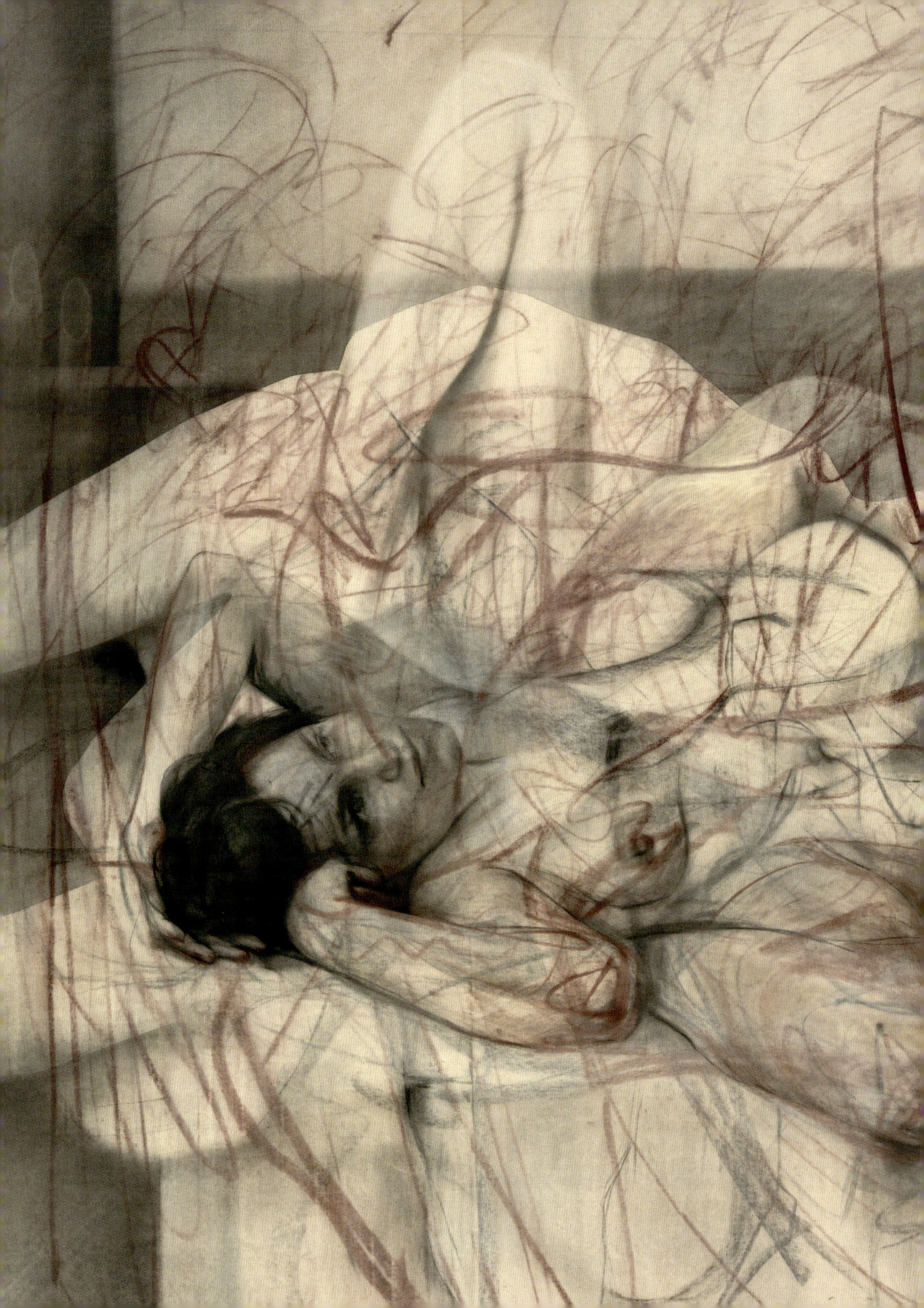

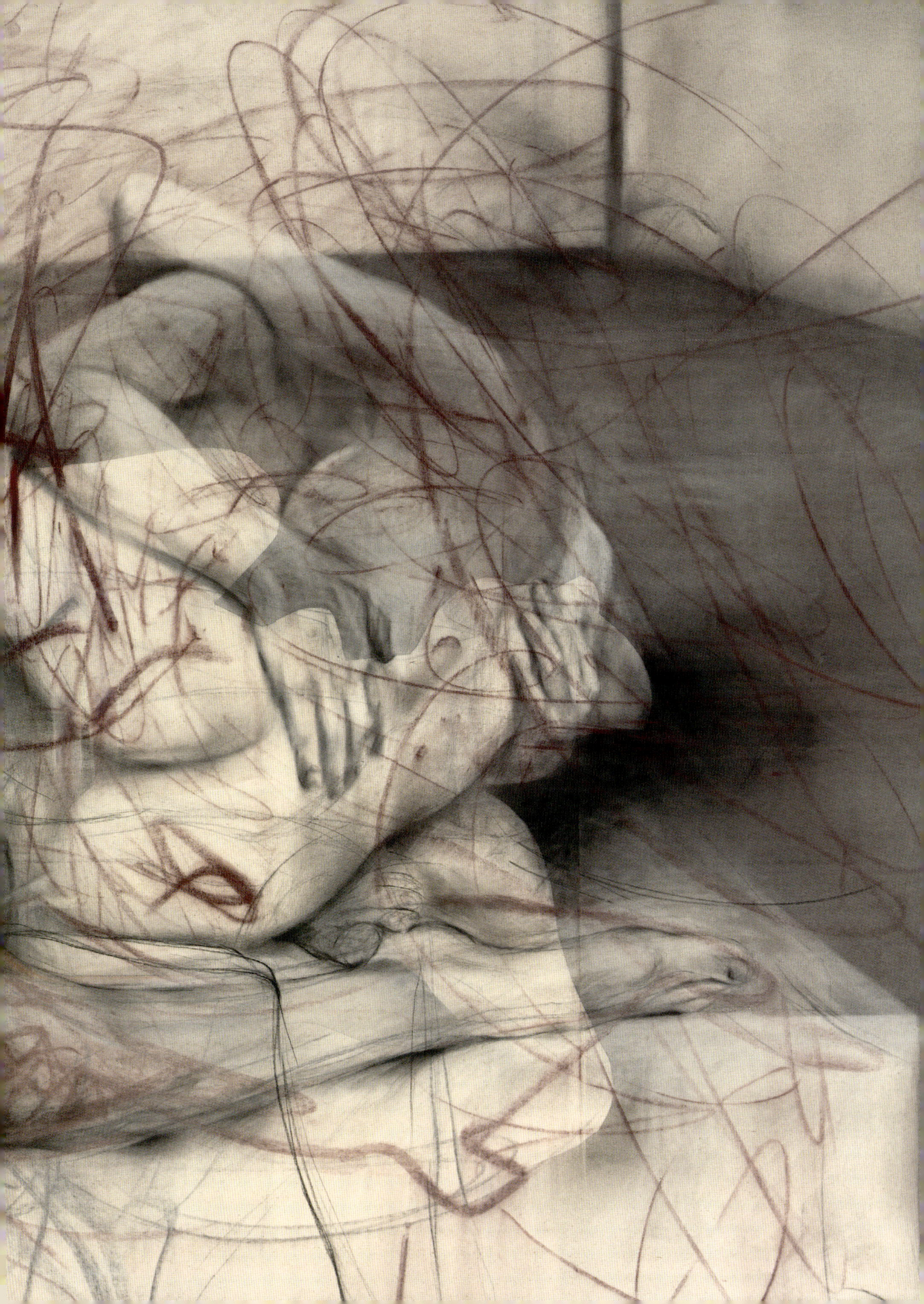

Yinka Shonibare

Yinka Shonibare MBE RA (b. 1962) examines ideas around authenticity, identity and post-colonialism in works that range across drawing, painting, sculpture, photography, film and installation. Shonibare was raised in Britain and Nigeria, and brightly coloured wax-printed fabric, exported from the Netherlands to Africa, is a signature element of his art.

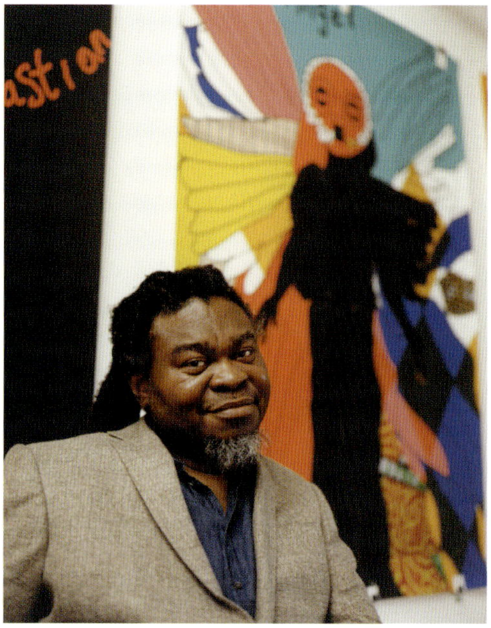

Yinka Shonibare's most celebrated work is a world away from the life class. His *Nelson's Ship in a Bottle* stood in London's Trafalgar Square from 2010 to 2012, one of the series of commissions for the square's empty Fourth Plinth. Now installed at the National Maritime Museum, Greenwich, this 1:30 scale model of the *Victory*, its bright batik sails filled by an invisible breeze, bobs within a great stoppered glass container. There is, though, says the British-Nigerian artist, an invisible kernel within the sculpture of his student days in the life class at the capital's Byam Shaw School of Art: 'I had a strict, formal training, which allows me to do what I do now,' he says. 'If you rebel, you need a point of reference to rebel against.' Shonibare's ship can be seen as the artist sailing away from those pencil-in-hand days.

The body nevertheless remains central to his work. With the help of 3D-scanning technology, Shonibare has made life-size copies of the Royal Academy's casts of the classical sculptures *Discobolus* and the *Townley Venus*. These are bodies that have already gone through a series of transformations. The forms of the ancient Greek originals, now lost, were reproduced in Roman marble copies; the artist-antiquary and Grand Tourist Gavin Hamilton (1723–98) discovered a Roman replica of each sculpture, and from those copies the casts were made that became part of the RA's collection.

Shonibare's own versions offered two more transformations. He covered his statues with the vividly coloured and patterned batik fabrics that are a characteristic of his work. Their convoluted Dutch, Indonesian and African heritage, he says, 'relates to my own history'. The ideal bodies that so fascinated classical sculptors have become emblems of Western civilisation in a globalised world of which the ancients could have barely conceived. 'People thought the original statues were marble-white,' he explains. 'But of course they weren't – that was [the German art historian and archaeologist] Winckelmann's influence in the 1750s and 1760s – they were coloured.'

Venus Presenting Helen to Paris (with Townley Venus)
2017
Virtual-reality presentation

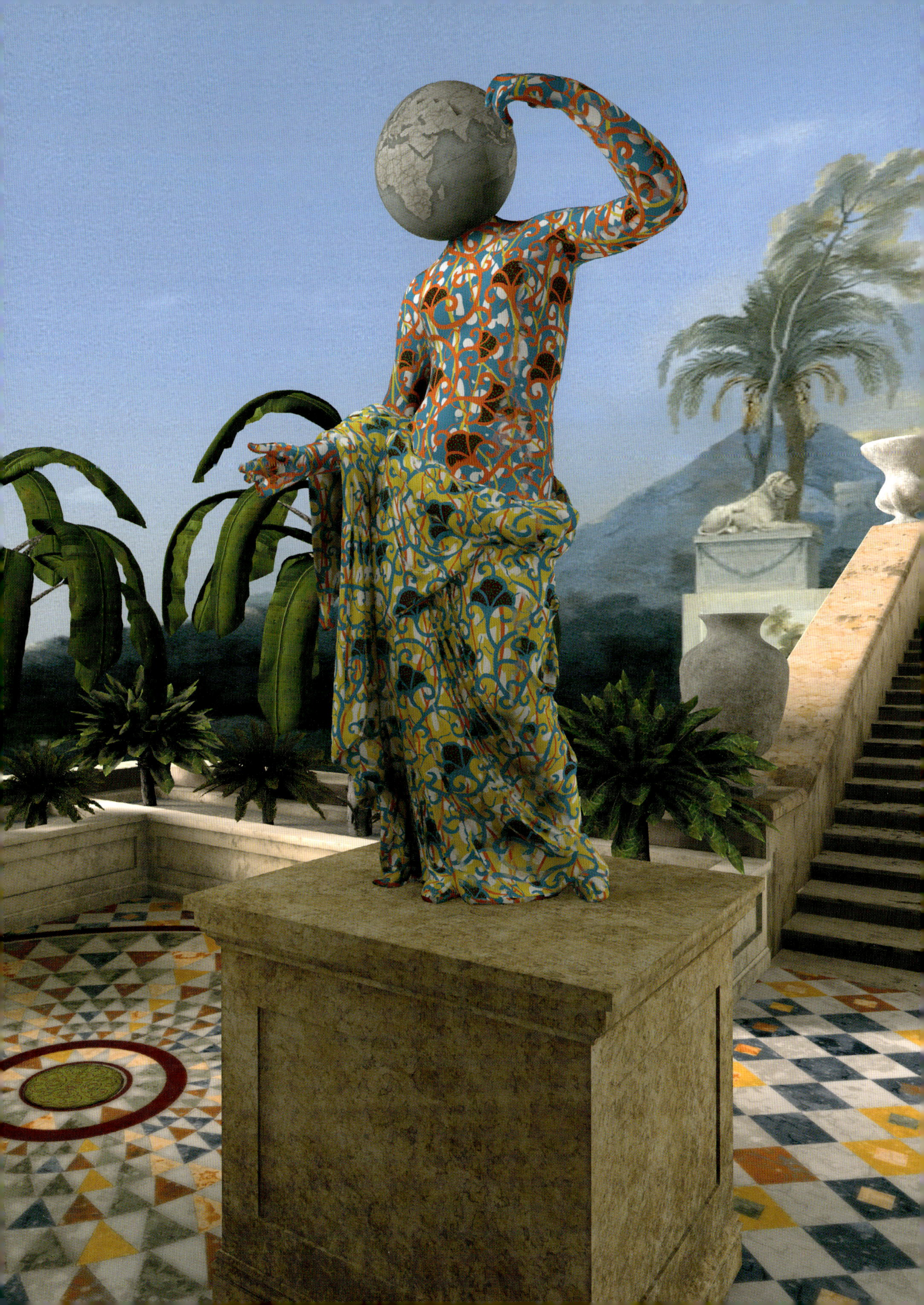

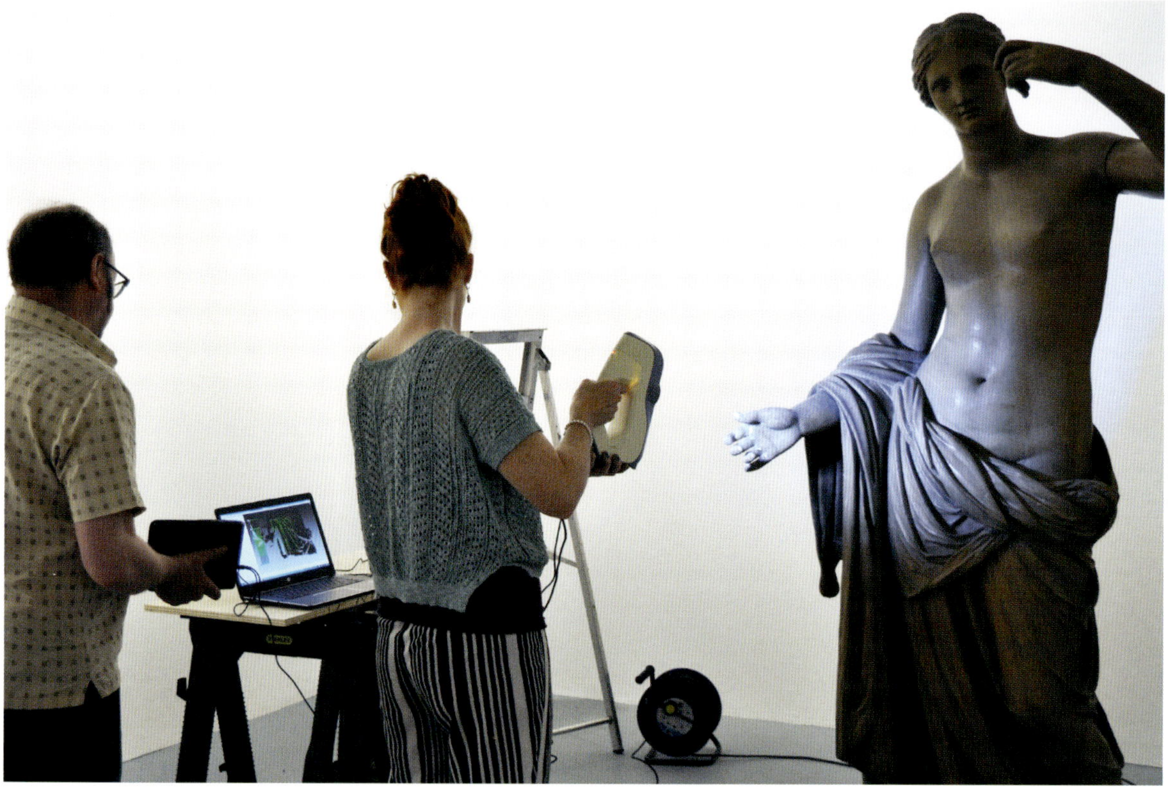

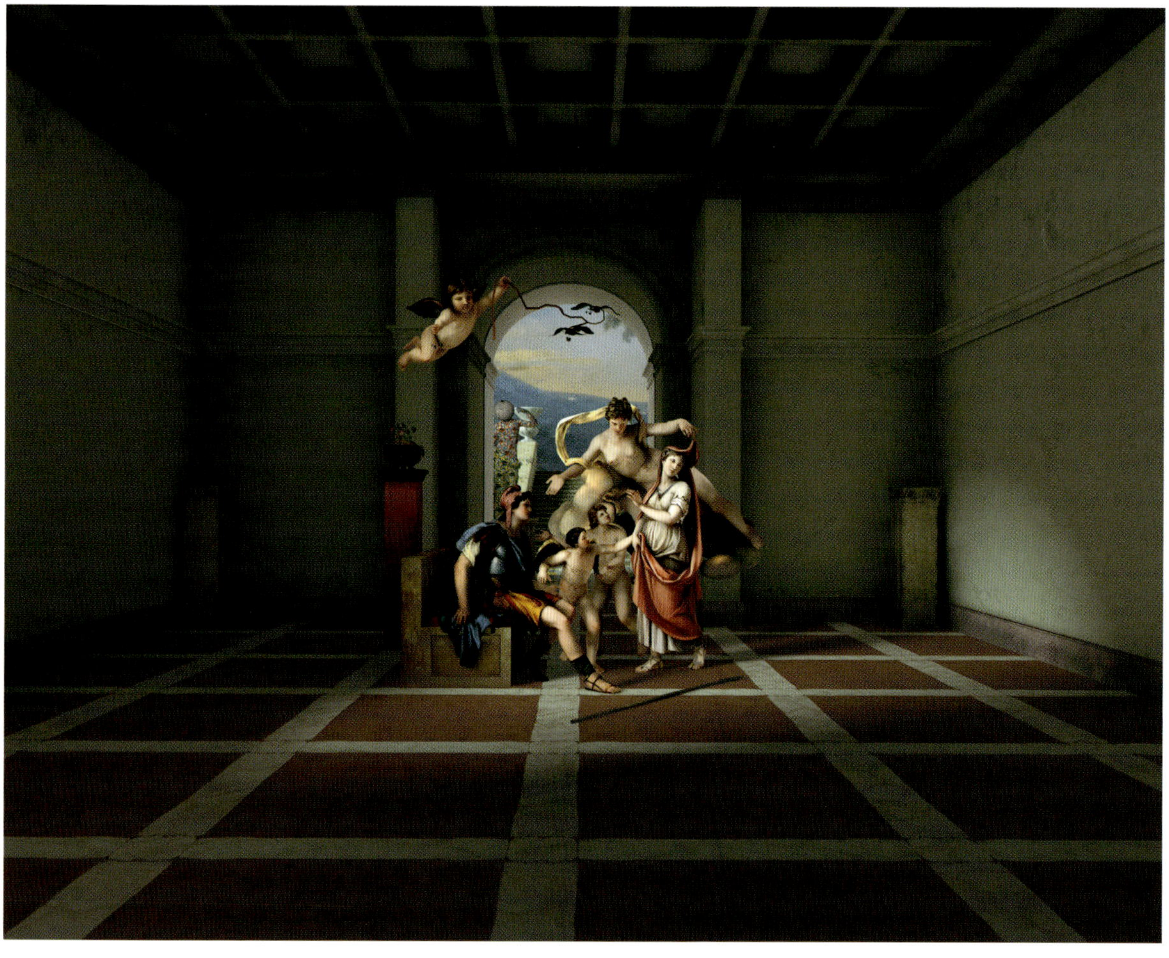

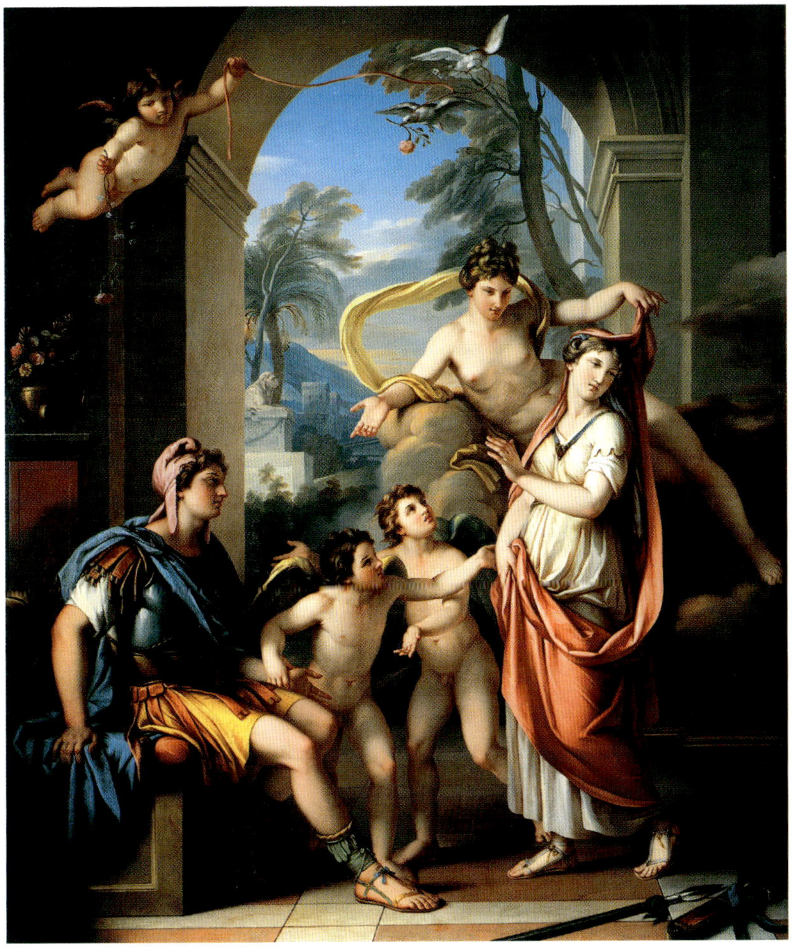

Shonibare's studio team make a 3D scan of the Royal Academy's cast of the *Townley Venus*, which was copied from a Roman replica found by Gavin Hamilton

Venus Presenting Helen to Paris (with Townley Venus)
2017
Virtual-reality presentation

Gavin Hamilton
Venus Presenting Helen to Paris
1785
Oil on canvas
306 x 259 cm
Museo Nazionale Romano, Rome

By transferring patterns onto his sculptures he is both nodding at their original, vibrant appearance and 'taking them away from classical art and making them universal bodies rather than racial ones'.

A further transformation has taken place in virtual reality (VR), using HTC Vive technology. Shonibare has imported his sculpture inspired by the *Townley Venus* into VR, where it has been 'installed' in a recreation of a painting by Hamilton that the user can navigate. This painting – *Venus Presenting Helen to Paris* (1785; Museo Nazionale Romano, Rome) – is one of Hamilton's series that depict scenes from Homer's *Illiad*. 'My idea is that people can enter Hamilton's painting and encounter my sculpture there,' says Shonibare. 'It's a way of showing that Hamilton was an antiquities dealer as well as a painter.'

The casts from the Royal Academy collection that Shonibare has used were among those acquired as teaching aids for the RA Schools. 'I'm interested in origins,' he continues, 'and in the Academy's relationship with antiquity.' Like Hamilton's paintings, the casts are testament to artists' prevailing interest in the classical world during the decades after the Royal Academy's foundation in 1768, an interest inherited from earlier European academies of art as well as the Renaissance masters, who remained exemplars of artistic practice. It was those casts – scrutinised, drawn and sculpted – that gave RA students the grounding from which they went on to experiment; indeed, before students were allowed to work from life models they were obliged to study the Academy's cast collection.

Shonibare contracted transverse myelitis at the age of 18, which left him with limited mobility. As a result, most of his work is now conceived on the computer and fabricated by assistants. He has in the past used his own body in his work, notably in a photographic series from 1998 in which he adopted the role of a Victorian dandy (see overleaf): 'Art never used to see a body like mine, certainly not in the life class.' By including it in his work

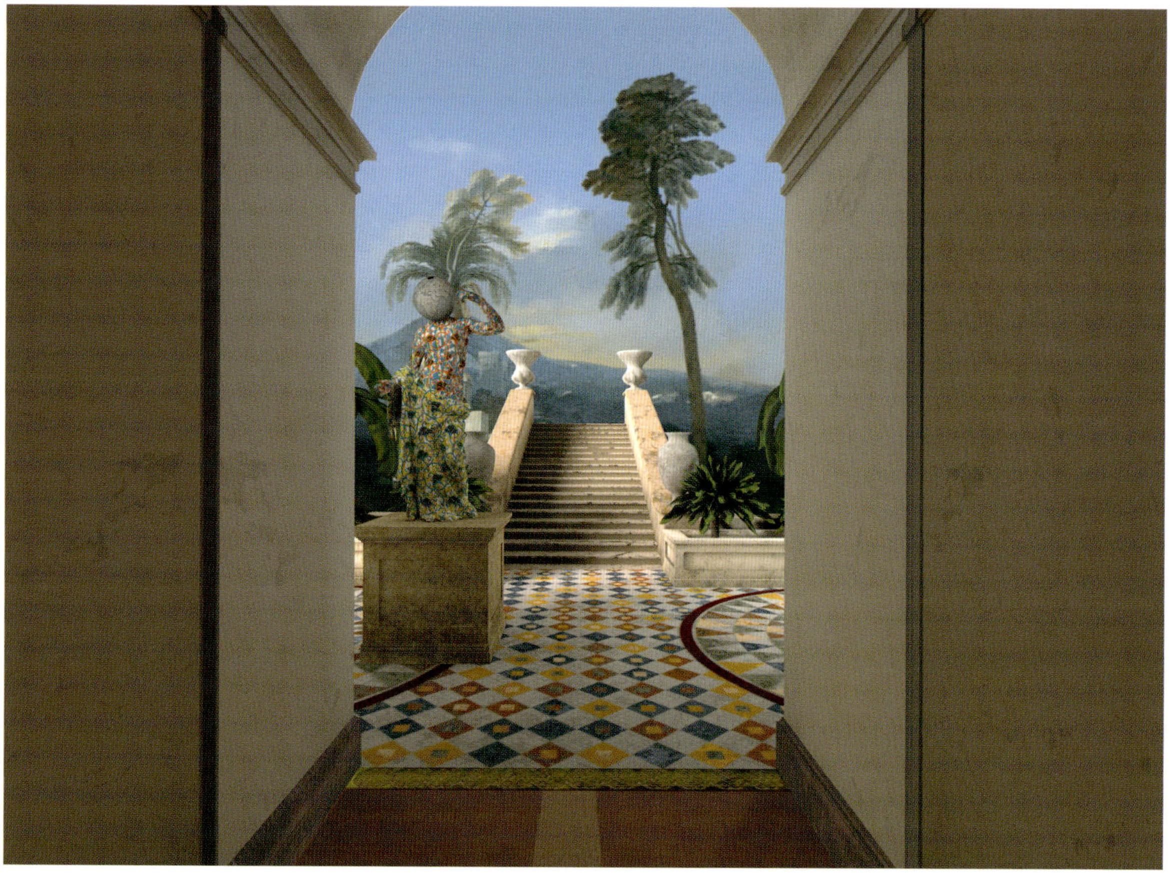

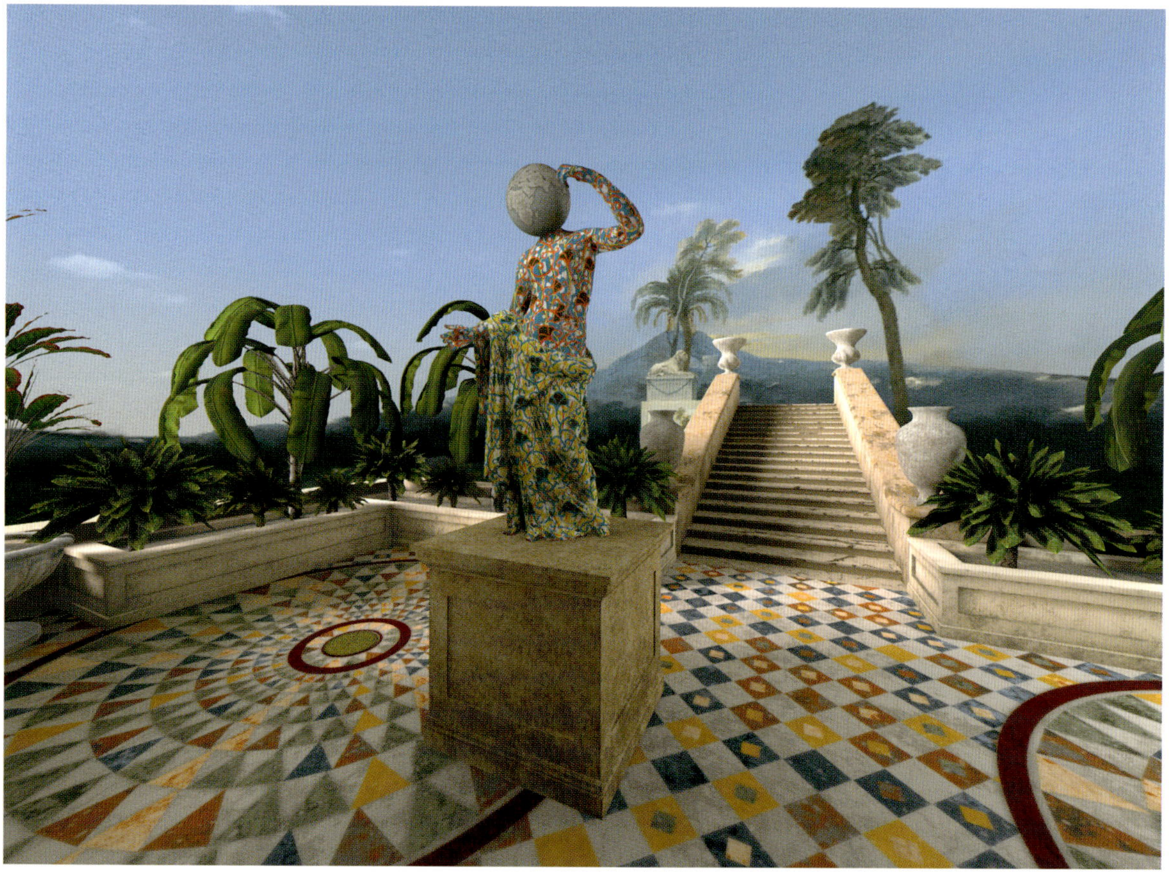

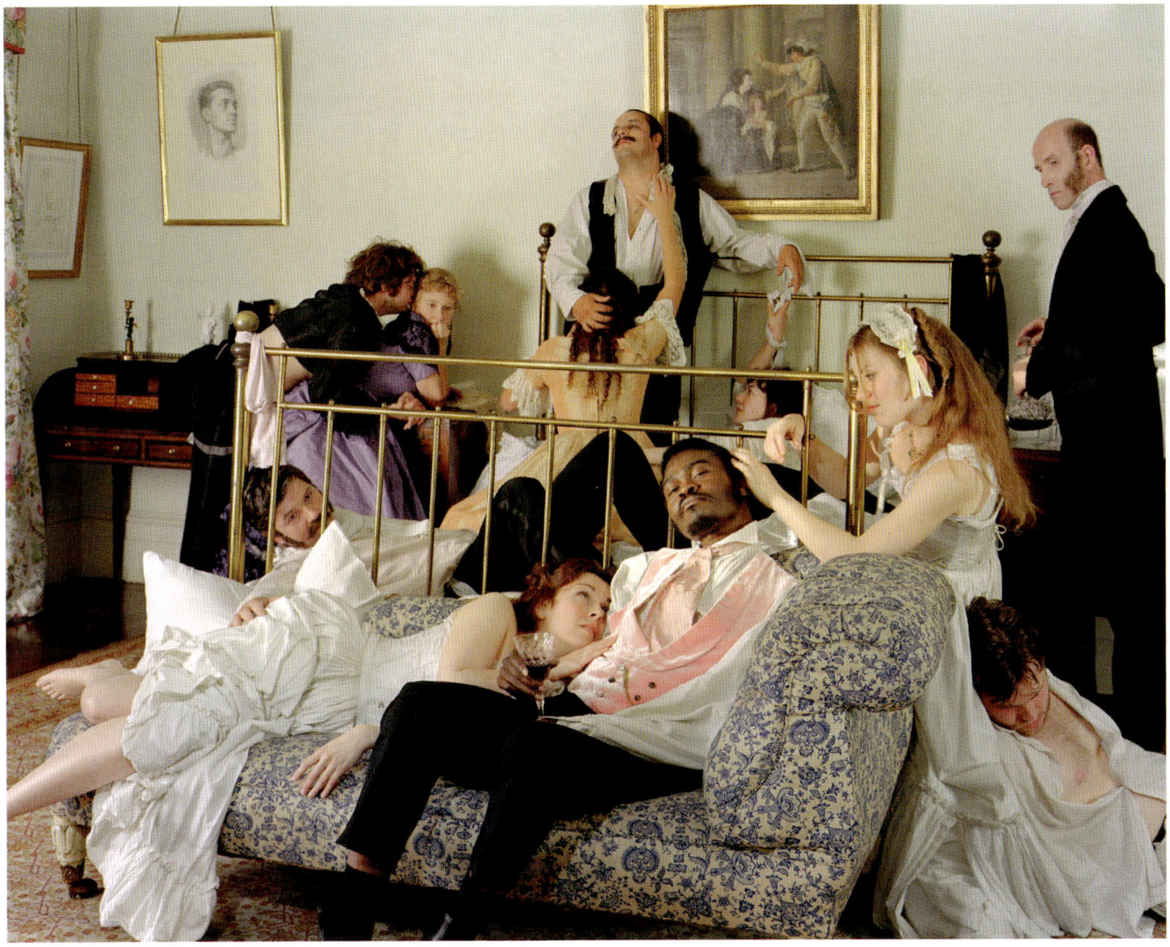

Diary of a Victorian Dandy: 03.00 Hours
1998
C-type print
122 x 183 cm

he intended to show that there is no such thing as the ideal body. 'I wanted the visual memory of people to be diverse.'

The role of working from life is different now from the more doctrinaire days of the RA's formation, Shonibare believes. Life drawing still has a role, he says, but only if it is relevant to an individual artist's work: 'Art is no longer about verisimilitude, the accurate depiction of the human body.' And there are aspects of life drawing of which he doesn't approve: 'A naked woman lying down and being drawn ... that's socially problematical.' He still sometimes draws from life, acknowledging that 'it is a very different process from using a computer. Computer work is not based on direct observation.'

Extending the possibilities of classical statuary has a strong appeal to the artist, and not just because he is fascinated by the way the eighteenth century shaped our perceptions of the world. Shonibare sees his art as 'a form of myth-making, fantasy rather than reality'. He makes works that he hopes will carry the atmosphere of a dream and make the viewer go 'Wow' (that urge is certainly behind his use of VR). For this he occasionally needs the body to assume unnatural poses, and mannequins and artificial figures can be made 'to do things that real people can't do – they'd do themselves an injury.'

'I've gone looking for the ideal body in art history,' he says, 'but it is a means to an end, the means by which to explore social and aesthetic issues. For me, it has never been about simple anatomy.' There are similarities, he believes, between the current objectification of the body – on billboards, television and in magazines – and life drawing. Eighteenth-century artists studied partially clothed or naked bodies only in life classes, but now we see them everywhere in every context. 'What's the difference between Hogarth and *Hello!* magazine?' he asks. 'They just use different media.'

Michael Prodger

Venus Presenting Helen to Paris (with Townley Venus)
2017
Virtual-reality presentation

Gillian Wearing

Conceptual artist Gillian Wearing OBE RA (b. 1963) uses elaborate masks, costumes and role-play in her work to explore personal and cultural histories, as well as the influence of the media. Awarded the Turner Prize in 1997, Wearing lives and works in London. She has been commissioned to create a sculpture of the suffragist leader Millicent Fawcett for Parliament Square.

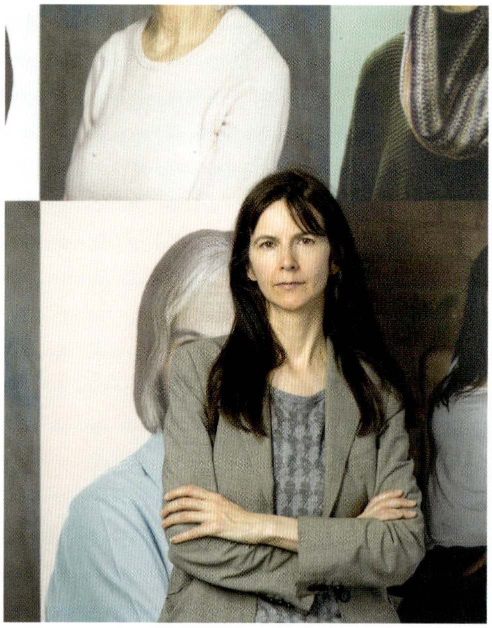

To create her photographs, which she describes as being akin to sculpture, Gillian Wearing makes and wears masks, complete with wigs, that represent members of her family – or her spiritual family, those artists who have been important to her. Only the subject's eyes are omitted from the mask, so that when Wearing takes the photograph, her own eyes are visible beneath the façade.

Confronting issues of identity and self-presentation, the photographs appear to be neither portrait nor self-portrait but rather something between the two. For Wearing there is no such ambiguity. 'I sometimes get asked what my family think about being in my work,' she explains, 'but I have to correct that question, as they are not and have never been in the work. All the portraits are of me.'

'I slip on a subjective identity of someone else, from my perspective,' she continues. 'The choices I make of the image I re-create, whether it's an actual existing image or an invented one, are also part of that process. I am creating the environment, the age I want to portray that person and the image that most sums up a bit of them and a bit of me. The masks I wear are hyper-real, the lines in each face modelled originally in clay before being cast in silicone. They are surfaces without blood or veins. My eyes are the only real feature; they are there to bring life to the inanimate mask.'

Despite their immediacy these works are far from spontaneous: 'When you work with the past you have to try and avoid the sentimental and find something else about the subject. *Self-portrait as My Brother Richard Wearing* (2003) is based on a snap my mother took in 1991. I loved it then because it felt very present. I wanted to do something with it, but like many ideas it took time to evolve, to find the perfect way to express something observed. In this case it took 12 years to come to fruition.'

Wearing's earliest formal training was at Sir John Cass School of Art in London, where she attended night classes in the 1980s. 'Being taught to draw or sculpt in those days was always with

Self-portrait as My Brother Richard Wearing
2003
Digital C-type print
191 x 130.5 cm

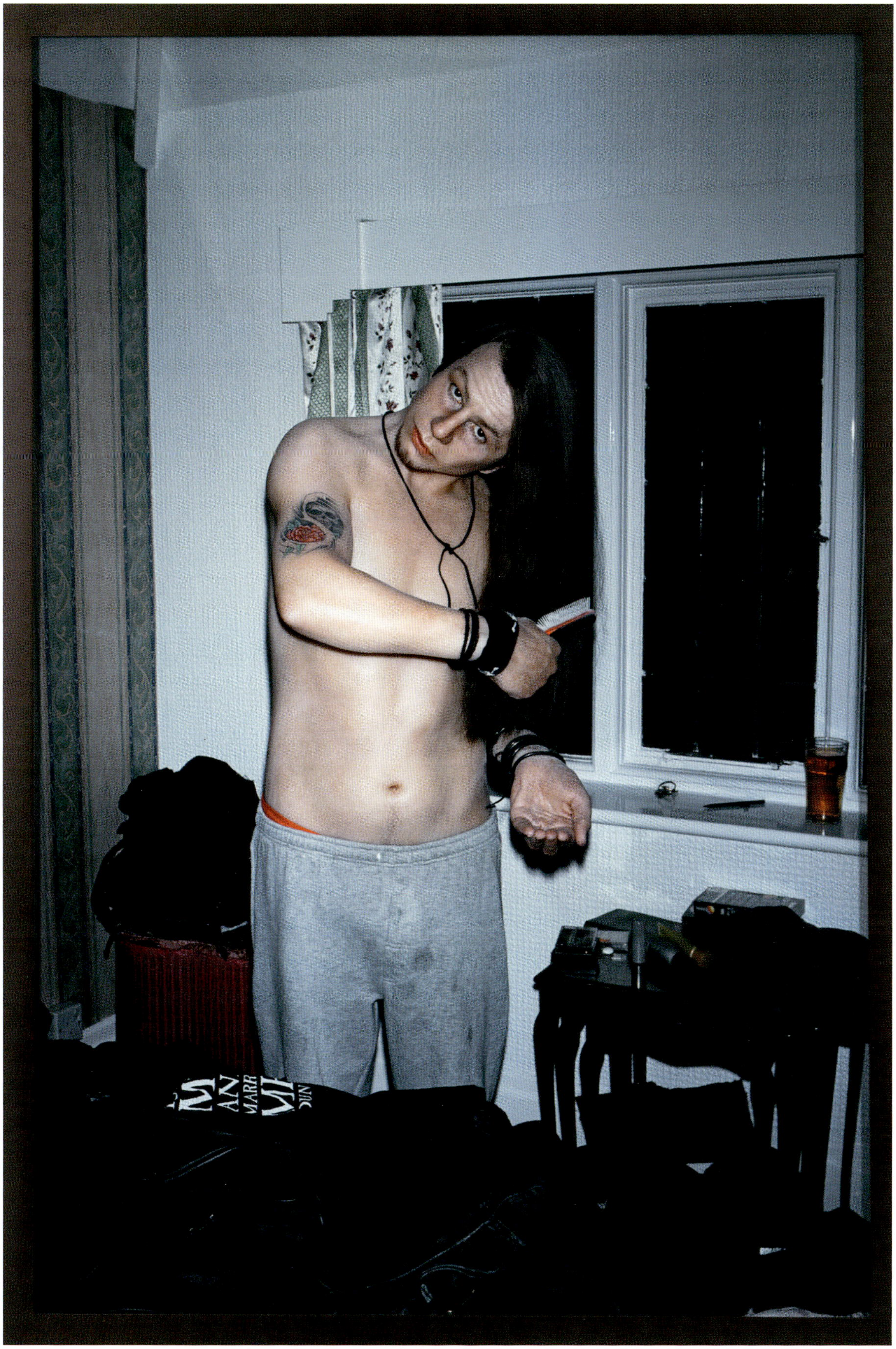

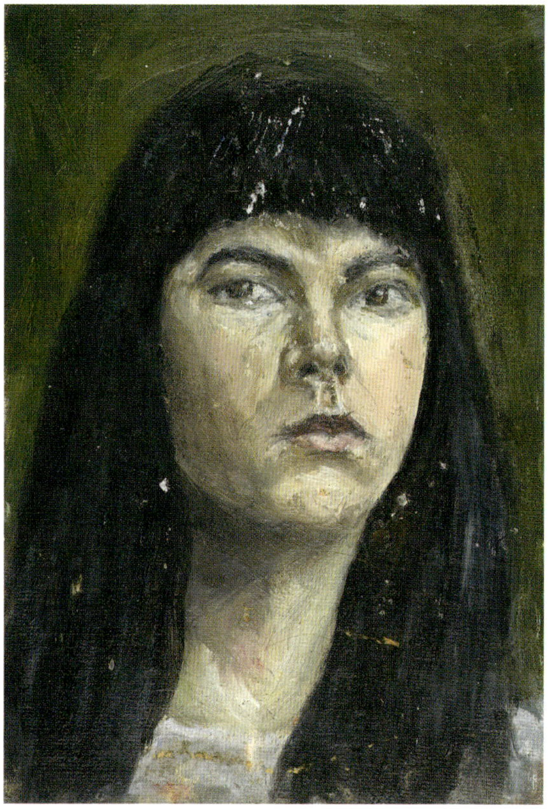

Self-portrait
1985
Oil on panel
25.4 x 17.5 cm

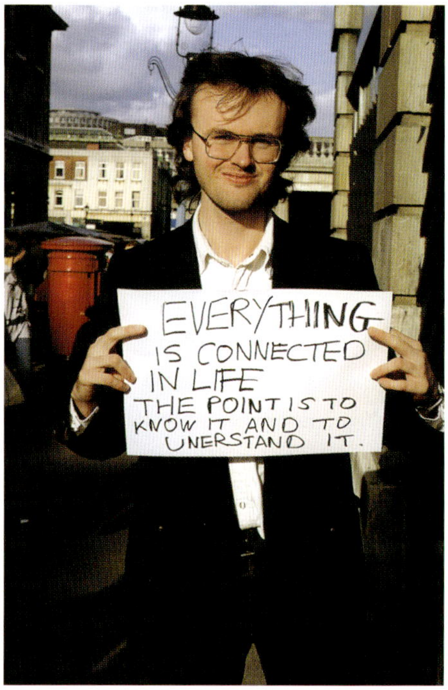

Signs that say what you want them to say and not Signs that say what someone else wants you to say (Everything is connected in life. The point is to know it and to understand it.)
1992–93
C-type print
119 x 79 cm

a life model,' she recalls. 'Drawing taught me to look. The habit at the beginning was to look up quickly and then draw what you thought you had seen, but the challenge is really to look and really try and draw what is there in front of you.'

When Wearing applied to Goldsmiths in 1987, life drawing had been banned because of its objectification of women. 'It was very conflicting for me, as my portfolio consisted of many life drawings of men and women. I tried to present a feminist argument for them at my application interview. I realised there and then that my art would change. I was becoming more attuned to the idea of questioning why I was making or wanted to make an artwork. I do, however, still believe that drawing – the head and hand connection – is really important and worthwhile.' Drawing also remains central to her creative process: 'I find I have a different way of thinking when I write words and ideas down as opposed to typing them. The same with drawing. You can try things out.' For example, before filming her video work *Sacha and Mum* (1994), she sketched out on paper the scenes of mother and daughter.

One of her most famous series is 'Signs that say what you want them to say and not Signs that say what someone else wants you to say' (1992–93), in which people are photographed on the street holding up handwritten signs expressing their thoughts. One woman she approached suggested that she draw Wearing's portrait rather than capture her thoughts on a piece of paper. 'She did a lovely simplified sketch of me,' Wearing recollects. 'So after that I asked some more strangers to draw me; some people got my likeness right and some less so. But what impressed me was everyone's willingness to try and draw me there on the spot, in the street.' The result, *Portraits of me, by people I don't know* (1993), is published here, alongside her own 'very earnest' self-portrait from 1985. Elsewhere we see *Landy Family. Gillian* (2007, see page 83), a portrait by Michael Landy RA, her partner. 'It was physically

Portraits of me, by people I don't know
1993
Pen on paper
12 parts
Each 29.7 x 21 cm

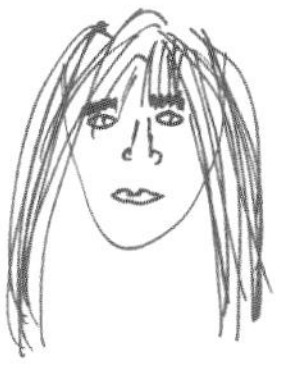

23-6-93

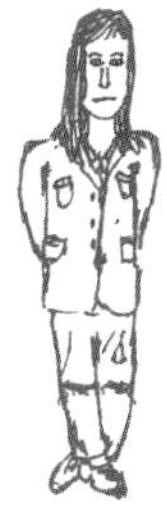

23/6/93

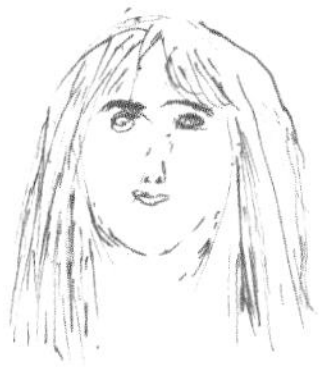

23/6/93

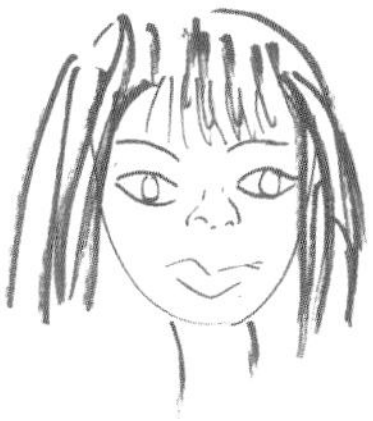

Nurun
23/6/93.

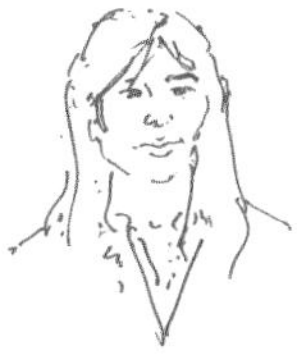

23/6/93

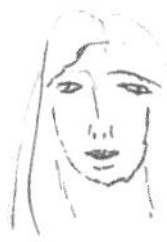

23-6-93

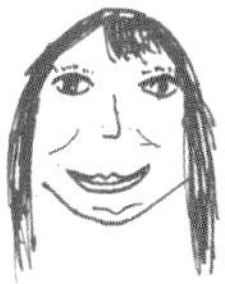

23/6/93

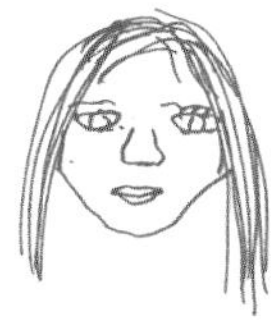

23/6/93

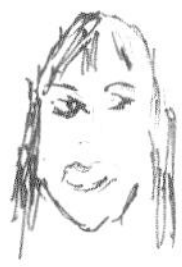

MICHAEL
23/6/93.

E YOUNGER 23-6-93

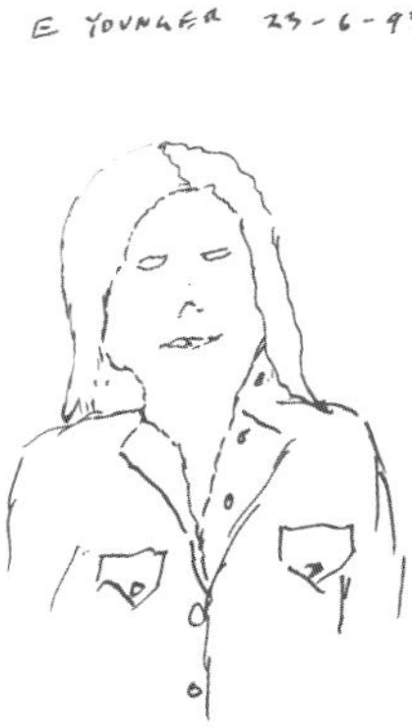

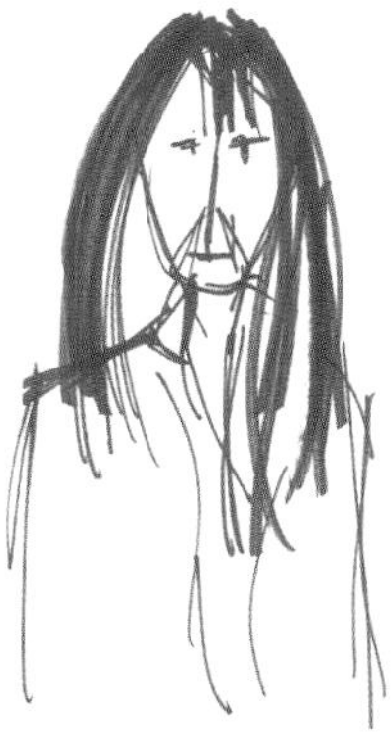

23/6/93

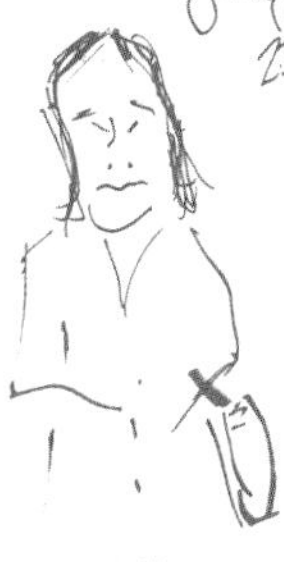

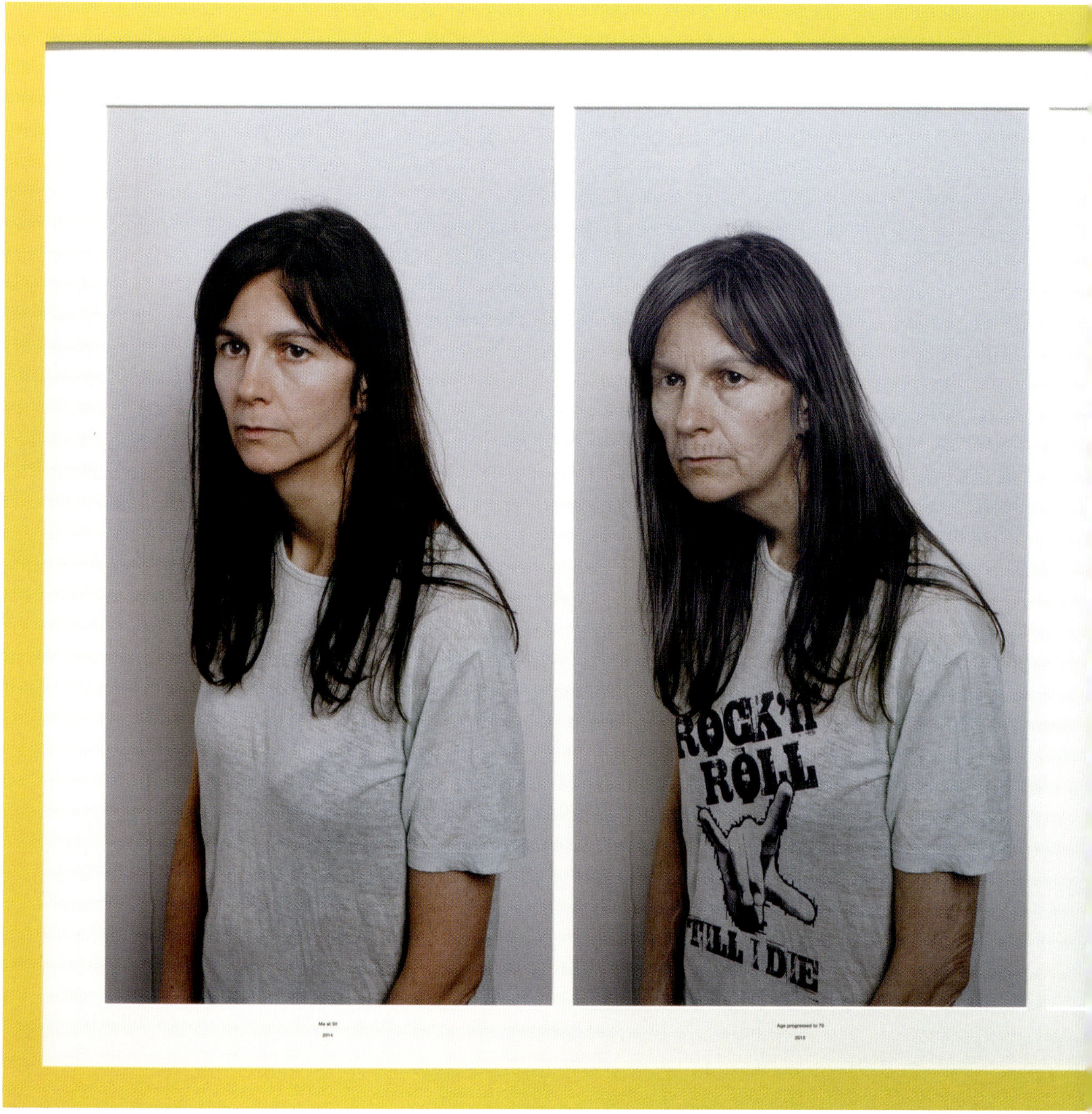

Rock 'n' Roll 70
2015
Framed C-type prints
131 x 192 cm

Texts, from left to right:
'Me at 50, 2014'
'Age progressed to 70, 2015'
'Me at 70, 2034'

Overleaf:
Rock 'n' Roll 70 wallpaper
2014
Printed wallpaper
Dimensions variable

challenging, sitting on a hard bench for two days solid, just staring. We had been partners for many years but had never spent that much time looking intently at each other, so it was rather a beautiful experience.'

For another work, *Rock 'n' Roll 70* (2015), Wearing collaborated with forensic artists working with age-progression technology, in order to represent how she might look at 70. However, she chooses carefully when to embrace technological innovation in her work. 'When you have a new idea, there are so many potential ways to create it. Lots of choices don't actually make you feel freer. It's tempting to think of technology over content, but I resist and just identify the right process. My experience from art school onwards has always been that art can be anything, so advances in technology are just another addition to a whole array of things that art can be made from.' Wearing's work focuses on life across time. Whether drawn from the past or projecting into the future, it is intensely personal, ultimately reflecting her life in the present.

Adrian Locke

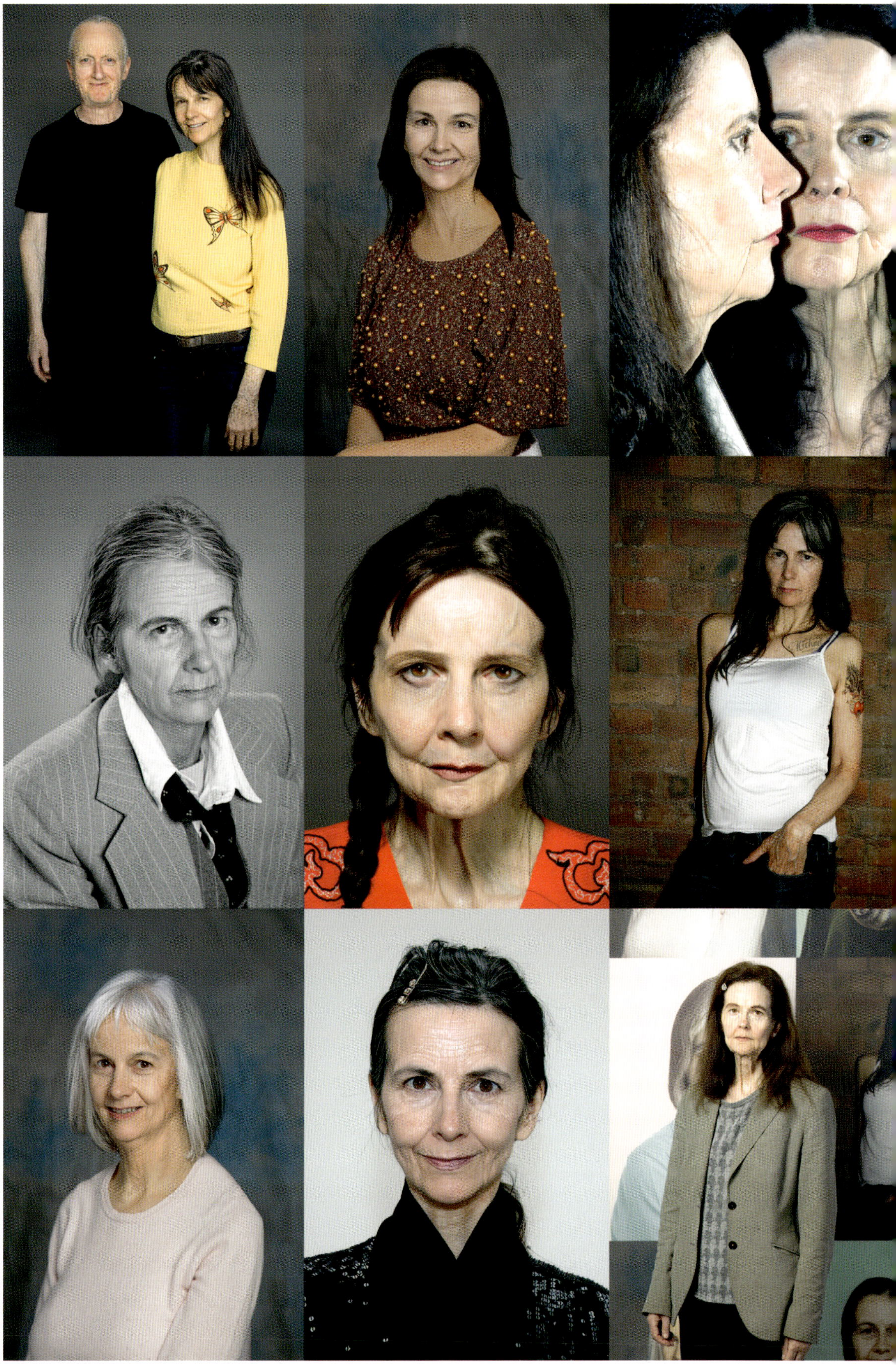

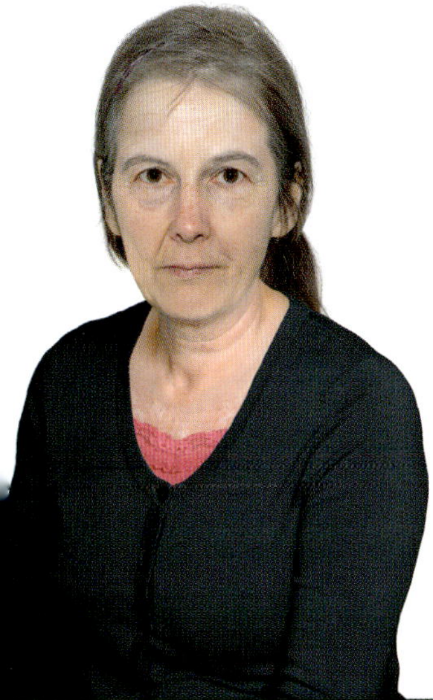
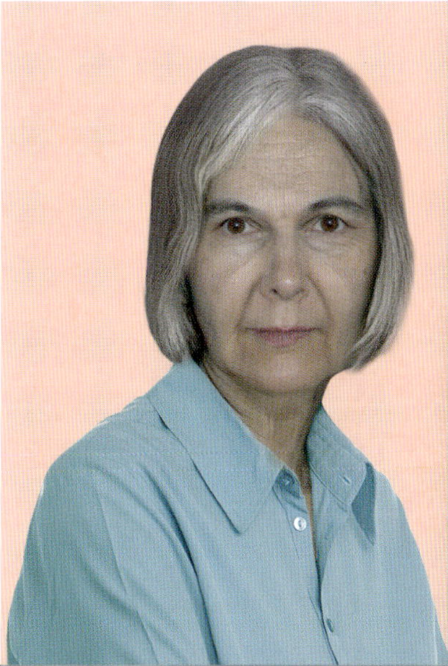
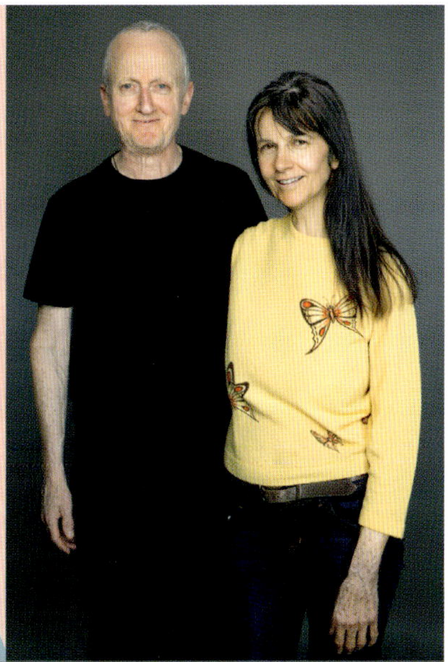
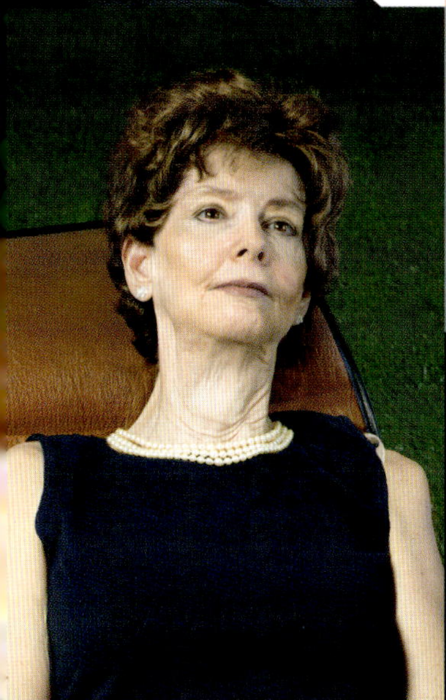
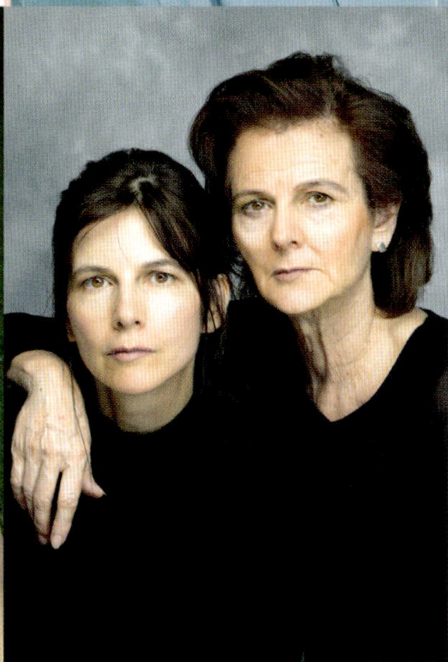
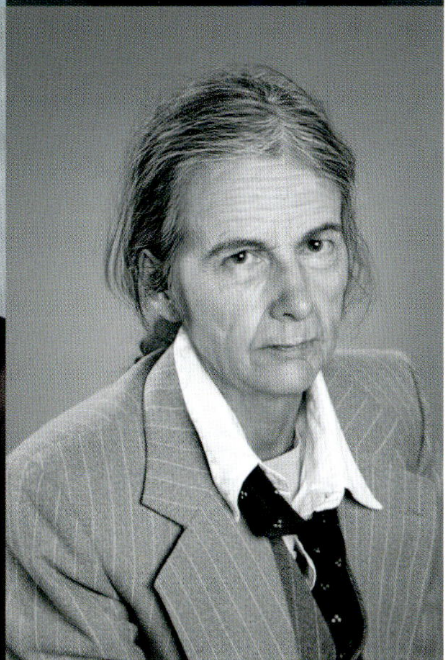
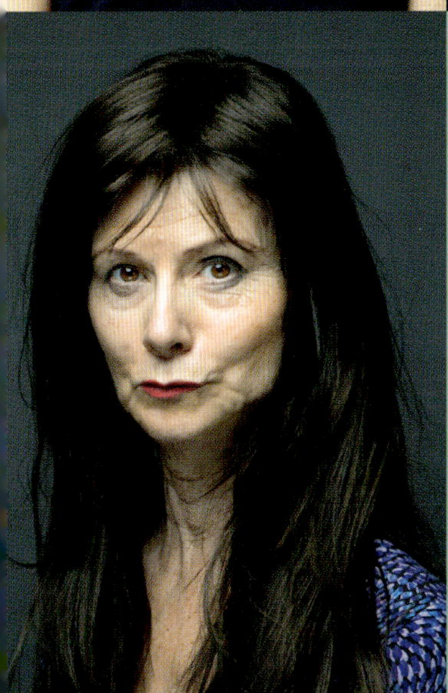
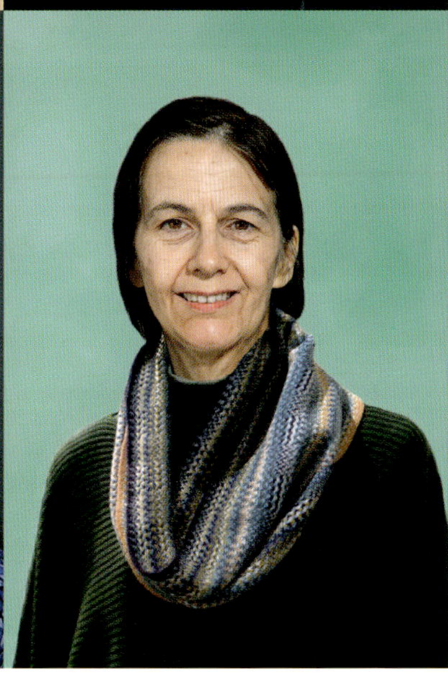
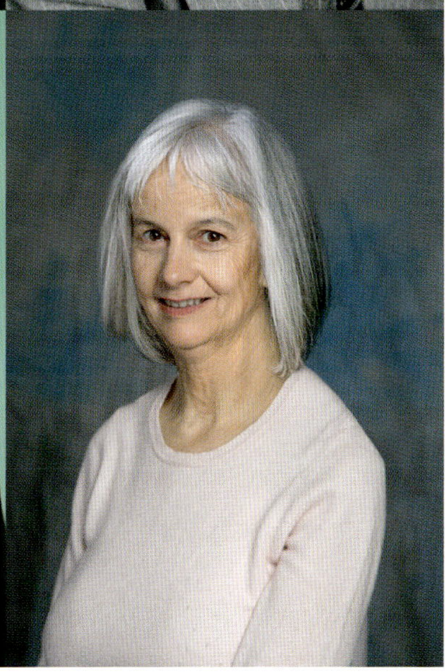

Jonathan Yeo

Jonathan Yeo (b. 1970) is renowned for portraits of well-known figures including Hollywood actors and British politicians. He embraces a wide range of techniques, expanding the traditional parameters of the genre with the use of emerging technology. The British painter was the subject of a retrospective at the National Portrait Gallery (2013–14) in London, where he lives and works.

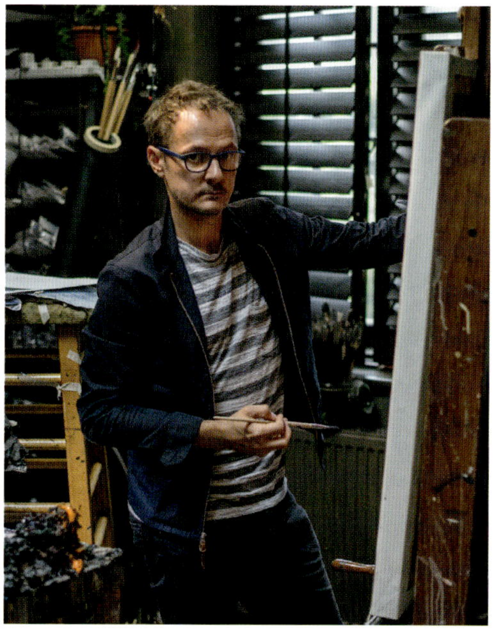

At first glance, Jonathan Yeo's painting studio seems a quite conventional portraitist's set-up. An easel supporting a canvas stands at its heart, with a palette lying next to it, congealed piles of blackening, discarded oil paint at its edges. A comfortable chair sits opposite the easel, waiting for a subject, and lights for the sitter and the painter surround the ensemble. Nearby, Yeo has arranged what he calls 'various objects and junk', a mini cabinet of curiosities that he has collected to distract his sitters and make them less self-conscious.

Yeo is entirely self-taught, and began his career making fairly orthodox, accomplished portraits – he came to prominence for his commissioned picture of the former British Prime Minister Tony Blair in 2007, and has since painted numerous leading public figures, ranging from royalty to actors, models and fellow artists. But now he rarely undertakes commissions and few paintings he makes in the studio today could be described as conventional. 'I was, in retrospect, quite fortunate to have spent several years just doing portraits,' he reflects, 'because it does force you to be quite precise about things, and gives you an understanding of a genre from which you can then deviate. I've always liked seeing it as a starting point for experimenting and playing with people's expectations.'

The idea of making work 'from life', and what that might mean, is at the core of Yeo's practice. His paintings of people are informed by formal sittings and photographs shot in the studio. He welcomes different lighting for different sittings, from natural light pouring in from the side of his subjects to artificial light from above, so that 'a sort of composite image' emerges of the person, reflecting multiple moods and shifts in appearance. 'The variation of light can be very helpful,' he explains. 'It helps make the painting come to life.'

But the final image is the result of what Yeo calls the 'live experience', which includes other, informal interactions. He speaks of how people relax at the end of a formal sitting, but the observation doesn't

The Preserving Machine
2017
Oil on canvas
101.5 x 76 cm

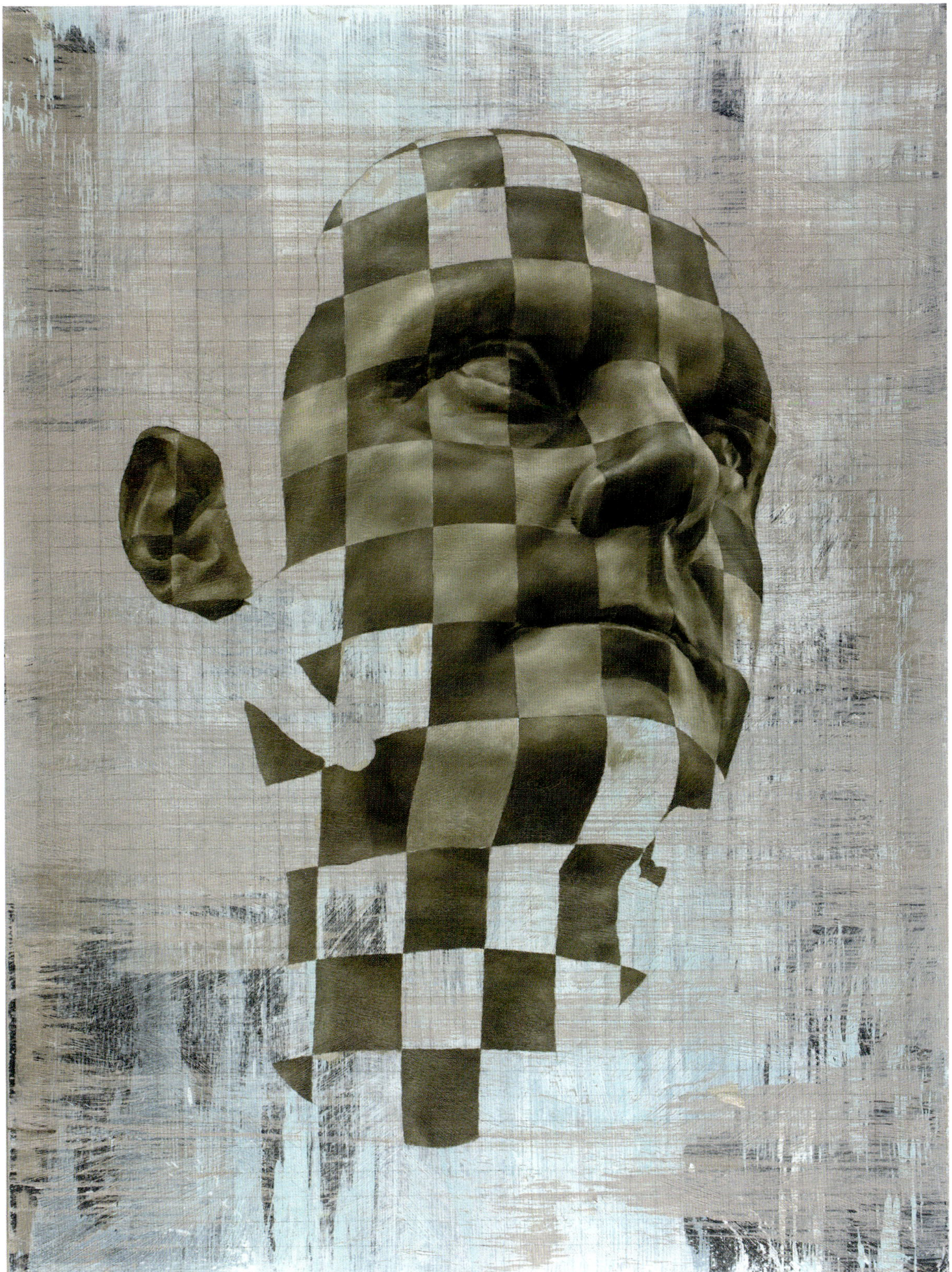

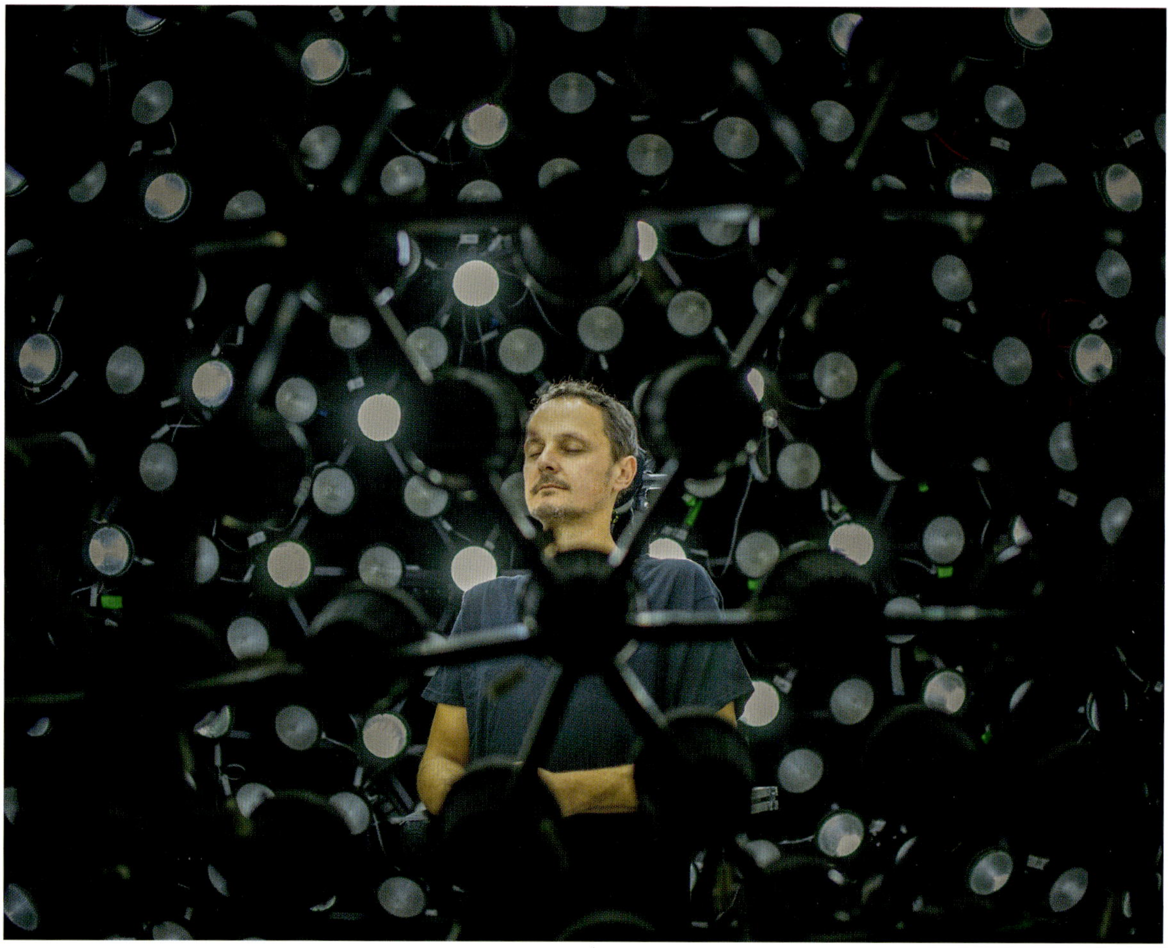

Jonathan Yeo prepares for facial scanning at OTOY LightStage in Burbank, California

end there. 'You go out for lunch, and then you can look at them, just when they think that you're no longer looking at them. That's when you see things that are much more relevant.' As he balances the formal and informal encounters, his paintings are increasingly concerned as much with what he omits as what he includes, with some elements of faces and figures precisely depicted and large areas of the canvas left more indistinct or inchoate. 'I've always preferred images where you get different elements, particularly things that are very sharp and in focus and things that are very abstract, within the same picture,' he says. 'I have always thought that must be closer to how we actually retain images in memory, which is something that I have tried to demonstrate in the work; it wasn't just an excuse for being lazy and not finishing certain bits.'

A recent series of self-portraits relate to body scans Yeo made of himself at OTOY, a California-based graphics company that pioneers some of the most sophisticated 3D scanning techniques on the planet. The artist captured himself in minute detail and high definition, in a process that avoided some of the traditional limitations of self-portraiture, such as when a likeness is necessarily reversed when painted from a mirror, or flattened and set at a single angle when represented in a photograph. Yeo studied the scans to paint self-portraits from different perspectives and in a range of styles: one engages with the idea of an artificial intelligence, casting him as a kind of robot; another evokes digital backgrounds, and accentuates the contours of his face, by covering his head with a chequerboard pattern (see page 151); and a third wittily plays on gaps in some of the scanned images by depicting his head almost as if it were a damaged ancient marble bust.

But the 3D scans offered even more possibilities when Yeo found out that they could be imported into the world of virtual reality (VR). Wearing an HTC Vive headset, he could observe a virtual representation of himself. 'You can look at yourself, walk all the way around yourself,

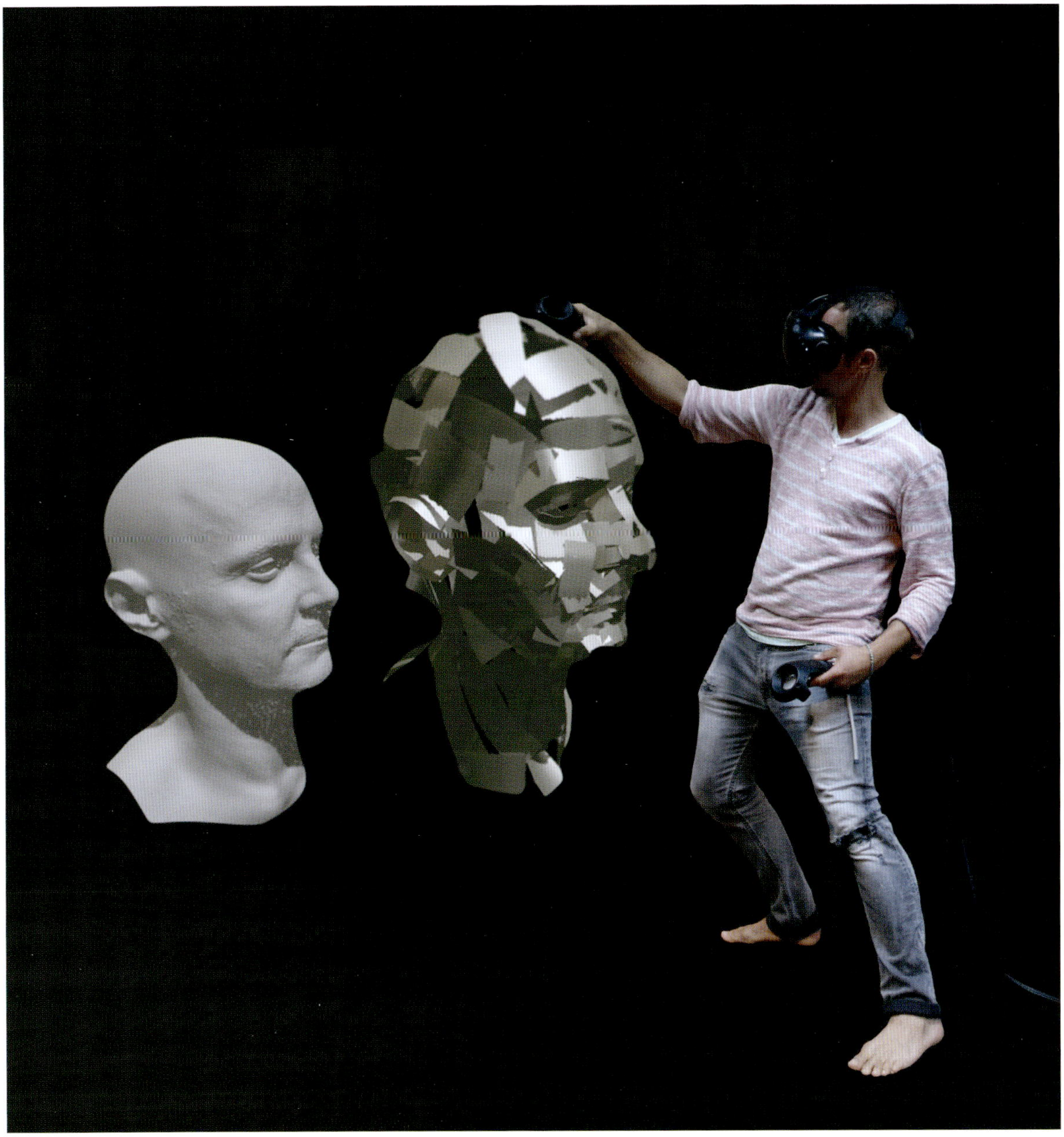

Yeo works from his facial scan inside virtual reality, using Google's Tilt Brush software to create self-portraits

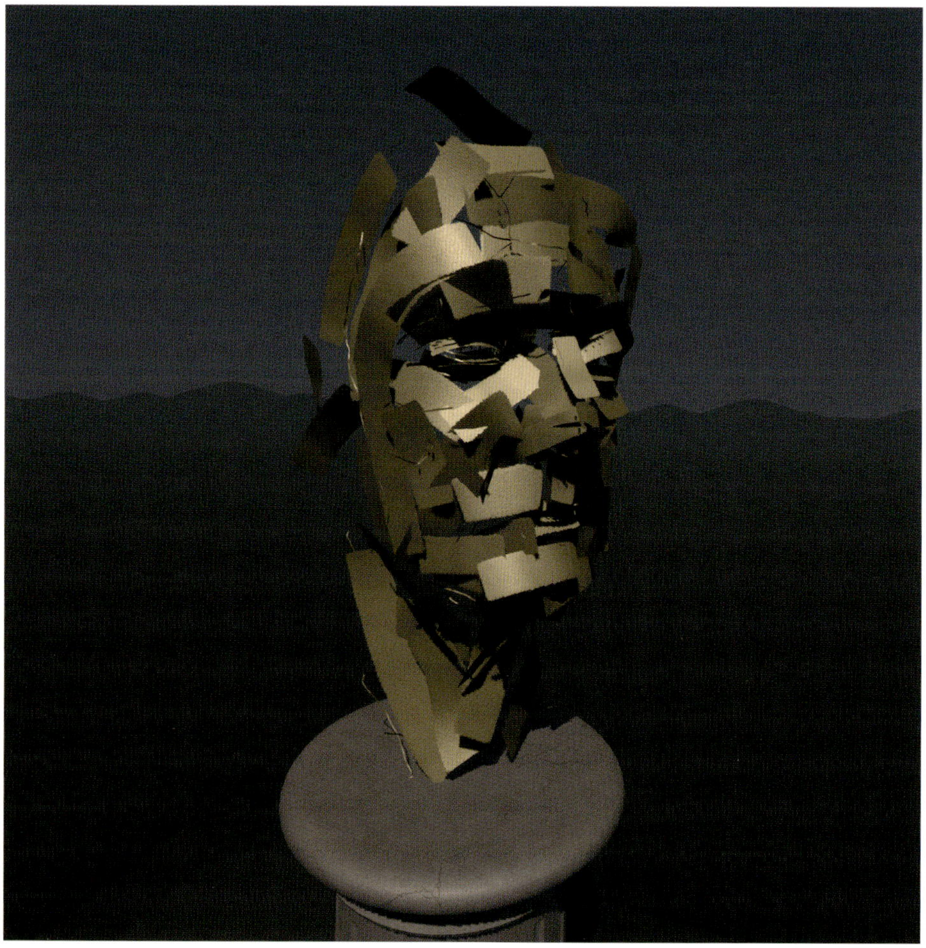

An experimental study for Yeo's virtual-reality self-portrait, using Google's Tilt Brush software

Homage to Paolozzi (Self-portrait)
2017
Bronze
100 x 66 x 56 cm

light yourself as if you were another person.' He was invited to experiment with Google's Tilt Brush software, using the wireless controllers that allow artists to make marks within a virtual space – when a headset is worn, the wireless controllers become palette and paintbrush. Yeo decided to make self-portraits with Tilt Brush; moving around the 3D scan of himself, he made likenesses of his likeness. 'These marks made in a gestural or free way are then locked in there, in VR, absolutely precisely – you can then move around them and view them from different angles, as if you were viewing a sculpture. So it seemed obvious that I should export my self-portrait out of VR and into physical reality, where it could take up real space.'

It is an entirely new artistic technique, but there is a characteristic twist in Yeo's approach to this new dawn: his virtual self-portrait has been cast in one of the most ancient materials, bronze. 'It just seemed logical to make it out of a material that is as old as any art material,' he says. He suggests that 'something that's irrefutably permanent and eternal is really important' for a project that is realised through virtual means. Yeo has collaborated on the bronze with Pangolin, the British sculpture foundry that works with leading international artists and is particularly associated with Damien Hirst. 'It's only in the last few months – weeks even – that it has been possible to extract and repurpose the VR files in this way,' Yeo explains. 'This development has also happened to coincide with the latest developments in 3D printing, which has made the casting possible.'

The resulting bust has a 'solidity but also a lightness', Yeo says, which evokes the fact that it has been made with Tilt Brush, a new medium that 'has much more in common with painting than sculpture,' he suggests. 'I am not a sculptor, so you get a sense by looking at the work that it must have been made in a different way – a sense of movement and energy and light.'

Ben Luke

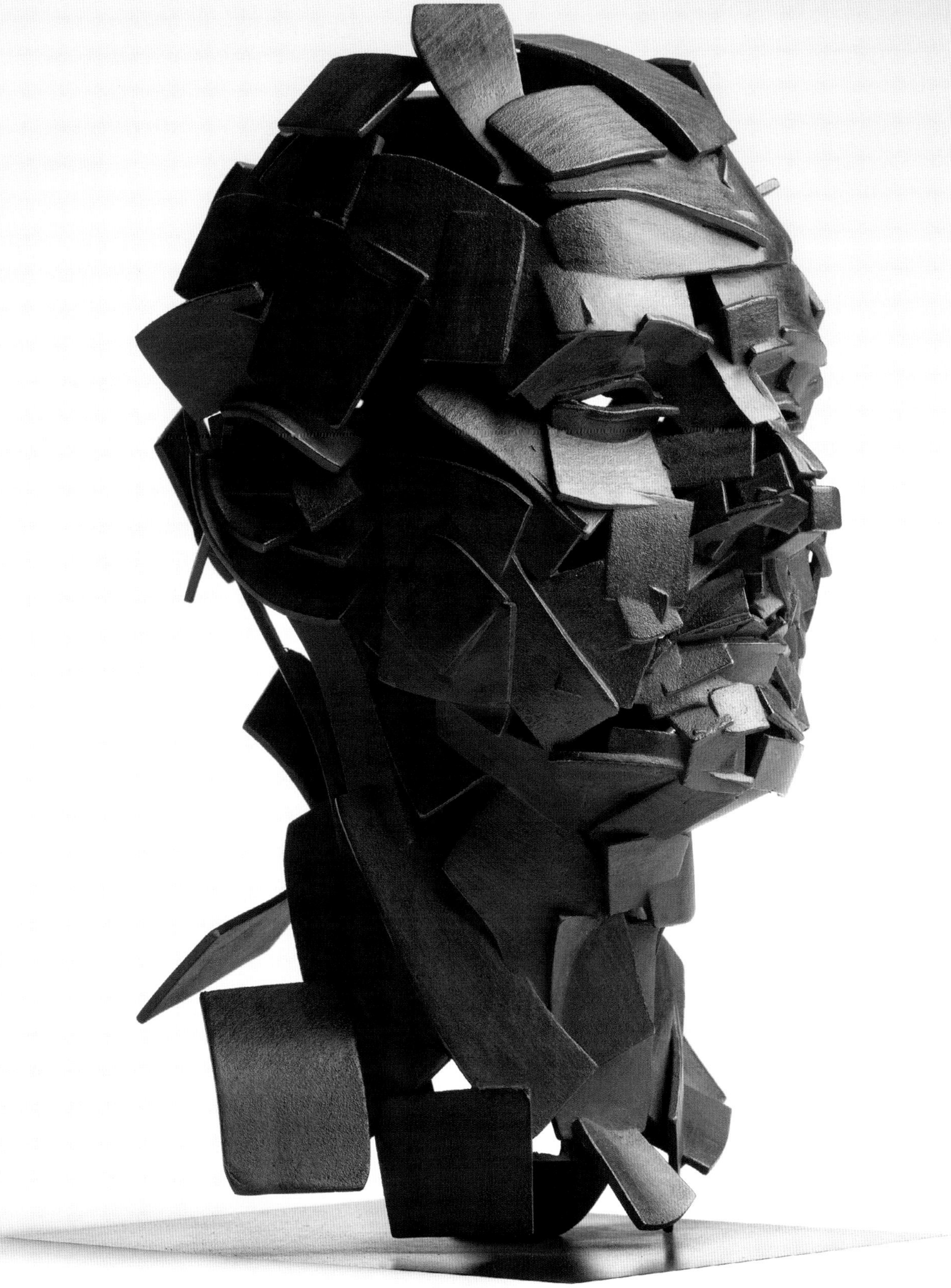

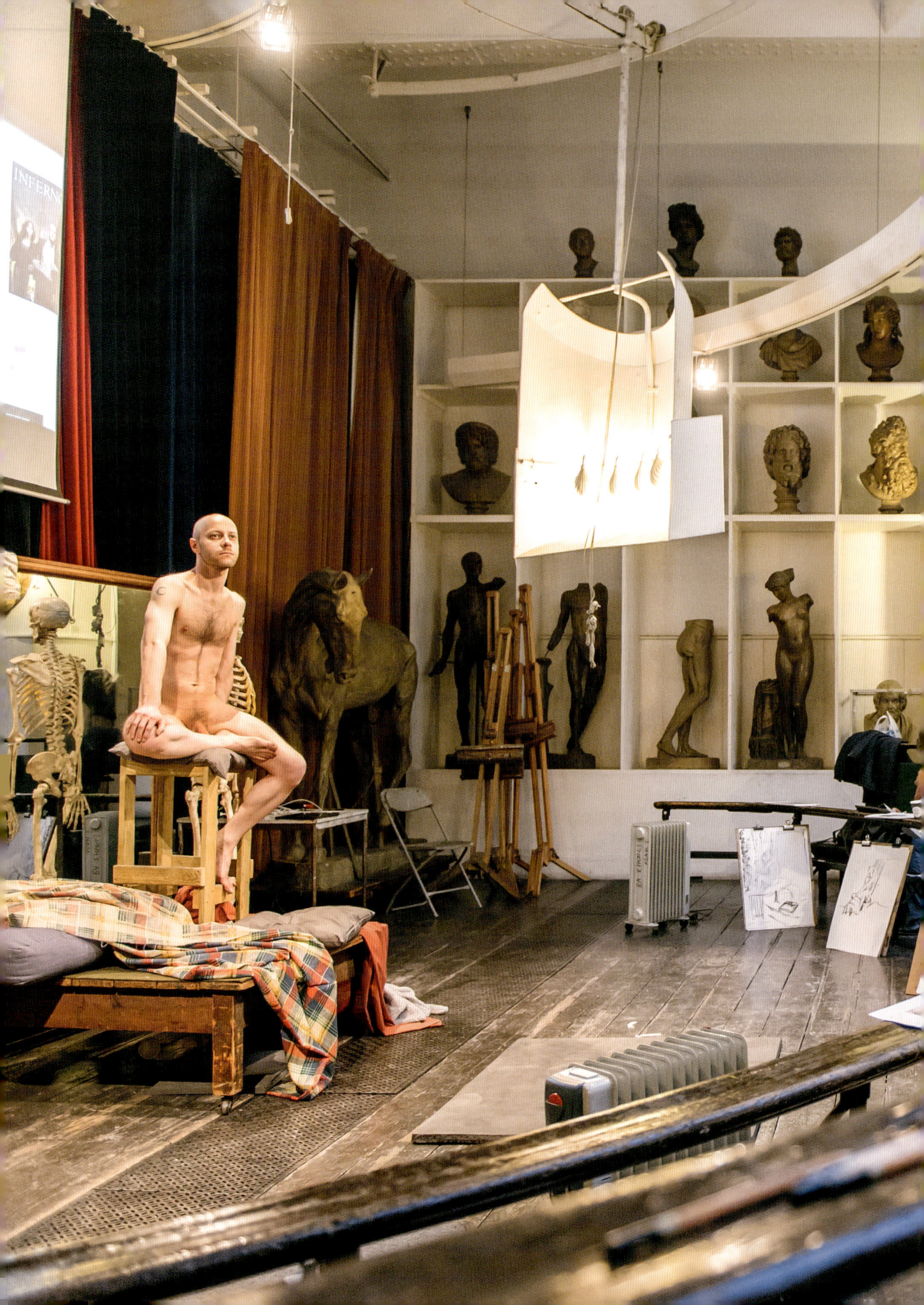

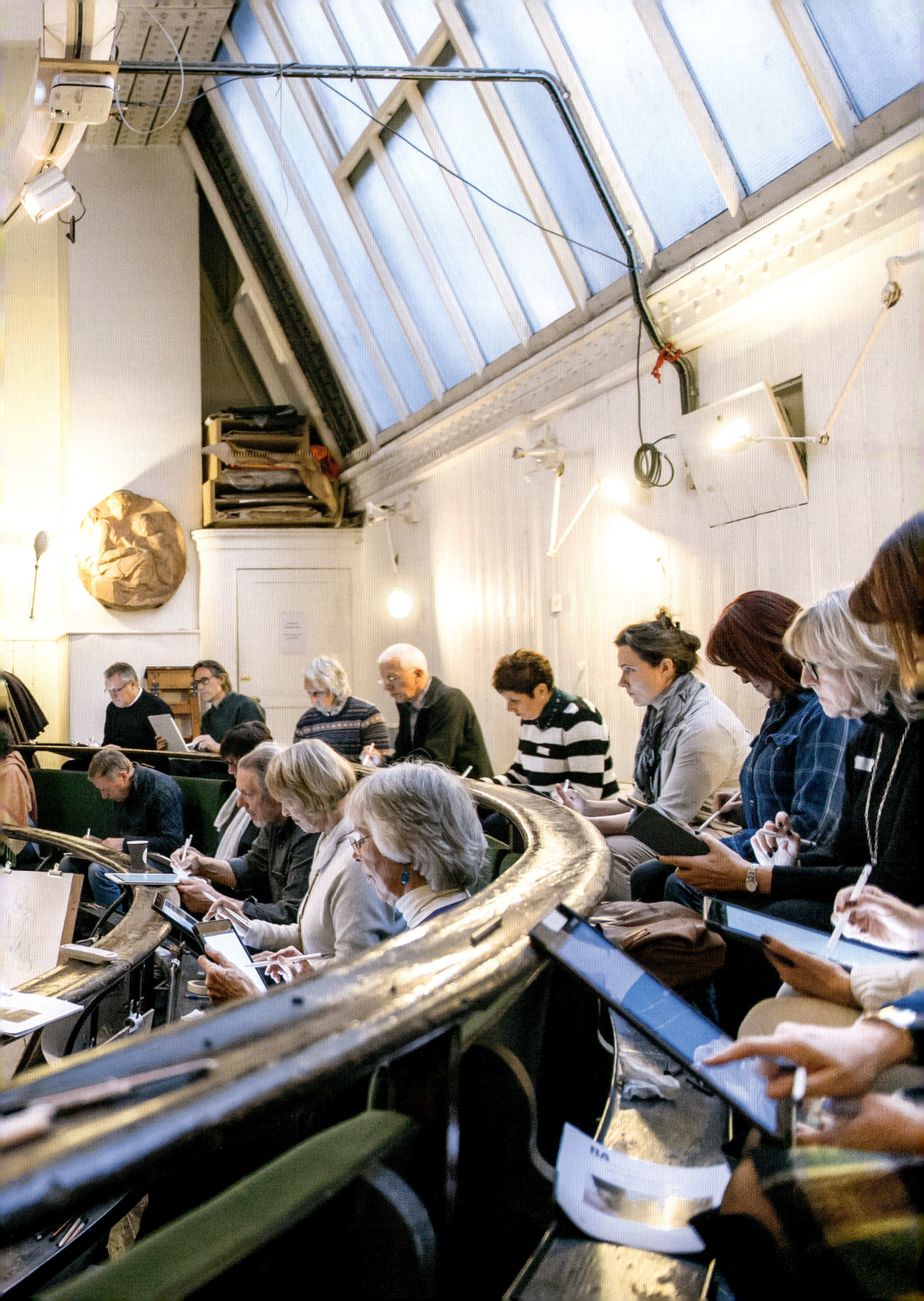

Contributors

Caroline Bugler is a writer and editor specialising in the visual arts. A former editor of the Art Fund's magazine *Art Quarterly*, she is a regular contributor to *Country Life*. She has edited several publications for the National Gallery, including the catalogue for Michael Landy RA's exhibition 'Saints Alive' in 2013.

Laura Gascoigne is a critic and commentator on the visual arts. A former editor of *Artists & Illustrators*, she writes for a range of magazines including *Apollo*, *The Spectator* and *RA Magazine*, and is the art critic of *The Tablet*. She is also the author of a novel about the art world, *The Horse's Arse*.

Martin Gayford is an art critic for *The Spectator* and the author of publications on Van Gogh, Constable and Michelangelo. His book *A Man with a Blue Scarf* records his experience of sitting for a portrait by Lucian Freud, and he has collaborated with David Hockney RA on publications including *A History of Pictures* and *A Bigger Message*.

Angela Kingston is a contemporary visual arts curator and writer. She has curated exhibitions including '3 am: Wonder, Paranoia and the Restless Night', touring from The Bluecoat, Liverpool (2013–14), and 'The First Humans', touring from Pump House, London (2015–16).

Adrian Locke is Senior Curator at the Royal Academy of Arts and curator of the RA's special exhibition project 'From Life' (2017–18). He has worked on a broad range of exhibitions since joining the Royal Academy in 2001; these include 'Anish Kapoor' (2009), 'Mexico: A Revolution in Art, 1910–1940' (2013) and 'Ai Weiwei' (2015).

Ben Luke is an art critic at the *London Evening Standard* and features editor at *The Art Newspaper*, whose podcast he also hosts. He has interviewed leading artists of different generations and from across the world and is a member of the Advisory Committee of the UK's Government Art Collection.

Sam Phillips is the editor of *RA Magazine*, the quarterly magazine of the Royal Academy of Arts. He is the author of a guide to the capital's art collections, *The Art Guide: London*, and *Isms: Understanding Modern Art*, an introduction to avant-garde art movements.

Michael Prodger is an art historian, a former literary editor and Senior Research Fellow at the University of Buckingham. He is the art critic of the *New Statesman* and *Standpoint* magazines and writes on art and books for, among others, *The Sunday Times* and *The Guardian*.

Rebecca Salter is a British painter and printmaker. She exhibits regularly internationally, and in 2011 had a major retrospective at the Yale Center for British Art, New Haven. In 2014 she was elected as a Royal Academician, and in 2017 she became Keeper of the Royal Academy, and thus responsible for the RA Schools.

Annette Wickham is Curator of Works on Paper at the Royal Academy. She has curated numerous exhibitions and displays highlighting works from the Academy's collections, including 'John Gibson RA: A British Sculptor in Rome' (2016). Her research focuses on the history of the Royal Academy and its Schools, as well as the history of drawing more generally.

Further reading on the history of working from life

Jeremy Deller, *Iggy Pop Life Class*, London, 2016

Adriano Aymonino and Anne Varick Lauder, *Drawn from the Antique: Artists and the Classical Ideal*, exh. cat., Sir John Soane's Museum, London, 2015

Tansy Curtin and Nicholas Savage (eds), *Genius and Ambition: The Royal Academy of Arts, London, 1768–1918*, exh. cat., Bendigo Art Gallery, Victoria, and other venues, 2015

Nigel Llewellyn, *The London Art Schools: Reforming the Art World, 1960 to Now*, London, 2015

Nikolaus Pevsner, *Academies of Art: Past and Present*, Cambridge, 2014 (reprint of original 1940 edition)

Frances Borzello, *The Naked Nude*, London, 2012

Tobias G. Natter and Elisabeth Leopold (eds), *Nude Men: From 1800 to the Present Day*, exh. cat., Leopold Museum, Vienna, 2012

Deanna Petherbridge, *The Primacy of Drawing: Histories and Theories of Practice*, New Haven and London, 2010

Jane Desmarais, Martin Postle and William Vaughan, *Model and Supermodel: The Artist's Model in British Art and Culture*, Manchester, 2006

James Fenton, *School of Genius: A History of the Royal Academy of Arts*, London, 2006

Alison Smith, *Exposed: The Victorian Nude*, exh. cat., Tate Britain, London, 2001

Martin Postle and William Vaughan, *The Artist's Model from Etty to Spencer*, London, 1999

Carl Goldstein, *Teaching Art: Academies and Schools from Vasari to Albers*, Cambridge, 1998

Ilaria Bignamini and Martin Postle, *The Artists' Model: Its Role in British Art from Lely to Etty*, exh. cat., University Art Gallery, Nottingham, and Iveagh Bequest, Kenwood, London, 1991

Photographic acknowledgements

All works of art are reproduced by kind permission of the owners. Every attempt has been made to trace copyright holders. We apologise for any inadvertent infringement and invite appropriate rights holders to contact us. Specific acknowledgements are as follows:

Photo credits

© Ami About-Bakr: p. 46

© Ashmolean Museum, University of Oxford: p. 50 (top)

© British Museum, London / Bridgeman Images: p. 64 (right)

Brooklyn Museum, New York: pp. 38–39, 43 (photo: © Elena Olivo); pp. 44–45

© Mike Bruce: pp. 103, 104 (bottom), 105, 106 (top)

© Alun Callender: p. 114

Alessandro Chiarini / Alamy Stock Photo: p. 96 (top)

The Samuel Courtauld Trust, The Courtauld Gallery, London: p. 13

© Kevin Cummins / Getty Images: p. 41

De Agostini Picture Library / A. Dagli Orti / Bridgeman Images: p. 139

© The Rob Dickins Collection at Watts Gallery / Bridgeman Images: p. 50 (bottom)

© Vincent Dilio: p. 26

Giulio Ercolani / Alamy Stock Photo: p. 96 (bottom)

© Robin Friend: p. 102

Kevin George / Alamy Stock Photo: p. 97

© Douglas R. Gilbert / Getty Images: p. 42

© Lars Gundersen: p. 60

© Adrian Locke: p. 106 (bottom)

© Scott Mead: p. 88

Metropolitan Museum of Art, New York / Bridgeman Images: p. 11

© David Parry: p. 68

© Paul Phung: p. 94

© Royal Academy Collection, London: pp. 9–10, 16, 18, 22, 24–25, 40; pp. 1–2, p. 76 (photo: © Marcus Leith); pp. 17, 21 (photo: © Prudence Cuming Associates Limited); p. 82 (photo: © Harriet Baker); p. 138 (photo: © Amy Macpherson)

Royal Collection Trust / © Her Majesty Queen Elizabeth II: pp. 14–15

© Carol Sachs: p. 108

© A. Saville: p. 128

© Tate, London: p. 20

© Justine Trickett: pp. 23, 156–57

Trinity Fine Art, London: p. 83

Victoria Miro, London: pp. 77–81

White Cube, London: p. 27 (photo: © Bill Orcutt); pp. 28–29 (photo: © Christopher Burke, New York); p. 30 (photo © Todd-White Art Photography); p. 31 (top and bottom) (photo: © Cary Whittier)

© Wen-You Cai: p. 32

© Wig Worland: p. 136

Additional copyright

Ellen Altfest © Ellen Alfest: pp. 6–7, 27–31

Cai Guo-Qiang © Cai Guo-Qiang, courtesy Cai Studio: pp. 33, 34 (bottom and top), 35; p. 36 (top) (photo: Andrey Parahin, courtesy IZOLYATSIA. Platform for Cultural Initiatives); p. 36 (bottom) (photo: Elio Montanari); p. 37 (Photo: On-Works International Multimedia Co., Ltd.)

Helen Clapcott © Helen Clapcott: p. 22

David Dawson © David Dawson: pp. 52, 58–59

Jeremy Deller © Jeremy Deller: pp. 39, 43

Stephen Farthing © Stephen Farthing: pp. 47–49, 51

Lucian Freud © The Lucian Freud Archive / Bridgeman Images: pp. 52–58

Alberto Giacometti © The Estate of Alberto Giacometti (Fondation Annette et Alberto Giacometti, Paris and ADAGP, Paris), licensed in the UK by ACS and DACS, London 2017: p. 64 (left)

Antony Gormley © Antony Gormley: pp. 61, 65, 67; pp. 62–63, 66 (photo: Stephen White)

David Hockney © David Hockney: pp. 68–70; pp. 71–72 (photo: Richard Schmidt); p. 73 (photo: Christie's); pp. 74–75 (photo: Prudence Cuming Associates Limited)

Chantal Joffe © Chantal Joffe, courtesy the artist and Victoria Miro, London: pp. 76–81

Michael Landy © Michael Landy, courtesy Thomas Dane Gallery, London: pp. 83–87

Liane Lang © Liane Lang: pp. 89–93

Maureen McAllister © Maureen McAllister: p. 45

Kallyiah Merilus © Kallyiah Merilus: p. 44

Farshid Moussavi, courtesy Farshid Moussavi Architecture: pp. 98–99; p. 95 (photo: Satoru Mishima/FOA); pp. 100–01 (photo: Stephen Gill)

Humphrey Ocean © Humphrey Ocean: p. 104 (top); pp. 103, 105, 106 (photo: Mike Bruce); p. 104 (bottom) (photo: Todd-White Art Photography)

Eddie Peake © Eddie Peake: p. 109 (photo: Adham Faramawy); p. 110 (top) (photo: Damian Jaques); p. 110 (bottom) (photo: Tristan Fewings / Getty Images / courtesy Barbican, London); p. 111 (photo: White Cube, London / Prudence Cuming Associates Limited); pp. 112–13 (photo: White Cube, London / Ben Westoby)

Cathy Pilkington © Cathy Pilkington: p. 118 (top and bottom); pp. 115–17, 119 (photo Graham Chalifour); pp. 120–21 (photo Perou)

Angel Ramirez © Angel Ramirez: p. 45

Bridget Riley © Bridget Riley / All rights reserved: pp. 122–27

Mauricio Rodriguez © Mauricio Rodriguez: p. 45

Jenny Saville © Jenny Saville, courtesy the artist and Gagosian: pp. 4, 129–32, 134–35 (photo: Mike Bruce); p. 133 (photo: Ashmolean Museum Photo Studio)

Yinka Shonibare © Yinka Shonibare: pp. 137, 138 (bottom), 140 (top and bottom) (courtesy the artist and Happy Finish, London); p. 141 (courtesy of the artist and Stephen Friedman Gallery, London)

Levan Songulashvili © Levan Songulashvili: p. 45

Gillian Wearing © Gillian Wearing: pp. 142, 144 (left), 145, 146–47 (courtesy Maureen Paley, London); pp. 143, 144 (right), 148–49 (courtesy Maureen Paley, London; Regen Projects, Los Angeles; and Tanya Bonakdar Gallery, New York)

Russell Westwood © The Estate of Russell Westwood: pp. 24–25

Jonathan Yeo © Jonathan Yeo studio: pp. 150–54; p. 155 (photo: Steve Russell Studios)

First published on the occasion of the special exhibition project 'From Life', Royal Academy of Arts, London, 11 December 2017 – 11 March 2018

Virtual Reality Partner

VIVE

Project Partners

Google Arts & Culture sky arts

EXHIBITION ARTISTS

Modern and contemporary artists whose works featured in the exhibition, alongside historic and documentary works from the Royal Academy Collection, included:

Ellen Altfest
Cai Guo-Qiang
David Dawson
Jeremy Deller
Lucian Freud
Antony Gormley
Chantal Joffe
Michael Landy
Liane Lang
Humphrey Ocean
Farshid Moussavi
Jenny Saville
Yinka Shonibare
Gillian Wearing
Jonathan Yeo

ARTISTIC DIRECTOR

Tim Marlow

EXHIBITION CURATOR

Adrian Locke

EXHIBITION ORGANISATION

Lucy Davis
Rebecca England
Rhiannon Hope
Cassandra Needham
Andrea Tarsia
Anna Testar

PHOTOGRAPHIC AND COPYRIGHT CO-ORDINATION

Caroline Arno

LIFE-DRAWING CLASSES

Artists who taught life-drawing classes as part of the special exhibition project included:

Francis Bowyer
Eliza Bonham Carter
Stephen Farthing
Michael Landy
Humphrey Ocean
Cathie Pilkington
Chris Wilkinson

ACADEMIC PROGRAMMES AND LEARNING

Mary Ealden
Ann Gilmore

EDITORS' NOTES

Unless otherwise stated, all works of art are by the artist whose interview they illustrate. Dimensions of works of art are given as height before width (before depth).

ILLUSTRATIONS

Cover and pages 2–3: the interior of the RA Schools Life Room. Photograph by Marcus Leith

Page 4: Jenny Saville, *Umbilical (Study)*, 2009. Graphite on watercolour paper, 89 x 70.7 cm

Pages 6–7: Ellen Altfest, *Torso*, 2011, Oil on canvas, 26 x 35.2 cm

Pages 156–57: a life-drawing class in which participants drew with iPads, in the Life Room of the Royal Academy Schools, 11 February 2017. Photograph by Justine Trickett

ROYAL ACADEMY PUBLICATIONS

Alison Hissey
Rosie Hore
Carola Krueger
Sam Phillips
Peter Sawbridge
Nick Tite

Design: Patrick Morrissey, Unlimited
Printed by Gomer Press, Llandysul, Wales

Some quotations in Martin Gayford's text on Bridget Riley were previously published in: Martin Gayford, 'Pitching opposites', *Modern Painters*, vol. 16, no. 2, Summer 2003, pp. 32–35.

ISBN 978-1-910350-90-4

Distributed outside the United States and Canada by ACC Distribution, Woodbridge

Distributed in the United States and Canada by ARTBOOK | D.A.P 155 6th Avenue, 2nd Floor, New York, NY 10013

ACKNOWLEDGEMENTS

The Royal Academy of Arts would like to thank the following individuals, studios, galleries and companies for their kind assistance during the making of the 'From Life' special exhibition project and this book:

Jason Araujo
Kitty Beamish
Anthony Bennett
Dan Bowmar
Brooklyn Museum: Elsie Alonso, Sharon Matt Atkins, Monica Park
Cai Studio Archives: Lydia Ohl, Yvonne Zhao
Jennifer Camilleri
Courtney Crichton-Turley
Dan Cowap
Maurice Davies
Elliot Dodd
Factory 42: John Cassy, James Hunt, Ruth Sessions, Dan Smith, Randall Wright, Louise Young
Gagosian: Cristina Colomar, Carlota Fernández de Córdoba, Miriam Perez, Robin Vousden
Panja Göbel
Antony Gormley Studio: Kerrie Bevis, Ondine Gillies, Pierre Jusselme
Vincent Grey
Mark Hampson
Happy Finish: Daniel Cheetham, Sebastian Kedra, Marco Marchesi, Alesandra Miro-Quesada, Christopher Peabody, Davide Preite, Amy Tinker, Richard Tisdall
David Hockney, Inc: Robert Berg, Julie Green
Hyperkit
ISelf Collection
Maureen Paley: Naja Bak Rantorp, Maureen Paley
Henry McGroggan
Farshid Moussavi Architecture: Philippe Dufour-Feronce, Sebastian Grey
OTOY
Pangolin Editions
Eddie Peake Studio: Will Davis
Iggy Pop
The Bridget Riley Art Foundation: Amelia Barratt, Natalia Naish, Amanda Sim
Jonathan Rowley
Shonibare Studio: Ailbhe Clyne, Ruth Hogan, Paula Morison, Imogen Wright, Yuki Yamamoto
Stephen Friedman Gallery
Thomas Dane Gallery: Saskia Coombs, Clare Morris, Olivia Rawnsley
Trinity Fine Art
Maciej Urbanek
Helen Valentine
Laura Valentine
Victoria Miro: Victoria Miro, Simona Pizzi, Rachel Taylor, Hannah van den Wijngaard, Glenn Scott Wright, Isabelle Young
White Cube: Steven Burridge, Susanna Greeves, Romilly Phillips
The Whitewall Company
Jonathan Yeo Studio: Jamie Barbor, Ruben Cooke, Will Graham, Sonia Lievaart, Jade Mitchell, Max Polak, Alberto Torres